DYNAMIC POLICY GAMES IN ECONOMICS

CONTRIBUTIONS TO ECONOMIC ANALYSIS

181

NORTH-HOLLAND
AMSTERDAM • NEW YORK • OXFORD • TOKYO

DYNAMIC POLICY GAMES IN ECONOMICS

Essays in Honour of Piet Verheyen

Edited by:
Frederick VAN DER PLOEG
Aart DE ZEEUW
Center for Economic Research
Tilburg University
Tilburg, The Netherlands

1989

NORTH-HOLLAND
AMSTERDAM • NEW YORK • OXFORD • TOKYO

ISBN: 0 444 87387 2

Publishers:
ELSEVIER SCIENCE PUBLISHERS B.V.
P.O. Box 1991
1000 BZ Amsterdam
The Netherlands

Sole distributors for the U.S.A. and Canada:
ELSEVIER SCIENCE PUBLISHING COMPANY, INC.
655 Avenue of the Americas
New York, N.Y. 10010
U.S.A.

PRINTED IN THE NETHERLANDS

Introduction to the series

This series consists of a number of hitherto unpublished studies, which are introduced by the editors in the belief that they represent fresh contributions to economic science.

The term 'economic analysis' as used in the title of the series has been adopted because it covers both the activities of the theoretical economist and the research worker.

Although the analytical methods used by the various contributors are not the same, they are nevertheless conditioned by the common origin of their studies, namely theoretical problems encountered in practical research. Since for this reason, business cycle research and national accounting, research work on behalf of economic policy, and problems of planning are the main sources of the subjects dealt with, they necessarily determine the manner of approach adopted by the authors. Their methods tend to be 'practical' in the sense of not being too far remote from application to actual economic conditions. In addition they are quantitative.

It is the hope of the editors that the publication of these studies will help to stimulate the exchange of scientific information and to reinforce international cooperation in the field of economics.

The Editors

Foreword

On the occasion of the 25th anniversary of Piet Verheyen's professorship in Business Econometrics the symposium on 'Dynamic Policy Games in Economics' was held at Tilburg University, on 19 and 20 May 1988. Bringing together a number of prominent scholars for discussion and exchange of ideas seems the best way to celebrate such an occasion.

Piet Verheyen has been the Dean of the Faculty of Economics, Tilburg University, until 1 january 1988. At present he is Chairman of the Board of Governors of the University.
Verheyen was the first to hold the chair of Business Econometrics at Tilburg University. The contents of his lectures greatly shaped the image of the young Department of Econometrics. In the Netherlands, econometrics is taught at undergraduate level at six universities. Tilburg was one of the first universities that organised courses in business econometrics, and there has been a steady inflow of students of this discipline. Within the department Verheyen has always been concerned with the supervision of the majority of the students graduating in econometrics, and through them he has had a considerable influence on the profession in the Netherlands.

Verheyen, born in 1931, favours a practical approach to problems. He started his career as a statistician at the Dutch State Mines. In 1962 he was nominated part-time associate professor, in 1963 he became professor of Business Econometrics. His pragmatic attitude to problem-solving was appreciated by his colleagues and his (18 PhD) students. Many administrative jobs were accomplished by him. From 1966 onward he served eight years as the Dean of the Faculty of Economics and three years as a member of the Board of Governors of the University. The chairmanship of the Board of Governors will probably set the seal on his work, although he has always greatly enjoyed his work as a professor.

The symposium on 'Dynamic Policy Games in Economics' can also be considered a milestone in the history of the Department of Econometrics. Today, it is the ambition of Tilburg University, and of the Department of Econometrics in particular, to promote high-quality theoretical research. One important result of these efforts was the establishment of the CentER for Economic Research, an institute affiliated to the Faculty of

Economics: it was during the symposium that the establishment of CentER was announced and the final decision of the Dutch Ministry of Education to support CentER was handed over to Piet Verheyen in his function of Chairman of the Board of Governors of the University. On behalf of the department I hereby express our gratitude for the contributions Piet Verheyen has made to our department and, more generally, to the promotion of our discipline in the Netherlands.

Pieter H.M. Ruys
Chairman of the Department of Econometrics

Preface

In September 1987 a committee was formed to think of a way of honouring Piet Verheyen on the occasion of the twenty-fifth anniversary of his professorship in business econometrics. This committee consisted of Arie Kapteyn, Paul van Loon, Pieter Ruys and Geert-Jan van Schijndel. The best way to thank Piet Verheyen was, in their view, to have an academic conference organised by the department in which he has invested so much of his time and energy. We were lucky enough to be asked by this committee to organise this conference. We chose to have a conference on dynamic policy games in economics, because this is an area in which there has been a lot of activity in recent years. We are therefore very grateful to the committee for entrusting us with this task. The committee has also raised the funds for the conference. We are indebted to Tilburg University, the Economics Institute Tilburg, the Dutch State Mines (D.S.M.), the Limburg Electricity Company (P.L.E.M.) and the Cobbenhagen Fund for sponsoring the conference and the preparation of this volume.

We are also grateful for all the efforts and the encouragement of our conference secretary, Jeanine Leytens. She has organised the dining, accommodation and administration of all the conference participants in a splendid manner. This book could not have been published without the detailed, thorough and diligent copy-editing of Hildegard Penn. She has ensured that all the papers are in the same format and style, and has clarified some of the papers in the process of copy-editing. We thank Petra Ligtenberg and Annemiek Dikmans for the quick and efficient typing of the volume, and Ralph van Delft for the preparation of the figures.

Last but not least, we thank the authors, discussants, anonymous referees and session chairmen for their contributions and cooperation in preparing this volume.

Tilburg, January 1989

Frederick van der Ploeg
Aart J. de Zeeuw

List of Participants

Tamer Başar, University of Illinois
Charles Bean, London School of Economics
Dagobert Brito, Rice University
Guillermo Calvo, University of Pennsylvania
Matthew Canzoneri, Georgetown University
Simone Clemhout, Cornell University
Eric van Damme, University of Bonn
John Driffill, Southampton University
Chaim Fershtman, Tel-Aviv University
Jörg Glombowski, Tilburg University
Michael Intriligator, University of California L.A.
Theo van de Klundert, Tilburg University
Finn Kydland, Carnegie-Mellon University
Ruud de Moor, Tilburg University
Torsten Persson, Stockholm University
Frederick van der Ploeg, Tilburg University
Berç Rustem, Imperial College London
Pieter Ruys, Tilburg University
Ron Smith, Birkbeck College London
Dolf Talman, Tilburg University
Stephen Turnovsky, University of Washington
Stef Tijs, Nijmegen University
Alistair Ulph, Southampton University
Piet Verheyen, Tilburg University
Henry Wan, Jr, Cornell University
David Webb, London School of Economics
Cees Withagen, Eindhoven University of Technology
Aart de Zeeuw, Tilburg University

CONTENTS

Dynamic Policy Games in Economics
F. van der Ploeg and A.J. de Zeeuw, (Editors)

INTRODUCTION

Frederick van der Ploeg

Aart J. de Zeeuw

CentER for Economic Research
Department of Economics
Tilburg University
5000 LE Tilburg, The Netherlands

This volume contains the revised versions of the papers presented at a conference held at Tilburg University, the Netherlands, 19 and 20 May 1988. The title of the conference and the volume was chosen to be 'Dynamic Policy Games in Economics', to reflect that the theme is to consider intertemporal and strategic issues in the formulation of economic policy so that dynamic game methodology is appropriate.

In the late seventies the Lucas critique of econometric policy evaluation (Lucas 1976) spread out to other fields of economics. The main point is that the reaction of other economic agents cannot be ignored when changes in economic policy are evaluated. An important example was the breakdown of the Phillips curve. The private sector expects that the government attempts to exploit an apparent short-run tradeoff between unemployment and inflation, and therefore the possible real effects of an expansive monetary policy will be nullified. This example also led to a discussion of the issue of time inconsistency (Kydland and Prescott 1977). If the private sector expects high inflation, the result of an optimal monetary policy will be high inflation without a reduction in unemployment. This is called the 'discretionary' outcome, because the government has no power to influence the formation of nominal wages. On the other hand, if the government can convince the private sector to expect low inflation, the result will be low inflation with the same level of unemployment. This is called the 'rules' outcome. Since the government takes its decision after the private sector has formed its expectations, the optimal policy of the government in the 'rules' outcome is time inconsistent. *Ex ante* it is optimal for the government to announce low inflation, but *ex post* it is optimal for the government to create high inflation. The issue of time inconsistency was developed and analysed in numerous subsequent papers. Calvo (1978) considers the time inconsistency of optimal dynamic taxation of a monetary economy with a Cagan-type money demand function. Fischer (1980) shows that *ex ante* it is optimal to choose a mix of taxation of capital income and labour income to induce sufficient savings now and sufficient work in the future. However, *ex post* it is optimal to tax only capital income as soon as the capital stock is in place. Fischer suggests some sort of time consistency requirement for optimal policy in a rational expectations framework. Ulph and Folie (1981) show that the *ex ante* optimal price and extraction policies of the cartel in a cartel versus fringe model for markets for raw materials from exhaustible resources also displays time inconsistency. The announcement of competitive prices induces the fringe to exhaust in a certain period, after which it is better for the cartel to renege and to jump to the monopoly price.

In the early eighties economists began to take these ideas to their logical conclusion, that is to model the relationship between, for example, the government and the private sector as a dynamic game. Indeed, Lucas already suggested in his famous interview with Klamer (1983: 55) that modern economic theory will make more and more use of dynamic game theory. The literature on optimal control just went through a revival of (non-zero-sum) differential/difference game theory starting with the seminal papers by Starr and Ho (1969a, b) and leading to the handbook by Başar and Olsder (1982). This literature shows that the assumptions of what information the players have about the state of the system and whether or not the players are committed to an announced strategy are crucial for the outcome of the game. Two solutions are typical. The first one is the open-loop solution, in which the players have no information about the state of the system and in which the players are committed to an announced strategy. The second one is the feedback solution, in which the players have information and are not committed. The low-inflation announcement of the government with the private sector expecting low inflation is the open-loop Stackelberg solution of the example above, described as a difference game. Simaan and Cruz (1973) show that the open-loop Stackelberg solution violates Bellman's principle of optimality. After some time has elapsed the Stackelberg solution of the game over the remainder of the planning period generally differs from the corresponding part of the Stackelberg solution over the whole planning period. To put it differently, the open-loop Stackelberg solution is time inconsistent. It may not be rational to carry out announced policies if called upon to do so in the future. The high-inflation policy of the government with the private sector expecting high inflation is the feedback Stackelberg solution, which in this case coincides with the open-loop Nash solution. The feedback solution concept resolves the time inconsistency of the outcome, but requires information about the state of the system. If the availability of this type of information is considered to be unrealistic, it is possible to find time-consistent equilibria in an open-loop setting (e.g. Fischer 1980). In the mid-seventies Selten (1975) introduced subgame perfectness as a refinement concept to resolve the multiplicity of Nash solutions for games in extensive form. With subgames defined as games at a certain point in time over the remainder of the planning horizon, the concept of subgame perfectness for extensive-form games comes close to the feedback Nash solution concept for differential/difference games. However, it is stronger than the time-consistency concept, as outcomes can be time consistent but not subgame perfect. Links were established between the Lucas critique of econometric policy evaluation and dynamic game theory, which gave rise to strategic analyses of a variety of economic policy issues such as monetary policy, government debt, optimal dynamic taxation, international policy coordination, the arms race and resource markets.

The inefficiency of the time-consistent or feedback Stackelberg outcome of the inflation/unemployment tradeoff under rational expectations was unsatisfactory. The question was whether the government can achieve a better outcome by building a reputation that the policy announcement is credible. This question can be analysed in the framework of repeating the game described above. In the case of an infinite horizon Barro and Gordon (1983) show that a better monetary policy rule is sustainable under rational expectations, because the temptation to cheat is outweighed by the threat of the time-consistent outcome in the next period. In the case of a finite horizon Selten's (1978) 'chain-store paradox' applies. Because no reputation can be gained in the last period, the time-consistent outcome is obtained. A backward recursive argument leads to the time-consistent outcome in every period. The same type of problem occurs in the industrial organisation literature, where a monopolist has to decide whether to fight a potential entrant or not, and where the potential entrant has to decide whether to enter ot not. Kreps and Wilson (1982) developed a model in which the monopolist can acquire reputation in the case of a finite horizon because the potential entrant has imperfect information about the type of monopolist he is playing against. Backus and Driffill (1985) use this model to show reputation effects in the Barro and Gordon monetary policy model with a finite horizon. The private sector does not know whether the government is of the type that has an inflation/unemployment dilemma or whether the government will fight inflation at all costs.

The authors in this volume have all been active in the revival of the game-theoretic approach to economic problems. They report on their recent research in their specific fields of interest.

Tamer Başar introduces the notions of weak time consistency and strong time consistency, to be able to determine whether the property of time consistency holds only on or also off an equilibrium path. He clarifies some of the underlying issues in both optimal control and dynamic game models (deterministic and stochastic) for different information patterns and under different equilibrium solution concepts. Furthermore, Başar introduces the notion of robustness of a solution and delineates its relationship with informational uniqueness, subgame perfectness and the two types of time consistency. The paper concentrates more on conceptual issues than on technical details.

Chaim Fershtman shows that the problem of time inconsistency not only occurs when the players are strategically asymmetric, by considering n-player Nash games with communication between the players but without binding agreements. More specifically he analyses the coalition-proof Nash equilibrium, in which no coalition of players can contemplate a credible or enforceable deviation, and the acceptable Nash equilibrium, in which a stronger definition of credible deviations is employed by allowing members of a deviating coalition to contemplate another deviation with players who are not in the original deviating coalition. In general, Fershtman advocates a stronger role of communications games in future research.

Michael Intriligator and Dagobert Brito analyse the arms race as a sequence of games in which the countries or alliances use heuristic decision rules in acquiring arms. Over time the heuristic rules can change as capabilities, perceptions, motivations, expectations, etc., change. These changes are treated as revisions in a plan which can be triggered by time or by events. Intriligator and Brito show that, in the case of the US-USSR arms race, if each attempts to deter the other and each uses a worst-case analysis to characterise the other, the result is arms race instability, with weapon stocks moving to higher and higher levels, but crisis stability, with each being deterred by the other.

Frederick van der Ploeg and Aart de Zeeuw analyse the arms race as a differential game between two countries facing a 'guns versus butter' dilemma. The government of each country maximises the utility of the representative consumer, which depends upon consumption, leisure and the characteristic defence. The first country is modelled as a decentralised market economy and the second country as a command economy. Van der Ploeg and de Zeeuw show that for non-separable utilities the feedback Nash equilibrium leads to less arms accumulation than the open-loop Nash equilibrium, which suggests that countries should be given the opportunity to monitor each other's weapon stocks.

Simone Clemhout and Henry Wan study methodological questions regarding the non-cooperative exploitation of a non-renewable common-property resource. This game of 'cake-eating' is structurally a twin of the Ramsey model and together this pair forms a natural bridge between control models and differential games. Clemhout and Wan study issues like existence, plausibility, uniqueness and robustness of the equilibrium concept, introduce the inverse-equilibrium concept and comment upon aspects of information structure. The first moral of their story is: don't rock the boat, the second one: don't you start to rock the boat, and the third one: on the right occasion, a bird in the hand is worth two in the bush.

Alistair and David Ulph analyse a market for an exhaustible resource where there are two large producers and a large number of small producers who act competitively. They distinguish two rather different sorts of commitments. The first one is the commitment of the large producers to a path of future outputs and prices. The second one is the commitment of the large producers to act cooperatively to maximise the joint profits of the cartel. Ulph and Ulph show that if one set of commitments can be made, it will always pay to enter into the other set of commitments, and they show that, if it is impossible to make one set of commitments, it may be undesirable to enter into the other set of commitments.

Stephen Turnovsky and Marcelo Bianconi address the issue of optimal wage indexation in a two-country stochastic model of a world economy in which both economies are subjected to stochastic disturbances in demand and supply, and in which expectations are rational. The gains from cooperation are assessed by comparing the non-cooperative Nash equilibrium and the Pareto-optimal cooperative equilibrium. Turnovsky and Bianconi show that in the case of a flexible exchange rate regime non-cooperative behaviour leads to overindexation of wages relative to cooperative behaviour, and that in the case of a fixed exchange rate regime the non-cooperative equilibrium and the cooperative equilibrium coincide.

Matthew Canzoneri and Dale Henderson consider the problem of instrument selection in a two-country version of the Barro and Gordon monetary policy game. Even if the policy-makers are sure of private sector behaviour, they will not be indifferent about the choice of an instrument, because this choice affects the opponent's inflation-employment tradeoff and, therefore, affects the outcome of the game. When each country has two instruments such as the money supply and the interest rate, there are four Nash solutions. Canzoneri and Henderson discuss this multiplicity problem by considering the possibility of institutional coordination, the restriction of the set of instruments and the reality of uncertainty.

Guillermo Calvo studies a model in which debt repudiation -directly, say, through interest rate taxes, or indirectly through inflation- is possible. The model is of the type where the government maximises the utility of the representative individual. The equilibrium concept is the one without precommitment. Calvo shows that there are cases in which the mere existence of government bonds generates a multiplicity of perfect-foresight equilibria. However, if the nominal return on government bonds is fully indexed to the price level and/or if the government refrains from issuing new bonds in case the interest rate exceeds some well-defined ceiling, this multiplicity problem may be solved.

Finn Kydland contrasts two approaches for analysing time-consistency issues in the context of monetary policy. The first one is based on the standard inflation-unemployment tradeoff with the private sector making decisions before the government does. The second one takes a public-finance approach. The latter approach is explicit, the models have parameters that can be measured, and monetary policy changes can imply real changes through any one of several channels. Kydland argues that capital-theoretic issues such as incentives for capital accumulation are at the heart of the problem of time inconsistency, and not only in the context of fiscal policy but also in the context of monetary policy.

John Driffill extends the reputation analysis in two ways. Firstly, he considers a model in which the uncertainty about the government's preferences is somewhat more broadly specified. Secondly, he considers a model in which some exogenous random shocks impinge on the economy and not only prevent the government from exercising perfect control but also prevent the private sector from exactly observing the policy measures. Driffill shows that the first extension reconciles earlier results on pooling and separating equilibria, and that the second extension tentatively indicates that the signal extraction problem faced by the private sector substantially reduces the discipline on policy-makers.

We hope that this volume will set some benchmarks and will provide a great deal of suggestions for the future development of economic research on the basis of dynamic game methodology.

References

Backus, D. and J. Driffill, 'Inflation and reputation', American Economic Review, vol. 75, no. 3, 1985, pp. 530-538.

Barro, R.J. and D.B. Gordon, 'Rules, discretion and reputation in a model of monetary policy', Journal of Monetary Economics, vol. 12, 1983, pp. 101-121.

Başar, T. and G.J. Olsder, Dynamic Noncooperative Game Theory, Academic Press, New York, 1982.

Calvo, G.A., 'On the time consistency of optimal policy in a monetary economy', Econometrica, vol. 46, 1978, pp. 1411-1428.

Fischer, S., 'Dynamic inconsistency, cooperation and the benevolent dissembling government', Journal of Economic Dynamics and Control, vol. 2, no. 1, 1980, pp. 93-108.

Klamer, A., Conversations with Economists, Rowman & Allanheld, Totowa, N.J., 1983.

Kreps, D.M. and R. Wilson, 'Reputation and imperfect information', Journal of Economic Theory, vol. 27, 1982, pp. 253-279.

Kydland, F.E. and E.C. Prescott, 'Rules rather than discretion: the inconsistency of optimal plans', Journal of Political Economy, vol. 85, no. 3, 1977, pp. 473-491.

Lucas, R.E., Jr, 'Econometric policy evaluation: a critique', in K. Brunner and A.H. Meltzer (eds), The Phillips Curve and Labor Markets, North-Holland, Amsterdam, 1976.

Selten, R., 'Reexamination of the perfectness concept for equilibrium points in extensive games', International Journal of Game Theory, vol. 4, 1975, pp. 25-55.

Selten, R., 'The chain-store paradox', Theory and Decision, vol. 9, 1978, pp. 127-159.

Simaan, M. and J.B. Cruz, Jr, 'Additional aspects of the Stackelberg strategy in nonzero-sum games', Journal of Optimization Theory and Applications, vol. 11, no. 6, 1973, pp. 613-626.

Starr, A.W. and Y.C. Ho, 'Nonzero-sum differential games', Journal of Optimization Theory and Applications, vol. 3, no. 3, 1969a, pp. 184-206.

Starr, A.W. and Y.C. Ho, 'Further properties of nonzero-sum differential games', Journal of Optimization Theory and Applications, vol. 3, no. 4, 1969b, pp. 207-219.

Ulph, A.M. and G.M. Folie, 'Dominant firm models of resource depletion', in D. Currie, D. Peel and W. Peters (eds), Microeconomic Analysis, Croom-Helm, London, 1981, pp. 77-106.

Dynamic Policy Games in Economics
F. van der Ploeg and A.J. de Zeeuw, (Editors)

TIME CONSISTENCY AND ROBUSTNESS OF EQUILIBRIA IN NON-COOPERATIVE DYNAMIC GAMES*

Tamer Başar

Decision and Control Laboratory
University of Illinois
Urbana, Illinois 61801, USA

Introduction

One of the major differences between static (or myopic) policies and dynamic ones is that a dynamic policy uses the available *a priori* information on the future evolution of the decision process, such as the decision (state) dynamics, the time horizon, the possibility of acquiring some dynamic information in the future, and the tradeoffs between current and future performances. In a way, a dynamic policy passively anticipates the future, and its construction is a result of the cooperative effort of individual decision units acting at different points in time. This is a cooperative effort because in any single-agent dynamic decision problem that stretches over several periods an 'optimal' decision at any point in time (chosen according to some quantitative or qualitative measure) cannot in general be determined without taking into account the effect of future decisions. A desirable feature of a dynamic policy is its consistency across time, in the sense that at any point in time, looking into the future, the decision-maker should have no rational reason to revise the future portion of the policy, provided that the truncated version of the policy is subjected to the same criteria as the original policy. This latter qualification is essential for such a consistency, because if either the underlying decision dynamics or the criteria according to which a policy is chosen (or both) abruptly change at some point in the decision horizon, and the possibility of such a change has not been built into the original formulation, then one cannot expect an optimal policy to retain its optimality for the new problem and under the new criteria. In other words, one cannot (and should not) expect (time) consistency of dynamic policies if the decision problem itself is not consistent over time.

The issue of time consistency of optimal or equilibrium policies in dynamic single-agent and multiple-agent (game) problems is a topic of major importance in economic decision-making, but in spite of the voluminous literature on the topic some of the basic issues have not yet been settled. This paper is aimed at clarifying some of the fundamental issues that arise in dynamic decision-making by presenting a unified framework in which both single and multiple agent, and deterministic and stochastic decision problems can be analysed, under different information patterns and using different solution concepts. We introduce two types of time consistency -weak and strong- and study them for various dynamic decision models involving single and multiple agents. We also introduce the notion of robustness of a solution, and discuss its relationship with informational uniqueness, subgame perfectness, and strong and weak time consistency. The main body of the paper has been devoted to models described in discrete time, with the counterparts of the results in continuous time briefly discussed in the next to the last section.

The organisation of the paper is as follows. The next section provides precise definitions for the two types of time consistency and robustness alluded to above, in a general framework, and studies them in the context of deterministic and stochastic single-agent dynamic optimisation problems. Section 2 extends this study to decision problems modelled as non-cooperative dynamic games, under the Nash equilibrium concept. The other equilibrium concept for non-cooperative games -the Stackelberg solution- has been covered in Section 3, and finally the parallel in continuous time has been developed in Section 4. The last section of the paper contains some brief concluding remarks, and is followed by a list of acronyms frequently used in the paper and some selective references.

1. Time Consistency and Robustness in Single-agent Dynamic Optimisation

1.1 Deterministic Systems

Perhaps the best starting point for a discussion of the notion of time consistency is the class of single-agent dynamic optimisation problems, since they provide an ideal setting for the introduction of some features common to all types of dynamic decision-making, without bringing in the structural complexities associated with dynamic games. Then, to move on to the dynamic game setting will be much easier, and this will also allow us to appreciate the new dimension of complexities offered by a dynamic game formulation.

A standard formulation of a single-agent optimisation problem, more commonly known as an optimal control problem, would involve a dynamic equation (called the state equation) which is driven by the instrument (control) variables, an objective functional (say, cost functional) defined in terms of the state and control variables and to be optimised by an appropriate selection of the latter, and some constraints imposed on the control as well as on the state variables. In a discrete-time framework, we would have

$$\text{state equation: } x_{t+1} = f_t(x_t, u_t), \quad t = 0,1,\ldots \tag{1.1a}$$

$$\text{cost function : } L(\underline{x},\underline{u}) = \sum_{t=0}^{T} g_t(x_{t+1}, u_t). \tag{1.1b}$$

where T is the time horizon, $\underline{u} := \{u_0,\ldots,u_T\}$ is the control sequence, with $u_t \in U_t$, and $\underline{x} := \{x_0,\ldots,x_{T+1}\}$ is the state sequence, with $x_t \in X_t$. Here, U_t and X_t are the control and state constraint sets, respectively, defined for each t. The objective is to obtain an appropriate sequence u that minimises L while meeting the several types of constraints imposed on the problem.

In characterising a solution $\underline{u}$ for such a problem, one might also require some specific dependence (of the solution) on the state variable sequence $\underline{x}$. This requirement manifests itself, among other things, in what we call the information pattern (IP) of the problem, which specifies what information (in this case, on the state sequence) the agent has acquired and therefore can use in the construction of a policy that will lead to the best (i.e. optimal) control sequence. Three standard types of IPs that arise in deterministic problems are

$$\eta_t = \{x_t, x_{t-1}, \ldots, x_0\} \qquad \text{closed-loop (CL)} \qquad (1.2a)$$

$$\eta_t = \{x_t\} \qquad \text{feedback (FB)} \qquad (1.2b)$$

$$\eta_t = \{x_0\} \qquad \text{open-loop (OL)} \qquad (1.2c)$$

but one could also have the fixed delay IP such as the n-step delay pattern

$$\begin{aligned} \eta_t &= \{x_{t-n}, x_{t-n-1}, \ldots, x_0\}, && t \geq n \\ &= \{x_0\}, && t < n. \end{aligned} \qquad (1.2d)$$

We assume throughout that the value of the initial state is not *a priori* information and can only be acquired as part of the (dynamic) information, provided that the given IP allows such an acquisition. Note that in the above, it is only the FB IP that does not allow the agent to know the value of the initial state x_0 at time $t > 0$.

Now, after specifying the IP, one introduces a class of mappings, $\gamma_t : \eta_t \to u_t \in U_t$, $t \in \underline{T} := \{0,\ldots,T\}$ belonging to some general class, and sometimes with some additional restriction on their structure. We denote the class of all such permissible mappings (called policies) at time t by Γ_t, and introduce the notation $\underline{\gamma}(\underline{\eta}) := \{\gamma_0(\eta_0),\ldots,\gamma_T(\eta_T)\}$, with $\underline{\gamma} \in \underline{\Gamma}$, the latter known as the policy space of the agent. Naturally, the policy space inherits all the constraints imposed on the control sequence u (as captured in U_t, $t \in \underline{T}$), but in addition it may involve some structural constraints, such as requiring the policy variable to be an affine function of the information. Under the FB IP, for example, this structural requirement would be given as

$$\gamma_t(x_t) = K_t x_t + k_t, \qquad (1.3)$$

where $\{K_t\}$ is a matrix sequence and $\{k_t\}$ is a vector sequence. Another type of a structural constraint, under the FB IP, would be to require the policies to be time-invariant, for example K_t and k_t in (1.3) to be constants.

Now, given the policy space $\underline{\Gamma}$, for each $\underline{\gamma} \in \underline{\Gamma}$ it is possible to express the cost function L solely in terms of $\underline{\gamma}$ and the initial state x_0:

$$J(\underline{\gamma},x_0) \equiv L(\underline{x},\underline{\gamma}(\underline{\eta})), \tag{1.4}$$

where $\underline{x}$ depends on $\underline{\gamma}$ and x_0, as obtained by substituting $u_t = \gamma_t(\eta_t)$ into (1.1a). The optimisation problem is then reformulated as

$$\min_{\underline{\gamma}\in\underline{\Gamma}} J(\underline{\gamma},x_0), \tag{1.5}$$

subject to the additional 'state' constraints $x^{\gamma}_{t+1} \in X_{t+1}$, $t \in T$, where x^{γ}_t is generated recursively by (1.1a), with $u_t = \gamma_t(\eta_t)$. In anticipation of some future need, we introduce here the notation $D(\underline{\gamma} \in \underline{\Gamma};\ \underline{X};\ [0,T];\ sol)$ to denote a dynamic decision problem (of, in fact, a more general type), where the arguments in D stand for the policy and the space where it lies, the state constraint set, the time horizon, and the solution concept adopted for the problem (where *sol* was taken as the minimisation of a function J in the formulation above).

We now note that the functional optimisation problem (1.5) is well defined only if γ_t is allowed to have x_0 as an argument, for all $t \in \underline{T}$ (as in the case of CL or OL IPs). For the FB IP, for example, (1.5) defines a vector-valued minimisation problem, requiring the optimal choice for $\underline{\gamma}$ to be the same for all $x_0 \in X_0$.

Let us leave this question of minimisation of vector-valued performance indices aside for the moment, and concentrate on the original optimisation problem (1.1), without paying attention to any informational restrictions that may be imposed on the problem. For a given $x_0 \in X_0$, denote the minimum[1] value of $L(\underline{x},\underline{u})$ over all permissible control sequences u by $L^*(x_0)$. [Note that this, in fact, corresponds to the OL IP since the optimal control sequence is allowed to depend only on x_0.] Then, it is a standard result of optimal control theory that

$$L^*(x_0) = V_0(x_0), \tag{1.6a}$$

where V_0 is the last step of the (backwards) 'dynamic programming' (DP) recursion

$$V_t(x) = \min_{u \in U_t} \{V_{t+1}(f_t(x,u)) + g_t(f_t(x,u),u)\}$$

$$V_{T+1} \equiv 0, \tag{1.6b}$$

where the minimisation is also subject to the constraint $f_t(x,u) \in X_{t+1}$. The right-hand-side of (1.6b) defines a mapping $\gamma_t^* : X_t \to U_t$, so that for each $x \in X_t$, $u_t = \gamma_t^*(x)$ is the minimising solution in (1.6b). Substituting this solution back into the state equation (1.1a), we obtain a sequence $\{x_t^*\}$ generated by

$$x_{t+1}^* = f_t(x_t^*, \gamma_t^*(x_t^*)), \qquad x_0^* = x_0, \tag{1.7}$$

which depends on the initial state x_0. Next, introduce the sequence $\underline{u}^* := \{u_0^*, \ldots, u_T^*\}$, where $u_t^* := \gamma_t^*\{x_t^*\}$, $t \in \underline{T}$, which can also be written as $u_t^* = \gamma_t^{OL}(x_0)$, for some $\gamma_t^{OL} : X_0 \to U_t$, $t \in \underline{T}$, which shows the explicit dependence on the initial state x_0.

1.1.1 Weak time consistency

For each fixed $x_0 \in X_0$, the sequence $\underline{u}^* \in \underline{U}$ above provides an optimal solution to (1.1), and $\{x_t^*\}$ is the corresponding optimal trajectory. If the IP is OL, then the sequence $\underline{\gamma}^{OL} := \{\gamma_0^{OL}, \ldots, \gamma_T^{OL}\}$ is the optimal (open-loop) control policy. Now, an important property of $\underline{u}^*$ or the optimal control policy $\underline{\gamma}^{OL}$ is the following: let $x_0 \in X_0$ be fixed, and suppose that the control sequence above has been applied to the system up to time $t = s - 1$, thus generating the sequence $x_0^*, \ldots, x_s^*$. At time s, the agent considers the possibility of revising his policy, and looking into the future he computes a (possibly new) set of policies by solving an optimisation problem which is identical with the original one except that it is now defined on the time horizon [s,T]:

$$\min_{\{u_t \in U_t\}_{t=s}^T} \sum_{t=s}^{T} g_t(x_{t+1}, u_t) \tag{1.8a}$$

subject to

$$x_{t+1} = f_t(x_t,u_t), \qquad x_s = x_s^*, \qquad t = s,s+1,\dots \tag{1.8b}$$

It is not difficult to see that the optimal control sequence here is precisely $\{u_t^*\}_{t=s}^T$, generating the same trajectory $\{x_{t+1}^*\}_{t=s}^T$, and hence there is no reason for the agent to change his (OL) policy *provided that he stays on the optimal path*. However, if $x_s \neq x_s^*$, i.e. there is some deviation from the optimal path, then the sequence $\{u_t^*\}_{t=s}^T$ will not, in general, be an optimum for (1.8), thus creating an incentive for the agent to revise his policy. This now motivates us to introduce the following definition, which is in fact more general than what the preceding discussion directly leads to:

DEFINITION 1.1. Let $D(\underline{\Gamma};\underline{X};[0,T];sol)$ be a dynamic decision problem which admits a solution $\underline{\gamma}^* \in \underline{\Gamma}$. Let s be an arbitrary point in (0,T], and consider the decision problem $D^*_{[s,T]} := D(\{\gamma_t = \gamma_t^*, t < s\};\{\gamma_t \in \Gamma_t, t \geq s\};\underline{X};[0,T];\ sol)$, which is derived from D by setting $\gamma_t = \gamma_t^*$, $t < s$. Then, $\underline{\gamma}^* \in \underline{\Gamma}$ is *weakly time consistent* (WTC) if the policy sequence $\{\gamma_t^*\}_{t=s}^T$ solves $D^*_{[s,T]}$, this being so for every $s \in (0,T]$. If a solution $\underline{\gamma}^* \in \underline{\Gamma}$ to D is not WTC, then it is *time inconsistent*. □

As we have already seen, the optimal open-loop solution for the discrete-time optimal control problem (1.1), or equivalently that of (1.5) under the OL IP, is WTC. In fact, it is not difficult to see that, given any information pattern and a corresponding policy space $\underline{\Gamma}$ (which also takes into account the structural restrictions that may have been imposed on the permissible policies), every solution of the minimisation problem (1.5) is WTC. This is true because if $\underline{\gamma}^* = \arg\min_{\underline{\gamma}\in\underline{\Gamma}} J(\underline{\gamma},x_0)$, then for any $s \in (0,T]$,

$$\{\gamma_t^*\}_{t=s}^T = \arg \min_{\{\gamma_t\in\Gamma_t\}_{t=s}^T} J(\{\gamma_t^*\}_{t=0}^{s-1},\{\gamma_t\}_{t=s}^T,x_0). \tag{1.9}$$

Note that this would hold even if the cost function in (1.1b) is not stage-decomposable, and/or the state equation in (1.1a) is replaced by one that incorporates 'lag' variables, such as

$$x_{t+1} = f_t(x_t, x_{t-1}, u_t), \qquad x_0 \text{ and } x_{-1} \text{ given} \tag{1.10a}$$

or

$$x_{t+1} = f_t(x_t, u_t, u_{t-1}), \qquad u_{-1} = 0. \tag{1.10b}$$

Hence, the above is an intrinsic property of dynamic optimisation problems. This brings us to the point where we state our first fact.

FACT 1. Every solution of a deterministic discrete-time dynamic optimisation problem is WTC. □

A number of single-agent dynamic decision problems which are not originally formulated as optimisation problems of the type (1.5), could be brought to that form, and hence their solutions satisfy the WTC feature. Typical examples are the target-reachability and worst-case design problems. For the former, the *sol* operator is the reachability of a target set $S \subset X_{T+1}$, at time T + 1, and hence the goal is to find a control sequence $\underline{\gamma}$ such that, using the evolution equation (1.1a), $x^{\gamma}_{T+1} \in S$. This can clearly be converted into a problem of the type (1.5), with the cost function to be minimised taken to be positive if the final state does not lie in S and zero otherwise. For the latter class, on the other hand, (1.1a) is replaced by

$$x_{t+1} = f_t(x_t, u_t, \alpha), \qquad t = 0,1,\ldots \tag{1.11a}$$

where α is an unknown parameter which lies in a given set $\underline{A}$. Working with the cost function (1.1b) and under a worst-case design philosophy which dictates the search of the best control sequence under worst (cost-maximising) choices for $\alpha \in \underline{A}$, the counterpart of (1.4) in this case will be

$$J(\underline{\gamma}, x_0) = \max_{\alpha \in \underline{A}} L(\underline{x}(\alpha, \underline{\gamma}, x_0), \underline{\gamma}(\underline{\eta})), \tag{1.11b}$$

where $\underline{x}$ now depends also on α. The problem then is in the same form as (1.5), and hence Fact 1 applies.

The reader may be aware of the considerable body of literature which either further studies or makes reference to the possibility that even in single-agent decision problems an optimal policy may be time inconsistent. Among the first to point out such a possibility (in a certain framework) were Kydland and Prescott (1977) and Calvo (1978), and for the past ten years or so this possibility of time inconsistency has been a major source of discredit for policies obtained as a result of the optimisation of a dynamic model. The question naturally arises as to how Fact 1 remains as a (universally valid) fact despite this evidence. This issue is addressed in the sequel where we first introduce a formulation which is a modified version of (1.1). This model will serve to delineate the underlying differences between Fact 1 above and the acknowledged 'time inconsistency' issue in what is known as 'rational expectations' models.

Consider again the dynamic optimisation problem formulated by (1.1), (1.4) and (1.5), but with the state equation (1.1a) replaced by

$$x_{t+1} = f_t(x_t, u_t, u_{t+1}), \qquad u_{T+1} = 0 \text{ for } T \text{ finite}, \tag{1.1a'}$$

and the cost function (1.1b) replaced by

$$L(\underline{x}, \underline{u}) = \sum_{t=0}^{T} g_t(x_{t+1}, u_t, u_{t+1}). \tag{1.1b'}$$

Note that, as a single-agent optimisation problem, the above formulation does not define a causal decision problem, since at any point in time the agent has to commit himself to the *value* of the action variable at the next time instant. Also, from an implementation point of view, a forward time realisation of the underlying decision process is not possible (in real time), especially under the CL or FB information patterns. However, as a purely mathematical optimisation problem in the policy space, the problem is generically well-defined and the optimal policies do satisfy (1.9), leading to weak time consistency under Definition 1.1, thereby not contradicting the statement of Fact 1.

In spite of this, the optimal policies (say, under the OL IP) to models of the type above have been referred to, by some authors, as time inconsistent, the 'rationale' behind it being the following: consider the formulation (1.1a') - (1.1b') under the OL IP, and let $u_t^* = \gamma_t^*(x_0)$, $t \in [0,T]$, be an optimal policy. This could be obtained, for example, through non-linear programming, by viewing the problem as a static optimisation problem, parameterised by the initial state x_0. Now let s be an arbitrary point in the discrete time interval (0,T], and consider the decision process from time s onwards, with the past decisions fixed at their optimal values, which also includes u_s^* since for transition to x_s its value is needed. In the truncated version defined on [s,T] the control u_s also appears, and if one considers this as a totally new problem and optimises also on u_s in addition to $u_{s+1},\dots,u_T$, the corresponding value for u_s in terms of x_0 will in general be different[2] from $u_s^* = \gamma_s^*(x_0)$, thus making the future decisions and the state trajectory different from their optimal values, which leads to 'time inconsistency'. Note, however, that if in the truncated problem we had respected the initial hypothesis that the two u_s's appearing in (1.1a') for t = s - 1 and t = s are in fact the same quantity which is selected once and for all, then the solution would still have featured *weak time consistency*, thus corroborating Fact 1. The question as to which interpretation one has to ascribe to the 'forward-looking' model above depends very much on the specific application that leads to that model, a case in point being the two-agent rational expectations formulation discussed below.

Consider again the state equation (1.1a'), but with the third argument of f_t replaced by v_t, which denotes the decision variable of a second agent:

$$x_{t+1} = f_t(x_t,u_t,v_t), \qquad x_0 \text{ given.} \tag{1.1a"}$$

The objective of the second agent is to choose the sequence $\{v_0,\dots,v_{T-1}\}$ in such a way that v_t stays as close (in value) to u_{t+1} as possible, with the 'rational expectations equilibrium' characterised by the identity $v_t \equiv u_{t+1}$, $t \in [0,T-1]$. If this identity is imposed on the problem, then we arrive at the single-agent optimisation problem discussed earlier; however, the solution of this problem is meaningfully related to that of the two-agent one only if there is a mechanism whereby such a constraint (which should be viewed as an end result rather than an *a priori* imposition) can be enforced. The underlying decision problem is in fact a two-person game, and should be analysed as such, using one of the equilibrium solution concepts for non-zero-sum dynamic games, such as the Nash or the Stackelberg equilibrium concepts, which will be discussed in the following sections. The time consistency of the equilibrium solution will then have to be evaluated in those contexts, and not in terms of the idealised single-agent problem. For two recent critiques on the time inconsistency issue in rational expectations models, we refer the reader to the articles by Wan (1985) and Cubitt (1986).

1.1.2 Strong time consistency

Now, to motivate a stronger notion of time consistency than the one given in Definition 1.1, let us go back to our original formulation, and consider the dynamic programming recursion (1.6b). Assume that we are operating under the CL or the FB IP, and that the policy $\underline{\gamma}^*$ introduced just following (1.6b) is an element of the corresponding policy space $\underline{\Gamma}$ (i.e. it meets all the additional structural restrictions that may have been imposed on the permissible policies). Such a policy is called an optimal FB control law, and in addition to being WTC it carries the additional appealing feature that, for any $s \in [0,T]$, its truncated version $\{\gamma_t^*\}_{t=s}^T$ solves the optimisation problem (1.8) not only when $x_s = x_s^*$ but for an arbitrary $x_s \in X_s$. Hence, even if the agent deviates (at some point in time) from the optimal path, the policy is still optimal for the remaining portion of the problem. This then motivates us to introduce the following stronger version of Definition 1.1.

DEFINITION 1.2. Let $D(\underline{\Gamma};\underline{X};[0,T];sol)$ be a dynamic decision problem which admits a solution $\underline{\gamma}^* \in \underline{\Gamma}$. Let s be an arbitrary point in (0,T], and consider the decision problem $D^{\beta}_{[s,T]} := D(\{\gamma_t = \beta_t \in \Gamma_t, t < s\}; \{\gamma_t \in \Gamma_t, t \geq s\};\underline{X}; [0,T];sol)$, which is derived from D by setting $\gamma_t = \beta_t$ which is taken as an arbitrary element of Γ_t, $t < s$, and generating a trajectory that lies in $\{X_t, t \leq s\}$. Then, $\underline{\gamma}^* \in \underline{\Gamma}$ is *strongly time consistent* (STC) if the policy sequence $\{\gamma_t^*\}_{t=s}^T$ solves $D^{\beta}_{[s,T]}$, this being so for every $s \in (0,T]$, and every $\underline{\beta} \in \underline{\Gamma}$ that generates a trajectory satisfying the state constraints. □

In a way, an STC policy is one that is not only independent of the initial state x_0 but also independent of other past values of the state, and the dynamic programming recursion (1.6b) is one way of obtaining such a solution, which is also known as the optimal FB solution. There may be some ambiguity in this latter terminology, however, especially if the initial state x_0 is a fixed known quantity. To make the point here, consider the optimal FB policy $\underline{\gamma}^* := \{\gamma_t^*, t \in T\}$ obtained from (1.6b), for a system the initial state x_0 of which is fixed and given, under which the optimal trajectory, $\{x_{t+1}^*, t \in T\}$, is just a sequence of known vectors. Now, if $\underline{\Gamma}$ is a policy space compatible with the FB IP, and we seek an optimal solution in the class $\underline{\Gamma}$, then not only $\underline{\gamma}^*$, but every $\underline{\gamma} \in \underline{\Gamma}$ given by $\gamma_t(x_t) = \psi_t(x_t, x_t^*)$, $t \in \underline{T}$, will be an optimal policy, where ψ_t is any function satisfying the boundary condition $\psi_t(x_t^*, x_t^*) = \gamma_t^*(x_t^*)$, $t \in \underline{T}$. Different choices of ψ lead to different *representations* of the same (optimal) policy on the optimal trajectory, and they all (in this case) depend only on the current value of the state. Because of this feature, one may be tempted to call all these different representations 'optimal FB policies', but this would not be correct because only one of them, namely $\underline{\gamma}^*$, is STC. The others cannot be obtained directly from (1.6b) and do not meet the 'permanent optimality' property we associate with an STC optimal solution. This latter point should become more clear later when we discuss STC solutions in stochastic systems.

There are two points worth mentioning here in connection with the notion of an STC optimal policy. The *first* one is that it is quite possible for a constant policy to be STC, which would arise if the optimisation problem in (1.6b) admits a solution which is independent of x for every t. In such a case, the optimal FB and the optimal OL solutions would coincide, and hence the OL solution would also be STC. The *second* point is that a given dynamic optimisation problem may not admit an STC optimal solution, even under the CL IP. This would arise if the policy space has additional structural restrictions imposed on the permissible policies. For example, one may require the policies to depend only linearly on the current value of the state, with no such restriction imposed on their dependence on past history. If the unique optimal FB solution obtained from (1.6b), i.e. $\underline{\gamma}^*$, is not linear in its argument, then the problem would not admit an STC solution. However, the problem would admit a WTC optimal solution, such as any policy of the form $\gamma_t(x_t, x_0) = K_t x_t + \gamma_t^*(x_t^*) - K_t x_t^*$, $t \in \underline{T}$, where $\{K_t\}$ is an arbitrary matrix sequence (of compatible dimensions) and $\{x_t^*\}$ is the trajectory generated by $\underline{\gamma}^*$, in general as a function of x_0.

1.1.3 Systems with lagged variables

The notions of weak and strong time consistency, as introduced above, are equally valid in systems which incorporate lag variables, either in the state or in the control, provided that one makes the appropriate identifications. Consider, for example, the system where the evolution is governed by (as a counterpart of (1.1a), and as in (1.10a)):

$$x_{t+1} = f_t(x_t, x_{t-1}, u_t), \qquad x_0 \text{ and } x_{-1} \text{ given.} \tag{1.12a}$$

This could be converted into the form (1.1a) by introducing a new state vector y_t which corresponds to the pair (x_t, x_{t-1}), thus making our earlier discussion apply here, with x_t replaced by y_t. Note that, in view of this, an STC optimal solution will exist (under the cost function (1.1b)) only if one allows the permissible policies at time t to depend not only on x_t but also on x_{t-1}. This can best be seen if one writes down the counterpart of the DP equation (1.6b) in terms of the original variables:

$$V_t(x_t, x_{t-1}) = \min_{u \in U_t} \{V_{t+1}(f_t(x_t, x_{t-1}, u), x_t) + g_t(f_t(x_t, x_{t-1}, u), u)\}$$

$$V_{T+1} \equiv 0. \tag{1.12b}$$

Clearly, an STC solution will have to be of the form $u_t = \gamma_t^*(x_t, x_{t-1})$. If the information pattern is FB, then the problem may not admit a solution at all.

For a second type of a 'lagged' dependence, consider the system introduced earlier by (1.10b):

$$x_{t+1} = f_t(x_t, u_t, u_{t-1}), \qquad u_{-1} = 0.$$

A type of argument similar to the above shows that every STC optimal policy for this system (under the cost function (1.1b)) has to be in the form $u_t = \gamma_t(x_t, u_{t-1})$, and hence the most recent past value of the control has to be included in the information set, along with the current value of the state. If a dependence on u_{t-1} at time t is not allowed, then in general no STC optimal solution will exist. Note that here we have departed from our original definition of an information pattern, which had included only (a subset of) the state vectors. As we will see in the next section, this departure will have significant implications in the case of dynamic games even if there is no lagged dependence. In the case of single-agent decision problems, inclusion of past control values in the information set does make a difference from the point of view of the 'time consistency' properties of the optimal solution. For the one extreme case when all past control values are included in $\underline{\eta}$, it is not difficult to see that (in the absence of any additional structural restrictions on the policies) every WTC optimal solution is also STC.

1.2 Stochastic Systems

We now extend the above observations to systems where the evolution of the dynamics is affected by additive shocks which can be modelled as elements of a random sequence. In particular, let us replace the system equation (1.1a) by

$$x_{t+1} = f_t(x_t, u_t) + w_t, \qquad t = 0,1,... \tag{1.13a}$$

where $\{w_t, t \in T\}$ is a sequence of zero-mean independent random vectors. The cost function L given by (1.1b) will now depend on $\underline{w} := \{w_0,...,w_T\}$, through $\underline{x}$ and also through $\underline{u} = \underline{\gamma}(\underline{\eta})$ if the IP is dynamic (i.e. not OL). To average out this dependence, (1.4) will have to be replaced by

$$J(\underline{\gamma}, x_0) \equiv E^{P_w}\{L(\underline{x}, \underline{\gamma}(\underline{\eta}))\}, \tag{1.13b}$$

where $E^{P_w}\{.\}$ is the expectation under P_w, which is the probability distribution of w. For the class of systems that we will be studying, the only randomness will come through $\underline{w}$, since the measurements will be noise-free (i.e. we will be working with the same type of IPs as in the deterministic case). Furthermore, we will drop the state constraint $x_t \in X_t$ since in stochastic problems it brings in additional degrees of complexity which would hinder the message we wish to convey here. Accordingly, we henceforth take $X_t = X$ for all t, where X is an appropriate dimensional Euclidean space wherein x_t takes values.

Now, the above formulation strips the problem off its random elements, and the resulting functional optimisation problem

$$\min_{\underline{\gamma}\in\underline{\Gamma}} J(\underline{\gamma},x_0) \tag{1.13c}$$

becomes no different from the earlier one (1.5). The notions of WTC and STC solutions, as introduced earlier, are equally applicable here, and so is Fact 1. However, even though the general definitions hold, some terminology used there and some specific conclusions arrived at will have no counterparts here, as we elucidate below. Foremost, we should mention that the statements 'being on or off an optimal path' cannot be used in the context of stochastic systems, because every path generated by (1.13a) (under different controls) will be a stochastic process. It was in anticipation of this difficulty that we have given Definition 1.1 and Definition 1.2 in terms of policies, and not trajectories. Another major difference between deterministic and stochastic problems arises in the existence and characterisation of different *representations* of a given policy. We now further elaborate on this point.

Firstly, we note that the counterpart of the DP algorithm (1.6b) in the stochastic case, and using the cost structure (1.1b), is

$$\begin{aligned} W_t(x) &= \min_{u\in U_t} E^{P_w}\{W_{t+1}(f_t(x,u)+w_t) + g_t(f_t(x,u)+w_t,u)\,|\,\eta_t\} \\ W_{T+1} &\equiv 0, \end{aligned} \tag{1.14}$$

where the expectation has been conditioned on the information available at time t, which we have assumed to include the current value of the state, as in the case of FB or CL IPs. Note that (because of independence) we could also have used P_{w_t} instead or P_w, the former being the probability distribution function of w_t. Now, the minimising control in (1.14), which we denote by $u_t = \gamma_t^*(x;P_w)$, will in general depend not only on $x_t = x$ but also on P_w (which explains the presence of the second argument in γ_t^*). If the information pattern is FB or CL or any other set that includes x_t at time t, and if furthermore $\underline{\Gamma}$ does not impose any structural restrictions on the permissible policies, then the sequence $\{\gamma_t^*(.;P_w),\ t\in\underline{T}\}$ provides an optimal FB solution to (1.13c). Such a solution is necessarily STC, since for any $s\in\underline{T}$, the truncation $\{\gamma_t^*(.;P_w),\ t\ge s\}$ minimises the truncated expected cost function

$$E^{P_w}\{\sum_{t=s}^{T} g_t(x_{t+1},u_t)\}$$

subject to (1.13a). What is different here from the deterministic case discussed earlier is that, provided that there is no open (Borel) set in X that receives zero probability under P_{w_t}, $t \in \underline{T}$, the policy $\underline{\gamma}^*(.;P_w)$ is *informationally unique*, i.e. it is not possible to generate other solutions to the problem from $\underline{\gamma}^*$ by constructing representations of it on the optimal trajectory. Before proceeding further with this discussion, let us pause to make the condition stated above precise, by introducing the notion of a 'distribution with full support'.

DEFINITION 1.3. A probability distribution (or measure) P_{w_t} for a random variable w_t defined on X is of *full support* if every open (Borel) subset of X receives positive probability from P_{w_t}. For an independent sequence $\underline{w} := \{w_0,\dots,w_T\}$, the probability distribution $P_w := \{P_{w_0},\dots,P_{w_T}\}$ is of *full support* if P_{w_t} is of full support for all $t \in T$. □

If the independent stochastic process driving the system (1.13a) is of full support, then there are no non-unique representations of a policy on the optimal trajectory, because every time a recursive substitution is made (of the type that led to non-uniqueness in deterministic systems) an element of uncertainty (and hence error) is introduced into the resulting policy. For a similar reason, if $\underline{\gamma}^*$ is an optimal policy in $\underline{\Gamma}$, and if $\underline{\Gamma}'$ is another policy space strictly included in $\underline{\Gamma}$, then the optimal solution in $\underline{\Gamma}'$ cannot, in general, be obtained from $\underline{\gamma}^*$ (which was possible in the deterministic case). For example, the optimal OL solution (which is only WTC) cannot in general be derived from the FB solution $\underline{\gamma}^*$, and its derivation involves the solution of a different stochastic optimisation problem[3]. We should point out that the condition that the sequence $\{w_0,\dots,w_T\}$ be of full support on X is only sufficient for informational uniqueness, but by no means necessary. We may, for example, have the stochastic version of the system described by (1.10a):

$$x_{t+1} = f_t(x_t,x_{t-1},u_t) + w'_t,$$

which could definitely be written in the form (1.13a) by introducing an additional state variable and an additional component for $\underline{w}$, which is a singular (in fact, zero) random process. In this case the process $\underline{w}$ is not of full support, but the informational uniqueness still holds whenever the process $\underline{w}'$ is independent and is of full support. What is actually needed is some form of 'stochastic controllability', which ensures that the noise diffuses throughout the state space at all points in time; delineation of the least stringent conditions for this requirement in precise mathematical terms and for general non-linear systems is a rather challenging task.

The following facts now summarise the main points of our discussion above for stochastic systems[4].

FACT 2. Every solution of a stochastic dynamic optimisation problem is WTC. □

FACT 3. Let the probability distribution of the independent sequence $\{w_t,\ t \in T\}$ be of full support. Then the following properties hold.

(i) Every solution of (1.13) under the FB or CL IP is STC.

(ii) For every fixed IP $\underline{\eta} := \{\eta_t,\ t \in \underline{T}\}$, such that $\eta_t \subseteq \{x_t,\dots,x_0\}$, every solution of (1.13) is informationally unique.

(iii) Given an IP $\underline{\eta} := \{\eta_t,\ t \in \underline{T}\}$, such that $\eta_t \subseteq \{x_{t-1},\dots,x_0\}$, the solution is generically not STC. □

In (ii) and (iii) above we have deliberately taken the IP to carry information only on the values of the state and not also on the past control values, because otherwise the statements there would not necessarily be true. To see this, consider again (1.13), this time under the one-step delay pattern, i.e.

$$\begin{aligned} \eta_t &= \{x_{t-1}, x_{t-2}, \dots, x_0\}, && t \geq 1 \\ &= \{x_0\}, && t = 0. \end{aligned} \tag{1.15a}$$

Since the value of x_t is not available at time t, the counterpart of the DP recursion (1.14) in this case would be

$$W_t(x_{t-1},u_{t-1}) = \min_{u \in U_t} E^{P_w}\{W_{t+1}(f_{t-1}(x_{t-1},u_{t-1})+w_{t-1},u)$$

$$+ g_{t+1}(f_t(f_{t-1}(x_{t-1},u_{t-1})+w_{t-1},u)+w_t,u)\,|\,\eta_t\} \tag{1.15b}$$

$$W_{T+1} \equiv 0,$$

which generates a solution in the form

$$u_t = \hat{\gamma}_t(x_{t-1},u_{t-1}), \qquad t = 1,2,\ldots$$

$$= \hat{\gamma}_0(x_0), \qquad t = 0, \tag{1.15c}$$

provided that the information set η_t also includes u_{t-1}. If this were the case (i.e. if η_t had also included u_{t-1}), then $\hat{\underline{\gamma}}$ would have been an optimal policy, which is also STC. In fact, assuming that the value of x_t is not available at time t, the set $\hat{\eta}_t \equiv \{x_{t-1},u_{t-1}\}$ is the least information needed for the characterisation of an optimal policy for this problem, which also turns out to be STC under the given IP. Now, returning to the original IP (1.15a), where u_{t-1} is not included in η_t, to construct the optimal policy we have to solve for u_t, $t \in \underline{T}$, recursively (in forward time) from (1.15c), which leads to

$$u_t = \tilde{\gamma}_t(x^{t-1}), \qquad t = 1,2,\ldots$$

$$= \tilde{\gamma}_0(x_0) \equiv \hat{\gamma}_0(x_0), \qquad t = 0, \tag{1.16}$$

where

$$x^{t-1} := \{x_{t-1},x_{t-2},\ldots,x_0\}.$$

Then, the policy sequence $\tilde{\underline{\gamma}} := \{\tilde{\gamma}_0,\ldots,\tilde{\gamma}_T\}$ constructed above constitutes an optimal solution under the information pattern (1.15a).

In this connection we now make two observations:

(i) The optimal solution under the IP (1.15a) is only WTC, and it uses full memory on the state. We may say that it is a representation of $\hat{\underline{\gamma}}$ on the policy space Γ which is compatible with (1.15a).

(ii) If the original IP is modified so as to include also past values of control, i.e. $\tilde{\eta}_t = \{x^{t-1}, u^{t-1}\}$, $t \geq 1$, $\tilde{\eta}_0 = \{x_0\}$, then the problem admits multiple (informationally non-unique) solutions, with $\hat{\underline{\gamma}}$ and $\tilde{\underline{\gamma}}$ constructed above being two such policies.

Similar features can be observed in the optimisation of (causal) forward-looking models, which is a topic recently discussed in Başar (1989b). In these models, the evolution dynamics are still given by (1.13a), but the cost function is different from (1.1a) in the sense that

$$L(\underline{x},\underline{u}) = \sum_{t=0}^{T} (x_{t+2}-u_t)^2, \tag{1.17a}$$

where we have taken all variables to be scalar quantities. If the IP is $\eta_t = \{x^t, u^{t-1}\}$, which allows for possible dependence on past control values, then it can be shown that a policy that minimises the expected value of (1.17a) is in the form

$$\begin{aligned} u_t &= \gamma_t(x_t, u_{t-1}), \qquad t = 1,2,\ldots \\ &= \gamma_0(x_0), \qquad t = 0, \end{aligned} \tag{1.17b}$$

which is STC. However, if we have the CL IP (1.2a), which does not allow for control dependence, then the optimal policy can be constructed from (1.17b), by recursively solving for u_t in terms of x^t:

$$u_t = \tilde{\gamma}_t(x^t), \qquad t \in T. \tag{1.17c}$$

Note that this policy is only WTC, and it requires full state memory.

1.3 Robustness of Optimal Policies

One relevant question to raise at this point is the relationship, if any, between the solutions of deterministic and stochastic problems, when the noise level in the system dynamics is 'low'. A mathematically precise way of asking this question would be the following:

Given a deterministic dynamic optimisation problem as described by (1.1), (1.4) and (1.5), with a fixed information pattern

$\underline{\eta} := \{\eta_t,\ t \in \underline{T}\}$, perturb the system dynamics by an additive independent zero-mean noise sequence as in (1.13a). Let $\underline{\gamma}(\underline{\eta};P_w)$ be a solution to the perturbed (stochastic) optimisation problem, where P_w is the probability distribution of the random sequence. Let $\{P_w^{(n)}\}_{n=1}^{\infty}$ be a sequence of probability distributions of full support that converges (in the supremum topology) to the singular distribution that assigns probability one to the point $\underline{w} = \underline{0}$, where $\underline{0}$ is the zero vector. Then the question is whether the limit of the sequence of policies $\{\underline{\gamma}(.;P_w^{(n)})\}$ provides a solution to the deterministic problem (provided that such a limit exists), and, if it does, which one of the solutions we capture.

The same question as above could be raised even for systems which have 'lagged' dependence in the evolution dynamics, such as the cases of (1.10a) and (1.10b). It is a valid one in view of the fact that deterministic dynamic optimisation problems admit multiple informationally non-unique optimal solutions (as we have seen earlier), some of which are STC and others only WTC. On the other hand, we know that the optimal solutions to the stochastic versions are informationally unique, provided that the random sequence has a probability distribution of full support, and only state information is allowed in the IP.

Now, since we have taken the state space (where x_t belongs) as a finite-dimensional (Euclidean) space, it is convenient to choose the distribution $P_{w_t}^{(n)}$ above as a Gaussian distribution with zero mean and positive-definite covariance, say $\Lambda_t^{(n)}$, for each $t \in \underline{T}$, and every finite n. Every such distribution is clearly of full support, and furthermore by taking $\{\Lambda_t^{(n)}\}$ as a sequence converging to the zero matrix for each $t \in \underline{T}$, we meet the requirement that the limiting distribution is totally singular, assigning probability one to the origin. Then, we can replace the notation $\underline{\gamma}(\underline{\eta};P_w^{(n)})$ above by $\underline{\gamma}(\underline{\eta};\Lambda^{(n)})$, and restrict the random perturbations around the deterministic system to Gaussian sequences as described above. We now introduce the terminology *robust* to refer to solutions of deterministic optimisation problems that are minimally sensitive to such perturbations. A precise definition follows, where again we hold the scope more general than that hinted at above, with 'optimisation' replaced by a more general notion of 'solution' as in Definition 1.1 and Definition 1.2.

DEFINITION 1.4. Let $\underline{\gamma}^* \in \underline{\Gamma}$ be a solution to a given deterministic dynamic decision problem $D(\underline{\Gamma};\underline{X};[0,T];sol)$ with an IP η, and let $\underline{\gamma}(\underline{\eta};\Lambda^{(n)})$ be any solution to a related stochastic decision problem which is the 'perturbed' version of the former, with an independent Gaussian sequence of positive-definite covariance $\Lambda^{(n)}$. Further let $\{\Lambda^{(n)}\}$ be a sequence converging monotonically to the zero matrix. Then, the policy $\underline{\gamma}^*$ is *robust* (under Gaussian perturbations) if a solution sequence $\underline{\gamma}(\underline{\eta};\Lambda^{(n)})$ exists such that

$$\underline{\gamma}^*(\underline{\eta}) = \lim_{n\to\infty} \underline{\gamma}(\underline{\eta};\Lambda^{(n)}). \qquad \square$$

The next result is a useful one which helps to establish some relationship between STC and robust solutions when the decision problem is a deterministic optimisation problem.

FACT 4. Let Γ_{sol} be the class of all solutions to a given deterministic optimisation problem with a fixed IP $\underline{\eta} := \{\eta_t,\ t \in T\}$, such that $\eta_t \subseteq \{x_t,\ldots,x_0\}$. Let Γ_{rob} be a non-empty subclass of Γ_{sol}, which consists of policies that are robust. Then,

(i) elements of Γ_{rob} are informationally unique;

(ii) if the problem admits STC solutions, at least one of them belongs to Γ_{rob}. $\square$

Perhaps the simplest illustration of the preceding result is provided by the standard formulation (1.1) under the CL IP (1.2a). For each $P_w^{(n)}$, we know that the solution to the stochastic problem can be obtained from (1.14), that it is informationally unique and that it is in the form $u_t = \gamma_t(x_t;P_w^{(n)})$, i.e. it is a function of only the current value of the state. Let us now take this policy to be the *unique* solution of the stochastic decision problem, without any loss of generality for the argument to follow. Denoting the corresponding solution of the DP recursion (1.14) (i.e. the value function) by $W_t(x_t;P_w^{(n)})$, it is not difficult to see that W_t is a continuous function of $\Lambda^{(n)}$ whenever f and g are continuous in their arguments. If we assume that the cost is bounded below, then as $n \to \infty$, $W_t(x;P_w^{(n)})$ converges, for each $x \in X$ and $t \in \underline{T}$, to $V_t(x)$ generated by (1.6b) - the DP recursion associated with the deterministic problem. Hence, if the right-hand side (RHS) of (1.6b) admits a unique solution for every $x \in X$, say $\gamma_t^*(x)$, and if the limit of the sequence $\{\gamma_t(.;P_w^{(n)})\}$ exists, then necessarily $\lim_{n\to\infty} \gamma_t(x;P_w^{(n)}) = \gamma_t^*(x)$, for every $t \in \underline{T}$, and therefore that the policy $\underline{\gamma}^*$ (which is STC) is *robust*[5]. Note that we do not rule out the possibility that there may be (other) STC optimal solutions to the problem which are not robust. This may arise, for example, if the stochastic problem admits a unique optimal solution for every finite n, whereas the solution to the RHS of (1.6b) is not unique, thus admitting structurally non-unique solutions all of which are STC. In a way, the notion of robustness also helps to make a selective choice out of a set of non-unique STC optimal solutions.

We should also note that Fact 4 above does not rule out the possibility that a problem may admit robust solutions while not admitting any STC optimal solution. A case in point is the class of dynamic optimisation problems with OL IP. If satisfying the right continuity and convexity assumptions, a given problem will admit a robust OL solution, but every such robust policy will only be WTC, because of the underlying IP.

As we have seen, there is some relationship between the two notions of strong time consistency and robustness, but they are not equivalent. Neither is every robust solution necessarily STC, nor is every STC solution necessarily robust. It is perhaps better to say that they complement each other in narrowing down the set of solutions to deterministic dynamic decision problems. A common feature of both is that they eliminate informational non-uniqueness when the IP is dynamic; but apart from that they eliminate solutions which show some sensitivity to inaccuracies in modelling and past strategy selection. A robust policy has a built-in safeguard against slight inaccuracies in the mathematical modelling of system dynamics, with these inaccuracies modelled as a random noise sequence with 'diminishing intensity'. An STC policy, on the other hand, provides a safeguard against inaccuracies in the past policy choices, which may arise, for example, because of errors brought in due to implementation constraints. Another positive feature of an STC policy is that it survives a reformulation of the original problem where explicit costs are attached (in the objective function) to the use of memory, with the penalties getting heavier as we go (relatively) farther into the past.

The notion of 'robustness' is applicable also to systems with lagged variables and/or IPs which also include (a subset of) the past control values. As an example of the former, consider the system described by

(1.10a), under the CL IP. The DP algorithm for its stochastic (perturbed) version is

$$W_t(x_t,x_{t-1}) = \min_{u \in U_t} E^{P_w^{(n)}} \{W_{t+1}(f_t(x_t,x_{t-1},u)+w_t,x_t)$$

$$+ g_t(f_t(x_t,x_{t-1},u)+w_t,u)|x^t\} \tag{1.18}$$

$$W_{T+1} \equiv 0,$$

which admits a solution only in the form

$$\gamma_t(x_t,x_{t-1};P_w^{(n)}), \qquad t \in \underline{T}.$$

If convergent, the limit will be in the form $\gamma_t^{\infty}(x_t,x_{t-1})$, which is exactly the form of the STC solution γ_t^* derived from (1.12b).

As an example of the latter (i.e. the case in which the IP also includes the past control values), consider the system (1.10b), with $\eta_t = \{x^t,u^{t-1}\}$. The corresponding DP equation under the cost function (1.1b) is

$$W_t(x,u_{t-1}) = \min_{u \in U_t} E^{P_w^{(n)}} \{W_{t+1}(f_t(x,u,u_{t-1})+w_t,u)$$

$$+ g_t(f_t(x,u,u_{t-1})+w_t,u)|\eta_t\} \tag{1.19}$$

$$W_{T+1} \equiv 0,$$

with the minimising solution being in the structural form

$$u_t = \gamma_t(x_t,u_{t-1};P_w^{(n)}), \qquad t \in \underline{T}. \tag{o}$$

This, however, is not the (structurally) unique solution on the strategy set $\underline{\Gamma}$, because u_t can be expressed in terms of the past values of control, without degrading the performance. For example, consider a policy in the form

$$u_t = \gamma_t(x_t,u_{t-1};P_w^{(n)}) + \Psi_t(u_{t-1},\gamma_{t-1}(x_{t-1},u_{t-2};P_w^{(n)})),\ t \geq 2, \qquad (oo)$$

where Ψ_t is any function on $U_{t-1} \times U_{t-1}$, with the property that $\Psi_t(u,u) = 0$ for all $u \in U_{t-1}$. For each Ψ_t, (oo) provides a representation of (o) in terms of the four variables $(x_t,x_{t-1},u_{t-1},u_{t-2})$. This shows that Fact 4(i) does not hold in the case of enlarged IPs, which is the reason why we had taken there η_t to be a subset of $\{x_t,\dots,x_0\}$. With such an enlarged IP that also includes past control values Fact 4(ii) still holds, i.e. one of the robust solutions is STC.

2. Non-cooperative Nash Equilibria in Dynamic Games

2.1 Deterministic Games

We now move on to dynamic games where we have multiple (say, M) agents, each having a (possibly) different cost function and a (possibly) different IP, of the type introduced in Section 1. For deterministic games, and in a discrete-time framework, the formulation follows that of (1.1), accommodating now M control sequences and M cost functions. Accordingly, we have

state equation: $$x_{t+1} = f_t(x_t,u_t), \qquad t = 0,1,\dots \qquad (2.1a)$$

cost function for agent m: $$L_m(\underline{x},\underline{u}) = \sum_{t=0}^{T} g_{mt}(x_{t+1},u_t),\ m \in \mathcal{M}, \qquad (2.1b)$$

where T is the time horizon, $\mathcal{M} := \{1,\dots,M\}$ is the set of agents, $\underline{u} := \{u_0,\dots,u_T\}$ is the composite control sequence (for all agents), $u_t := (u_{1t},\dots,u_{mt},\dots,u_{Mt})$ is the composite control of the M agents at the time step t, and u_{mt} is the control of agent m at time t, belonging to the control constraint set U_{mt} for that agent. Finally, $\underline{x} := \{x_0,\dots,x_{T+1}\}$ is the state sequence, with $x_t \in X_t$.

To introduce the non-cooperative Nash equilibrium solution, we let η_{mt} denote the information available to agent m at time t, and $\underline{\eta}_m$ denote the information pattern for the same agent. Compatible with this information pattern is the policy space $\underline{\Gamma}_m$ for agent m, with elements $\underline{\gamma}_m$, their restriction to the time point t being the space Γ_{mt}, with elements γ_{mt}, where the latter is the policy variable of agent m at time t; note the relationship $u_{mt} = \gamma_{mt}(\eta_{mt})$. We also adopt the notation $\gamma_t := (\gamma_{1t},\ldots,\gamma_{Mt}) \in \Gamma_t$ and $\underline{\gamma} := (\underline{\gamma}_1,\ldots,\underline{\gamma}_M) \in \underline{\Gamma}$, for the corresponding composite quantities. Now, given the composite policy space $\underline{\Gamma}$, it is possible to convert the above extensive form of the game into the normal form, by simply expressing the cost functions L_m, m = 1,...,M, solely in terms of the composite policy variable $\underline{\gamma}$ and the initial state x_0:

$$J_m(\underline{\gamma},x_0) \equiv L_m(\underline{x},\underline{\gamma}(\underline{\eta})). \tag{2.2}$$

In the above, $\underline{x}$ depends on $\underline{\gamma} \equiv (\underline{\gamma}_1,\ldots,\underline{\gamma}_M)$ and x_0, as obtained by substituting $u_{mt} = \gamma_{mt}(\eta_{mt})$, $m \in \mathcal{M}$, into (2.1a). Finally, let $(\underline{\gamma}^m,\underline{\beta}_m)$ denote the composite policy

$$(\underline{\gamma}_1,\ldots,\underline{\gamma}_{m-1},\underline{\beta}_m,\underline{\gamma}_{m+1},\ldots,\underline{\gamma}_M),$$

that is with the m'th component of $\underline{\gamma}$ replaced by a new policy $\underline{\beta}_m \in \underline{\Gamma}_m$ (for agent m). Then, a Nash equilibrium solution (NES) to this dynamic decision problem is a composite policy $\underline{\gamma}^* \in \underline{\Gamma}$ satisfying

$$\min_{\underline{\beta}_m \in \underline{\Gamma}_m} J_m((\underline{\gamma}^{m^*},\underline{\beta}_m),x_0) = J_m(\underline{\gamma}^*,x_0), \qquad m = 1,\ldots,M. \tag{2.3}$$

Using the earlier notation, we can now compactly represent this multiple-agent decision problem as $D(\underline{\gamma} \in \underline{\Gamma};\underline{X};[0,T];sol)$, where *sol* stands for NES.

The first observation we make is that Definition 1.1 and Definition 1.2, thereby the notions of WTC and STC solutions are equally applicable here. The second observation is that a natural counterpart of Fact 1 holds here, asserting that every NES is necessarily WTC. To see this, note that for any NES $\underline{\gamma}^*$, and for any $m \in \mathcal{M}$ and $s \in (0,T]$, it follows from (1.9) that

$$\{\gamma^*_{mt}\}_{t=s}^T = \arg \min_{\{\underline{\beta}_{mt} \in \underline{\Gamma}_{mt}\}_{t=s}^T} J_m((\underline{\gamma}^{m^*},\{\gamma^*_{mt}\}_{t=0}^{s-1},\{\beta_{mt}\}_{t=s}^T),x_0). \tag{2.4}$$

Hence, for any s, the truncated NES $\{\gamma^*_t\}_{t=s}^T$ provides a solution (in the NES sense) to the decision problem (the truncated game) $D^*_{[s,T]}$ introduced in Definition 1.1. Note that the 'asterisk' on D designates the convention that in the construction of the truncated game the past choices for the policies of the M agents have been fixed at their values dictated by $\underline{\gamma}^*$. We now formalise this result, which in fact holds (as in the case of Fact 1) even if the cost functions (2.1b) are not stage-decomposable.

FACT 5. Every NES of a discrete-time deterministic dynamic game is WTC. □

It is now worth pointing to two major differences between the solution properties of the single-agent decision problem of Section 1 and the multiple-agent decision problem of this section. For the former, and in a deterministic framework, if the solution is *optimisation* of a single-cost function, then every *representation* of the solution on the corresponding optimal trajectory is also a solution to the problem (provided that it lies in Γ); furthermore, if the problem admits more than one solution, then (as a natural consequence of the notion of optimality) they all lead to the same value for J. These two features generally fail to hold in dynamic games under the NES, as has been documented in the literature (see Başar and Olsder 1982). Hence, we have the following two important facts which differentiate single-agent problems from multiple-agent multiple-cost problems.

FACT 6. If $\underline{\gamma}^* \in \underline{\Gamma}$ and $\underline{\gamma}^{**} \in \underline{\Gamma}$ are two solutions to the dynamic multiple-agent decision problem of this section, it is not necessarily true that $J_m(\underline{\gamma}^*,x_0) = J_m(\underline{\gamma}^{**},x_0)$, for every $m \in \mathcal{M}$. □

FACT 7. If $\underline{\gamma}^* \in \underline{\Gamma}$ is a solution, with a corresponding trajectory $\underline{x}^*$, and $\underline{\beta}^* \in \underline{\Gamma}$ is an arbitrary representation of $\underline{\gamma}^*$ on $\underline{x}^*$, then $\underline{\beta}^*$ need not be a solution. □

Now, to construct an STC solution, we first write down the counterpart of the DP recursion (1.6b) for the dynamic game with the stage-additive cost functions (2.1b) and evolution dynamics (2.1a):

$$\{V_{mt}(x)\}_{m=1}^{M} = sol_{u \in U_t} \{\underbrace{V_{m,t+1}(f_t(x,u)) + g_{mt}(f_t(x,u),u)}_{\tilde{V}_{m,t+1}(x,u)}\}_{m=1}^{M} \tag{2.5}$$

$$V_{m,T+1} \equiv 0, \qquad m = 1,\dots,M.$$

Here, the *sol* operator on the RHS determines a NES for the M-person non-zero-sum (NZS) game which is defined by the cost M-tuple $\{\tilde{V}_{m,t+1}\}_{m=1}^{M}$ in terms of the state $x \in X_t$, and using the decision variables $\{u_{mt} \in U_{mt}\}_{m=1}^{M}$. The M-tuple on the LHS of (2.5) is the corresponding value of this static NZS game. Note that (in view of Fact 6) neither the NES nor the resulting values for each of these static games need be unique, in which case one has to keep track of the different solutions generated by (2.5) in the construction of the NES of the original dynamic game - provided that the policies obtained are compatible with the assumed IP.

To elaborate further on the above point, let a NES to the RHS of (2.5) be given by $\{u_{mt} = \gamma_{mt}(x)\}_{m=1}^{M}$, where t is arbitrary in [0,T] and x stands for an arbitrary value of x_t at time t. Note that this solution will in general show dependence on the (current value of) state, x, but there could also be instances in which it is independent of x (i.e. a constant) for some or all m and t. Such a dependence (on the current value of the state) would be compatible with a CL IP, which we henceforth adopt for the discussion to follow. Let $\underline{\Gamma}_{DP}$ be the class of all composite policies (out of $\underline{\Gamma}$) which can be generated from (2.5) as above. Furthermore, let $\underline{\Gamma}_{CL}$ be the class of all solutions of the same game (under the CL IP for all agents). Then we have the following result.

FACT 8. For a deterministic dynamic game (2.1) with CL IP for all agents, and using the NES concept:
(i) $\underline{\Gamma}_{DP} \subset \underline{\Gamma}_{CL}$;
(ii) every element of $\underline{\Gamma}_{DP}$ *is STC.* □

The inclusion in (i) above is generally a strict one, since $\underline{\Gamma}_{CL}$ is a much richer set, also including policies which incorporate state memory. Solutions which show explicit dependence on past values of the state cannot be derived from (2.5) (see also Fact 7), and they are normally not STC (but only WTC). A case in point is the class of dynamic games where one or more agents have delayed IPs of the type (1.2d), where the derivation of a NES involves quite intricate arguments. The solution will generally not be STC, unless it turns out to be a constant and a solution of the sequence of games defined in (2.5).

An STC NES of the type covered by Fact 8 above is also known as a *subgame-perfect equilibrium* of the underlying dynamic game with CL information (which actually makes the game a *feedback* game), since any truncated version (in forward time) constitutes a NES to the corresponding truncated version of the game[6] regardless of the past policy choices.

A question may be raised now as to whether Fact 8 above covers every possible scenario concerning the STC solution. The answer is yes, if we restrict ourselves only to systems defined by the first-order dynamics (1.1a). The conclusion there is that the STC NES will show explicit dependence on only the current value of the state (as a special case it could also be a constant, as discussed earlier) - provided that the IP allows knowledge of x_t at time t, such as the case of CL IP or FB IP. For other types of state information, the NES will not generally be STC. However, the story is different if the system evolution involves some 'lagged dependence', as in (1.10a) or (1.10b). Consider first (1.10a), where u_t is now the composite control vector. In this case, the DP recursion (2.5) will be replaced by (as the counterpart of (1.12b)):

$$\{V_{mt}(x_t,x_{t-1})\}_{m=1}^{M}$$

$$= sol_{u\in U_t} \underbrace{\{V_{m,t+1}(f_t(x_t,x_{t-1},u),x_t) + g_{mt}(f_t(x_t,x_{t-1},u),u)\}_{m=1}^{M}}_{\tilde{V}_{m,t+1}(x_t,x_{t-1},u)} \tag{2.6}$$

$$V_{m,T+1} \equiv 0, \qquad m = 1,\dots,M.$$

Since the cost M-tuple $\{\tilde{V}_{m,t+1}\}_{m=1}^{M}$ now depends on both x_t and x_{t-1}, the solution generated from (2.6) will generally be of the form $u_{mt} = \gamma^*_{mt}(x_t,x_{t-1})$, $m \in \mathcal{M}$, and hence all agents have to have access to the current as well as the most recent past value of the state vector, in order to realise an STC NES; this, of course, is compatible with the CL IP.

As a second example of 'lagged dependence', consider the system evolving according to (1.10b), where again u_t and u_{t-1} are the composite control vectors. Under the cost functions (2.1b), every STC NES for this dynamic game (with the IP as yet arbitrary) will be in the form $u_{mt} = \gamma_{mt}(x_t, u_{t-1})$, $m \in \mathcal{M}$, and hence the information set η has to include (in addition to the current value of the state) the most recent past value of the composite control, for all agents. If such information is not available to the agents (it is, in fact, quite unreasonable in a game situation for agents to observe each others' past control values), then the problem will generally admit no STC NES. For the extreme case in which the IP allows for the entire past composite control values to be common knowledge, then every NES will be STC. Such a common knowledge, however, brings in an additional degree of complication, since even for a system of the type (2.1a) the extra knowledge of past control values enriches the set of NESs, creating a plethora of new informationally non-unique equilibria. The best choice out of this set then becomes a difficult (and an ambiguous) one, also in view of Fact 6. Note that no such complication arises in single-agent optimisation problems.

Before moving on to stochastic games, it would be worth commenting on the 'rational expectations model' (1.1a'), (1.1b'), (1.1a"), when formulated (and solved) as a non-cooperative game between two agents. To complete the description of the problem as a *quantitative game*, we introduce (along with the decision dynamics (1.1a")) two cost functions, one for agent 1 and one for agent 2:

$$L_1(\underline{x},\underline{u},\underline{v}) = \sum_{t=0}^{T} g_t(x_{t+1},u_t,v_t)$$

$$L_2(\underline{x},\underline{u},\underline{v}) = \sum_{t=0}^{T} (u_{t+1}-v_t)^2,$$

where L_1 is the counterpart of (1.1b') under the game interpretation, and L_2 is chosen so as to reflect the second agent's true objective which is to guess correctly the true value of u_t at each point in time and through a causal process. Now we observe that, given any causal information pattern, the above is a well-defined dynamic game, and hence (from Fact 5) every Nash equilibrium solution for it is WTC.

2.2 Stochastic Games

We now consider stochastic systems of the type (1.13a) where u_t is the composite control, and with M average (expected) cost functions

$$J_m(\underline{\gamma},x_0) \equiv E^{P_w}\{L_m(\underline{x},\underline{\gamma}(\underline{\eta}))\}, \qquad m = 1,\ldots,M, \tag{2.7}$$

where L_m is as defined in (2.1b). The sequence of zero-mean random variables $\{w_t,\ t \in T\}$ is assumed to satisfy the same independence conditions as in Section 1. Following an argument similar to the one that led to Fact 5, we first have:

FACT 9. Every NES of a discrete-time stochastic dynamic game is WTC. □

Toward obtaining STC NESs, we first write down the counterpart of the DP recursion (2.5) in the stochastic case (see also (1.14)):

$$\{W_{mt}(x)\}_{m=1}^{M}$$

$$= sol_{u \in U_t} \underbrace{\{E^{P_w}\{W_{m,t+1}(f_t(x,u)+w_t) + g_{mt}(f_t(x,u)+w_t,u) \mid \eta_{mt}\}\}_{m=1}^{M}}_{\widetilde{W}_{m,t+1}(x,u;P_w)} \tag{2.8}$$

$$W_{m,T+1} \equiv 0, \qquad m = 1,\ldots,M,$$

where we have taken the information set for each agent to carry perfect knowledge on the current value of the state, which we have denoted by x. Note that the NZS game $\{\widetilde{W}_{m,t+1}\}_{m=1}^{M}$ defined by the RHS of (2.7) for each t depends not only on the current composite control and the current value of the state, but also on the probability distribution P_w. Hence, the solution sequence to these stochastic static games will be in the form $\{\gamma^*_{mt}(x_t;P_w)\}_{m=1}^{M}$ which is indeed a NES for the stochastic dynamic game, which we also call *feedback solution*. Such a construction also readily leads to the conclusion that the generated NES is STC. This then signals a result similar to Fact 8 in the deterministic case, but in fact we could make a stronger statement, provided that P_w is of full support (cf. Definition 1.3). Toward this end, let $\underline{\Gamma}_{SDP}$ denote the class of all composite policies (out of $\underline{\Gamma}$) which can be constructed through (2.8). Further let $\underline{\Gamma}_{SCL}$ be the class of all solutions to the same stochastic game. Then the following result follows, basically because every composite policy for a stochastic game of the type above is informationally unique - the details of the verification, however, are somewhat involved (Başar and Olsder 1982).

FACT 10. Consider the stochastic dynamic game defined by (1.13a) and (2.7), with CL IP for all M agents. Let the probability distribution of the independent sequence $\{w_t, t \in \underline{T}\}$ be of full support. Then the following properties hold:

(i) $\underline{\Gamma}_{SDP} \equiv \underline{\Gamma}_{SCL}$;

(ii) every element of $\underline{\Gamma}_{SDP}$ is STC;

(iii) given an IP $\underline{\eta} := \{\eta_{mt}, t \in T, m \in \mathcal{M}\}$, such that $\eta_{mt} \subseteq \{x_t, \ldots, x_0\}$ for all $m \in \mathcal{M}$, and $\eta_{mt} \cap \{x_t\} = \emptyset$ (empty set) for at least one $m \in \mathcal{M}$, the solution is generically not *STC.* □

The above result no longer holds if the IP carries control information, particularly with regard to the past actions of the other agents. In this case, the stochastic dynamic game will in general admit (other) NESs (explicitly depending on the past actions) which are not STC. In some cases, however, past control information will be required in order to ensure that the problem admits at least one STC NES. This would arise, for example, if for a stochastic dynamic game of the type covered by Fact 10 there is a one-step delay in the receipt of state information (see (1.15a)). In such a case, the counterpart of the DP recursion (2.8) would admit a solution only in the form

$$u_{mt} = \hat{\gamma}_{mt}(x_{t-1}, u_{t-1}), \qquad t = 1,2,\ldots$$

$$= \hat{\gamma}_{m0}(x_0), \qquad t = 0, \quad m \in \mathcal{M},$$

provided that the information set η_{mt} for each agent m also includes u_{t-1}. With this additional 'control' information, $\hat{\underline{\gamma}}$ above is an STC NES; however, the problem admits a plethora of other NESs all of which are only WTC - that is, with the additional redundant information, $\underline{\Gamma}_{SDP} \subset \underline{\Gamma}_{SIP}$ with a strict inclusion. Here SIP refers to the NESs obtained for the stochastic game under the given IP and SDP refers to the solutions constructed using a DP-type recursion under the same IP. Now, if the control information were not available then the NES would depend (in general) on the entire past history of the state vector and not only on x_{t-1} at time t. Such a policy would not be STC but only WTC.

2.3 Robust Equilibrium Solutions

We now use the above stochastic framework to introduce the notion of *robust* NESs for deterministic games. The procedure follows the one given in Section 1, and Definition 1.4 equally applies here. The following result is the counterpart of Fact 4 in the context of dynamic games.

FACT 11. Let $\underline{\Gamma}_{sol}$ *be the class of all solutions to a given deterministic dynamic game with a fixed IP* $\underline{\eta} := \{\eta_{mt}, t \in T, m \in \mathcal{M}\}$, *such that* $\eta_{mt} \subseteq \{x_t, \ldots, x_0\}$, $m \in \mathcal{M}$. *Let* $\underline{\Gamma}_{rob}$ *be a non-empty subclass of* $\underline{\Gamma}_{sol}$, *which consists of policies that are robust. Then, if the problem admits STC solutions, at least one of them belongs to* $\underline{\Gamma}_{rob}$. □

The discussion following Fact 4 in Section 1 equally applies here, with some obvious modifications stemming from the fact that we now have M value functions $\{W_{mt}\}_{m=1}^{M}$, instead of one. Furthermore, as in single-agent problems, neither is a robust NES necessarily STC (e.g. the NES under the OL IP), nor is an STC NES necessarily robust[7]. But again, together, they tend to narrow down the set of solutions by elimininating those that are either sensitive to small modelling errors or sensitive to 'non-optimal' play in the past. Note that 'robustness' is defined using an *extensive* form of a game (and hence, whether a NES for a dynamic game is robust or not may depend on the specific extensive form adopted), whereas 'strong time consistency' employs the *normal* form; hence, in this sense also the two notions complement each other.

Before concluding the discussion on 'robustness' for dynamic games, it is worth mentioning two more points here. The first is that, as in the single-agent case, the notion is applicable also to games the description of which involves lagged variables. As a specific illustration of this, we could consider the deterministic game which led to the DP recursion (2.6). If the system (1.10a) (with u_t taken as a composite control vector) is perturbed by a noise sequence w, then the associated DP recursion is (as the counterpart of (2.6)):

$$\{W_{mt}(x_t,x_{t-1})\}_{m=1}^{M} = sol_{u\in U_t}\{\widetilde{W}_{m,t+1}(x_t,x_{t-1},u;P_w^{(n)})\}_{m=1}^{M}$$

$$W_{m,T+1} \equiv 0, \qquad m = 1,\dots,M. \tag{2.9a}$$

where, with $x := x_t$, $u := u_t$ and $y := x_{t-1}$,

$$\widetilde{W}_{m,t+1}(x,y,u;P_w^{(n)}) \equiv E^{P_w^{(n)}}\{W_{m,t+1}(f_t(x,y,u)+w_t,y)$$

$$+ g_{mt}(f_t(x,y,u)+w_t,u)\,|\,x^t\}. \tag{2.9b}$$

As in Fact 10(i), the NESs of the perturbed game (with CL IP) for each non-singular (full support) distribution P_w can only be generated from (2.9) by solving the static games $\{\widetilde{W}_{m,t+1}\}_{m=1}^{M}$, and therefore every NES will be in the form $\{\gamma_{mt}(x_t,x_{t-1};P_w)\}_{m=1}^{M}$. This then shows that a robust NES can only show dependence on the current and most recent past values of the state, as in the case of the STC NESs constructed from (2.6).

The second point is that the notion also extends to IPs which include, in addition to the state, (a subset of) the past controls of the agents[8]. As an illustration of this type of generalisation we can consider, as in Section 1, an evolution dynamics described by (1.10b), with the IP $\eta_{mt} = \{x^t,u^{t-1}\}$ for each agent m. Adopting again the cost functions (2.1b), the associated DP equation for the perturbed version will be given as follows:

$$\{W_{mt}(x_t,u_{t-1})\}_{m=1}^{M} = sol_{u\in U_t}\{\widetilde{W}_{m,t+1}(x_t,u_t,u_{t-1};P_w^{(n)})\}_{m=1}^{M}$$

$$W_{m,T+1} \equiv 0\ , \qquad m = 1,\dots,M. \tag{2.10a}$$

where, with $x := x_t$, $u := u_t$ and $v := u_{t-1}$,

$$\widetilde{W}_{m,t+1}(x_t,u_t,u_{t-1};P_w^{(n)}) := E^{P_w^{(n)}}\{W_{m,t+1}(f_t(x,u,v)+w_t,u)$$

$$+ g_{mt}(f_t(x,u,v)+w_t,u)\,|\,\eta_{mt}\}. \tag{2.10b}$$

Every NES constructed from the static games defined by (2.10b) will be in the structural form

$$u_{mt} = \gamma_{mt}(x_t, u_{t-1}; P_w^{(n)}), \qquad m \in \mathcal{M}, \qquad t \in T,$$

but this will not be the only class of NESs the stochastic game will admit. In fact, it is possible to generate additional equilibria by using also the memory on both the state and composite controls (see Başar and Olsder 1982); this is possible because of the redundancy in the acquired information. Hence, for the corresponding deterministic game, in general a plethora of robust NESs will exist. Some of these will depend only on (the entire past history of) the state, which correspond to the robust solutions of the same deterministic game under the CL IP. These, however, will not be STC under the new IP.

It may be interesting to note that the 'forward-looking' model discussed briefly in Section 1 (see the cost function (1.17a)) and the solution of which was shown to be either WTC or STC, depending on the information pattern, also admits a counterpart in the game framework. This game formulation has recently been studied in Başar (1989a) and has been shown to admit a WTC NES when the state dynamics are linear. More precisely, let the decision dynamics be described by

$$x_{t+1} = ax_t + bu_{1t} + cu_{2t} + w_t,$$

where $\{u_{1t}\}$ and $\{u_{2t}\}$ are the decision variables of agents 1 and 2, respectively, which are chosen based on CL state information. Furthermore, let the loss functions for the two agents be given respectively by

$$L_1(\underline{x},\underline{u}) = \sum_{t=0}^{T+1} \{x_{t+1}^2 + ku_{1t}^2\}\rho_1^t$$

and

$$L_2(\underline{x},\underline{u}) = \sum_{t=0}^{T} [u_{2t} - x_{t+2}]^2 \rho_2^t,$$

where ρ_1 and ρ_2 are discount factors, lying in (0,1).

As shown in Başar (1989a), the unique NES of this game requires full memory on the state; it is robust and WTC, but it is not STC.

2.4 Other Ways of Eliminating Non-uniqueness

The two notions that we have discussed heretofore, namely robustness and strong time consistency, help to narrow down the number of NESs a dynamic game may admit, but they do not necessarily lead to a unique equilibrium. Additional non-uniqueness may arise mainly due to one or both of the following two reasons:

(i) *Structural non-uniqueness*: the static games constructed in the DP type recursions may admit more than one equilibrium, in both deterministic and stochastic cases.

(ii) *Informational non-uniqueness*: the IP may involve also control information (in addition to state information), thus exhibiting redundancy in dynamic information. This gives rise to non-unique equilibria, with some NESs depending on a larger number of variables than others.

We will not further deal with the 'non-uniqueness' issue here. But it is worth mentioning that several different approaches exist towards further shrinking the set of NESs, most of which have been developed for finite games and do not carry over so easily to the 'infinite games' domain. Among these, we can list the notions of perfect equilibrium (Selten 1975), quasi-perfect equilibrium (van Damme 1984), proper equilibrium (Myerson 1978), sequential equilibrium (Kreps and Wilson 1982) and strategic stability (Kohlberg and Mertens 1986), all of which bring in some refinement of the basic notion of a NES, based on introducing either *vanishing* 'noise' into the consequences of the agents' actions and/or *shrinking* 'elements of irrationality' into the decision process (such as making a wrong decision with non-zero probability). Other possible approaches would be the use of computational stability (Başar 1986), or the incorporation of additional costs into the objective functions due to strategy implementation and use of memory (Abreu and Rubinstein 1988). The application of these as well as the earlier approaches to infinite dynamic games, so as to further shrink the NES set is an open, highly promising research area.

3. Stackelberg Equilibria in Dynamic Games

In this section we present a brief discussion of the 'time consistency' and 'robustness' properties of an asymmetric equilibrium, namely the Stackelberg equilibrium, in non-zero-sum two-person games. The scenario here allows one of the agents (called 'the leader') to be the dominant player, able to announce in advance and dictate his policies to the other player (called 'the follower').

Consider the multiple-agent formulation of Section 2, along with the state equation (2.1a) and cost functions (2.1b), but with M = 2. Designate agent 1 as the leader and agent 2 as the follower. Given an IP $\underline{\eta}$ and a corresponding composite policy space $\underline{\Gamma}$, consider the normal form $\{J_1, J_2; \underline{\Gamma}\}$ where J_m is given by (2.2). For each $\underline{\gamma}_1 \in \underline{\Gamma}_1$, introduce the reaction set $\underline{R}(\underline{\gamma}_1) \subset \underline{\Gamma}_2$ for the follower by

$$\underline{R}(\underline{\gamma}_1) \equiv \{\underline{\beta} \in \underline{\Gamma}_2 : J_2(\underline{\gamma}_1, \underline{\beta}, x_0) = \min_{\underline{\gamma}_2 \in \underline{\Gamma}_2} J_2(\underline{\gamma}_1, \underline{\gamma}_2, x_0)\}. \tag{3.1}$$

Finally let $\underline{\gamma}_1^{op}$ and $\underline{\gamma}_1^{ps}$ be two policies for the leader -to be called *optimistic Stackelberg solution* (OSS) and *pessimistic Stackelberg solution* (PSS), respectively- defined by

$$\underline{\gamma}_1^{op} \equiv \arg\min_{\underline{\beta} \in \underline{\Gamma}_1} \inf_{\underline{\gamma}_2 \in R(\underline{\beta})} J_1(\underline{\beta}, \underline{\gamma}_2, x_0), \tag{3.2a}$$

$$\underline{\gamma}_1^{ps} \equiv \arg\min_{\underline{\beta} \in \underline{\Gamma}_1} \sup_{\underline{\gamma}_2 \in R(\underline{\beta})} J_1(\underline{\beta}, \underline{\gamma}_2, x_0). \tag{3.2b}$$

Note that these correspond to the two extreme cases in a Stackelberg game, where the follower either cooperates with the leader on the reaction set $\underline{R}$ (the optimistic scenario), or chooses the worst policy for the leader (the pessimistic scenario)[9]. Of course, if $\underline{R}(\underline{\beta})$ is a singleton for every $\underline{\beta} \in \underline{\Gamma}_1$, then the two extreme scenarios coincide.

For the above class of dynamic games, we can still use the general notation (and characterisation) $D(\underline{\Gamma}, \underline{X}, [0,T]; sol)$, where *sol* now stands for either (3.2a) or (3.2b), i.e. OSS or PSS. Hence, all the previous definitions (of WTC, STC and robust solutions) are equally applicable here. It turns out, however, that since neither OSS nor PSS admits a 'recursive definition', we have:

FACT 12. Generically, neither OSS nor PSS is WTC. □

This implies that while the decision process is evolving under either OSS or PSS, at any time $t \in [0,T]$ there will be some incentive for the leader to modify his future policies again under the same solution concept - this being so even if the process has not deviated from the trajectory dictated by the initially adopted solution. In other words, the leader would be tempted to reoptimise his policy along the way, even if he does not make any state measurements (for example, under the OL IP) but operates under the assumptions that the follower has responded rationally and the system dynamics used in the initial computations were accurate. The presence of such an incentive to renege by the leader also brings with it a loss in reputation that he may have built with the follower, so that he may no longer be able to convincingly dictate policies to the latter and expect him to respond optimally. This initiates a 'second guessing' process whereby each side will attempt to forecast the future moves of each other, For example, if the follower places some weight on the possibility that the leader may not abide by the announced policy, his response will not necessarily be determined through (3.1), which is another factor that the leader has to take into account while determining his policy (initially). It would be interesting to study the possible ramifications of such 'second-order' effects on the Stackelberg solution, and particularly whether the deterrence provided by these second-order effects would lead to time consistency.

An exception to the general rule that OSS and PSS are generically time inconsistent, is the class of problems where the leader can use his CL information to force the follower to a team solution to his benefit. Whenever this happens (i.e. when the global minimum of J_1 can be achieved under γ_1^{op}) then the corresponding policy for the leader will be WTC (Başar and Selbuz 1979), and in some cases even STC (Tolwinski 1981). Such policies for the leader have close connections with the so-called *incentive policies* (Başar and Olsder 1982; Ho, Luh and Olsder 1982; Başar 1985b; Zheng, Başar and Cruz 1984).

A solution concept that generally leads to time consistency (and in the strong sense), while preserving the stipulated decision hierarchy (though only stagewise), is the so-called *feedback Stackelberg solution* (FSS) (Başar and Olsder 1982), which is applicable to feedback games (with both agents having CL or FB IP). The STC FSS can be obtained from the DP recursion (2.5) where the *sol* operator now stands for either the OSS or PSS solution concepts, applied to the sequence of static games $\{\tilde{V}_{m,t+1}\}_{m=1}^{2}$.

One could even extend the notion of FSS to systems with lagged variables, such as those described by (1.10a) or (1.10b). In the case of (1.10a), and under the CL IP for both agents, the FSS can be obtained from (2.6), with *sol* again interpreted as above. In the case of (1.10b), and with $\eta_{mt} = \{x^t, u_{t-1}\}$ for m = 1,2, the DP recursion will be

$$V_{mt}(x,u_{t-1}) = sol_{u\in U_t}\{V_{m,t+1}(f_t(x,u,u_{t-1}),u) + g_t(f_t(x,u,u_{t-1}),u)\}_{m=1}^{2}$$
$$V_{m,T+1} \equiv 0, \qquad m = 1,2, \tag{3.3}$$

the solution of which will be in the form $u_{mt} = \gamma_{mt}(x_t, u_{t-1})$, m = 1,2.

Further extensions are possible, to stochastic systems of the type discussed in Section 1 and Section 2 - a framework that allows the introduction of the notion of 'robustness' as before. In general robust solutions will exist under both FSS and OSS/PSS concepts, though proving the existence of a limit to the solution sequence obtained for the (stochastically) perturbed game is more difficult for the latter than for the former. A complete theory for this is yet not available.

In principle, it is also possible to extend the notions of time consistency and robustness to dynamic games with more than two agents and with a blend of Nash and Stackelberg modes of play and/or multiple hierarchies; but the conclusions are not as clean there (for some possibilities see Başar and Olsder 1982). Another possible extension would be to the *consistent conjectural variations equilibrium* (Başar 1986), which is again generally not WTC, but its FB version is.

4. Time Consistency in Continuous-time Systems

The results presented in the earlier sections on the time consistency and robustness of solutions to single- or multiple-agent decision problems are valid, at the conceptual level, even if the discrete-time interval is replaced by a continuous interval. Letting [0,T] denote, this time, the continuous closed interval, the counterparts of (1.1a) and (1.1b) in the continuous time would be:

$$\dot{x}_t = f(t,x_t,u_t), \qquad t \geq 0 \tag{3.4a}$$

$$L(\underline{x},\underline{u}) = \int_0^T g(t,x_t,u_t)dt, \tag{3.4b}$$

and the counterpart of (1.2a) (the CL IP) would be the following:

$$\eta_t = \{x_s,\ 0 \leq s \leq t\}.$$

The dynamic programming recursion (1.6b) would then be replaced by the partial differential equation

$$\frac{\partial V(t,x)}{\partial t} + \min_{u \in U_t} \{\nabla_x V(t,x) f(t,x,u) + g(t,x,u)\} \equiv 0 \tag{3.5}$$

the boundary condition of which is $V(T,x) \equiv 0$[10].

With these changes, Definitions 1.1 and 1.2 are equally applicable, Fact 1 remains valid, and the control that is obtained from (3.5) constitutes an STC solution under the FB or CL IPs. For the stochastic version, on the other hand, (3.4a) is replaced by the stochastic differential equation

$$dx_t = f(t,x_t,u_t)dt + \sigma dw_t \tag{3.6}$$

where σ is an appropriate dimensional square matrix and $\{w_t,\ t \geq 0\}$ is a vector-valued standard Wiener process. The corresponding dynamic programming algorithm (the Hamilton-Jacobi-Bellman equation), as the counterpart of (1.14) in the continuous-time case, is

$$\frac{\partial W(t,x)}{\partial t} + \frac{1}{2} \sum_{i,j} \sigma_{ij} \frac{\partial^2 W(t,x)}{\partial x_i \partial x_j} + \min_{u \in U_t} \{\nabla_x W(t,x) f(t,x,u) + g(t,x,u)\} \equiv 0 \tag{3.7}$$

with a boundary condition $W(T,x) \equiv 0$, where σ_{ij} denotes the ij'th entry of the matrix σ and x_i stands for the i'th component of x. Note that in contrast with (1.14), the 'averaging' over the statistics of the noise (Wiener) process has already been done in (3.7), which is the reason why it does not involve an expectation operator as in (1.14).

Definition 1.3 has a natural counterpart here, and the noise process has full support if, and only if, the matrix σ is non-singular[11]. Hence, whenever this condition holds, the only solution of the single-agent optimisation problem will be the one obtained from (3.7), $u_t = \gamma(t,x_t)$, $t \in [0,T]$, which is STC. Facts 1 and 2 are equally valid here, and the notion of robustness has a natural counterpart, with the sequence $\{\Lambda^{(n)}\}$ in Definition 1.4 replaced by a sequence $\{\sigma^{(n)}\}$ converging to the zero matrix.

The continuous-time dynamic game (more commonly known as 'differential game') formulation also follows the previous lines (see Başar and Olsder 1982 for details), with the state equation again given by either (3.4a) or (3.6), under the interpretation that u is now the composite control for all agents, the m'th one having the loss function

$$L_m(\underline{x},\underline{u}) = \int_0^T g_m(t,x_t,u_t)dt.$$

Facts 5 to 11 inclusive are equally valid in the continuous time, under the Nash equilibrium solution concept, with the two dynamic programming recursions (2.5) and (2.9) replaced, respectively, by

$$\left[\frac{\partial V_m(t,x)}{\partial t}\right]_{m=1}^M + sol_{u\in U_t}\{\nabla_x V_m(t,x)f(t,x,u) + g_m(t,x,u)\}_{m=1}^M \equiv 0 \tag{3.8a}$$

with boundary condition $V_m(T,x) \equiv 0$, $m = 1,\ldots,M$;
and

$$\left[\frac{\partial W_m(t,x)}{\partial t} + \tfrac{1}{2}\sum_{i,j} \sigma_{ij} \frac{\partial^2 W_m(t,x)}{\partial x_i \partial x_j}\right]_{m=1}^M + sol_{u\in U_t}\{\nabla_x W_m(t,x)f(t,x,u) + g_m(t,x,u)\} \equiv 0 \tag{3.8b}$$

with boundary condition $W_m(T,x) \equiv 0$, $m = 1,\ldots,M$, where the *sol* operator in each case determines the NESs of the corresponding static game.

For the Stackelberg solution concept, Fact 2 is valid with *sol* again standing for either (3.2a) or (3.2b), making the Stackelberg solution generally non-credible also in the continuous-time case. The STC solution in this case is again the feedback Stackelberg solution, for which a rigorous definition (in the continuous time) can be found in Başar and Haurie (1984). Assuming full state information, the partial differential equation in this case is identical with (3.8a) or (3.8b) above (depending on whether we have a deterministic or a stochastic formulation), with the only difference being that now the sol operator computes the Stackelberg solution of the corresponding (two-person) static game. We should mention, in this context, three recent references, Miller and Salmon (1985), Dockner and Neck (1988) and Cohen and Michel (1988), which deal with the time-consistency issue in continuous-time dynamic games with an infinite time horizon.

5. Concluding Remarks

Our main objective in this paper has been to provide a unified description of time consistency in dynamic decision problems, so as to encompass both stochastic and deterministic models, and a variety of information patterns and solution concepts. As we have mentioned in the Introduction, for a meaningful study of time consistency it is essential that the problem formulation be consistent across time; accordingly, we have not included decision problems with ambiguity in termination, or in the evolution of the decision dynamics, or in the information acquisition of the agents. Consider, for example, a stochastic single-agent policy optimisation problem where initially the decision-maker constructs a policy over a given horizon under the assumption that full state information will be available at all points in time, but then experiences a blackout as regards some (or all) of the information channels. Under such a scenario the initially constructed policy will no longer be feasible and will definitely need to be revised, unless such a contingency was accounted for (by the assignment of some probability weights) in the original formulation of the problem. Without a reliable probabilistic assessment of such deviations from a nominal model, it would not be possible to accommodate such problems in the general framework of this paper.

Acronyms

IP : Information pattern
CL : Closed-loop
FB : Feedback
OL : Open-loop
WTC: Weakly time consistent
STC: Strongly time consistent
DP : Dynamic programming
NES: Nash equilibrium solution
OSS: Optimistic Stackelberg solution
PSS: Pessimistic Stackelberg solution
FSS: Feedback Stackelberg solution

Notes

* The current version of this paper has benefited from comments received from the audience at the Conference on 'Dynamic Policy Games in Economics' and from the two referees. I am also grateful to Mark Salmon, of the University of Warwick, for several constructive suggestions on an earlier version of the paper. The work was partially conducted while the author was spending a sabbatical year at INRIA, Sophia Antipolis, France. Our research in the area of multiple-agent decision-making, some of which has been reported here, has been partially supported by the Air Force Office of Scientific Research under Grants AFOSR 84-0056 and AFOSR 88-0178, through the University of Illinois at Urbana-Champaign.

1. We assume here, and throughout, that the infimum can always be replaced by a minimum, since our main objective in this paper is to study salient features of optimal policies, whenever they exist, and *not* to study their existence.

2. For the truncated version, the open-loop solution will first depend on the x_s^*, but since all the past decisions have been fixed at their optimal values, x_s^* can be expressed in terms of the initial state x_0, thus making the future decisions depend only on x_0.

3. For some special structures, such as the case of linear f_t and quadratic g_t, the OL solution can be derived from the FB solution, using the 'certainty equivalence' property of the optimal solution. For general non-linear problems, however, such a derivation would not be valid. Also, even in the linear-quadratic case, the FB solution is *informationally unique*, provided that the system noise is of the type described above.

4. Fact 2 is valid also for stochastic policy optimisation problems where the dynamic information available is of the 'noisy' type, provided that a full statistical description of the noisy measurements is available as *a priori* information.

5. For some classes of problems, such as those described by linear f and quadratic g, the minimising solution in (1.14) is independent of $P_w^{(n)}$, and hence the solution coincides with $\underline{\gamma}^*$ for all n, which makes it unnecessary to go to the limit.

6. This truncated version is in fact the decision problem $D^{\beta}_{[s,T]}$ introduced in Definition 1.2. For a feedback game such a truncation leads to a subgame which itself is a feedback game with fewer stages (time steps).

7. For example, for a game with CL IP for all agents, (2.8) may admit a unique solution for every non-singular P_w -since inclusion of small noisy perturbations tends to smoothen the value function- while its deterministic counterpart (2.5) generates non-unique NESs all of which are STC.

8. We do not allow the IPs to carry full information on the past control values while carrying only partial information on state variables, because such formulations would lead to 'games with imperfect information' which is a topic beyond the scope of our coverage here.

9. Note that by the rules of the game, at the time he chooses and announces his policy, the leader does not actually know which scenario the follower will adopt. But once he fixes his policy, the follower is indifferent to different choices out of $\underline{R}$. Of course, the two

scenarios given constitute the two extremes; there could be several other possibilities which fall somewhere in between.

10. The boundary condition is zero here because we have not placed any costs on the terminal state in the loss functional (3.4b); if there had been an additional additive term such as $q(x_T)$ in L, then the boundary condition would be equal to that function at time T.

11. Here we have abused the terminology somewhat and have considered the coefficient matrix σ as a part of the noise (Wiener) process, so that as $\sigma \to 0$ (the zero matrix) we recover the deterministic formulation.

References

Abreu, D. and A. Rubinstein, 'The structure of Nash equilibrium in repeated games with finite automata', Econometrica, vol. 56, no. 6, 1988, pp. 1259-1281.

Başar, T., 'On the uniqueness of the Nash solution in linear-quadratic differential games', International Journal of Game Theory, vol. 5, no. 2/3, 1976, pp. 65-90.

Başar, T., 'Informationally nonunique equilibrium solutions in differential games', SIAM Journal on Control, vol. 15, no. 4, 1977, pp. 636-660.

Başar, T., 'Informational uniqueness of closed-loop Nash equilibria for a class of nonstandard dynamic games', Journal of Optimization Theory and Applications, vol. 46, no. 4, 1985a, pp. 409-419.

Başar, T., 'Dynamic games and incentives', in A. Bagchi and H.Th. Jongen (eds), Systems and Optimization, Lecture Notes on Control and Information Sciences, vol. 66, Springer-Verlag, Berlin, 1985b, pp. 1-13.

Başar, T., 'A tutorial on dynamic and differential games', in T. Başar (ed.), Dynamic Games and Applications in Economics, Lecture Notes on Economics and Mathematical Systems, vol. 265, Springer-Verlag, Berlin, 1986, pp. 1-25.

Başar, T., 'Some thoughts on rational expectations models, and alternate formulations', invited contribution to a special issue of S. Mittnik (ed.), Computer and Mathematics with Applications, 'System-theoretic methods in economic modelling, II', forthcoming August 1989b.

Başar, T., 'Dynamic optimization of some forward-looking stochastic models', in A. Blaquière (ed.), Modeling and Control of Systems, Proceedings of the Bellman Continuum, Lecture Notes on Information

Sciences and Systems, Springer-Verlag, Berlin, forthcoming February 1989b.

Başar, T. and A. Haurie, 'Feedback equilibria in differential games with structural and modal uncertainties', in J.B. Cruz, Jr (ed.), Advances in Large Scale Systems, JAI Press, Greenwich, Connecticut, 1984, pp. 163-201.

Başar, T. and G.J. Olsder, Dynamic Noncooperative Game Theory, Academic Press, London/New York, 1982.

Başar, T. and H. Selbuz, 'Closed-loop Stackelberg strategies with applications in the optimal control of multilevel systems', IEEE Transactions on Automatic Control, vol. AC-24, no. 2, 1979, pp. 166-179.

Başar, T., S.J. Turnovsky and V. d'Orey, 'Optimal strategic monetary policies in dynamic interdependent economies', in T. Başar (ed.), Dynamic Games and Applications in Economics, Lecture Notes on Economics and Mathematical Systems, vol. 265, Springer-Verlag, Berlin, 1986, pp. 134-178.

Calvo, G., 'On the time consistency of optimal policy in a monetary economy', Econometrica, vol. 46, 1978, pp. 1411-1428.

Cohen, D. and P. Michel, 'How should control theory be used to calculate a time-consistent government policy?', Review of Economic Studies, vol. LV, 1988, pp. 263-274.

Cubitt, R.P., 'Two perspectives on the time inconsistency problem', Greek Economic Review, vol. 8, no. 1, 1986, pp. 1-20.

Damme, E. van, 'A relation between perfect equilibria in extensive games and proper equilibria in normal form games', International Journal of Game Theory, vol. 13, issue 1, 1984, pp. 1-13.

Dockner, E.J. and R. Neck, 'Time-consistency, subgame-perfectness, solution concepts and information patterns in dynamic models of stabilisation policies', Internal report, Institut für Volkswirtschaftstheorie und -politik, Wirtschaftsuniversität Wien, Austria, 1988.

Ho, Y.-C., P.B. Luh and G.J. Olsder, 'A control theoretic view on incentives', Automatica, vol. 18, no. 1, 1982, pp. 167-180.

Kohlberg, E. and J.-F. Mertens, 'On the strategic stability of equilibria', Econometrica, vol. 54, no. 5, 1986, pp. 1003-1037.

Kreps, D.M. and R. Wilson, 'Sequential equilibria', Econometrica, vol. 50, no. 4, 1982, pp. 863-894.

Kydland, F. and E.C. Prescott, 'Rules rather than discretion: the inconsistency of optimal plans', Journal of Political Economy, vol. 85, 1977, pp. 473-491.

Miller, M. and M. Salmon, 'Policy coordination and the time inconsistency of optimal policy in open economies', Economic Journal, vol. 95, (Supplement), 1985, pp. 124-137.

Myerson, R.B., 'Refinement of the Nash equilibrium concept', International Journal of Game Theory, vol. 7, issue 2, 1978, pp. 73-80.

Selten, R., 'Reexamination of the perfectness concept for equilibrium points in extensive games', International Journal of Game Theory, vol. 4, issue 1, 1975, pp. 25-55.

Tolwinski, B., 'Closed-loop Stackelberg solution to multistage linear quadratic games', Journal of Optimization Theory and Applications, vol. 34, no. 4, 1981, pp. 485-502.

Wan, H.Y., Jr, 'The new classical economics - a game-theoretic critique', in G. Feiwel (ed.), Issues in Macro-Economics, MacMillan, London, 1985, pp. 235-257.

Zheng, Y.P., T. Başar and J.B. Cruz, Jr, 'Incentive Stackelberg strategies for deterministic multi-stage decision processes', IEEE Transactions on Systems, Man and Cybernetics, vol. SMC-14, no. 1, 1984, pp. 10-20.

Dynamic Policy Games in Economics
F. van der Ploeg and A.J. de Zeeuw, (Editors)

SELF-ENFORCEABLE AGREEMENTS IN AN N-PLAYER DYNAMIC GAME*

Chaim Fershtman

Department of Economics
Tel-Aviv University
Tel-Aviv 69978, Israel

Introduction

Dynamic game theory provides an analytical framework for modelling interaction among players in which the structure of the interaction may change over time and the changes are governed by the players' actions. In applying dynamic games to economic situations, one may consider a cooperative environment in which the players have to agree on a time path of actions or on a set of rules, and once the decision is made the agreement is binding and enforceable. On the other hand, the players sometimes face a non-cooperative situation in which communication and a binding agreement are not feasible. Many economic problems, however, fall into a class of games in which the players can communicate with one another, i.e. they can discuss possible solutions, but they cannot sign a binding agreement. Dynamic policy games are a good example of such a class of games, for when agreements have no legal standing, players must look for agreements which are self-enforceable.

The equilibrium concept most frequently used in dynamic game theory is the Nash equilibrium concept. The rationale of this concept is that no player can gain from a unilateral deviation from the prescribed equilibrium strategies. Thus it is clear that a self-enforceable agreement should satisfy the Nash condition. When we consider, however, an n-player game we should also consider joint deviations by a coalition of several players. If a coalition of players can credibly deviate from a proposed agreement then the agreement is not self-enforceable.

Consider, for example, an exchange rate policy coordination game. Discussing such a problem as a dynamic game and adopting the Nash equilibrium concept can be misleading. When n countries negotiate their joint exchange rate policy they will not consider an agreement on the basis of which a coalition of countries can benefit by a credible joint deviation from the proposed agreement. Channels of communication exist between all the countries. Moreover the countries can continue their communication throughout the game and discuss possible deviations at some future periods. Countries can also condition deviation on the realisation of some state of the world through contemplating conditional deviations. Clearly any such self-enforceable agreement should be a Nash equilibrium, otherwise there is at least one player who will benefit from a unilateral deviation. However, not all the Nash equilibria are good candidates for such a self-enforceable multiple country agreement[1].

The equilibrium concept when deviation of coalitions is feasible has been discussed already in the literature. Aumann (1959) and Rubinstein (1980) define and discuss the strong Nash equilibrium and the perfectly strong Nash equilibrium. A strong Nash equilibrium is a strategy profile such that there is no coalition of players that can increase the payoffs of its members by a joint deviation. When we discuss a strong equilibrium we consider all possible deviations including non-credible deviations, i.e. we allow players to contemplate deviations even if they know that there will be a deviation from the deviation. Bernheim, Peleg and Whinston (1987) and Bernheim and Whinston (1987) define and discuss the coalition-proof Nash equilibrium which is an n-tuple of strategies according to which no coalition of players can contemplate an enforceable deviation. The present paper is much in the spirit of these works as it tries to examine the conditions under which an agreement is self-enforceable.

The concept of coalition-proof equilibrium is based on the assumption that players are able to terminate their communication channels with other players, i.e., for example, to leave the room in which they negotiate. This assumption draws criticism since, if it is possible to do so, it should be part of the game and not a condition for the equilibrium concept. Van Damme[2] elaborates on this issue and demonstrates that, once the communication among the players is modelled in such a way that the order in which players leave the room is part of the equilibrium behaviour, then the resultant equilibrium is different from the coalition-proof equilibrium. We will discuss van Damme's criticism and show the relationship between the assumptions regarding the communications game and the definition of self-enforceable agreement. Subsequently we will discuss the concept of acceptable equilibrium in which we use a stronger definition of credible deviations. In this definition we allow members of a deviating coalition to contemplate another deviation with players who are not in the original deviating coalition.

Adopting equilibrium concepts, such as the coalition-proof equilibrium or the acceptable equilibrium, in a dynamic game setting raises many interesting issues. Since in dynamic games the structure of the game, i.e. the payoff functions as well as the sets of admissible actions, changes along time, the incentives that different coalitions have to deviate may change over time. If we consider a potential deviation of a coalition at the beginning of the game, it is possible that such a deviation is credible in the first stages of the game but that, as the game proceeds, members of the deviating coalition will have incentives to join other coalitions and to contemplate other deviations. Moreover, since the evolution of the game (and the state variables) is determined by the player's action, each player must take into account the effect of his current action on future incentives to form deviating coalitions.

The problem of time inconsistency in dynamic policy games usually occurs when the players are strategically asymmetric. One is the leader while the other is the follower (see Kydland and Prescott 1977). Changing this assumption and assuming symmetry leads to a time-consistent equilibrium (see, for example, Buiter 1983). The question is whether this property is generalised to an n-player game in which coalition-proof or acceptable Nash equilibria are considered. We examine the problem of time consistency in such an n-player game and conclude that a coalition-proof (or acceptable) Nash equilibrium might be time inconsistent.

Before we proceed to more formal definitions we would like to emphasise that this paper does not suggest a specific equilibrium concept that should be used in all n-player dynamic games. Clearly the definitions of credible deviation and self-enforceable agreement depend on the model under investigation. Moreover, the research on n-player dynamic games and enforceable overtime agreements is in its early stages. We hope, however, that this discussion will assist in modelling dynamic economic interaction and, in particular, dynamic policy games in which assuming communications among players throughout the game is a natural assumption.

1. Notation and Definitions

Let $G(N,\Gamma,J)$ be an n-player game such that N is the set of players, $\Gamma = (\Gamma_1,\ldots,\Gamma_n)$ are the players' strategy spaces, $J = (J_1,\ldots,J_n)$ such that $J_i : \Gamma \to R$ is the i'th player's payoff function. A Nash equilibrium is an n-tuple of strategies $\gamma^* = (\gamma_1^*,\ldots,\gamma_n^*) \in \Gamma$, such that for every i

$$J_i(\gamma^*) \geq J_i(\gamma_1^*,\ldots,\gamma_{i-1}^*,\gamma_i,\gamma_{i+1}^*,\ldots,\gamma_n^*)$$

for all possible $\gamma_i \in \Gamma_i$, i.e. no player can benefit from a unilateral deviation. Clearly, a necessary condition for self-enforceability is that the agreement is a Nash equilibrium in the game among the players. However, as has been argued previously, this condition is insufficient.

For an n-player game G, let P be the set of all possible coalitions. For a given $\gamma \in \Gamma$ and $p \in P$ we denote as G/γ_{-p} the game among the players of coalition p when non-members of p play γ_{-p}.

A *strong equilibrium* (Aumann 1959) is an n-tuple of strategies such that no coalition can benefit by changing its strategies. Clearly this requirement implies that a strong Nash equilibrium is Pareto efficient among all the feasible outcomes since, if not, a coalition consisting of all the players can deviate. Formally a strong equilibrium is a strategy profile γ^* such that there is no $p \in P$ and strategies $\gamma_p \in \Gamma_p$ for which $J_i(\gamma_{-p}^*,\gamma_p) \geq J_i(\gamma^*)$ for all members of p and there is at least one player $i \in p$ for whom we have strict inequality.

2. Coalition-proof Nash Equilibria (Bernheim, Peleg and Whinston 1987)

In defining 'strong equilibrium' we allow players to deviate from any strategy profile without examining whether their deviation is credible or not. The environment in which the players negotiate is such that there is no binding agreement. Thus, if we consider a possible joint deviation of a particular coalition, we should check whether the members of the deviating coalition will indeed follow their deviating strategy. To overcome this difficulty Bernheim, Peleg and Whinston (1987) define the coalition-proof Nash equilibrium. Here we follow their definition with a slight change of presentation.

DEFINITION 1. A (weakly) *credible deviation* is defined as follows:

(i) In a single-player problem, a (weakly) credible deviation from a strategy $\tilde{\gamma} \in \Gamma$ is a strategy $\hat{\gamma} \in \Gamma$ such that $J_i(\hat{\gamma}) > J_i(\tilde{\gamma})$ and $J_i(\hat{\gamma}) \geq J_i(\gamma)$ for every $\gamma \in \Gamma$.

(ii) Let $n > 1$ and assume that a (weakly) credible deviation is defined for games with fewer than n players. Then, for any game with n players a (weakly) credible deviation from $\tilde{\gamma} \in \Gamma$ is a coalition $p \in P$ and strategies $\{\hat{\gamma}_j\}_{j \in p}$ such that there is no (weakly) credible deviation from $\{\hat{\gamma}_j\}_{j \in p}$, $J_i(\hat{\gamma}_p, \tilde{\gamma}_{-p}) \geq J_i(\tilde{\gamma})$ for all $i \in p$ and there is at least one player $j \in p$ for whom we have strict inequality.

DEFINITION 2. Let G be an n-player game. $\gamma^* \in \Gamma$ is a *coalition-proof Nash equilibrium* if (i) there is no (weakly) credible deviation from γ^*; (ii) γ^* is not Pareto dominated by another strategy profile from which there is no (weakly) credible deviation.

When n = 3, a coalition-proof Nash equilibrium is $\gamma^* = (\gamma_1^*, \gamma_2^*, \gamma_3^*)$ such that (i) γ^* is a Nash equilibrium; (ii) for every j, $k \neq i$, (γ_j^*, γ_k^*) is a Nash equilibrium in G/γ_i^* and it is not dominated by any other Nash equilibrium in the game G/γ_i^*.

In order to illustrate this notion of equilibrium, Bernheim et al. presented the following three-player game. Player A chooses rows, player B chooses columns and player C chooses boxes. The payoffs are specified in Table 1 below.

Table 1: Illustration of a coalition-proof Nash equilibrium

	C_1			C_2	
	B_1	B_2		B_1	B_2
A_1	8, 8, 0	0, 0, 5	A_1	3, 3, 8	0, 0, 5
A_2	0, 0, 4	5, 5, 12	A_2	0, 0, 5	2, 2, 5

There are two Nash equilibria in pure strategies in the above game: (A_2,B_2,C_1) and (A_1,B_1,C_2). If we adopt a criterion which selects a Pareto-dominant Nash equilibrium, then (A_2,B_2,C_1) is chosen. But, as Bernheim et al. argue, (A_2,B_2,C_1) is not coalition proof. Since any subgroup of players has the opportunity to communicate, players A and B can agree on a joint deviation and play A_1 and B_1 instead of A_2 and B_2. This deviation is weakly credible since, given the third player's strategy C_1, (A_1,B_1) is a Nash equilibrium in the induced two-player game. Thus, (A_2,B_2,C_1) is not a coalition-proof Nash equilibrium. The difference between a coalition-proof equilibrium and a strong equilibrium is that, in defining a coalition-proof Nash equilibrium, we consider only a weakly credible deviation, while in defining a strong equilibrium there is no such credibility requirement. In the above game, for example, there is no strong equilibrium, since players A and B can deviate from (A_2,B_2,C_1) and (A_1,B_1,C_2) is Pareto dominated.

3. The Communications Game

The notion of coalition-proof Nash equilibria was developed in order to capture the view that a meaningful agreement should be self-enforceable. In order to capture this property the definition of coalition proof specifies the condition that the agreed strategy profile should satisfy. Although the communication among the players is what motivates the discussion, it is not modelled and the conditions are specified directly on the equilibrium strategies. Bernheim et al., however, describe a simple scenario that provides some intuitive explanation of the notion of coalition-proof Nash equilibrium.

Consider a group of players meeting in a room and discussing possible agreements. Any player may choose his own strategy and then leave the room. Once he leaves the room he is forbidden to come back and to change his decision. Thus, if the players reach an agreement and one of them leaves the room, the remaining players take his action as given and may reach a new agreement among themselves. A coalition-proof Nash equilibrium is an agreement that is self-enforceable regardless of the order of exit.

Van Damme pointed out that in order to develop a notion of self-enforceable agreement one should also model the communications game between the players. If players are meeting in a room negotiating an agreement and they are allowed to leave the room, this stage of the interaction should be modelled as part of the game. Using the three-player game described in Table 1, van Damme shows that in equilibrium, player C is not the first to leave the room; thus, the equilibrium of the extended game is (A_2, B_2, C_1) which is not the coalition-proof equilibrium.

Specifically, if player A is the first to leave the room, he can choose either A_1 or A_2. If he chooses A_1, then players B and C face the following game:

	C_1	C_2
B_1	8, 0	3, 8
B_2	0, 5	3, 5

The equilibrium of this game is (B_1, C_2) and the players' payoffs are (3,3,8).

If player A chooses A_2 instead, players B and C face the game:

	C_1	C_2
B_1	0, 4	0, 5
B_2	5, 12	3, 5

The equilibrium of this game is (B_2, C_1) which yields the payoffs (5,5,12). Thus we can conclude that, if player A is the first to leave the room, his strategy choice will be A_2. Similar arguments hold for player B.

Now let us follow the same steps for player C. If he leaves the room and chooses C_1, players A and B face the game:

	B_1	B_2
A_1	8, 8	0, 0
A_2	0, 0	5, 5

and choose to play (A_1, B_1) which yields the payoffs (8,8,0). If player C chooses C_2 instead, players A and B face the game:

	B_1	B_2
A_1	3, 3	0, 0
A_2	0, 0	2, 2

which yields the payoffs (3,3,8). Thus, it is clear that if player C is the first to leave the room he chooses C_2.

So far we may summarise the analysis as follows: when player A (or B) leaves the room first, the final equilibrium payoffs are (5,5,12) while when player C leaves the room first the final payoffs are (3,3,8). Thus, van Damme concludes that it is a dominant strategy for all the players to let player A (or B) leave the room first, which implies that (A_2, B_2, C_1) is an enforceable agreement.

4. Acceptable Nash Equilibria

What characterises the above game is that players are allowed to terminate their channel of communication. One may think of a different scenario in which cutting communication channels or leaving the room is not feasible or cannot be done credibly. If, for example, the European finance ministers negotiate an exchange rate coordination policy, they can talk among themselves without the possibility of leaving the conference room and of credibly promising that they will not call, or talk with, one of their colleagues. If communication among any subset of players is always possible, one can specify conditions of self-enforceability that take into account this 'unlimited' communication possibility. In defining the coalition-proof Nash equilibrium we require that only weakly credible deviations be considered. That is to say that, once a coalition deviates, it cuts off all communication with the other players. Thus only members of the deviating coalitions may continue to deviate from the original deviation. The concept of coalition-proof equilibrium therefore embodied in its definition the possibility of cutting communication channels without a proper modelling of this possibility.

Now consider the case in which every coalition that plans to deviate from a certain strategy profile, knows that the channels of communication between every group of players are still, and will always be, open. Thus, if a particular player is a member of a deviating coalition, he may still communicate with players who are not in this coalition and may thus be tempted to collaborate with another coalition that contemplates a different kind of deviation. This coalition may also consist of some players who are not in the original deviating coalition. Thus, in order to make a deviation credible, we should also consider, in this case, a collaboration of members of the deviating coalition with players not in that coalition. We thus modify the definition of coalition-proof Nash equilibrium by considering only credible deviations and we denote such an equilibrium as an 'acceptable equilibrium'.

In modelling an n-player economic interaction the definition of credible deviation depends, of course, on the problem under discussion. The members of the deviating coalition have first-hand information regarding the deviation scheme while a non-member does not have the means of verifying the strategies that were agreed upon by the deviating coalition. Thus, if we think about a deviation from the deviation, it is easier to assume that only members of the original deviating coalition can contemplate further deviations. However, we may think of a model in which any deviation becomes public knowledge. In a dynamic game setting this argument is even stronger, since non-members can observe past actions of the deviating coalition and realise that there is a deviation.

To illustrate the different types of equilibria, consider the three-player game specified in Table 2.

Table 2: A three-player game

	C_1			C_2	
	B_1	B_2		B_1	B_2
A_1	8, 8, 0	0, 0, 5	A_1	3, 3, 8	0, 0, 5
A_2	0, 0, 4	5, 5, 12	A_2	9, 0, 13	3, 3, 5

The strategy profile (A_2,B_2,C_1) is a Nash equilibrium for this game. Let us now examine whether it is also a coalition-proof or acceptable Nash equilibrium. Once (A_2,B_2,C_1) is agreed upon, players A and B can deviate by playing (A_1,B_1), and increase their payoffs from (5,5) to (8,8). This deviation is (weakly) credible as (A_1,B_1) is a Nash equilibrium in the game between players A and B induced by player C's choice of C_1. Thus (A_2,B_2,C_1) is not a coalition-proof Nash equilibrium. In order to find out if (A_2,B_2,C_1) is an acceptable equilibrium, let us check whether the deviation of players A and B to the strategies (A_1,B_1) is credible. After the deviation to (A_1,B_1,C_1) players A and C can benefit from deviating again and play (A_2,C_2). In this case the payoffs will be (9,0,13). The deviation of players A and C is credible since it yields to them the highest possible payoffs in this game. Since player C is not part of the original deviating coalition, such a deviation is not considered when we discuss (weakly) credible deviations. Thus the original deviation of players A and B is weakly credible, but not credible, which implies that (A_2,B_2,C_1) is an acceptable Nash equilibrium but not a coalition-proof equilibrium.

REMARK: The definition of credible deviation can be modified by considering a second-order deviation of any possible coalition and not just a coalition in which there are members of the original deviating coalition. For example, in the game discussed above, the original deviating coalition is (A,B) and we consider a second-order deviation by

(A,C). Changing the definition as suggested in this remark implies that we should also consider a deviation of player C alone.

5. Time Consistency and Other Dynamic Aspects

In many cases players negotiate their time-dependent behaviour. If the interaction has a dynamic structure, it is possible that a certain deviation is credible at the outset of the game, but once the dynamic system reaches certain states, the members of the original deviating coalition have incentives to join another coalition. Players in joining certain agreements should thus consider the effect of their actions on the evolution of the game and on the future incentives of players to form different coalitions.

There are two major strategy spaces (or information structures) which are most commonly used in the application of dynamic games[3]: (i) the open-loop strategy space which is the set of all admissible time paths of actions; (ii) the closed-loop no-memory or feedback strategy space which is a set of Markovian decision rules specifying at every t the players' actions as a function of time and the observed state variables. One may also define different strategy spaces that are associated with different information structures.

Let us now modify the one-shot three-player game described in the previous sections and consider a game which is infinitely repeated.

Table 3: An infinitely repeated three-player game

	C_1			C_2	
	B_1	B_2		B_1	B_2
A_1	$a(\tau)$, $b(\tau)$, 0	0, 0, 5	A_1	3, 3, 8	0, 0, 5
A_2	0, 0, 4	5, 5, 12	A_2	0, 0, 5,	3, 3, 8

The one-period payoff matrix is defined in Table 3. Let τ be a state variable such that when the game starts $\tau = 0$. Every time (A_1,B_1,C_1) is played, the state variable τ is changed by one. Thus, τ is not a calender time, but a clock that ticks only when the relevant box, i.e., (A_1,B_1,C_1) is played. We let

$$a(\tau) \equiv 8 - \tau, \qquad b(\tau) = 8 - \tau.$$

At the beginning of the game, $\tau = 0$ and $a(0) = b(0) = 8$. We assume that the players wish to maximise their discounted profits. For such a dynamic game the open-loop strategies of playing (A_2,B_2,C_1) or (A_1,B_1,C_2) every period constitute a Nash equilibrium. Moreover, defining closed-loop no-memory strategies such that (A_2,B_2,C_1) or (A_1,B_1,C_2) are played at every time and state yields a subgame-perfect Nash equilibrium. As before, the open-loop strategies of playing (A_2,B_2,C_1) every period is not coalition proof as players A and B can deviate in the first three periods and play (A_1,B_1). After three periods of deviations $a(3) = b(3) = 5$ and there is no reason for further deviations. Now let us examine the open-loop strategies of playing (A_1,B_1,C_1) for three periods and then switching to (A_2,B_2,C_1) for the rest of the game. These strategies are not a coalition-proof Nash equilibrium as player C prefers to deviate in the first three periods and play C_2. But if we assume a discount factor close enough to one, this sequence of actions can be the outcome of a coalition-proof Nash equilibrium with closed-loop no-memory strategies. Let $\gamma_i(\tau,t)$ be a typical closed-loop no-memory strategy that specifies the i'th player's action at state τ and at time t. Now consider the strategies $\gamma_A(\tau,t) = A_1$ for $\tau = 0, 1, 2, 3$ and every t and $\gamma_A(\tau,t) = A_2$ for $\tau \geq 4$ and every t. γ_B and γ_C are defined in a similar way. Note that, since the discount factor is close enough to one, player C cannot benefit from deviating from his strategy and play C_2 for $\tau \leq 3$. Any such deviation results in an unchanged level of τ which yields a delay in moving to (A_2,B_2,C_1) in which player C's payoffs are 12. Note also that for a discount factor close enough to one the closed-loop strategies of playing (A_1,B_1,C_2) is not a coalition-proof Nash equilibrium, because it is Pareto dominated by the coalition-proof Nash equilibrium suggested above.

Consider now the dynamic game defined in Table 4. The game is played over time and the state variable τ is defined as in our previous game.

Players are assumed to maximise discounted payoffs and the discount factor is assumed to be close enough to one.

Table 4: Another infinitely repeated three-player game

	C_1			C_2	
	B_1	B_2		B_1	B_2
A_1	$8-\tau$, $8-\tau$, 0	0, 0, 5	A_1	3, 3, 8	0, 0, 4
A_2	0, 0, 4	5, 5, 12	A_2	0, 0, 5,	3, 3, $11+\tau$

As before, consider the agreement of playing (A_2,B_2,C_1) every period. Any deviation of player A and B to (A_1,B_1) leads to a higher τ. If A and B deviate for two periods, the payoff from playing (A_2,B_2,C_2) becomes (3,3,13) which implies that (A_2,B_2,C_1) ceases to be a Nash equilibrium. Thus, players A and B, in deciding on deviations, should consider the implications of their deviation for the payoffs structure of the game. For example, if they deviate for three periods, (A_2,B_2,C_1) ceases to be a Nash equilibrium and there is a new Nash equilibrium (A_2,B_2,C_2) in which players A and B get only 3. Thus, after having played (A_1,B_1,C_1) for three periods, they cannot switch back to (A_2,B_2,C_1) since player C will deviate and play C_2. Note that, if the payoff function at (A_2,B_2,C_2) would be $(3,3,12+\tau)$, then the agreement of always playing (A_2,B_2,C_1) is coalition proof.

The problem of time inconsistency has been the focus of many recent studies. This problem occurs when the players are strategically asymmetric. One is a leader while the other is a follower (see Kydland and Prescott 1977). The best response property of the Nash equilibrium implies immediately that every n-player Nash equilibrium is time consistent (see, for example, Buiter 1983 and Fershtman 1988). The question is whether this well-known observation can be generalised to the coalition-proof or acceptable Nash equilibrium.

DEFINITION 3. A coalition-proof (or acceptable) open-loop Nash equilibrium is time consistent if at every (x,t) *along* the equilibrium path the truncated open-loop strategies constitute a coalition-proof (acceptable) open-loop Nash equilibrium for the truncated game.

THEOREM. A coalition-proof open-loop Nash equilibrium is not necessarily time consistent.

PROOF. Consider the following dynamic three-player game:

Table 5: Time inconsistency of a coalition-proof open-loop Nash equilibrium

	C_1			C_2	
	B_1	B_2		B_1	B_2
A_1	$2-3\tau_2+\tau_3$, $2+3\tau_2+\tau_3$, 8	0, 0, 5	A_1	3, 3, 8	0, 0, 4
A_2	0, 4, 4	5, 5, 12	A_2	0, 2, 5	3, 3, 8
	(τ_2)	(τ_3)			

There are two state variables τ_2 and τ_3. τ_2 is a clock that ticks if (A_2,B_1,C_1) is played while τ_3 is a clock that ticks only if (A_2,B_2,C_1) is played. We assume, however, that both τ_2 and τ_3 can tick only in the first four periods. Now consider the 3-tuple open-loop strategies such that (A_2,B_2,C_1) is repeated forever. We claim that this is a coalition-proof Nash equilibrium. First note that player C will not join any coalition that deviates from this strategy profile. What about a joint deviation of players A and B? It seems that when τ_3 is high enough they can benefit from a joint deviation to (A_1,B_1,C_1). Thus let us consider the following deviation from the above open-loop strategy. Player A plays A_2 for four periods and then switches to A_1 forever; player B plays B_2 for four periods and then switches to B_1. Clearly both players can benefit from such a deviation. But this deviation is not (weakly) credible. Player B, who is a member of the deviating coalition, will deviate from such an agreement and play B_1 instead of B_2 in the first four periods.

The strategy profile (A_2,B_2,C_1), although a coalition-proof Nash equilibrium, is not time consistent. After four periods $\tau_3 = 4$, $\tau_2 = 0$, the game now repeats itself identically for every period and the deviation of players A and B to play (A_1,B_1) forever is a credible deviation. □

REMARK. In the above example, playing (A_2,B_2,C_1) is also a subgame-perfect Nash equilibrium. We can therefore conclude that subgame perfection does not necessarily imply that the equilibrium is coalition-proof time consistent.

Let us now discuss the intuition behind the above result. Let $(\gamma_1,\gamma_2,\gamma_3)$ be an open-loop Nash equilibrium of a three-player dynamic game. For every $(\tilde{x},\tilde{t})$ which is reached along the equilibrium path the truncated strategies continue to constitute a Nash equilibrium. If player j can benefit from deviating at $(\tilde{x},\tilde{t})$ and playing $\tilde{\gamma}_j$, it implies that the original strategy profile is not a Nash equilibrium and the best response to γ_{-j} is not γ_j. Now observe that we cannot follow similar arguments when we consider a coalition-proof equilibrium. Let $(\hat{\gamma}_1,\hat{\gamma}_2,\hat{\gamma}_3)$ be a coalition-proof open-loop Nash equilibrium. Now assume that $(\tilde{x},\tilde{t})$ is on the equilibrium path and that there are two players (j,k) that can benefit from a joint (weakly) credible deviation $(\tilde{\gamma}_j,\tilde{\gamma}_k)$ at $(\tilde{x},\tilde{t})$. Does the existence of such a deviation contradict the statement that $(\hat{\gamma}_1,\hat{\gamma}_2,\hat{\gamma}_3)$ is a coalition-proof equilibrium? Not necessarily. Let us take, as in the Nash equilibrium case, the combined strategies $(\bar{\gamma}_j,\bar{\gamma}_k)$ such that $(\bar{\gamma}_j(\tau),\bar{\gamma}_k(\tau)) = (\hat{\gamma}_j(\tau),\hat{\gamma}_k(\tau))$ for every $\tau < \tilde{t}$ and for $\tau \geq \tilde{t}$ let $(\bar{\gamma}_j(\tau),\bar{\gamma}_k(\tau)) = (\tilde{\gamma}_j(\tau),\tilde{\gamma}_k(\tau))$. Clearly $J_k(\hat{\gamma}_i,\bar{\gamma}_j,\bar{\gamma}_k) > J_k(\hat{\gamma})$ and similarly for player j. But the deviation of players (j,k) to $(\bar{\gamma}_j,\bar{\gamma}_k)$ at time zero is not necessarily (weakly) credible. It is possible that player j can benefit from deviating from $\bar{\gamma}_j$ if he knows that the other players play according to $(\hat{\gamma}_i,\bar{\gamma}_k)$. Clearly such a deviation should occur before the state $(\tilde{x},\tilde{t})$ is reached since we know from the (weak) credibility of the deviation $(\tilde{\gamma}_j,\tilde{\gamma}_k)$ that, once the state $(\tilde{x},\tilde{t})$ is reached, player j will not deviate from the strategy $\bar{\gamma}_j$.

COROLLARY. Since we can follow the same arguments when we discuss the acceptable Nash equilibrium, we conclude that an acceptable open-loop Nash equilibrium is not necessarily time consistent.

6. Concluding Remark

In situations in which agents need to reach a non-binding agreement they will consider only agreements which are self-enforceable. The main objective of this work is to contribute to the discussion about the meaning of 'self-enforceability'. Generally, a self-enforceable agreement is an agreement such that no coalition deviates from it. A coalition of players deviates only if the players benefit from the deviation and if there is some credibility to their deviation. The notion of credibility, however, can be defined in different ways, depending on the possible types of second-order deviations which are allowed in the model. I would like to emphasise that the adequate definition of credible deviation depends on the economic problem which is being analysed, and on the specific assumption regarding the existing communication channels among the players. As was demonstrated in this paper, however, the final outcome of the interaction crucially depends on the assumed notion of credible deviation.

Notes

* The author is grateful to Eric van Damme and participants in the Conference for valuable comments.

1. Allowing communication and negotiation among the players does not affect only the equilibrium of an n-player game. As a matter of fact, if we consider even a two-player dynamic game and allow for communication throughout the game, it is plausible that the players will not follow a mutually unpleasant subgame-perfect equilibrium path. They can renegotiate and choose an alternative path which is favourable to both of them. This argument suggests that the players will look for an agreement which is renegotiation proof. There is no reason for them to choose an agreement which they know will not

follow. For more details on renegotiation-proof equilibria in repeated game frameworks, see Farrell and Maskin (1987), Pearce (1987) and van Damme (1986). The focus of this paper, however, is not on renegotiation proof but on the potential deviation of a coalition of players. It is important to note, however, that the notion of renegotiation proof was discussed only in repeated game frameworks. To the best of my knowledge it has not been discussed yet within the context of a dynamic game setting.

2. Private communication (1988).

3. For more details see Başar (1986), Başar and Olsder (1982) and Fershtman (1987).

References

Aumann, R., 'Acceptable points in general cooperative n-person games', in A.W. Tucker and R.D. Luce (eds), Contributions to the Theory of Games IV, Princeton University Press, 1959.

Başar, T., 'A tutorial on dynamic and differential games', in T. Başar (ed.), Dynamic Games and Applications in Economics, Lecture Notes on Economics and Mathematical Systems, vol. 265, Springer-Verlag, Berlin, 1986.

Başar, T. and G.J. Olsder, Dynamic Noncooperative Game Theory, Academic Press, New York, 1982.

Bernheim, B.D., B. Peleg and M.D. Whinston, 'Coalition-proof Nash equilibrium: I Concepts', Journal of Economic Theory, 42, 1987, pp. 1-12.

Bernheim, B.D. and M.D. Whinston, 'Coalition-proof Nash equilibria: II Application', Journal of Economic Theory, 42, 1987, pp. 13-29.

Buiter, W., 'Optimal and time-consistent policies in continuous time rational expectation models', Technical Working Paper no. 29, NBER, 1983.

Damme, E. van, 'Renegotiation-proof equilibria in prisoners' dilemma', (mimeo), 1986.

Farrell, J. and E. Maskin, 'Renegotiations in repeated games', Discussion Paper no. 1335, Harvard University, 1987.

Fershtman, C., 'Alternative approaches to dynamic games', in R. Bryant and R. Portes (eds), Global Macroeconomics: Policy, Conflict and Cooperation, MacMillan Press, London, 1987.

Fershtman, C., 'Fixed rules and decision rules: subgame perfection and time consistency', Economic Letters, forthcoming.

Kydland, F.E. and E.C. Prescott, 'Rules rather than discretion: the inconsistency of optimal plans', Journal of Political Economy, 85, 1977, pp. 473-492.

Pearce, D.G., 'Renegotiation proof equilibria: collective rationality and intertemporal cooperation', (mimeo), 1987.

Rubinstein, A., 'Strong perfect equilibrium in supergames', International Journal of Game Theory, 9, 1980, pp. 1-12.

Dynamic Policy Games in Economics
F. van der Ploeg and A.J. de Zeeuw, (Editors)

A DYNAMIC HEURISTIC GAME THEORY MODEL OF AN ARMS RACE*

Michael D. Intriligator

Department of Economics
University of California, Los Angeles
Los Angeles, CA 90024-1486, USA

Dagobert L. Brito

Department of Economics
Rice University
Houston, TX 77001, USA

1. Arms Race Models versus Defence Decision-making

Models of the arms race are typically based on the Richardson model or on rational choice models. The Richardson model is one in which each side acquires weapons in response to the numbers of weapons held by the other side, in response to its own holdings of weapons, and in response to other factors, with the process of arms acquisition treated as a mechanistic and autonomous one[1]. Rational choice models, by contrast, allow for optimising behaviour, where arms procurements are choice variables in the maximisation of a certain objective function subject to certain constraints with regard to production possibilities and the reaction of the opponent, and with the process of arms acquisition embedded in the larger problem of welfare maximisation[2]. Neither of these models, however, takes explicit account of the *institutions* involved in defence decision-making, which are probably not adequately represented as either mechanistic or explicitly optimising in their procurement decisions.

Defence decision-making is typically conducted by institutions that are large, complex and bureaucratic. These organisations tend to rely on neither passive mechanical responses nor explicit optimisation rules. They rather tend to use 'rules of thumb' or *heuristic decision rules* for weapons procurement, which guide their choices with regard to arms acquisitions[3]. These heuristic decision rules may be based, in part, on mechanistic responses and, in part also, on optimising behaviour over some long horizon. They may also, however, be based on history, attitudes of decision-makers, interservice rivalry, and a variety of other institutional factors.

An example of a heuristic decision rule for weapons procurement is that used by the British navy in the period before World War I, when the navy was the principal means for projecting force worldwide. The British policy at that time was to have a navy capable of defeating the combined fleets of the next two largest naval powers. This decision rule was based on institutions, history and an analysis of the capabilities required for Britain to retain its naval preeminence and to meet its global colonial responsibilities. A second example of a heuristic decision rule is the US policy on conventional force capabilities in the 1970s and early 1980s, which called for forces sufficient to fight one and one-half wars at the same time, i.e., a major conflict plus a separate local conflict. A third example, which will be analysed in detail below, is the current US policy on strategic forces, which calls for sufficient capabilities to enable the United States to survive a Soviet first strike and inflict unacceptable levels of damage on the Soviet Union on a retaliatory second strike, i.e., a policy of deterrence by assured destruction. In all three examples the decisions on weapons procurement can be described by a two-stage process: firstly, a bureaucratic-political decision to establish a certain rule or goal and, secondly, an economic decision on the rate of accumulation of weapons needed to achieve this rule or goal.

This paper treats heuristic decision rules for weapons accumulation in an arms race and analyses their implications for stability in the context of a dynamic game. The dynamic game is one in which defence planners revise their heuristic rules over time using revisions in the plan, which can be triggered by time itself, as in the budget cycle, or by events, such as perceived changes in the capabilities or intentions of the enemy[4]. The resulting sequence of heuristic arms race games is studied for its stability properties, including both arms race stability and crisis stability.

The treatment of crisis stability, involving the chance of a war, leads to a related game, namely the war-fighting game. The arms race game and the war-fighting game are linked in three important ways. Firstly, defence planners use backward induction from the war-fighting game to determine required stocks in the arms race game via simulating a potential war-fighting game. Secondly, it is possible to move from the arms race game to the war-fighting game if the imbalance in levels of weapons gives a sufficient advantage to one side. This is the problem of crisis instability. Thirdly, there are random shocks to the system which can influence not only the arms race, via crises or the introduction of new types of weapons, but also the chance of moving from the arms race game to the war-fighting game due to accidental or inadvertent war[5].

2. The Arms Race

The arms race involves interactions between two or more countries in the acquisition of weapons. In a two-power arms race involving countries A and B, each country has at any instant of time t a certain number of weapons, here called 'missiles', country A having $M_A(t)$ missiles and country B having $M_B(t)$ missiles. The pair (M_A, M_B) represents a point in the weapons plane of all such pairs. An *arms race* is the interactive acquisition of weapons by the two nations, and it is summarised by the paths over time of the numbers of weapons on both sides, given by a trajectory over a time interval in the weapons plane $\{M_A(t), M_B(t)\}$ for t between t_0 and t_1. An example is the arms race between the superpowers of the United States and the Soviet Union, each of which acquires weapons, possibly in reaction to the other.

A general formulation of the two-power arms race which allows for possible interaction would be the system of two coupled differential equations

$$\dot{M}_A = F_A(M_A, M_B), \tag{2.1}$$

$$\dot{M}_B = F_B(M_A, M_B), \tag{2.2}$$

where $\dot{M}_A$ and $\dot{M}_B$ represent the (net) change in missiles on both sides (e.g., $\dot{M}_A \equiv dM_A/dt$); the F_A and F_B functions relate these changes to current (and possibly lagged) levels of weapons on both sides; and, for simplicity, the time dependency of all variables has been omitted. the *Richardson model* is then the linear variant of this system

$$\dot{M}_A = a_1 M_B - a_2 M_A + a_3, \quad a_1, a_2 > 0, \tag{2.3}$$

$$\dot{M}_B = b_1 M_A - b_2 M_B + b_3, \quad b_1, b_2 > 0, \tag{2.4}$$

where a_1 and b_1 are the *defence coefficients,* a_2 and b_2 are the *fatigue coefficients,* and a_3 and b_3 are the *grievance terms*. An equilibrium, at which $\dot{M}_A$ and $\dot{M}_B$ are both zero, exists, and it is stable, in that small deviations from the equilibrium lead to forces that restore it, provided the stability condition

$$a_1 b_1 < a_2 b_2 \tag{2.5}$$

is met.

3. Heuristic Decision Rules

Heuristic decision rules with regard to weapons procurement can be described, as already noted, as a two-stage process. In the first stage a bureaucratic-political decision is made to establish a certain rule or goal, while in the second stage an economic decision is made, using this rule or goal, to allocate resources to weapons acquisition. The decision rule established in the first stage can be considered one defining a desired level of weapons as a function of the weapons levels on both sides. For country A, if M_A^* is its desired level of weapons (at a particular time t), then

$$M_A^* = G_A(M_A, M_B), \tag{3.1}$$

where G_A is the goal function of A, relating its desired level of missiles to the actual number on each side. The implied gap for country A is the difference between desired and current missiles

$$M_A^* - M_A = G_A(M_A, M_B) - M_A. \tag{3.2}$$

The second stage of resource allocation for weapons procurement is then driven by this gap, with the rate of accumulation of weapons a function of the gap

$$\dot{M}_A = R_A(M_A^* - M_A) = R_A[G_A(M_A, M_B) - M_A]. \quad (3.3)$$

An example is the *stock adjustment model* where $R_A(z) \equiv k_A z$, so that a certain fraction of the gap is eliminated in each period.

An important class of heuristic decision rules is that for which the decision rule chosen by the bureaucratic-political establishments is linear. In this case the goal function in (3.1) is a linear function of the weapons held by the opponent, so

$$M_A^* = \alpha_1 M_B + \alpha_2 \quad (3.4)$$

represents the *linear decision rule*. For example, the US strategic goal of having sufficient capabilities to enable it to have enough forces to deliver a retaliatory strike on the Soviet Union on a second strike, that is, the goal of deterrence, leads to a linear decision rule as in (3.4). The desired level of missiles for A is then the linear function[6]

$$M_A^* = f_B(1-\exp(-\bar{\beta}\vartheta_B))M_B + \bar{C}_B/[v_A(1-\exp(-\bar{\alpha}\psi_A))]. \quad (3.5)$$

Here, in the anticipated two initial strikes of the war, country B strikes first, firing its missiles at the (maximum) rate $\bar{\beta}$ over the time interval from 0 to ϑ_B and using a counterforce strike against A missiles, where f_B is the counterforce effectiveness of B missiles as measured by the number of A missiles destroyed per B counterforce missile. Then country A strikes B in a retaliatory second strike, firing its missiles at the (maximum) rate $\bar{\alpha}$ over the time interval from ϑ_B to $\vartheta_B + \psi_A$ using a countervalue strike against B cities, where v_A is the countervalue effectiveness of A missiles as measured by the number of B casualties inflicted per A countervalue missile. The number of desired A missiles M_A^* in (3.5) is the number of A missiles needed at the outset of the war for A, after having lost missiles due to the B first strike, to have enough missiles left to inflict $\bar{C}_B$ casualties in B on its own second strike. The level of B casualties $\bar{C}_B$ is the minimum unacceptable level of casualties in country B which, as estimated by A, would deter it from starting the war. Equation (3.5) therefore represents a *deterrence decision rule*, a special case of the linear deterrence rule in (3.4). The region defined by $M_A \geq M_A^*$ is one in which A deters B. Similarly, defining M_B^* for the case in which B has enough weapons to deter an A first strike, the region defined by $M_B \geq M_B^*$ is one in which B deters A. The region of *mutual deterrence* is then that in which both $M_A \geq M_A^*$ and $M_B \geq M_B^*$. In this region A has sufficient missiles to deter B and, in addition, B has missiles to deter A. Thus each deters the other.

Another example of the linear decision rule is one for which the desired number of missiles is that required to attack the opponent. It is convenient to state this rule for country B since it involves the same scenario used in the previous case, namely one in which B strikes first and A retaliates on a second strike. For B to have enough missiles to carry out a successful first-strike attack, its desired level of missiles is the linear function of A missiles

$$M_B^{**} = M_A/[f_B(1-\exp(-\bar{\beta}\vartheta_B))] + \hat{C}_B/[f_B(1-\exp(-\bar{\beta}\vartheta_B))v_A(1-\exp(-\bar{\alpha}\psi_A))]. \tag{3.6}$$

The notation in (3.6) is the same as in (3.5), except that here $\hat{C}_B$ is the maximum acceptable level of casualties which B would accept on a retaliatory strike, as estimated by B. The number of desired B missiles M_B^{**} in (3.6) is the number country B needs at the outset of the war to have enough to destroy sufficient numbers of A missiles and to prevent A from inflicting an unacceptable level of casualties on its second strike. Thus equation (3.6) represents an *attacking decision rule*. The region defined by $M_B \geq M_B^{**}$ is one in which B can attack A. Similarly, the region defined by $M_A \geq M_A^{**}$ is one in which A can attack B, where M_A^{**} is defined symmetrically as in (3.6).

A third example of the linear decision rule is that for parity or superiority, where

$$M_A^{***} = \alpha M_B \qquad (\alpha \geq 1) \tag{3.7}$$

is the *parity* or *superiority decision rule*, so the desired level is simply the number of the opponent's weapons or a multiple of this number and the gap in (3.2) is the difference $\alpha M_B - M_A$. The parameter α is a measure of the degree of superiority desired. For example, if $\alpha = 1.1$ then A seeks to have 10 per cent more missiles than B.

4. Planning and Revisions in Plans

Planning refers to the elaboration of a set of decisions over time by a decision-maker or planner[7]. In the case of weapons planning, defence planners make decisions on weapons procurement via arms acquisitions. Plans extend over a certain period of time, and they can be revised in one of two ways. In *time planning* plans are revised at fixed time intervals, such as after a certain number of days or years. Examples include buying inventory on the first of the month; using annual budgets or five-year plans; and setting a fixed term of office for government, as in a presidential system. By contrast, in *event planning*, plans are revised in response to specific events, the time for revision being the time when the time path for the vector of state variables describing the system hits a revision manifold in the space of state variables. Examples include the (s,S) inventory policy of buying inventory when its levels fall to s and reordering enough to have S available; budgets being revised in the event of a major change in the system; and having the opportunity to change a government on a vote of no confidence, as in a parliamentary system. In general, time planning and event planning are equivalent in yielding a similar outcome for total net benefits in the case of certainty, where there is no uncertainty in the dynamical system that describes the movement of the state variables[8]. By contrast, in the case of uncertainty, where there is a stochastic element in the dynamical system, event planning is superior to time planning in yielding a greater expected net benefit[9].

In the case of weapons planning the state variables include the level of weapons on both sides and possibly other variables. There are major uncertainties in changes over time in the level of weapons. In peacetime these changes are described by the arms race, as in (2.1), (2.2), where there is uncertainty over the weapons acquired by the opponent. In wartime these changes are determined by decisions to launch and by counterforce strikes destroying missiles, which again are subject to uncertainty. The result is that armaments dynamics involve uncertainty, so event planning is superior to time planning.

If country A seeks to deter B and uses the deterrence decision rule in (3.5), one type of event planning would involve selecting a desired number of weapons, as given by M_A^* in (3.5); building weapons levels to this number, following the resource allocation rule in (3.3); and keeping this number of weapons roughly constant (e.g., only replacing weapons that become obsolete) unless there is a major change in M_A^*. A major change in M_A^* would result from several possible causes. One would be a buildup of missiles on the other side, changing M_B (or its perceived value) in a significant way. A second cause would be a change in enemy capabilities through weapons improvements, such as via changes in the counterforce effectiveness of B weapons in destroying A weapons, as measured by f_B (e.g., due to improvements in accuracy or yield) or via changes in the rate of fire of B missiles $\bar{\beta}$ or the time interval for the first strike ϑ_B (e.g., due to improvements in command and control). A third cause would be a change in own capabilities through weapons improvements, such as via changes in the countervalue effectiveness of A weapons in inflicting B casualties, as measured by v_A (e.g., due to changes in yield) or via changes in the rate of fire of A missiles $\bar{\alpha}$ or the time interval for the retaliatory second strike ψ_A or via changes in A missiles that affect f_B (e.g., due to hardening, mobility, or concealment of A missiles). A fourth cause would be a change in the A estimate of the minimum level of casualties in B required to deter B from initiating the war, $\bar{C}_B$.

The historical pattern of US-Soviet arms interaction is consistent with this type of event planning. Rather than continuous increases in weapons levels, certain shocks, which involved major changes in elements of the deterrence decision rule (3.5), had profound and long-lasting effects in the pattern of arms acquisition. The 1953 Soviet May Day flyby of long-range bombers spurred US arms acquisitions (and also the US development of the ICBM) by demonstrating Soviet long-range capabilities. The 1957 Soviet launch of Sputnik similarly spurred US arms acquisitions. The 1962 Cuban missile crisis spurred both Soviet and US arms acquisitions by demonstrating to both a willingness to use strategic weapons if necessary. The development of MIRV technology affected arms deployments in both the United States and the Soviet Union in the early 1970s. More recently, President Reagan's SDI programme for strategic defence, which started in 1983, has resulted in a shock to Soviet defence planners, who see this programme as not only a strategic threat, but also a technological, political and economic challenge. In all these cases defence planners revise their estimates of the desired number of weapons and, accordingly, change their procurement plans. It is reasonable to assume that in the absence of a shock planners continue their previous planned allocations without revision, which is consistent with both the concept of event planning and the historical record.

5. Sequence of Heuristic Games: the Case of Certainty

At any one time defence planning uses heuristic decision rules, so the combination of two players, namely the defence planners in each of the two countries, are playing a heuristic game. Over time, as each uses event planning for the revision of its plans, the result is a sequence of heuristic games. Of particular interest for this sequence of heuristic games are its implications for the existence of equilibrium and for stability, including both arms race stability and stability against the outbreak of war. First of all, does an equilibrium exist at which neither side will change its stock of weapons? Secondly, assuming that an equilibrium exists, is there *arms race stability* for which small changes from the equilibrium level lead to forces restoring the equilibrium? Alternatively, is there *arms race instability* in that small changes from the equilibrium level lead to movement further and further away from the equilibrium? Thirdly, what are the implications for *crisis stability*, that is, is there stability against the outbreak of war? Alternatively, is there *crisis instability* in which war is probable or likely?

Suppose each country uses a linear decision rule, as in (3.4), establishing the desired number of weapons for each side as a linear function of the number held by the other side:

$$M_A^* = \alpha_1 M_B + \alpha_2, \qquad M_B^* = \beta_1 M_A + \beta_2. \tag{5.1}$$

If each uses a stock adjustment model, then

$$\dot{M}_A = k_a[\alpha_1 M_B + \alpha_2 - M_A], \qquad \dot{M}_B = k_B[\beta_1 M_A + \beta_2 - M_B], \tag{5.2}$$

so the acquisition of weapons is proportional to the gap between desired and actual levels of weapons. The factors of proportionality k_A and k_B are the adjustment coefficients, which are assumed to be positive.

If there is no uncertainty in the system -so, in particular, each side knows the number of weapons of the other side and all the relevant parameters (such as those in (3.5) or (3.6))- and if there is no cost of planning, then the optimal plan is chosen at the outset and is never revised[10]. If this plan involves the linear decision rule and the stock adjustment model, then the pair of differential equations in (5.2) are followed. These equations imply an equilibrium which is stable if the coefficients satisfy

$$\alpha_1\beta_1 < 1. \tag{5.3}$$

If both sides use a deterrence decision rule, as in (3.5), then condition (5.3) is likely to be met, since then[11]

$$\alpha_1\beta_1 = f_A f_B(1-\exp(-\bar{\alpha}\vartheta_A))(1-\exp(-\bar{\beta}\vartheta_B)). \tag{5.4}$$

If it takes more than one missile to destroy an enemy missile, then f_A and f_B are both less than one, so condition (5.3) is met. Even if f_A and f_B are larger than one, the condition can still be met if $\bar{\alpha}\vartheta_A$ or $\bar{\beta}\vartheta_B$ are small enough, due to either the rate of fire or the time intervals for the first strike being small. In this case of mutual deterrence each side approaches a stable equilibrium at a point of minimal mutual deterrence. Not only does a stable equilibrium exist but it is also a point of minimal mutual deterrence, which is stable against war initiation.

If both sides use an attacking rule, as in (3.6), by contrast, then condition (5.3) is not likely to be met since then the product $\alpha_1\beta_1$ is simply the reciprocal of the value in (5.4). In this case the outcome depends on the starting point. Because the equilibrium is an unstable one, if the process starts at low levels, then the dynamics of the system drive it to lower and lower levels of weapons, and at these levels neither side can deter the other. If, however, the process starts at high levels, then the process drives the system to higher and higher levels of weapons on both sides, involving an unstable arms race 'trap'. In this case the levels of weapons move upward in regions in which there is a relatively low chance of deliberate war since at these levels each side deters the other. Thus if both sides seek to attack, there is a genuine dilemma between seeking arms race stability at the disarmed point but which involves a relatively high probability of war outbreak in the absence of deterrence, or, alternatively, seeking stability against war outbreak but at the cost of a continuing arms race involving higher and higher levels of weapons on both sides.

In the asymmetric case where one side uses a deterrence decision rule and the other uses an attacking decision rule the result is an unstable arms race trap, with no equilibrium and with levels of weapons spiralling to higher and higher levels. The attacker attempts to build up weapons levels to be able to attack, but the deterrer then counters by building up its weapons to deter, leading to yet further increases in weapons levels by the attacker.

6. The Case of Uncertainty

Now consider the case of uncertainty in the system where there is uncertainty about the weapons of the other side and/or uncertainty about the relevant parameters, such as those in (3.5) or (3.6). The optimal planning procedure is then that of event planning, with plans revised when there is information that triggers such a revision. If each side wants to deter the other, then a reasonable planning procedure is to keep the stock of weapons constant if it deters the other and to increase the number of weapons if it does not have enough to deter. The revision manifold for this case of event planning is thus the barrier between deterring and not deterring the other side. Thus, in this case of event planning for country A

$$\dot{M}_A = 0 \quad \text{if} \quad M_A \geq M_A^*, \tag{6.1}$$

$$\dot{M}_A = k_A(M_A^*-M_A) \quad \text{otherwise} \quad (\text{if } M_A < M_A^*), \tag{6.2}$$

where M_A^* is defined in (3.5). According to (6.1), country A keeps its weapons levels unchanged if it has enough to deter B, since its goal is deterrence, only replacing weapons that are becoming obsolete. According to (6.2) country A augments its weapons levels according to the stock adjustment rule if it does not have enough to deter B, building up its weapons to levels that could deter B[12]. According to (3.5), M_A^* depends on M_B and on technical parameters such as f_B and v_A, the missile effectiveness parameters; $\bar{\alpha}$ and $\bar{\beta}$, the rates of fire parameters; and ϑ_B and ψ_A, the time interval parameters. Thus as A receives new information about the B weapons levels and/or the technical parameters, it may switch from not building weapons, as in (6.1), to building weapons, as in (6.2).

This approach to weapons procurement is a reasonable one, given the goal of deterrence, and it is consistent with the optimality of event planning in the case of uncertainty. It is also consistent with the historical record of the superpower arms race, with certain relatively stable periods interrupted by shocks, which led to weapons buildups[13]. These shocks convey information to one side or both sides about the capabilities of the other, triggering an arms race. Consider, for example, the development of MIRV technology in the 1970s and the increased accuracy of missiles in the 1980s. The result in (3.5) is an increase in f_B, the number of A missiles destroyed per B counterforce missile, where A could be either the United States or the Soviet Union. As a consequence there is an increase in the desired number of missiles on both sides, triggering a new round of the arms race. As another example, consider the Reagan SDI programme. Suppose there is an effective US defence against Soviet missiles, rendering these missiles 'impotent and obsolete'. The result, now treating the Soviet Union as country A, is a fall in v_A in (3.5), i.e., reduced casualties inflicted in the US per Soviet countervalue missile. The result is again an increase in M_A^*, leading to a new arms race[14].

Another important aspect of the uncertain case is uncertainty about the weapons held by the opponent and, of even greater relevance, the decision rule used by the opponent in its plans for weapons procurement. The usual response to this uncertainty is to rely on *worst-case analysis*, where each assumes the worst from its own perspective in terms of enemy capabilities and/or intentions: this approach is, in fact, widely used in the military and, in particular, in weapons procurement. Then (6.1) and (6.2) hold as stated, with M_A^* as defined in (3.5) but with the further assumption in (3.5) that M_B is defined not as the actual stock of missiles in B but rather as the level B needs to attack A, that is, by M_B^{**} in (3.6). The result of such an arms race is a continuous arms buildup, where M_A^* always exceeds M_A and (6.2) becomes

$$\dot{M}_A = k_A(M_A^* - M_A) = k_A(\hat{C}_A + \bar{C}_B)/[v_A(1-\exp(-\bar{\alpha}\psi_A))]. \quad (6.3)$$

If both countries act in this manner, then there is a continuous arms race, building arms up to higher and higher levels. At the same time, however, each side is deterred by the opponent's weapons, as they move higher and higher into the region of mutual deterrence, for which $M_A \geq M_A^*$ and $M_B \geq M_B^*$. This type of outcome, accelerated by shocks at certain points, probably comes closest to describing the superpower arms race. It results in arms race instability but, at the same time, stability against war outbreak (crisis stability).

7. Conclusions

Because the institutions of defence decision-making are large, complex, and bureaucratic, it is more appropriate to model the arms race as a heuristic game, in which each side uses heuristic decision rules, than to model it as either a mechanistic Richardson model process or as the result of a rational choice model. Because of the inherent uncertainty about technical parameters in arms procurement decisions, defence planning is more appropriately characterised by event planning, in which decisions are triggered by events, than by time planning, in which decisions are made at fixed times. Because of uncertainty about the other side, each side tends to rely on worst-case analysis, in which it treats the other as attempting to achieve a level of weapons for which the other could successfully attack it. Thus, the analysis of the arms race leads to the case of an arms race in which each side uses heuristic rules for weapons procurement, each side uses event planning, and each side uses worst-case analysis. If each side in such a two-country arms race seeks to deter the other, then the outcome is a continuous arms race, accelerated at certain times by shocks to the system, in which each side is deterred by the other.

This case is probably the most relevant since it uses assumptions that are reasonable in describing the superpower arms race, and its results are consistent with the historical record of US-USSR arms interactions. The outcome is an unusual coupling of an instability result and a stability result, with *arms race instability* but *crisis stability*. As each side seeks a level of weapons that would deter the other, given its suspicion or fear that the other is trying to build up its weapons to attack it, each side builds up its own level of weapons. The actions of each side thus reinforce the suspicions or fears of the other. The result is an unstable *arms race trap*, escalating levels of weapons to higher and higher levels but at the same time ensuring that there is mutual deterrence in that each side deters the other from initiating a war. Thus there is crisis stability but arms race instability, as each side acquires considerably more than enough weapons to deter the other but continues nevertheless to acquire yet even more weapons (or superior weapons).

From the viewpoint of arms control the problem in this case is then not one of incentives to strike or to preempt, which have totally disappeared in view of the overwhelming ability of each side to deter the other. Rather, the problem becomes one of accidental or inadvertent initiation, particularly given the large stocks of weapons. While neither side would deliberately strike the other, there is a chance that either would launch by accident, e.g., due to human error or to technical failure in warning systems or in command and control systems. It is the treatment of this type of problem of accidental/inadvertent nuclear war and other problems, such as the potential erosion of deterrence due to defensive systems or to antisatellite or antisubmarine weapons and the proliferation of weapons of mass destruction and delivery systems, rather than negotiated weapons reductions, that should be at the forefront of the arms control agenda, including bilateral, multilateral and unilateral approaches to arms control initiatives[15].

Notes

* The authors are indebted to Ron Smith and an anonymous referee for extremely valuable suggestions on the first draft of this paper.

1. For a discussion of the Richardson model of the arms race see Richardson (1951, 1960), Intriligator (1975, 1982), Intriligator and Brito (1976b, 1988a) and Anderton (1985).

2. For a discussion of optimising models of the arms race see Brito (1972), Brito and Intriligator (1973), Intriligator (1982) and Intriligator and Brito (1976b, 1988a).

3. For a discussion of heuristic decision rules see Intriligator and Brito (1985a).

4. For a discussion of the theory of planning, including revisions of plans as triggered by time or events see Intriligator and Sheshinski (1986) and Sheshinski and Intriligator (1988).

5. In moving from the arms race game to the war-fighting game there is a major problem of time inconsistency. *Ex ante*, it is optimal for each side to commit itself to respond to a first strike by the other side, but *ex post* it would never be rational to do so. Thus the commitment to retaliate lacks credibility despite being optimal within the model in maintaining (mutual) deterrence. This problem is, of course, a very old one in the deterrence literature. Proposed solutions, such as precommitments in alliances, doomsday machines, which make retaliation automatic, or irrational behaviour generate problems of their own, particularly those of compounding the danger of accidental or inadvertent war.

6. The derivation of (3.5) follows from a system of four coupled differential equations describing the evolution of a missile war over time, as described in Intriligator (1967, 1968, 1975), Saaty (1968), Brito and Intriligator (1973, 1974), and Intriligator and Brito (1976a, 1984, 1985a).

7. See Intriligator and Sheshinski (1986) and Sheshinski and Intriligator (1988).

8. Ibid.

9. Ibid.

10. See Intriligator and Sheshinski (1986).

11. The notation is explained below equation (3.5) for f_B, $\bar{\beta}$, ϑ_B. The terms f_A, $\bar{\alpha}$, ϑ_A are the corresponding concepts for the scenario in which A attacks B first, then B retaliates, where $\bar{\alpha}$ is the A rate of

fire, ϑ_A is the time interval for the A strike on B, and f_A is the number of B missiles destroyed per A counterforce missile.

12. Omitted from consideration here are resource constraints and the technology of weapons building, which could be treated as a separate intertemporal game. One way in which resource constraints could be taken into account is to allow the parameter k_A in (6.2) to vary with the available level of resources. In the superpower arms race, however, defence expenditure and military technology are typically top priority items for resource allocation.

13. In the theory of evolution this type of path is referred to as one of 'punctuated equilibrium', where long stable periods are interrupted by relatively short periods of dramatic change.

14. Note that the defence of missiles, by contrast to population defence, has the effect of reducing f_B in (3.5), e.g., a US defence of its missiles reduces the number of US missiles destroyed per Soviet counterforce missile, where A is the US and B is the USSR. Thus defence of missiles will reduce rather than increase the desired number of missiles.

15. See Intriligator and Brito (1985b, 1986, 1987, 1988b, 1988c).

References

Anderton, C., 'A selected bibliography of arms race models and related subjects', Conflict Management and Peace Science, 8, 1985, pp. 99-122.

Brito, D.L., 'A dynamic model of an armaments race', International Economic Review, 13, 1972, pp. 359-375.

Brito, D.L. and M.D. Intriligator, 'Some applications of the maximum principle to the problem of an armaments race', Modeling and Simulations, 4, 1973, pp. 140-144.

Brito, D.L. and M.D. Intriligator, 'Uncertainty and the stability of the armaments race', Annals of Economic and Social Measurement, 3, 1974, pp. 279-292.

Intriligator, M.D., Strategy in a Missile War: Targets and Rates of Fire, Security Studies Project, University of California, Los Angeles, 1967.

Intriligator, M.D., 'The debate over missile strategy: targets and rates of fire', Orbis, 11, 1968, pp. 1138-1159.

Intriligator, M.D., 'Strategic considerations in the Richardson model of arms races', Journal of Political Economy, 83, 1975, pp. 339-353.

Intriligator, M.D., 'Research on conflict theory: analytic approaches and areas of application', Journal of Conflict Resolution, 26, 1982, pp. 307-327.

Intriligator, M.D. and D.L. Brito, 'Strategy, arms races, and arms control', in Gillespie and Zinnes (eds), Mathematical Systems in International Relations, Praeger, New York, 1976a.

Intriligator, M.D. and D.L. Brito, 'Formal models of arms races', Journal of Peace Science, 2, 1976b, pp. 77-88.

Intriligator, M.D. and D.L. Brito, 'Can arms races lead to the outbreak of war?', Journal of Conflict Resolution, 28, 1984, pp. 63-84.

Intriligator, M.D. and D.L. Brito, 'Heuristic decision rules, the dynamics of an arms race, and war initiation', in Luterbacher and Ward (eds), Dynamic Models of International Conflict, Lynne Rienner, Bolder, 1985a.

Intriligator, M.D. and D.L. Brito, 'Non-Armageddon solutions to the arms race', Arms Control, 6, 1985b, pp. 41-57.

Intriligator, M.D. and D.L. Brito, 'Arms races and instability', Journal of Strategic Studies, 9, 1986, pp. 113-131.

Intriligator, M.D. and D.L. Brito, 'Arms control: problems and prospects', IGCC Research Paper No. 2, Institute on Global Conflict and Cooperation, University of California, San Diego, 1987.

Intriligator, M.D. and D.L. Brito, 'The Richardson arms race model', in M.I. Midlarsky (ed.), Handbook of War Studies, Allen and Unwin, Boston, 1988a.

Intriligator, M.D. and D.L. Brito, 'Arms control', in E.A. Kolodziej and P. Morgan (eds), National Security and Arms Control, Greenwood Press, Westport, CT, 1988b.

Intriligator, M.D. and D.L. Brito, 'Accidental nuclear war: a significant issue for arms control', Current Research on Peace and Violence, vol. 11, 1988c, pp. 14-23.

Intriligator, M.D. and E. Sheshinski, 'Toward a theory of planning', in W. Heller, R. Starr and D. Starrett (eds), Essays in Honor of Kenneth J. Arrow, Cambridge University Press, New York, 1986.

Richardson, L.F., 'Could an arms race end without fighting?', Nature, no. 4274, 29 September, 1951.

Richardson, L.F., Arms and Insecurity, Boxwood Press, Pittsburgh, 1960.

Saaty, T., Mathematical Models of Arms Control and Disarmament, John Wiley & Sons, Inc., New York, 1968.

Sheshinski, E. and M.D. Intriligator, 'Cost-benefit analysis with switching regimes: an application of the theory of planning', Computers and Mathematics with Applications, forthcoming 1988.

Dynamic Policy Games in Economics
F. van der Ploeg and A.J. de Zeeuw, (Editors)

CONFLICT OVER ARMS ACCUMULATION IN MARKET AND COMMAND ECONOMIES*

Frederick van der Ploeg

Aart J. de Zeeuw

CentER for Economic Research
Department of Economics
Tilburg University
5000 LE Tilburg, The Netherlands

Introduction

Conflict over arms accumulation has in recent years become a more prevalent feature of the relations between West and East. The political aspects of the arms race receive a great deal of attention both in the press and in academic studies (e.g. Richardson 1960; Boulding 1961; McGuire 1965; SIPRI 1982). Much of the theoretical analysis of arms conflict has a game-theoretic nature (e.g. Schelling 1980). The welfare of one country depends on the level of security, which is perceived as an increasing function of its own weapon stock and a decreasing function of the foreign weapon stock. This may be because any imbalance in weapon stocks increases the likelihood of loosing a possible war and it also increases the likelihood that a war might in fact be initiated. Alternatively, a country may simply feel that it gains international prestige from having a more superior army than its rivals. Both of these factors can in principle lead to a balance of terror. Such defence externalities can also be shown to lead to prisoner's dilemma situations. In the absence of cooperation each country builds up a larger weapon stock than with cooperation, because in the absence of commitments no country trusts the other countries to stick to a negotiated level of lower or zero weapon stocks. Other studies concentrate on the technological and strategic aspects of arms and the relationship to the probability that war breaks out (Saaty 1968; Intriligator 1975; Brito and Intriligator 1976; Intriligator and Brito 1982).

From the point of view of an economist, the purely political analyses of conflict over arms do not pay adequate attention to the 'guns versus butter' dilemma. A higher level of investment in weapons eventually increases security and welfare, but it also means that there are less resources available for private sector consumption and therefore welfare diminishes. A variety of studies employs optimal control and differential game theory to analyse the intertemporal tradeoffs inherent in such 'guns versus butter' dilemmas (e.g. Brito 1972; Deger and Sen 1984). The main problem with these studies is that they consider open-loop Nash equilibrium solutions while feedback Nash equilibrium solutions would in most cases be more appropriate (e.g. Simaan and Cruz 1975). The advantage of the latter type of solution concept is that the resulting equilibrium relies on more realistic information sets, since each country is assumed to be able to monitor the current levels of weapon stocks rather than to be able to observe only the initial weapon stocks. The informational non-uniqueness resulting from closed-loop information sets with memory (Başar and Olsder 1982, Section 6.3) is resolved when the principle of subgame perfection (Selten 1975) is imposed, which has the added advantage that the resulting equilibrium strategies are credible. It is clear that the importance of informational assumptions requires more attention than the literature has given it so far. For example, each country may be able to observe its own weapon stock accurately and to observe the foreign weapon stock not at all or inaccurately.

In an earlier paper (van der Ploeg and de Zeeuw, forthcoming 1989) the conflict between a decentralised market economy (the West) and a command economy (the East) is considered when the western government has the possibility of levying non-distortionary (lump-sum) taxes to finance the investment in arms, when households have quadratic utility functions, and when firms have linear technologies. The open-loop Nash equilibrium solution concept assumes that governments precommit themselves to a given sequence of levels of investment in arms and that governments cannot monitor the weapon stocks of the other countries. The feedback Nash or subgame-perfect equilibrium solution concept assumes that the governments' announcement about investment levels in arms are credible and that governments can monitor the weapon stocks of rival countries at any point in time. The main conclusion of the earlier research is that monitoring leads to lower stocks of weapons and to higher consumption of goods and leisure, so that monitoring of each other's weapon stocks is a good thing and is a feasible and desirable form of unilateral disarmament. It can also be argued that the subgame-perfect equilibrium provides a strategic underpinning of the Richardson equations, which give the change in weapon stocks as the sum of a constant, called the 'grievance' or 'hatred' coefficient, a term that depends negatively on the product of the own weapon stock and the 'fatigue' coefficient, and a term that depends positively on the product of the rival weapon stock and the 'defence' coefficient. The desired lead of weapons over the rival country and the relative priority of 'guns' over 'butter' increases the grievance coefficients and thus the steady-state levels of weapon stocks. The discount rate, depreciation rate and the relative priority of 'butter' over 'guns' diminish the defence coefficients and thus the steady-state levels of weapon stocks. The sum of the defence coefficients and physical depreciation rates gives the fatigue coefficients. Hence, with quadratic preferences, linear technologies and non-distortionary taxes, weapon stocks increase proportionately to the level of weapon stocks of the rival nation (defence), decrease proportionately to the economic burden of its own weapon stock (fatigue) and increase due to the desired lead of weapons over the rival nation (grievance or hatred). Furthermore, there is less arms accumulation and higher welfare when monitoring is permitted.

One important shortcoming of the research described above and in van der Ploeg and de Zeeuw (forthcoming 1989) is that it is not really concerned with conflict between a decentralised market economy and a command economy, because the assumption of non-distortionary taxes allows one to invoke the fundamental theorem of welfare economics which says that market economies are efficient and thus equivalent to command economies. The main objective of this paper is to allow for distortionary taxes on labour income, which is an important asymmetry between the West and the East. In addition, the unrealistic assumption of quadratic preferences is replaced by the more realistic assumption of Cobb-Douglas or CES preferences in order to investigate the robustness of previous results. Hence, this paper reconsiders the 'guns versus butter' dilemma, allows for conflict between a decentralised market economy (the West) and a command economy (the East), and contrasts open-loop and subgame-perfect Nash equilibrium solutions with outcomes under coordination. Section 1 formulates a simple general equilibrium model of a market economy and

Section 2 formulates a simple model of a command economy. Each government maximises the discounted utility of the representative household, which depends on consumption, leisure and defence. Defence is a characteristic good which depends positively upon the own weapon stock and negatively upon the foreign weapon stock. The government of the West uses distortionary taxes on labour income to finance the provision of arms, whereas the government of the East commands its constituents directly. Section 3 discusses coordinated decision-making and shows that, under special circumstances, cooperation leads to a gradual running down of weapon stocks via wear and tear. Section 4 analyses decentralised decision-making. The equilibrium for the open-loop information pattern corresponds to a saddlepoint in which the accumulated weapon stock in the East for similar preferences and technologies is larger than the accumulated weapon stock in the West. It is argued that when utilities are separable in home and foreign weapon stocks, as is the case for Cobb-Douglas utility functions, the open-loop Nash equilibrium and the subgame-perfect equilibrium must coincide. Finally, it is shown that closed-loop equilibria which are based on investment strategies with threats can induce a cooperative outcome. Section 5 considers the more general situation in which utility is not separable in defence. This is accomplished with a nested utility function; for example a CES utility function that depends on a composite commodity, given by a Cobb-Douglas sub-utility function that depends on consumption and leisure, and defence. For this more general case, subgame-perfect equilibria lead to less arms accumulation than open-loop Nash equilibria. This suggests that countries should be encouraged to monitor the weapon stocks of their rivals, since this leads to less arms. Section 6 concludes the paper with a summary and some suggestions for further research.

1. Optimal Dynamic Taxation and the Provision of Arms in a Market-oriented Economy

Consider a decentralised market economy with a representative household, a representative firm and a government. There are no domestic or foreign financial assets and the economy does not engage in international trade. There is no private sector capital accumulation, although the government invests in weapon stocks. There is only one domestically produced commodity, which is like 'jelly' as it can be used for both consumption and investment purposes. The government demands goods for investment purposes, the household supplies labour and demands goods for consumption purposes, and the firm demands labour and supplies goods. The real wage adjusts in order to ensure labour market equilibrium. The government finances the provision of public goods, i.e., weapon stocks, by means of distortionary taxes on labour income and maximises the utility of the representative household. The problem of optimal taxation is that the household values spending on public goods, but that it is not prepared to pay for it.

The representative household maximises its utility subject to its budget constraint. The main analysis in this paper is based upon a Cobb-Douglas utility function, although the expressions for general utility functions are also given. This utility function is increasing in consumption of goods, leisure and defence and, what will be important, it is separable in defence. Section 5 extends the analysis for a CES utility function, which allows for non-separability between goods and leisure on the one hand and defence on the other hand. Both of these utility functions lead to linear Engel curves, so that aggregation across households is possible and therefore the assumption of a representative household is justified. Utility is assumed to be homogeneous of degree one in consumption and leisure. Defence is a characteristic (cf. Lancaster 1966), which is an increasing function of the own weapon stock and a decreasing function of the foreign weapon stock. It is assumed to be homogeneous of degree one in the respective weapon stocks. Consumption cannot exceed disposable income, which consists of after-tax wages and dividends. The household's problem is therefore:

$$\underset{c,\ell}{\text{Maximise}}\ U(c,\bar{\ell}-\ell,d(a,a^*)) \equiv \alpha_1 \ln(c) + \alpha_2 \ln(\bar{\ell}-\ell) + \alpha_3 \ln(a/a^*),$$

$$\alpha_i \geq 0, \quad \alpha_1 + \alpha_2 = 1, \tag{1.1}$$

subject to the household's budget constraint

$$0 \leq c \leq w\ell(1-\tau) + \pi \equiv y, \tag{1.2}$$

where

c : real consumption of goods
ℓ : supply of labour
$\bar{\ell}$: total amount of time available to the household
d : level of defence or security
w : real wage rate
τ : rate of taxation on labour income
π : real profits or dividends
y : real disposable income
a : weapon stock of the decentralised market economy
a^* : weapon stock of the command economy.

For an interior solution, the marginal rate of substitution between leisure, $\bar{\ell}-\ell$, and consumption equals the real opportunity cost of leisure:

$$U_{\bar{\ell}-\ell}/U_c = w(1-\tau). \tag{1.3}$$

Because utility is homogeneous of degree one, this yields consumption

$$c = (\bar{\ell}-\ell)\ h(w(1-\tau)) = \varphi(w(1-\tau))y_0, \quad \varphi' \lesseqgtr 0, \quad h' > 0 \tag{1.4}$$

and the supply of labour

$$\ell = \bar{\ell} - \varphi(w(1-\tau))y_0/h(w(1-\tau)), \tag{1.5}$$

where $h^{-1}(c/(\bar{\ell}-\ell)) \equiv U_{\bar{\ell}-\ell}/U_c$, $y_0 \equiv w(1-\tau)\bar{\ell} + \pi$ is full-employment income and

$$\varphi(w(1-\tau)) = h(w(1-\tau))/\{h(w(1-\tau)) + w(1-\tau)\}.$$

An increase in profits (or time available to the household) increases income, so that consumption increases and labour supply falls as both consumption and leisure are normal goods given the assumption of homogeneous utility functions. For Cobb-Douglas utility functions,

$h(w(1-\tau)) = \alpha_1 w(1-\tau)/\alpha_2$ and $\varphi(w(1-\tau)) = \alpha_1$ so that an increase in the after-tax wage increases consumption and the supply of labour.

The representative firm (with linear technology) chooses the demand for labour to maximise profits:

$$\underset{\ell}{\text{Maximise}}\ \pi \equiv f(\ell) - w\ell = \beta\ell - w\ell, \qquad f' > 0, \qquad f'' \le 0, \tag{1.6}$$

so that $f'(\ell) = \beta = w$ and $\pi = 0$.

Labour market equilibrium gives $w = W(\tau) = \beta$, employment

$$\ell = L(\tau) = \alpha_1 \bar{\ell}, \tag{1.7}$$

and consumption

$$c = C(\tau) = \alpha_1 \beta(1-\tau)\bar{\ell}. \tag{1.8}$$

For Cobb-Douglas utility functions and constant-returns-to-scale production functions, a tax cut increases the opportunity cost of leisure so that the household substitutes away from leisure towards consumption. Labour supply is unaffected, since the substitution effect is exactly offset by the income effect.

Upon substitution of (1.7) and (1.8) into (1.1), one obtains the indirect utility function:

$$\hat{U}(\tau,a,a^*) \equiv U(C(\tau),\bar{\ell}-L(\tau),d(a,a^*)) = \alpha_1 \ln(1-\tau) + \alpha_3 \ln(a/a^*) + \alpha_0,$$

$$\hat{U}_a > 0, \quad \hat{U}_{a^*} < 0, \quad \hat{U}_\tau < 0, \tag{1.9}$$

where $\alpha_0 \equiv \alpha_1 \ln(\alpha_1\beta) + \alpha_2 \ln \alpha_2 + \ln \bar{\ell}$. The role of the government is to provide the public good, defence, and finance it with taxes on labour income. Government investment, g, leads to the accumulation of weapon stocks,

$$\dot{a} = g - \delta a, \qquad a(0) = a_0, \tag{1.10}$$

where δ is the depreciation rate, and needs to be financed by distortionary taxation,

$$g = \tau\, W(\tau)\, L(\tau) = \tau\, \beta\, \alpha_1\, \bar{\ell} \, . \tag{1.11}$$

Note, that summing of the household budget constraint, (1.2), and the government budget constraint, (1.11), yields the familiar national accounting identity:

$$c + g = w\ell + \pi = f(\ell). \tag{1.12}$$

The government of the market economy chooses the tax rate in order to maximise the discounted utility of the representative household,

$$\underset{\tau}{\text{Maximise}} \int_0^\infty \exp(-rt)\, \hat{U}(\tau,a,a^*)dt, \tag{1.13}$$

where r is the pure rate of time preference, subject to (1.10) and (1.11). The dilemma of 'guns versus butter' for a market economy is that high tax rates are required to ensure a large build-up of weapons, but that this necessarily implies less private sector consumption.

It could have been argued that the arms accumulation game should be modelled as an insurance where the level of defence decreases the probability of being attacked and therefore increases the probability that nobody survives and the utility of the current and all future generations is zero (see Shepherd 1988). This argument suggests that, if an attack only affects the utility of the current generation, an appropriate utility function might be $P(a-a^*)\hat{U}(\tau)$, where $P(.)$ denotes the instantaneous probability of not being attacked, $P' > 0$, and $\hat{U}(\tau)$ denotes the indirect utility function. Taking logarithms yields (1.9) with $\hat{U}(\tau,a,a^*) = \ln[P(a-a^*)] + \ln(\hat{U}(\tau))$. A proper analysis of the probabilities of survival, when an attack destroys the current and all future generations, requires an intertemporal and stochastic framework, but this leads to a differential game formulation which is extremely difficult to solve. In any case such an intergenerational analysis is more appropriate for a nuclear than for a conventional arms build-up. However, if the analysis allows for nuclear attacks where all future generations can be destroyed, then the only credible, non-cooperative equilibrium is for neither country to accumulate missiles. When the build-up of nuclear weapons leads to a finite probability of an attack which is too horrendous to contemplate and when there is a zero probability of attack, there is no incentive to accumulate arms. In other words, deterrence requires the probability of a commitment to investments which in the future may imply launching missiles and blowing up the world, and which is therefore not rational to be carried out. This seems to exclude perfect equilibrium as an appropriate solution concept for deterrence games.

2. The 'Guns versus Butter' Dilemma in a Command Economy

The previous section discussed a stylised model of the market-oriented Western economies (e.g. the USA). The objective of this paper is to analyse conflict over arms accumulation between the Western economies and the Eastern economies (e.g. the USSR). It is probably more realistic to describe the Eastern bloc by a command or centrally planned economy than by a decentralised market economy. The effects of such asymmetries in economic organisation on the arms race have not been discussed previously in the literature. For simplicity, it is assumed that the two economies have identical tastes, technologies and population sizes. The variables and expressions describing the Eastern bloc will be distinguished from the ones describing the West by an asterisk.

The government of the centrally planned economy does not levy taxes, but commands the household how much to consume and how much to work and commands the firm how many workers to hire and how much to produce. The optimal plan follows from maximising the utility of the representative household, $U^*(c^*,\bar{\ell}-\ell^*,d^*)$, subject to the material balance condition, $f(\ell^*) = c^* + g^*$. Hence, the marginal rate of substitution between leisure and consumption equals the marginal productivity of labour, so that

$$c^* = (\bar{\ell}-\ell^*)\, h^*(f'(\ell^*)), \qquad h^{*\prime} > 0 \tag{2.1}$$

holds. With the material balance condition this yields

$$\ell^* = L^*(g^*) = \alpha_1\, \bar{\ell} + \alpha_2\, g^*/\beta \tag{2.2}$$

and

$$c^* = C^*(g^*) = \alpha_1(\beta\bar{\ell}-g^*), \tag{2.3}$$

where $L^*_{g^*} = \{f'(\ell^*) + h^* - (\bar{\ell}-\ell^*)\, h^{*\prime} f''(\ell^*)\}^{-1} > 0$ and

$C^*_{g^*} = -\{h^* - (\bar{\ell}-\ell^*)\, h^{*\prime} f''(\ell^*)\}L^*_{g^*} < 0.$

Consumption and employment do not depend directly on the level of security, since it has been assumed that utility is separable in defence. When the central planning authority allocates more resources to investment in weapon stocks, there are less resources available for consumption purposes and, consequently, the people consume less and work more hours. This one-to-one crowding out captures the 'guns versus butter' dilemma for the Eastern bloc. Note that for identical levels of investment in weapons (and identical tastes and technologies), the Eastern bloc employs more labour and consumes more than the West:

$$c^* = C^*(g^*) = \alpha_1(\beta\bar{\ell}-g^*) > c = C(\tau) = \alpha_1\, \beta\bar{\ell} - g, \tag{2.4}$$

when $g(=\alpha_1\tau\beta\bar{\ell}) = g^*$. The reason for this result is that the Western economy levies distortionary taxes on labour income, which reduces the real opportunity cost of leisure and therefore Western households supply less labour and consume less. Obviously, if the West has a more productive technology (say, $\beta > \beta^*$), it is possible for the West to be more affluent than the Eastern bloc ($c > c^*$ yet $\ell < \ell^*$).

Using (2.2) and (2.3), one obtains the indirect utility function:

$$\hat{U}^*(g^*,a^*,a) \equiv U^*(C^*(g^*),\bar{\ell}-L^*(g^*),d^*(a^*,a))$$

$$= \ln(1-g^*/\beta\bar{\ell}) + \alpha_3 \ln(a^*/a) + \alpha_0,$$

$$\hat{U}^*_{a^*} > 0, \quad \hat{U}^*_a < 0, \quad \hat{U}^*_{g^*} < 0. \tag{2.5}$$

The optimal defence strategy of the central planning authority of the Eastern bloc follows from maximising the discounted utility of the representative household,

$$\underset{g^*}{\text{Maximise}} \int_0^\infty \exp(-rt)\ \hat{U}^*(g^*,a^*,a)dt, \tag{2.6}$$

subject to

$$\dot{a}^* = g^* - \delta a^*, \qquad a^*(0) = a_0^*. \tag{2.7}$$

3. Cooperative Behaviour

Before the problems of conflict over weapons accumulation are discussed, it seems appropriate to consider briefly the coordination of arms accumulation. Pareto-efficient outcomes for the Western and Eastern blocs may be found from choosing τ and g^* to maximise joint welfare,

$$\int_0^\infty \exp(-rt)\ \{\vartheta\ \hat{U}(\tau,a,a^*) + (1-\vartheta)\ \hat{U}^*(g^*,a^*,a)\}\ dt, \tag{3.1}$$

subject to τ, $g^* \geq 0$, (1.9) - (1.11), (2.5) and (2.7). This yields

$$\left.\begin{aligned} \vartheta\ \hat{U}_\tau + \lambda\{W(\tau)\ L(\tau) + \tau\ W_\tau(\tau)\ L(\tau) + \tau\ W(\tau)\ L_\tau(\tau)\} &\leq 0 \\ \tau &\geq 0 \end{aligned}\right\}\ \text{c.s}, \tag{3.2}$$

$$\left.\begin{aligned} (1-\vartheta)\ \hat{U}^*_{g^*} + \lambda^* &\leq 0 \\ g^* &\geq 0 \end{aligned}\right\}\ \text{c.s.}, \tag{3.3}$$

$$\dot{\lambda} = (r+\delta)\ \lambda - \vartheta\ \hat{U}_a(\tau,a,a^*) - (1-\vartheta)\ \hat{U}^*_a(g^*,a^*,a),$$

$$\lim_{t\to\infty} e^{-rt}\ \lambda(t)\ a(t) = 0, \tag{3.4}$$

$$\dot{\lambda}^* = (r+\delta)\ \lambda^* - \vartheta\ \hat{U}_{a^*}(\tau,a,a^*) - (1-\vartheta)\ \hat{U}^*_{a^*}(g^*,a^*,a),$$

$$\lim_{t\to\infty} e^{-rt}\ \lambda^*(t)\ a^*(t) = 0, \tag{3.5}$$

(1.10) and (2.7), where λ and λ^* are the marginal values of the weapon stocks of the Western and Eastern blocs, respectively. Under the assumption that the 'world peace authority' attaches equal weight to the Western and Eastern blocs, i.e. $\vartheta = \frac{1}{2}$, and using the specific functional forms for the utility functions adopted in the previous sections, it follows that $\lambda(t) = \lambda^*(t) = 0$, for all t. This result holds whenever $\hat{U}_a = -\hat{U}^*_a$ and $\hat{U}^*_{a^*} = -\hat{U}_{a^*}$, that is whenever the game between the two economies is zero-sum at the margin with respect to a and a*. It implies that $\tau(t) = g^*(t) = 0$, for all t, so that the cooperative outcome for both economies is to stop investing in arms and to run down weapon stocks (via the natural process of wear and tear) until they have fallen to zero. This outcome is probably close to one's intuition, although it should be noted that it pertains only under rather special conditions. Due to the asymmetry in economic organisation of the West and the East, it may well be that the Nash bargaining solution does not coincide with $\vartheta = \frac{1}{2}$. Furthermore, the utility functions may not be separable or homogeneous of degree one in a and a* and then the cooperative outcome need not necessarily lead to a moratorium on investment in weapons. The cooperative outcome is not sustainable, since each country has an incentive to deviate from it and increase its security at the expense of its rival by investing more in weapons.

4. Competitive Behaviour and the Arms Race

Consider the situation in which the Western and the Eastern blocs do not cooperate when they accumulate weapon stocks. Since there is a unilateral incentive to deviate from the cooperative outcome, there are serious problems with implementing and sustaining the cooperative outcome and therefore non-cooperative outcomes may be more relevant. It seems reasonable to consider Nash equilibria, since neither the Western nor the Eastern bloc is dominant in the arms race. This implies that there should be no unilateral incentive to deviate from the equilibrium. Typically, there are an infinite number of Nash equilibrium solutions in differential games. Sometimes uniqueness can be obtained for special information sets. For example, with open-loop information sets, i.e. the information set of each country at any point of time is assumed to be $\{a_0, a^*_0\}$, the unique open-loop Nash equilibrium solution (OLNES) can be obtained (e.g. Starr and Ho 1969a). In general multiple Nash equilibrium solutions exist. For example, with closed-loop (memory) information sets, i.e. the information set of each country at time t is assumed to be $\{t, a(s), a^*(s), 0 \le s \le t\}$, an infinite number of closed-loop Nash equilibrium solutions (CLNES) exist (Başar and Olsder 1982). However, if one restricts the class of CLNES to subgame-perfect equilibria (Selten 1975), one can obtain uniqueness within the class of CLNES. The resulting outcome will be called the subgame-perfect Nash equilibrium solution (SPNES). Starr and Ho (1969b) and Simaan and Cruz (1975) refer to the SPNES as the feedback (stagewise) Nash equilibrium solution.

4.1 Nash Equilibrium with Open-loop Information Sets

The OLNES implies that each country conditions its optimal investment strategy on the initial stocks of weapons and therefore commits itself to a path of levels of investment in weapons. The expected investment strategy of the rival country only depends on initial weapon stocks and not on past or current weapon stocks or on past or current investment levels of the country under consideration. It follows that Pontryagin's Maximum Principle can be used, hence

$$\left.\begin{array}{r} \hat{U}_\tau + \lambda\{w\ell + \tau(W_\tau \ell + wL_\tau)\} = \alpha_1\{\beta\bar{\ell}\lambda - (1-\tau)^{-1}\} \le 0 \\ \tau \ge 0 \end{array}\right\} \text{c.s.,} \tag{4.1}$$

$$\left.\begin{array}{r} \hat{U}^*_{g^*} + \lambda^* = \lambda^* - (\beta\bar{\ell} - g^*)^{-1} \le 0 \\ g^* \ge 0 \end{array}\right\} \text{c.s.,} \tag{4.2}$$

$$\dot{\lambda} = (r+\delta)\,\lambda - \hat{U}_a = (r+\delta)\,\lambda - \alpha_3/a,$$

$$\lim_{t\to\infty} e^{-rt}\,\lambda(t)\,a(t) = 0, \tag{4.3}$$

$$\dot{\lambda}^* = (r+\delta)\,\lambda^* - \hat{U}^*_{a^*} = (r+\delta)\,\lambda^* - \alpha_3/a^*,$$

$$\lim_{t\to\infty} e^{-rt}\,\lambda^*(t)\,a^*(t) = 0, \tag{4.4}$$

(1.10), (1.11) and (2.7), where λ (λ^*) is the marginal value of the Western (Eastern) weapon stock to the Western (Eastern) bloc, are necessary conditions. The interpretation of (4.3) and (4.4) is that the marginal utility of weapons of each country has to equal the rate of time preference plus the depreciation charge minus the rate of capital gains in the marginal value of its weapons. Equation (4.1) says that no taxes will be levied in the West when the marginal indirect disutility of the tax rate ($-\hat{U}_\tau$), arising from lower consumption, exceeds the marginal value of the increase in investment in arms made possible by a marginal increase in the tax rate. Otherwise, the marginal indirect disutility equals the marginal shadow value of the tax rate which gives the tax rate as an increasing function of the marginal value of Western weapon stocks:

$$\tau = T(\lambda) = 1 - (\beta\bar{\ell}\lambda)^{-1}, \qquad T_\lambda > 0. \tag{4.5}$$

It follows that private sector consumption is a decreasing function of the marginal value of weapons, $c = \alpha_1/\lambda$, which is of course quite intuitive. Upon substitution of (4.5) into (1.11), one obtains

$$g = G(\lambda) \equiv T(\lambda)\ W(T(\lambda))\ L(T(\lambda)) = \alpha_1(\beta\bar{\ell}-\lambda^{-1}). \tag{4.6}$$

Equation (4.2) says that the Eastern bloc does not invest in arms when the marginal disutility of arms expenditure, in terms of foregone consumption, exceeds the marginal value of weapon stocks. In general, $-\hat{U}^*_{g^*} = \lambda^*$ and consequently Eastern bloc investment in arms is an increasing function of the marginal value of weapon stocks:

$$g^* = G^*(\lambda^*) = \beta\bar{\ell} - \lambda^{*-1}, \qquad G^*_{\lambda^*} > 0. \tag{4.7}$$

It turns out that the OLNES can be easily characterised, since the policy instrument, weapon stock and shadow price of each country are independent of the corresponding foreign variables. This is a direct consequence of the assumption that the utility function is separable in a and a*. The game is in a sense degenerate. The OLNES for the West follows from

$$\dot{a} = G(\lambda) - \delta a = \alpha_1(\beta\bar{\ell}-\lambda^{-1}) - \delta a, \qquad a(0) = a_0 \tag{4.8}$$

and (4.3). The $\dot{a}$ = 0-locus is upward-sloping and the $\dot{\lambda}$ = 0-locus is downward-sloping. The full phase-diagram is given in Figure 1.

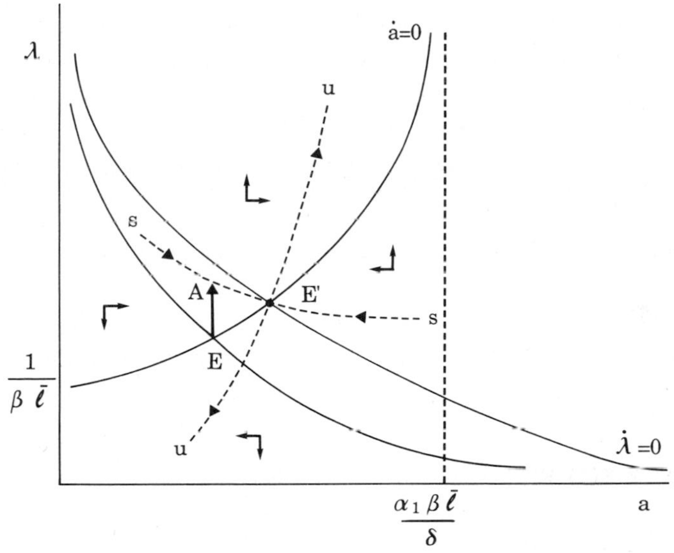

Figure 1: Phase-diagram for the open-loop Nash equilibrium - Increase in α_3

The equilibrium is a saddlepoint, which follows from $\det(J) = -\delta(r+\delta) - \alpha_1\alpha_3(\lambda a)^{-2} < 0$, where J is the Jacobian of (4.8) and (4.3) evaluated at the equilibrium. The equilibrium is given by $\lambda(\infty) = \alpha_3/\{(r+\delta)\ a(\infty)\}$, where

$$a(\infty) = \alpha_1\alpha_3\ \beta\bar{\ell}/\{(\alpha_1+\alpha_3)\delta + \alpha_1 r\}. \tag{4.9}$$

Hence, the steady-state weapon stock of the West is an increasing function of productivity (β) and the weights attached to security (α_3) and private sector consumption (α_1), but a decreasing function of the weight attached to leisure (α_2), the rate of depreciation (δ) and the rate of impatience (r).

The OLNES for the East follows from

$$\dot{a}^* = G^*(\lambda^*) - \delta a^* = (\beta\bar{\ell} - \lambda^{*-1}) - \delta a^*, \qquad a^*(0) = a_0^* \tag{4.10}$$

and (4.4). This yields a similar phase-diagram, where $\det(J^*) = -\delta(r+\delta) - \alpha_3(\lambda^* a^*)^{-2} < 0$. The steady-state weapon stock of the East is given by

$$a^*(\infty) = \alpha_3 \; \beta\bar{\ell}/\{(1+\alpha_3)\delta + r\} > a(\infty). \tag{4.11}$$

Since $\lambda^*(\infty) = \alpha_3/(r+\delta)\; a^*(\infty)$, $g(\infty) = \delta a(\infty)$ and $g^*(\infty) = \delta a^*(\infty)$, it follows that $\lambda^*(\infty) < \lambda(\infty)$ and $g^*(\infty) > g(\infty)$. Also,

$$\ell^*(\infty) = \frac{(\alpha_1+\alpha_3)\delta + \alpha_1 r}{(1+\alpha_3)\delta + r}\,\bar{\ell} > \ell(\infty) = \alpha_1\,\bar{\ell} \tag{4.12}$$

and

$$c^*(\infty) = \frac{(r+\delta)\alpha_1\;\beta\bar{\ell}}{(1+\alpha_3)\delta + r} > c(\infty) = \frac{(r+\delta)\alpha_1^2\;\beta\bar{\ell}}{(\alpha_1+\alpha_3)\delta + \alpha_1 r}\,. \tag{4.13}$$

An unanticipated increase in the weight attached to security (α_3) leads in both countries to an immediate increase in the marginal value of weapon stocks from E to A (see Figure 1), which causes an immediate increase in investment in arms and associated reduction in consumption. Afterwards, the marginal value of weapons falls gradually until the weapon stocks have reached their new higher equilibrium values at E' (see Figure 1).

Since the West has to levy distortionary taxes to finance the provision of arms, employment and therefore output, consumption, investment in arms and the eventual weapon stock are clearly below the corresponding levels attained in the East. However, the West may have a more productive technology ($\beta > \beta^*$ rather than $\beta = \beta^*$) in which case consumption, leisure and arms in the West may exceed the levels attained in the East. It is obvious that competitive arms accumulation leads to excessive investment in weapons relative to the cooperative outcomes of Section 3, since competitive arms accumulation does not lead to a moratorium.

4.2 The Subgame-perfect Nash Equilibrium

The CLNES implies that each country conditions its optimal investment strategy on the current and, possibly, past stocks of weapons. This type of information structure admits, among other things, threat strategies which are briefly considered in Section 4.3. The solution set under CLNES is typically non-unique. However, if the principle of subgame perfection is applied, uniqueness might result. An equilibrium solution is subgame perfect, if the relevant part of this solution is also a Nash equilibrium for each subgame. A subgame in this respect is a game over a remainder of the planning period, say over $[\bar{t},\infty)$ rather than over $[0,\infty)$. The subgame-perfect equilibrium must be a Nash equilibrium for any $\bar{t} \in [0,\infty)$ and for any $\{a(\bar{t}),\ a^*(\bar{t})\}$. Considered this way Selten's (1975) principle of subgame perfection is very similar to Bellman's principle of optimality, which is now assumed and not concluded. The solution technique follows dynamic programming. This implies that each country uses information on the current weapon stocks and does not commit itself to a fixed investment strategy from the beginning. In fact the principle of subgame perfection rules out threat equilibria which rely on information patterns with memory, and rules out equilibria which cease to be equilibria when something unexpected occurs. Under closed-loop information patterns there might be different sets of equilibrium strategies which yield the same equilibrium path of arms accumulation. This is a problem of non-uniqueness in representation of the optimal policies. The only set of equilibrium strategies, which remains an equilibrium solution when mistakes or disturbances cause a deviation from the expected equilibrium path, is the subgame-perfect Nash equilibrium solution (SPNES).

Although Pontryagin's Maximum Principle is primarily constructed for problems with an open-loop information pattern, an extended version can be used to find equilibrium solutions for closed-loop (no-memory) information patterns. To the right-hand sides of equations (4.3) and (4.4) the extra terms $(-g^*_a\lambda_*)$ and $(-\tau_{a^*}\lambda^*_*)$ have to be added respectively, where λ_* (λ^*_*) is the marginal value of the Eastern (Western) weapon stock to the Western

(Eastern) bloc and where λ_* and λ^*_* have to satisfy the additional necessary conditions

$$\dot{\lambda}_* = (r+\delta)\,\lambda_* + \alpha_3/a^* - g^*_{a^*}\lambda_*, \qquad \lim_{t\to\infty} e^{-rt}\,\lambda_*(t)\,a^*(t) = 0, \tag{4.14}$$

$$\dot{\lambda}^*_* = (r+\delta)\,\lambda^*_* + \alpha_3/a - \tau_a\lambda^*_*, \qquad \lim_{t\to\infty} e^{-rt}\,\lambda^*_*(t)\,a(t) = 0. \tag{4.15}$$

Note that the user cost of defence, that is the rental plus depreciation charges minus capital gains $((r+\delta-\dot{\lambda}/\lambda)\lambda)$, now has to match the marginal benefit of weapons (α_3/a) plus an extra term to allow for the closed-loop nature of the information patterns $(g^*_a\lambda_*)$. Since one normally expects the rival country to step up its investment in arms when the home country's weapon stock increases $(g^*_a>0)$, and the marginal value of the Eastern weapon stock to the West to be negative $(\lambda_*<0)$, one expects this extra term to reduce the marginal benefit of weapons. Hence, one expects less weapon stocks and therefore greater welfare when countries can monitor their rival's weapon stock. Indeed, van der Ploeg and de Zeeuw (forthcoming 1989) prove this for a symmetric model with lump-sum taxation and quadratic preferences. However, these insights only hold when defence is not separable in home and foreign weapon stocks.

The SPNES is expressed in terms of the value functions $V(t,a,a^*)$ and $V^*(t,a^*,a)$ which are the equilibrium values for the indirect intertemporal utility functions when the game would start in time period t with weapon stocks a and a^*. Note that $V_a = \lambda$, $V_{a^*} = \lambda_*$, $V^*_a = \lambda^*_*$ and $V^*_{a^*} = \lambda^*$ establishes the relationship between the SPNES and the extended Maximum Principle above. The value functions V and V^* have to satisfy the Hamilton-Jacobi-Bellman equations

$$V_t - rV + \max_{\tau} \{V_a[\tau\, W(\tau)\, L(\tau) - \delta a] + V_{a^*}[g^*-\delta a^*] + \hat{U}(\tau,a,a^*)\} = 0, \tag{4.16}$$

$$V^*_t - rV^* + \max_{g^*} \{V^*_a[\tau w\ell-\delta a] + V^*_{a^*}[g^*-\delta a^*] + \hat{U}^*(g^*,a^*,a)\} = 0, \tag{4.17}$$

yielding

$$\left.\begin{aligned} \hat{U}_\tau + V_a\{w\ell + \tau(W_\tau\ell + wL_\tau)\} = \alpha_1\{\beta\bar{\ell}V_a - (1-\tau)^{-1}\} \le 0 \\ \tau \ge 0 \end{aligned}\right\} \text{c.s.,} \tag{4.18}$$

$$\left.\begin{aligned} \hat{U}^*_{g^*} + V^*_{a^*} = V^*_{a^*} - (\beta\bar{\ell}-g^*)^{-1} \le 0 \\ g^* \ge 0 \end{aligned}\right\} \text{c.s.} \tag{4.19}$$

Even for the stationary situation with interior solutions the explicit functional forms of the value functions V and V* are very difficult to find. However, on the basis of two specific aspects of the present problem it can be concluded that the equilibrium paths for the weapon stocks and the equilibrium values for the investments in arms of the SPNES and the OLNES must coincide. These specific aspects are the separability of the indirect utility functions in the weapon stocks a and a* and the absence of a direct influence of each investment and stock on the accumulation of arms in the rival country. These aspects imply a decoupling of the dynamic game, which restores the one-player property that subgame-perfect control and open-loop control yield the same control values. The decoupling can also be recognised in the analysis of the stationary OLNES in Section 4.1. In Section 5 the separability is relaxed by considering the more general CES utility function instead of the Cobb-Douglas utility function.

4.3 Threats as an Inducement of Cooperative Behaviour

Suppose each country aims at the results of cooperative behaviour but cannot rely on a cooperative agreement with the rival country, because the rival country then has an incentive to deviate by accumulating more weapons than the level agreed upon in the cooperative outcome. In other words, the cooperative outcome is in general not sustainable under competitive arms accumulation. However, if each country can employ memory strategies, threats can be formulated in such a way that the cooperative outcome can be sustained. Each country announces that, if the rival country deviates from the cooperative equilibrium, it will invest so heavily in arms accumulation, that the rival country is deterred from deviating. The structure of such a threat equilibrium is given by:

$$\tau = 0, \qquad \text{if } a^*(t) = e^{-\delta t} a_0^*,$$

$$\tau \text{ big}, \qquad \text{if } a^*(t) > e^{-\delta t} a_0^*,$$

$$g^* = 0, \qquad \text{if } a(t) = e^{-\delta t} a_0,$$

$$g^* \text{ big}, \qquad \text{if } a(t) > e^{-\delta t} a_0.$$

There are two possibilities. Either each country submits to the threat and the cooperative equilibrium results or a country does not submit to the threat (because it is not credible and thus not optimal to execute it when called upon to do so) and then anything can happen.

5. Consequences of Non-separable Preferences

In Section 4.2 it was argued that the separability of the Cobb-Douglas utility function is one of the reasons why the OLNES and the SPNES coincide. This section therefore considers a more general nested CES utility function:

$$U(c,\bar{\ell}-\ell,d(a,a^*)) = \left\{\frac{1}{1+\alpha_3}\left[c^{\alpha_1}(\bar{\ell}-\ell)^{\alpha_2}\right]^{-\alpha_4} + \frac{\alpha_3}{1+\alpha_3}[a/a^*]^{-\alpha_4}\right\}^{\frac{-1}{\alpha_4}},$$

$$\alpha_1,\ \alpha_2,\ \alpha_3 \geq 0, \qquad \alpha_4 \geq -1, \qquad \alpha_1 + \alpha_2 = 1, \tag{5.1}$$

where $\sigma \equiv 1/(1+\alpha_4)$ is the elasticity of substitution between private goods, a composite of consumption and leisure, and defence. The special case of a unit elasticity of substitution ($\alpha_4 \to 0$) yields the Cobb-Douglas utility function employed so far. This nested approach has the advantage that the logarithm of the sub-utility function is still separable, so that the choices for consumption and leisure are unaffected. Upon substitution into (5.1), one obtains the indirect utility functions

$$\hat{U}(\tau,a,a^*) \equiv \left\{\frac{1}{1+\alpha_3}\left[\hat{\alpha}_0(1-\tau)^{\alpha_1}\right]^{-\alpha_4} + \frac{\alpha_3}{1+\alpha_3}[a/a^*]^{-\alpha_4}\right\}^{\frac{-1}{\alpha_4}} \tag{5.2}$$

and

$$\hat{U}^*(g^*,a^*,a) \equiv \left\{\frac{1}{1+\alpha_3}\,[\hat{\alpha}_0(1-\alpha_1 g^*)]^{-\alpha_4} + \frac{\alpha_3}{1+\alpha_3}\,[a^*/a]^{-\alpha_4}\right\}^{\frac{-1}{\alpha_4}}, \qquad (5.3)$$

where $\hat{\alpha}_0 \equiv \exp(\alpha_0)$. As before, the OLNES is found with the aid of Pontryagin's Maximum Principle and the SPNES with the aid of dynamic programming. Since an analytical treatment becomes very cumbersome, a numerical example will be discussed in such a way that the length of the working day in the West will be eight hours and the normalisation $\alpha_1 \beta \bar{\ell} = 1$ is used.

EXAMPLE.

$\bar{\ell} = 24$, $\alpha_1 = 1/3$, $\beta = 1/8$, $\delta = 0.1$, $r = 0.1$.

The indirect instantaneous utility functions for this example are

$$\hat{U}(\tau,a,a^*) = \left\{\frac{1}{1+\alpha_3}\,[(1-\tau)^{1/3}\,16^{2/3}]^{-\alpha_4} + \frac{\alpha_3}{1+\alpha_3}\,[a/a^*]^{-\alpha_4}\right\}^{\frac{-1}{\alpha_4}}$$

and

$$\hat{U}^*(g^*,a^*,a) = \left\{\frac{1}{1+\alpha_3}\,[(1-g^*/3)16^{2/3}]^{-\alpha_4} + \frac{\alpha_3}{1+\alpha_3}\,[a^*/a]^{-\alpha_4}\right\}^{\frac{-1}{\alpha_4}}.$$

5.1 Nash Equilibrium with Open-loop Information Sets

The first-order conditions describing the OLNES are (1.10) - (1.11), (2.7), $H_\tau = 0$, $H^*_{g^*} = 0$, $r\lambda - \dot{\lambda} = H_a$, $r\lambda_* - \dot{\lambda}_* = H_{a^*}$, $r\lambda^* - \dot{\lambda}^* = H^*_{a^*}$ and $r\lambda^*_* - \dot{\lambda}^*_* = H^*_a$, where the Hamiltonians for the Western and Eastern blocs are given by $H \equiv \hat{U} + \lambda(\tau-\delta a) + \lambda_*(g^*-\delta a^*)$ and $H^* \equiv \hat{U}^* + \lambda^*(g^*-\delta a^*) + \lambda^*_*(\tau-\delta a)$, respectively. Again, the equations describing the dynamic behaviour of λ_* and λ^*_* are decoupled from the other equations. The OLNES for the example above is a saddlepoint and its steady state can be shown to satisfy the following set of equations:

$$\frac{1}{3}(r+\delta)16^{-\frac{2}{3}\alpha_4}(1-\delta a)^{-\frac{1}{3}\alpha_4-1} = \alpha_3 a^{*\alpha_4} a^{-\alpha_4-1} \tag{5.4}$$

and

$$\frac{1}{3}(r+\delta)16^{-\frac{2}{3}\alpha_4}(1-\delta a^*/3)^{-\alpha_4-1} = \alpha_3 a^{\alpha_4} a^{*-\alpha_4-1}. \tag{5.5}$$

The values of the weapon stocks and utilities in equilibrium for $\alpha_3 = 0.2$ and for different values of the parameter α_4 have been calculated and are:

α_4	σ	$a(\infty)$	$a^*(\infty)$	$\hat{U}$	$\hat{U}^*$
-0.5	2.00	0.514	2.526	4.651	5.660
0	1.00	2.308	2.727	4.219	4.431
0.5	0.67	4.303	5.183	3.353	3.764
1	0.50	6.337	8.042	2.532	3.219

The values for $\alpha_4 = 0$ correspond to the results (4.9) and (4.11) which were obtained for Cobb-Douglas utility functions. An increase in α_4 or, alternatively, a decrease in the elasticity of substitution between, on the one hand, consumption and leisure and, on the other hand, defence leads to larger weapon stocks in equilibrium. The reason for this is that less substitution possibilities between private goods and defence makes each country more vulnerable to increases in foreign weapon stocks, so that each country escalates its accumulation of arms. As before, for any given value of the elasticity of substitution, except for $\sigma \to \infty$, the East is more efficient and therefore has more weapons and a higher level of welfare.

5.2 The Subgame-perfect Nash Equilibrium

The SPNES is considerably more difficult to calculate. In fact, it has proven impossible to find the asymptotic solution to the coupled system of partial differential equations describing the SPNES for the example discussed in this section. One possibility is to solve a linear-quadratic approximation of the problem, since then the value functions associated with the SPNES can be found. It is not clear that this is a very satisfactory approach, hence some progress has been made in the development of a computer algorithm for solving discretised finite-horizon dynamic games.

Each country is given a limited set of investment possibilities and for a finite number of stages a 'game-tree' is built in which the branches represent the investment choices with the corresponding utility levels and the nodes represent the resulting weapon stocks. The algorithm solves backwards recursively for each node the remaining subgame starting at the end of the tree. In this discretised setting these subgames take the form of bimatrix games. The horizon is set at 7 stages and the security parameter α_3 is given a value of at least 0.2 in order to evoke positive investments in arms. Suitable discrete investment possibilities were experimentally established at 0.1 and 0.3 and the initial values of the weapon stocks, a_0 and a_0^*, are set at the equilibrium values of the corresponding OLNES.

The purpose of this section is to compare, for non-separable preferences, the SPNES, in which the countries are able to observe each other's weapon stocks, and the OLNES, in which the countries precommit themselves to a sequence of investment choices and cannot monitor foreign weapon stocks. Therefore, the OLNES is also calculated for the same discretised finite-horizon dynamic game which implies solving one large bimatrix game for the Nash equilibrium. Thus the OLNES solves one 128×128 bimatrix game and the SPNES solves 5461 (i.e., $(4^7-1)/3$) 2×2 bimatrix games. Even for this simple example, the computational costs of calculating the OLNES and the SPNES are considerable. When the horizon or the number of investment possibilities goes up, the computational cost goes up exponentially.

Three typical situations occur for the following three sets of parameter values: $\{\alpha_3 = 0.2, \alpha_4 = 1.0\}$, $\{\alpha_3 = 0.2, \alpha_4 = 0.5\}$ and $\{\alpha_3 = 0.3, \alpha_4 = 0.5\}$, labelled I, II and III, respectively.

The results are:

	Case I		Case II		Case III	
	SPNES	OLNES	SPNES	OLNES	SPNES	OLNES
$\tau(1)$ $g^*(1)$	0.3 0.1	0.3 0.3	0.3 0.1	0.3 0.3	0.1 0.3	0.3 0.3
$\tau(2)$ $g^*(2)$	0.3 0.3	0.3 0.3	0.1 0.3	0.3 0.3	0.3 0.3	0.3 0.3
$\tau(3)$ $g^*(3)$	0.3 0.1	0.3 0.3	0.1 0.3	0.3 0.3	0.3 0.3	0.3 0.3
$\tau(4)$ $g^*(4)$	0.3 0.3	0.3 0.3	0.3 0.1	0.1 0.1	0.3 0.3	0.3 0.3
$\tau(5)$ $g^*(5)$	0.3 0.3	0.3 0.3	0.1 0.1	0.1 0.1	0.3 0.1	0.3 0.1
$\tau(6)$ $g^*(6)$	0.3 0.1	0.3 0.1	0.1 0.1	0.1 0.1	0.1 0.1	0.1 0.1
$\tau(7)$ $g^*(7)$	0.1 0.1	0.1 0.1	0.1 0.1	0.1 0.1	0.1 0.1	0.1 0.1
$a(7)$	4.396	4.396	2.832	2.935	3.618	3.724
$a^*(7)$	4.794	5.032	3.250	3.356	4.279	4.279
$\hat{U}$	14.326	14.033	15.015	14.906	10.469	10.520
$\hat{U}^*$	17.423	17.527	16.770	16.599	12.720	12.577
$\hat{U} + \hat{U}^*$	31.749	31.560	31.785	31.505	23.189	23.097

The most remarkable conclusion is that the SPNES leads to less arms accumulation in both the West and the East than the OLNES and is therefore better for the world as a whole. This is exactly what one expected from Section 4.2, since closed-loop information effectively reduces the marginal benefit of weapons as each country now takes account of the fact that, when it invests in an additional weapon, the rival will react and escalate its arms accumulation. It is clear that a unilateral arms treaty should give each country the opportunity to monitor the rival's weapon stocks. The familiar result that the East has more weapons, greater security and therefore greater welfare than the West is also illustrated in this discretised version of the dynamic game. The general pattern in each case is that heavy investments in arms take place in the early periods of the game and that more consumption takes place later on. This is not unreasonable in view of the fact that the marginal value of weapons after the game is zero. In situation II both countries invest less in guns in the SPNES and thus consume more butter than in the OLNES and both countries achieve a higher level of welfare. In situation I the East invests less in guns in the SPNES and thus consumes more butter. However, because the West invests the same in weapons in the SPNES as in the OLNES, the East feels less secure and the tradeoff between more butter and less security results in a lower level of welfare for the East. The West consumes the same amount of butter but feels more secure, so that the West achieves a higher level of welfare in the SPNES than in the OLNES. In situation III it is just the other way around. Situations I and III are peculiar to asymmetric economies and discretised games and cast doubt on the robustness of the result obtained in Situation I.

6. Concluding Remarks

This paper tries to contribute to the literature on the arms race in two ways. Firstly, the arms race is modelled from an economic point of view so that adequate attention is given to the 'guns versus butter' dilemma and to the way in which investment in arms is realised. A decentralised market economy where distortionary taxes finance the investment in arms is contrasted with a centrally planned economy. The analysis is based on a utility function, which depends on consumption, leisure and defence. Secondly, the impact of information on the investment strategies is investigated where especially information on both the own and the foreign weapon stock over time is considered. For Cobb-Douglas utilities the separability ensures that there are no differences in the outcomes under precommitment with static information patterns and in the subgame-perfect outcomes with dynamic information patterns. However, more general CES utilities lead to different equilibrium solutions. It has been argued that the subgame-perfect Nash equilibrium leads to lower stocks of weapons than the open-loop (or precommitment) Nash equilibrium. This implies that the previous literature (e.g. Brito 1976) has tended to overestimate the extent of the accumulation of arms. As far as policy is concerned, this suggests that countries should be given the opportunity to monitor each other's weapon stocks as this will lead to less arms accumulation and therefore to a safer world. It has also been shown that a decrease in the elasticity of substitution between private goods, consumption and leisure on the one hand, and defence on the other, leads to larger weapon stocks.

In this paper it has been argued that monitoring of each other's weapon stocks may be a good thing, because it leads to smaller weapon stocks, higher consumption levels and greater welfare. However, monitoring is not necessarily the same thing as verification. Historically, verification has been endogeneous in the sense that once countries agree on less arms accumulation they agree on verification by formalising how the results of monitoring procedures should be interpreted. Verification was a major issue prior to SALT, but once the limits had been agreed both sides accepted that existing monitoring methods, National Technical Means (satellites), were adequate for verification which is something they could have accepted before. Likewise scientists apparently think that a Comprehensive Test Ban Treaty can be monitored, but governments refuse this and use verification as a major argument against an agreement. Hence, verification should really be considered a bargaining issue rather than the provision of public information. Another problem is that monitoring itself, i.e. counting weapons, is not so much of a problem, but agreeing on what the numbers mean (given different capabilities of the weapon stocks) is almost always a problem. Such problems may make feedback more difficult.

There are at least four directions for future research. The first is to extend the framework to allow for international trade between the West and the East. This would make the welfare of each country depend on the government policies of the rival country. For example, an increase in foreign government spending or taxes might lead to a reduction in foreign consumption and the resulting balance of payments deficit might be choked off by a depreciation of the real exchange rate and therefore home welfare might fall. Such trade wars introduce flow externalities over and above the stock externalities caused by conflict over arms accumulation, but they do not change the qualitative character of the results described in this paper. The second direction is to think more carefully about the asymmetries between the West and the East. It seems more reasonable to assume that the West is in a regime of Keynesian unemployment and the East is in a regime of repressed inflation (e.g. Malinvaud 1977). Since the West has an excess supply of goods and labour, Western arms now have benefits not only in terms of higher security but also in terms of Keynesian employment-generating effects. However, the East has an excess demand for goods and labour, so that expenditure on arms in the East increases security but leads to longer queues and inflation. This seems to suggest that the West may have more of an incentive to invest in arms than the East. The third direction is to consider extensions that allow the private sector to accumulate assets and the government to issue debt. This may introduce problems of time inconsistency and credibility of each government vis-à-vis its private sectors. For example, the government might announce to levy low capital taxes and high labour taxes in order to encourage investment. However, once the machines have been accumulated, the government has an incentive to renege and levy higher capital taxes than promised. Another example is a surprise inflation tax. It may well be that, when there is international trade and governments cannot credibly precommit themselves, international cooperation is counter-productive as multilateral reneging does not induce a depreciation of the exchange rate and therefore inflation costs (see Rogoff 1985; van der Ploeg, 1988). It would be exciting to investigate whether such counter-intuitive results can be obtained in multi-country models of arms conflict. It would also be interesting to analyse reputational equilibria within the context of such models. The final direction of future research extends the economic framework of competitive arms accumulation from two to more than two countries. It may well be that, if the analysis is restricted to two countries, important adverse responses from third countries are overlooked. Cooperation may no longer lead to multilateral disarmament, i.e. a moratorium on investment in weapons, as this might provoke an arms build-up or even an attack of third countries. The economic analogue of this result for international monetary coordination between three countries is provided by Canzoneri and Henderson (forthcoming).

Note

* An earlier version of this paper was presented at a meeting of the European Public Choice Society, 2-5 April 1986, Noordwijkerhout, the Netherlands, and at a Conference on International Economic Security organised by the Centre for Economic Policy Research, June 1986, London. The authors are grateful to the participants in those meetings, to two referees, to Simone Clemhout and Ron Smith for their comments, and to Anton Markink for his excellent computational assistance for Section 5.2.

References

Başar, T. and G.J. Olsder, Dynamic Noncooperative Game Theory, Academic Press, New York, 1982.

Boulding, K.E., Conflict and Defence, Harper and Row, Boston, 1961.

Brito, D.L., 'A dynamic model in an armaments race', International Economic Review, 13, 2, 1972, pp. 359-375.

Brito, D.L. and M.D. Intriligator, 'Formal models of arms races', Journal of Peace Science, 2, 1976, pp. 77-88.

Canzoneri, M.B. and P.W. Henderson, Noncooperative Monetary Policies in Interdependent Economies, (forthcoming).

Deger, S. and S. Sen, 'Optimal control and differential game models of military expenditure in less developed countries', Journal of Economic Dynamics and Control, 7, 1984, pp. 153-169.

Intriligator, M.D., 'Strategic considerations in the Richardson model of arms races', Journal of Political Economy, 83, 1975, pp. 339-353.

Intriligator, M.D. and D.L. Brito, 'Nuclear proliferation and the probability of nuclear war', Public Choice, 37, 1982, pp. 247-260.

Lancaster, K., 'A new approach to consumer theory', Journal of Political Economy, 24, 1966, pp. 132-157.

Malinvaud, E., The Theory of Unemployment Reconsidered, Basil Blackwell, Oxford, 1977.

McGuire, M.C., Secrecy and the Arms Race, Harvard University Press, Cambridge, MA, 1965.

Ploeg, F. van der, 'International policy coordination in interdependent monetary economies', Journal of International Economics, 25, 1988, pp. 1-23.

Ploeg, F. van der and A.J. de Zeeuw, 'Perfect equilibrium in a competitive model of arms accumulation', International Economic Review, (forthcoming 1989).

Richardson, L.F., Arms and Insecurity, Boxwood Press, Chicago, 1960.

Rogoff, K., 'Can international monetary policy cooperation be counterproductive?', Journal of International Economics, 18, 1985, pp. 199-217.

Saaty, T.L., Mathematical Models of Arms Control and Disarmament, John Wiley, New York, 1968.

Schelling, T.C., The Strategy of Conflict, Harvard University Press, Cambridge, MA, 1980.

Dynamic Policy Games in Economics
F. van der Ploeg and A.J. de Zeeuw, (Editors)

ON GAMES OF CAKE-EATING

Simone Clemhout

Henry Wan, Jr

Department of Economics
Cornell University
Ithaca, New York 14853-7601, USA

Introduction

This study focuses upon a very simple problem in resource economics: the exploitation of a non-renewable common-property resource. An example of such resources is the ground water originated in geological time, and freely accessible to various parties. Problems of this type are of interest in their own right. But more importantly, their extreme simplicity provides the opportunity to probe into some conceptual and methodological issues in dynamic games.

At this moment, the bulk of publications in our profession is primarily concerned with casting specific tools or performing specific tasks, rather than studying methodological questions. On this happy occasion of honouring the lifetime accomplishments of Professor Piet Verheyen, we are inspired not to stop at 'how', but to reflect on 'why'.

Game theory studies the resolution of conflicting interests among rational individuals. As long as the players differ ever so slightly in their preferences over how the resources should be allocated, some conflict inherently arises. Whether and how much the players may 'care' for each other, like members in a family in the theory of Becker (1981), do not change the situation. Two friends can reach a deadlock at the doorway, each insisting 'after you'. Cooperative *modus vivendi* may arise frequently in real life. But by Nash (1953), what dictates the terms of every realised cooperation is the perceived outcome of an *unplayed non-cooperative* game of threats. In *non-cooperative* games, players only reach self-enforcing accommodations, and not arrangements which become binding only by an appeal to external power.

In our problem, conflicts arise from the shared access to a scarce resource. We study how players operate non-cooperatively.

The static common property problem may appear simplistic: players always 'grab' as much as they can. The dynamic version is less straightforward. A player may deny his rival any future consumption only by exhausting all of the resource in one stroke, but then he must accept the same irreversible, total privation for himself, from now on. Here comes the first moral: don't rock the boat.

But the matter does not end there. How much a person would save for the future depends on how much that act of saving can benefit his own future, and this benefit becomes less if the other players take more in the meantime. What is the prudent consumption of a Crusoe may trigger all players into a stampede, causing immediate resource exhaustion. Here comes the second moral: don't *you start* to rock the boat.

Thus, the concepts of retaliation and deterrence, brought to prominence by Friedman (1971), Radner (1980), and Rubinstein and Yaari (1983), with history-dependent *trigger strategies* in repeated games, are also present in many 'dynamic games', where only state-dependent strategies are in use. Of course, Pareto-superior results may be achieved by specifying additional history-dependent state variables, to enrich the opportunities for mutual behaviour modification.

There is a proviso, however, to our first and second morals. If the marginal returns decline very mildly, and the time preferences are sufficiently high, immediate resource exhaustion can be an equilibrium behaviour pattern (Clemhout and Wan 1985a). Here then is the third moral: on the right occasion, a bird in the hand is worth two in the bush.

The dynamic common property problem may involve either a non-renewable resource (like ground water or petroleum), or a renewable resource, like a fishery. Analytically, the former is a special case of the latter, see, for instance, Clemhout and Wan (1985b). In the case of a fishery, the conserved resource may be used not only for future consumption but also as an investment in biological reproduction. In studying certain conceptual problems, we shall focus upon the simpler structure.

This simpler problem is known as *cake-eating* (see Gale 1967; Kemp and Long 1980). It is attractive not only because of its utter simplicity. By happy coincidence, this model is structurally a twin of the Ramsey model, known to most economists. Together this pair forms a natural bridge between the control models which are familiar to us all, and the differential games which are probably not. We found this problem helpful in shedding light on some issues about difference/differential games, which are especially relevant for economists. These include,

(i) the existence,

(ii) the plausibility,

(iii) the uniqueness and

(iv) the robustness

of the equilibrium concept. We now study these issues not in the abstract, but in the context of a single stylised problem in real life. We further introduce the concept,

(v) inverse equilibrium,

and comment upon aspects of

(vi) information structure.

On (i), (ii) and (iii) we shall present a viewpoint, illustrated with an example. On (iv) we suggest a technique (state transformation) together with some robustness results. To our knowledge, with the exception of Arrow and Kurz (1970), (v) has not yet been studied very much in the game-theoretic context. Our observations on (vi) may help to clarify certain issues.

We outline the main points of this study in the ensuing section, to be followed by the formal model specification. Next, we introduce the inverse equilibrium problem, and analyse the class of models with linear equilibrium strategies. By the technique of state transformation, this is then generalised to the class of models with share-preserving equilibrium strategies. The latter in turn provides the basis for discussing the question of robustness. Finally, we comment upon the use of history-dependent state variables, as introduced by Başar and Olsder (1982).

1. The Quality of Existence: Our Personal View

As Aumann (in Arrow and Honkapohja 1985) observes, ultimately, game theory -like all scientific studies- must be justified by its contribution to our understanding of reality. A game-theoretic model is the idealisation of real-life conflicts; its solution mirrors the predicted outcome. What insight one may obtain depends on what kind of solution one is looking for. For convenience, we call this issue the choice of *solution concept*.

Any non-cooperative game x, in 'normal form' is decided by (i) the set of choices (action or control) $C_i(x)$, available to each player i, (ii) the outcome function $\omega(c_1,c_2,\ldots;x)$, dependent upon both the game x and choices c_i, one selected by each player, and finally (iii) the payoff functions $u_i(\omega)$, one for each player i, pertaining to that outcome. For such games, the natural solution concept is the Nash equilibrium. This specifies a list (or profile) of choices, one for each player, such that no player can gain by switching to another choice all by himself.

If c_i is a once-for-all action for each player i, the game is called a one-shot game, and the choice may be called either an action or a strategy. We are interested in dynamic games, which evolved from stochastic games (see Owen 1982). Here we depict the real-life situation (say, playing chess) with a class of games. Each game is characterised by the index x, the state of the game, which may be a point (vector) in some Euclidean state space (for chess, it is the configuration on the board, and such facts as whether the king or rook has already moved). Time itself may enter as a component of the state vector. Players choose actions in each game, and the outcome is an ordered pair (u,T), where $u = (u_1,u_2,\ldots)$ is a list of instant rewards (in chess, pieces taken), one for each player, and T is a transition rule, deciding which subsequent games are to be played (in chess, how does the configuration on the board evolve), or alternatively, whether all is over. For the play to continue, the transition rule takes the form:

$$x_{t+1} = T(c_{1t},c_{2t},\ldots;x_t)$$

for difference games where time is discrete, and

$$dx/dt = T(c_{1t},c_{2t},\ldots;x_t)$$

for differential games where time is continuous. The payoff for each player is related to his instant rewards over the play, often the sum or integral over the reward stream (in chess, the taking of the rival king). The decision rule of player i in such models is a strategy (or policy),

$p_i(.)$, where $c_{it} = p_i(x_t)$. This specifies what action to take in each game, i.e., in each state of the game (in chess, such a contingent plan would call for different moves in different variations). Note that by now the terms strategy and action are clearly not equivalent. By deciding what form such functions $p_i(.)$ can take, we impose restrictions on the rules of the game (in chess, such rule of game decides when a player can castle).

Recall that a Nash equilibrium is a 'strategy profile' from which no player wishes to deviate alone. Equivalently, it can be defined as an N-tuple of strategies, such that the strategy of each player is the best reply to the strategies of all other players. An equilibrium play describes the evolution of the state when players use their equilibrium strategies. The value of a game-theoretic model rests on the hope that the essence of real-life events is mirrored in an equilibrium play among the rational agents. Such a model allows researchers to predict. The researcher has more predictive power if the equilibrium is unique.

For the same problem, by imposing different restrictions on the forms of the strategies, entirely different sets of equilibria may emerge. This is why the choice of solution concept is critically important.

Three types of restrictions have been considered.

Firstly, there are conceptual restrictions, the most important one being the requirement of subgame perfection, introduced by Selten (1965, 1975). The issue here is *credibility*. Initially, at time t_1 and state x_1, player i may adopt a strategy which promises a particular action when the state becomes x_2. Such a promise is credible only if it is to the interest of i to carry it through when state x_2 arrives. An equilibrium is subgame perfect, if all strategies are credible. In principle, one may precommit oneself to certain actions. A notable example is entry deterrence through irreversible investment (Dixit 1980). Or else, one may try to bluff an imperfectly informed rival (see Milgrom and Roberts 1982, for instance). But such possibilities must be explicitly specified, rather than loosely implied. The concept of perfection originally arose from extensive games. More related discussions can be found in van Damme (1983).

Secondly, there are informational constraints. The conventional preference in differential games is to assume that a player must adopt the same action when confronting the same 'state of the game'. This is referred to as *feedback strategies*, by the usage of Başar and Olsder (1982), and closed loop strategies (see, e.g., Clemhout and Wan 1979).

This allows for the use of state-space representation in the engineering literature.

Some researchers advocate, instead, the use of 'memory strategies' which are 'history-dependent', and not contingent upon the present state only (e.g. Shubik 1982). For our chess analogy, this may mean to take advantage of the known stamina, or the lack of it, of a rival. In terms of traditional game theory in extensive form, a player may condition his choices on all his information, which is precisely specified by his 'information set'. By the usual postulation of 'perfect recall', what a player has known once, can always be the basis to select a later move. Thus, in this view, the notion 'state' in differential games is far too restrictive. For example, it requires the traffic court to give equal treatment to first offenders and all repeated offenders. Many deterrence opportunities are omitted in such modelling.

At the opposite end, largely because of tractability, other researchers prefer to deal only with those strategies which depend solely on time. These are referred to in the literature *as open-loop strategies* (see e.g., Fudenberg and Tirole 1985). By Fleming and Rishel (1975), this exclusive use of such strategies means that players only act upon their initial knowledge, but not upon any subsequent information. Whatever news about subsequent rival action would not elicit 'mid-course adjustments' (for more technical details, see Başar and Olsder 1982).

Thirdly, there are analytical constraints, which are adopted either to assure that the problems are well posed, or that the analysis is tractable. In differential games, the use of continuous time obligates us to insist that the 'strategies' must be measurable functions over their domain. Otherwise the outcome of the game may be mathematically undefined. One may further require the strategies to be piece-wise continuous, or smooth (i.e., twice continuously differentiable, or in the class C").

For us, as economists, the only concern is to develop our insight, using whatever conceptual tools suit our purpose. For this objective, we need solution concepts which are meaningful in the following senses.

Firstly, it must be a plausible representation of rational behaviour. Rational individuals neither take seriously incredible threats nor exclude information just because it comes at a wrong time. Hence, we deal with feedback strategies in equilibria which are subgame perfect.

Secondly, it must be conceptually simple to perceive. Nash strategies are best replies to each other. But one replies only to what one perceives. Given our limited perceptual capabilities, the simplest strategies are the likeliest to prevail in real life. Such considerations are not new in the literature. They gave rise to the focal point notion of Schelling (1960), the machine game model of Rubinstein (1986) and the motivation of Başar (1977) to model memory strategies with history-dependent state variables rather than past histories themselves.

Thirdly, the solution should be reasonably tractable. Above all, only what is easy to analyse for the researcher is easy to perceive by the player. Moreover, there is little point in limiting one's attention to solutions promising existence under the broadest circumstances. To prove the existence of something totally inscrutable does not contribute all that much to science. A viable alternative is to consider first the solutions with easy tractability. Our purpose is served either by proving the existence of something simple outright, or by acquiring such insight in some unsuccessful first try, so that a successful model reformulation would follow naturally. Focusing on the tractability has one more justification. More than just in the normative questions of feasibility and efficiency, economists are often interested in such descriptive questions as sensitivity analysis: what would happen if such and such were the case. Thus, equilibria may best be studied constructively. A pure existence proof does not help all that much.

Based upon the above considerations, we prefer to start with an equilibrium concept which is subgame perfect, and a class of strategies which is feedback Nash and also smooth, and states of the game which may be partly history dependent.

Like in one-shot games, how players in difference/differential games arrive collectively at an equilibrium is a question defying satisfactory answers. Rarely does a model have a dominant strategy equilibrium, where each player has a strategy which is the best reply to any combination of strategies of all the others. Pre-game communication may supply the answer, but such acts of communication should be included as part of the game. Other things being equal, the simpler are the equilibrium strategies, the more plausible is an equilibrium.

Technically, the differential game differs from the difference game in one major aspect. With continuous time, one can be sure that the equilibrium play is mathematically defined only if the strategies are measurable. This restriction appears unnatural to some economists. It is one of the reasons that they prefer to work with discrete time.

Moreover, for both difference and differential games, the characterisation of the equilibrium is not easy. The open-loop equilibrium is tractable but economically unappealing, as we have explained above. The feedback equilibrium is conceptually more acceptable but analytically quite intractable. Unlike the control models, the first-order necessary condition for an equilibrium takes the form of partial differential equations, due to the presence of the cross-influence term, see, e.g., Fudenberg and Tirole (forthcoming). One may first propose certain solutions and then attempt their analytic verification. In the past, verification is possible only if we assume (a) certain particular functional forms for the payoff indices and the production technology (see, for example, Reinganum 1982, references in Clemhout and Wan 1979, 1987, Dockner, Feichtinger and Jørgenson 1985, and for difference games see Levhari and Mirman 1980) or that (b) players are identical (see Stokey 1985, Clemhout and Wan 1985a, and for difference games see Sundaram 1989). Even this approach is not entirely satisfactory. It leaves open the crucial question of the robustness of the existence result; to be specific, whether the existence result can survive any small perturbations of the specific functional forms in such models. This is a serious matter, since all these special functional forms and special assumptions (e.g., all players are identical and like players use like strategies) are proposed for their analytic convenience and not because of any empirical evidence.

In economics, functional form-specific results are valuable in two capacities, either as counter-examples against some unfounded conjecture, or as an illustration of some generic result. The unavailability of robust existence results is perhaps a principal reason that dynamic games (especially with continuous state and controls) have not yet been studied more widely. It is against this background that we offer our tentative approach below.

For continuous time models, we shall tentatively assume, for simplicity, that all strategies are smooth (twice-continuously differentiable). This permits us to follow a two-step approach. Firstly, using results from the theory of differential equations, one can construct with relative ease, a unique candidate function for equilibrium, and one can then verify whether this candidate is truly an equilibrium. By its very nature, this constructive approach, unlike the existence approach, offers a specific solution which may be scrutinised for questions of sensitivity analysis.

Not all games have equilibria in smooth strategies. But one may look for a smooth equilibrium first, by adopting the working hypothesis that all admissible strategies are C". In our case below, the unsuccessful search yields the insight allowing us to reformulate and establish an equilibrium of another type. To us, this procedure offers something most important: the equilibria it isolates are readily characterisable, and even the non-existence of a smooth equilibrium may provide meaningful information.

Of course, no concept is infallible. If the state-space representation and smooth strategies fail to capture some plausible solution, one must consider alternative approaches (see Fudenberg and Tirole, forthcoming).

For our problem, we shall first prove the existence result for a model with specific functional forms, but without requiring that players are identical. Next, by a monotonic transformation of the state variable, we extend the existence proof to a broader class of models. Finally, starting from a subset of such extended models, we show that minor perturbations will not affect the existence result.

In the above studies, we have isolated two classes of strategies: in one, the equilibrium exploitation strategies of all players are linear in the state variable, and in the other, the players' equilibrium exploitation rates are all proportional to each other.

We then consider the new problem (inverse equilibrium): whether the observed behavioural patterns are an equilibrium for some particular model. In our case, the answer is a qualified yes. There is an entire class of games which may share one observed pattern as their equilibrium. The payoff indices can be determined if, and only if, we know the ratio between the time-preference rates of the two players.

Finally, we shall comment in passing on the issue of information structure. It is usually believed that the feedback Nash strategies cannot convey the notion of self-enforcing equilibrium among the players based upon past performance. This turns out to be not quite the case.

2. Model Description

Consider a model with a non-replenishable common-property resource, x, with initial level, $x(0)$, and two players, $i = 1,2$, each one is associated with:

a decision variable: the consumption level, $c_i \in R_+$,

a payoff index, $V_i = \int_0^\infty \exp(-r_i t) U_i(c_i(t))dt$,

where t stands for time, $r_i > 0$ is the time preference rate, and the felicity index,

$$U_i : R_+ \to R$$

is strictly increasing, strictly concave, and twice-continuously differentiable.
The dynamics of the model are described by the equation:

$$dx/dt = -\Sigma c_i.$$

We study such solutions in which the chosen level of consumption depends only upon the state x, and not on time t. Write now such a relationship between c_i and x as $c_i = p_i(x)$, where $p_i(.)$ is the strategy of i, then,

$$dx/dt = -\Sigma p_i(x).$$

At any equilibrium, each player solves an optimal control problem,

$$\max \int_0^\infty \exp(-r_i t) U_i(c_i(t))dt,$$

subject to

$$dx/dt = -\Sigma_{j \neq i}\, p_j(x) - c_i,$$

given the strategies of all others. This resembles the discounted Ramsey problem:

$$\max \int_0^\infty \exp(-rt)U(c(t))dt,$$

subject to

$$dx/dt = f(x) - c.$$

The distinction between the two is that f is a known function, but the term $\Sigma_{j\neq i}[-p_j(x)]$ is not. It is to be simultaneously determined among all players. The former model is said to be an 'N-coupled control problem': each player faces an optimisation problem, taking for granted the equilibrium strategies of all other players.

Since one can always choose a unit for time without losing generality, we suppose that the length of a unit of time is such that the time preference rates of the two players sum up to unity. Furthermore, player 1 is no more 'impatient' than player 2 ($r_1 \leq r_2$):

$$r_1 = 1 - r_2 = r \in (0,1/2].$$

Since the choices of the origin are arbitrary for the players' utility indices, we may set:

$$U_i(1) = 0$$

with no effect on the marginal utilities, U_i', which we focus on.

Since the units of both the utility indices and the consumption good are arbitrary, we can focus attention on their relative magnitudes, log U_i', and log c_i, and require that:

$$U_i'(1) = 1.$$

To facilitate analysis, from now on, we shall operate in terms of a more convenient form, the 'elasticity of the marginal utility function'. This is defined as follows:

$$E_i(c_i) = [c_i U_i''(c_i)/U_i'(c_i)], \qquad E_i : R_{++} \to -R_{++}, \qquad i = 1,2,$$

where the utility index can be expressed in terms of E_i:

$$U_i(c_i) = \int_1^c \{\exp[\int_1^v (E_i/w)dw]\}dv. \tag{2.1}$$

In Figure 1: a, b, c and d below we display two specimens of utility indices in their total, marginal and elasticity forms. Note that if the 'Inada condition':

$$U_i'(0) = \infty$$

is not satisfied, then $E_i(0) = 0$.

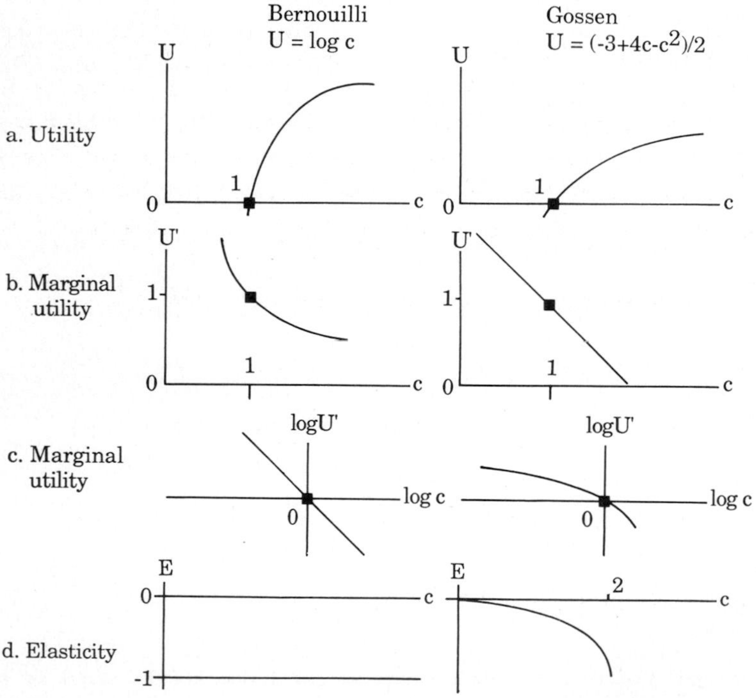

Figure 1: Utility indices

EXAMPLES. The canonical example is the Bernouilli utility function:

$$U(c) = \log c, \qquad E(c) = -1.$$

For other constant-elastic utility functions, we have:

$$U(c) = c^{1-k}, \qquad 0 < k < 1, \qquad E = -k,$$

and

$$U(c) = -c^{1-k}, \qquad 1 < k, \qquad E = -k.$$

For the Gossen utility function,

$$U(c) = -3 + 4c - c^2, \qquad E(c) = -c/(2-c).$$

We now proceed to construct a candidate solution, which is to be verified later on, as a Nash equilibrium. This candidate must be an ordered pair of twice-continuously differentiable functions, $p(x) = c \in R_+^2$. To construct $p(x)$, we use the Euler equation, which is a first-order necessary condition for an optimum. In verifying that $p(x)$ is truly an equilibrium, sufficiency conditions for a global optimum will be invoked.

To begin with, each cake-eating model is characterised as a triplet,

$$(r,E_1,E_2) \in (0,1) \otimes (C''[R_{++},-R_{++}])^2, \tag{2.2}$$

where $C''[R_{++},-R_{++}]$ is the space of twice-continuously differentiable functions from positive reals to negative reals.

At any equilibrium, player i = 1 or 2 faces the variational problem:

$$\begin{aligned} &\text{Max} \int_0^\infty (\exp(-r_i t)\int_1^c \{\exp[\int_1^v (E_i[-p_j(x)-(dx/dt)]/w)dw]\}dv)dt, \\ &x(0) = 1,\ x(\infty) = 0, \end{aligned} \tag{2.3}$$

where $j = 2$, or 1; $j \neq i$.

For expository convenience, we first state the Euler equation for i in U_i:

$$p_j' \exp(-r_i t)U_i' = (d/dt)[\exp(-r_i t)U_i'],$$

or,

$$r_i + p_j' = (d/dt)[\log U_i'] \qquad \text{(Rearrangement)}$$

$$= -[U_i''/U_i'][p_j'(dx/dt) + (d^2x/dt^2)] \qquad \text{(Differentiating)}$$

$$= -[U_i''/U_i'][-p_i'(dx/dt)] \qquad \text{(Differentiating } dx/dt \equiv -(p_i+p_j) \text{ and substituting in the result)}$$

$$= -[U_i''/U_i'](p_i')(p_i+p_j), \qquad (dx/dt \equiv -(p_i+p_j))$$

which is equivalent to

$$p_i(r_i+p_j') = -(p_i+p_j)(p_i')E_i(p_i) \tag{2.4}$$

for $i,j = 1,2,\ i \neq j$.

Rearranging, we have the first-order simultaneous differential equations:

$$\begin{aligned} (p_1+p_2)E_1(p_1)p_1' + p_1p_2' &= -p_1r_1, \\ p_2p_1' + (p_1+p_2)E_2(p_2)p_2' &= -p_2r_2, \end{aligned} \tag{2.5}$$

which may be simplified to:

$$\begin{aligned} p_1' &= -s_1[E_2r_1 - s_2r_2]/[E_1E_2 - s_1s_2], \\ p_2' &= -s_2[E_1r_2 - s_1r_1]/[E_1E_2 - s_1s_2], \end{aligned} \tag{2.6}$$

where

$$s_1 = p_1/(p_1+p_2), \qquad s_2 = 1-s_1. \tag{2.7}$$

Since exploitation rates must be zero as the resource stock becomes zero, we have the transversality conditions, usable as initial conditions for (2.6),

$$p_1(0) = p_2(0) = 0. \tag{2.8}$$

Direct substitution of (2.8) into (2.7) seems to imply that s_1 takes the indeterminate form of zero divided by zero. But, by L'Hôpital's rule, at $x = 0$,

$$s_1 = p_1'(0)/[p_1'(0) + p_2'(0)], \qquad s_2 = p_2'(0)/[p_1'(0) + p_2'(0)].$$

Further progress is possible by concentrating on the equilibrium value for $p_1'(0)$, by a fixed point argument given below.
Define

$$F : R \to R,\ z \to z[-E_2r_1 + (1-z)r_2]/\{z[-E_2r_1 + (1-z)r_2]$$
$$+ (1-z)[-E_1r_2 + zr_1]\}.$$

At any fixed point, we must have

$$z^* = -E_2 + (1-r)(1+E_1+E_2). \tag{2.9}$$

Equations (2.6), (2.7), (2.8) and (2.9) can thus be solved to obtain a candidate pair. Our model description is now complete.

Of course, candidate pairs need not always be genuine equilibrium pairs. A solution z^* consistent with (2.9) must further satisfy the restriction:

$$z^* \in (0,1). \tag{2.10}$$

Furthermore, as we have said before, we are interested not only in the existence of any solution, but of a robust solution. For illustration, we shall establish 'robust existence' for a particular class of cases, in three steps over the next three sections.

REMARKS.

1. So far, most studies of the feedback equilibrium in dynamic games are hampered by the unavailability of globally analytic tools, such as the phase diagram, extensively used in control theoretic applications (for an exception, see Clemhout and Wan 1985a). The difficulty is the dependence of the adjoint equation of one player upon the strategy used by another (the cross-influence term). In the present example, this happens with the appearance of the term $p_j' = dp_j/dx$ causing the Euler equation for player i to become a partial differential equation (for intuition, see the 'second moral' mentioned in the Introduction).
2. The manipulations leading to equation (2.4) have changed the independent variable from t to x. In lieu of two partial differential equations, we now have two simultaneous ordinary differential equations, making it possible to study the global properties of the problem.
3. The derivation of (2.4) depends upon the use of continuous time. On balance, it seems a small price to pay for avoiding the intractable partial differential equations inherent in such problems.

3. Constant-elastic Utility and Linear Strategy

We shall first show that under some restrictions, a class of 'parameter-contingent' models has a unique Nash equilibrium, with the rates of exploitation proportional to the remaining resource level. This class is of some interest in its own right. It also forms the first step of our quest for 'robust existence'.

Consider the case where

$$E_i = -k_i, \quad i = 1,2.$$

Substitution into (2.5) and (2.7) transforms the latter into

$$\begin{aligned} p_1' &= s_1[k_2 r_1 + s_2 r_2]/[k_1 k_2 - s_1 s_2], \\ p_2' &= s_2[k_1 r_2 + s_1 r_1]/[k_1 k_2 - s_1 s_2]. \end{aligned} \qquad (3.1)$$

For (2.9), we then have

$$z^* = r_1k_2 + r_2(1-k_1)$$
$$= k_2 - r_2(k_1+k_2-1) \qquad (\text{recall } r_1 + r_2 = 1). \tag{3.2}$$

Set

$$s_1 = z^*, \qquad s_2 = 1-z^*,$$

one can show,

$$k_2r_1 + s_2r_2 = k_2r_1 + k_1r_2 - r_1r_2(k_1+k_2-1) = k_1r_2 + s_1r_1,$$

and

$$k_1k_2 - s_1s_2 = [k_2r_1 + k_1r_2 - r_1r_2(k_1+k_2-1)](k_1+k_2-1).$$

Next, set

$$H = 1/(k_1+k_2-1),$$

and (3.1) simplifies to:

$$p_1' = z^*H, \qquad p_2' = (1-z^*)H.$$

Assume that (i), (2.10) holds true, i.e.,

$$0 < z^* < 1,$$

and (ii),

$$k_1 + k_2 > 1, \tag{3.3}$$

so that $H > 0$, then (3.1) implies proportional Nash strategies:

$$p_1(x) = z^*Hx, \qquad p_2(x) = (1-z^*)Hx, \tag{3.4}$$

with an exponentially declining resource stock:

$x(t) = x(0)\exp(-Ht)$.

The restrictions on r, k_1 and k_2 are summarised graphically in Figure 2 below.

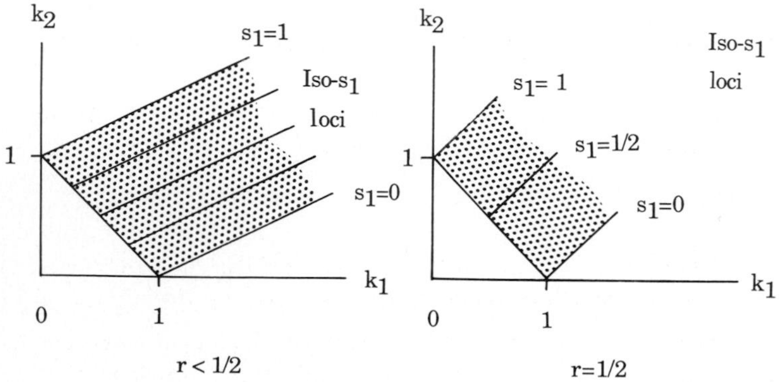

Figure 2: Admissible parameters

We now state formally:

PROPOSITION 1. If both players have payoffs with constant elasticities of marginal utility, then:

(a) any C" feedback Nash (equilibrium) strategy pair must be unique and linear, and the factors of proportionality are as specified in (3.4);
(b) if both (2.10) and (3.3) are satisfied, such an equilibrium exists.

Both the elasticities (of marginal utilities) and the time-preference rates may vary from player to player.

SKETCH OF A PROOF. (a) follows from (2.6) to (2.9). To prove (b), that is that the candidate strategies in (3.4) are equilibrium strategies, we observe that:

(i) taking the linear strategy of player 1 (resp. 2) as given, the strategy of player 2 (resp. 1) satisfies the Euler equation, by construction;
(ii) the integrand of the payoff index for player 2 (resp. 1),

$$\exp(-rt)U(c)$$

is concave in the control variable c; and finally

(iii) the dynamic constraint for player 2 (resp. 1):

$$dx/dt = -p_1(x) - c \qquad (\text{resp. } -p_2(x) - c)$$

has a right-hand side expression which is linear (thus, concave) in x and c.

By the Mangasarian sufficient condition (see, e.g., Kamien and Schwartz 1982), $c = p_2(x)$ [resp. $c = p_1(x)$] is optimal for player 2 (resp. 1), given the strategy $p_1(x)$ [resp. $p_2(x)$]. □

REMARK. In a discrete time fishery model, Levhari and Mirman (1980) assume logarithmic utilities for both players, with time-preference rates potentially different from each other. For simplicity, our formulation does not postulate any 'recruitment function' (see a Remark later), but we allow players to have different utility indices, i.e., different values for E_i.

Proposition 1 deals with the characterisation of an equilibrium. We now explore the question of an inverse equilibrium: given the observed behavioural patterns of the players, what preferences must they possess so that their behaviour is an equilibrium play? For the model under consideration, we can present

PROPOSITION 2. If the two players adopt linear exploitation strategies:

$$p_1(x) = zHx \text{ and } p_2(x) = (1-z)Hx,$$

then, given that the two players' time-preference rates are r and (1-r) respectively, the observed behaviour represents an equilibrium play of a game, where the players have the constant-elastic utilities with

$$E_1 = -k_i, \qquad i = 1,2,$$

such that,

$$k_1 = (1-z) + r/H,$$

$$k_2 = z + (1-r)/H.$$

SKETCH OF A PROOF. Apply Proposition 1. □

REMARKS.

1. Unless the relative impatience of the two players (i.e., the value of r) is known, it is not possible to deduce the exact values of k_1 and k_2 from the observed values of H and z.
2. For models with constant-elastic marginal utilities, we can deduce from the derivation of Proposition 1, that every equilibrium C"-strategy pair is a linear strategy pair. Figure 3 depicts such an equilibrium in the space of strategy pairs.

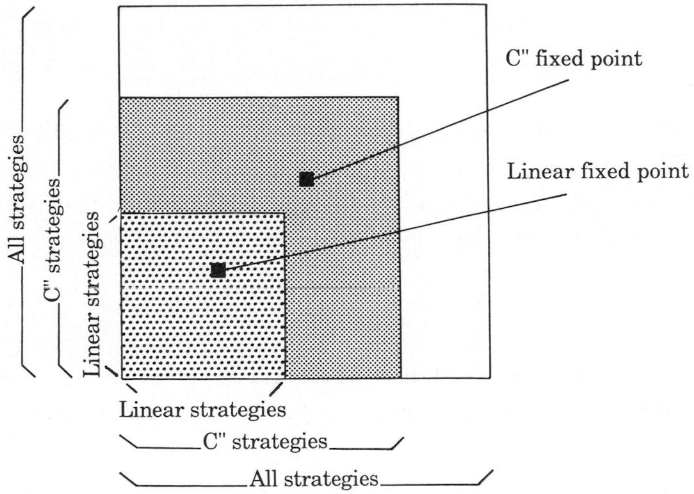

Figure 3: Strategy pairs and fixed points

As we realise, a fixed point in a game-theoretic model corresponds to an equilibrium outcome in real life. The non-existence of a fixed point in smooth strategies, for the case $k_1 + k_2 < 1$, also merits further analysis.

Our study follows Cournot, through graphic and sequential analysis (see Brito and Intriligator (1977) for an earlier application of the latter procedure).

Set

$E_i = -k_i$, (the utility of player i is constant elastic)

and

$p_j = m_j x$, $m_j > 0$ (assuming the strategy of player j is linear)

in equation (2.4), then we have a transformed Euler equation:

$$p_i(r_i+m_j) = -(p_i+m_j x)(p_i')(-k_i),$$

together with the boundary condition:

$$p_i(0) = 0.$$

It can be easily verified that this first-order differential equation has the solution:

$$p_i(x) = \{[r_i + (1-k_i)m_j]/k_i\}x.$$

Again invoking the Mangasarian sufficiency test, one can state formally:

PROPOSITION 3. For a player with a constant-elastic utility, the 'best reply' to a rival's linear strategy, is a linear strategy of his own.

One may proceed with a sequential analysis: a player offers the 'best reply' to the rival who has offered his best reply to oneself, etc. Either this process comes to an end, in a full circle within two iterations, or it will not converge at all. In the former case, one has:

$$p_i' = [r_i + (1-k_i)m_j]/k_i$$

$$= \{(r_i/k_i) + [(1-k_i)/k_i](r_j/k_j)\} + [(1-k_i)/k_i][(1-k_j)/k_j]p_i',$$

or, on rearrangement,

$$p_i' = \{(r_i/k_i) + [(1-k_i)/k_i](r_j/k_j)\}k_ik_j/(k_i+k_j-1).$$

This reaffirms the necessity of the condition, $k_i + k_j > 1$, for the existence of an equilibrium.

More intuitively, one can emulate the 'reaction curve' analysis, in Figure 4, for the following example.

EXAMPLE. $k_i = k_j = 1/3$, $r_i = r_j = 1/2$, thus

$$p_1' = (3/2) + 2p_2', \qquad p_2' = (3/2) + 2p_1'.$$

Since linear strategies may be completely characterised by their slope coefficients, we may depict the best reply functions of the two players graphically, not different from the traditional treatment of the Cournot duopoly.

Formally, there is a 'fixed point', (-3/2, -3/2), for the 'best reply' mapping, which is obviously inadmissible as an equilibrium for this game. In Figure 4 we consider a hypothetical sequence of strategies by the two players, each being the best reply to the strategy of the other, in alternating moves. Without losing generality, let the first player move first. His initial plan is based on the assumption that he would enjoy the resources alone. In that case, one can easily verify that his optimal policy is:

$$p_1(x) = (3/2)x.$$

The appearance of player 2 leads to the following alternating sequence of plans:

$$p_1(x) = (3/2)x,$$

$$p_2(x) = (9/2)x,$$

$$p_1(x) = (21/2)x,$$

$$p_2(x) = (45/2)x, \text{ etc.}$$

Each player realises that the resource is rapidly disappearing, due to rival action. He would then escalate this exploitation race. The result is a stampede toward immediate exhaustion. Although each player is aware of the desirability of conservation, rapid depletion will prevail. Interestingly, should there be only one player, or should joint maximisation be feasible, the optimal strategy is to set the exploitation rate to $p(x) = (3/2)x$.

The non-existence of any 'smooth strategy' equilibrium may be counted as a blessing in disguise. In the process of searching for an equilibrium, we have obtained the following insight:

> *The mildlier the marginal utilities diminish, the less undesirable is the feast-then-famine outcome to players. Given both the time preference and the rival depredation, the exploitation race may become the best option.*

The non-existence of a smooth equilibrium induces us to reformulate the problem by embedding the differential game within a multi-stage game, S.

3.1 The Two-stage Game Reformulation

In the first stage, two players play the following bi-matrix game:

Player One's Choices	Player Two's Choices: withdraw	conserve	deplete
withdraw	(m,m)	(m,M)	(m,D)
conserve	(M,m)	(G,G)	(g,D')
deplete	(D,m)	(D',g)	(D",D"),

where the following preference ranking (<) always holds:

$$m < g < D'' < D' < D < M; \; m < g < M.$$

Option 'deplete' stands for the fastest exploitation, option 'conserve' stands for the exploitation at a positive but finite rate, and option 'withdraw' stands for no exploitation at all. 'Withdraw' is strictly dominated by 'conserve'. It is included here only for expository convenience. The payoffs to 'conserve' and 'deplete' vary inversely to the exploitation rate of the other player. If the other player refrains from any exploitation, then 'deplete' is less rewarding than 'conserve'. If both players choose to 'conserve', then they go to the differential game as the second-stage game, with reward (G,G).

We conclude that (a) 'deplete' versus 'deplete' is always an equilibrium: faced with a prodigal rival, there is no alternative but to reciprocate; (b) a Pareto-superior alternative, in the form of a differential game (G,G), becomes an equilibrium, if and only if $G > D'$, i.e., when it is preferable to conserve resources in the presence of a conservation-minded rival.

Note that the intuition behind (a) becomes obvious only after the model is reformulated into a multi-stage game.

REMARKS.

1. The generalisation to $N > 2$ players is straightforward.
2. For renewable resources associated with a recruitment function,

$$f(x) = x(q-\log x), \qquad q \in R_+, \tag{3.5}$$

   the above results can be routinely extended.
3. In the above example, the 'best reply' mapping happens to take extremely simple forms over the subclass of linear strategies. In general, the best reply mapping is not well behaved over the space of strategy pairs. Specifically, fixed point theorems are hard to apply since the mapping lacks the closure property. See the penetrating analysis by Sundaram (1989).

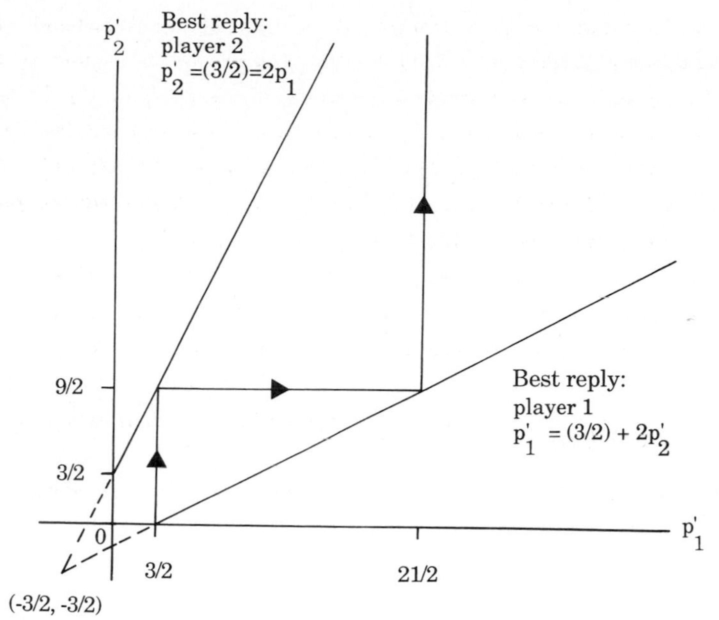

Figure 4: An anatomy of non-existence

4. Share-preservation Strategies

As a second step in our quest for robustness, we now turn to a more general inverse equilibrium problem. This is whether one can characterise the utility indices of the players, given that their exploitation rates are always observed to be proportional to each other, i.e.,

$$p_1(x) = sH(x), \qquad p_2(x) = (1-s)H(x).$$

Here $H(x)$ is positively valued, strictly increasing, and twice-continuously differentiable. It may not be linear.

We first note that if the aggregate exploitation rate were x, rather than H(x), then at any given value of r, Proposition 2 implies that these players have constant elastic utility indices with

$$k_1 = 1 - r + s, \qquad k_2 = 1 - s + r.$$

We now set aside the actual system for a moment, and consider the 'idealised' system instead.

$$dx/dt = -x.$$

Next, by a change of variable, we shall attempt to show that the actual system is no more than the 'idealised' system in disguise. This is a technique long in use for the analysis of production functions (see Clemhout 1968 and Sato 1981).

Define first a function, G, such that,

$$G(y) = \exp[\int_0^y d\xi/H(\xi)],$$

and next a variable, X, such that,

$$x = G(X).$$

Now, rewrite the two sides of our 'idealised' system as follows:

$$dx/dt = G'dX/dt, \quad -x = -G(X).$$

By substitution

$$G'dX/dt = -G(X),$$

or

$$dX/dt = -G/G'$$

$$= -H(X).$$

Since $G' > 0$, the increasing monotonic transformation between x and X is one-to-one, preserving the optimisation operations.

By Proposition 2, there is a unique, mutually proportional C"-strategy pair, as a feedback Nash solution for the inverse equilibrium problem, with the dynamics:

$$x' = -x.$$

Such facts are invariant over the state-representation transformation, from x to X. They are carried over to the actual system with the dynamics:

$$X' = -H(X).$$

EXAMPLE. $H(X) = X^2/(X+1)$ and $G(X) = X\exp(-1/X)$.
Since $G'(X) = [1 + (1/X)]\exp(-1/X)$, the transformation from X to x is one-to-one. Since $H'(X) = X(X+2)/(X+1)^2 > 0$, $H''(X) = 2/(X+1)^3 > 0$, H is increasing and convex, a crucial property for the next section. As X declines asymptotically toward zero, $s_jH(X)$, the rate of exploitation for firm $j = 1,2$, declines relatively to the stock X, over time.

One can also characterise the payoffs of the players as follows. Let $U_i'(C_i)$ be the marginal utility for player i, then the following relationship must hold:

$$(\partial\log U_i'/\partial\log C_i)(\partial\log C_i/\partial\log X)$$

$$= (\partial\log u_i'/\partial\log c_i)(\partial\log c_i/\partial\log x)(\partial\log x/\partial\log X),$$

or, on rearrangement,

$$(\partial\log U_i'/\partial\log C_i) = (-k_i)(1)(XG'/G)/(XH'/H)$$

$$= -k_i/H'(X)$$

$$= -k_i/H'[P_i - 1(C_i)], \tag{4.1}$$

say, where

$$P_i(X) = s_iH(X)$$

is the optimal consumption policy for i. Thus, we have characterised the felicity index for i in its elasticity form. It is straightforward to show that over an equilibrium play, the ratio between two players' elasticities of marginal utilities must be constant, since:

$$(\partial \log U_1'/\partial \log C_1)/(\partial \log U_2'/\partial \log C_2) = k_1/k_2 = (1-r+s)/(1-s+r).$$

We now have established

PROPOSITION 4. If the two players adopt share-preserving exploitation strategies:

$$p_1(x) = sH(X), \quad p_2(x) = (1-s)H(x), \quad H' > 0 \text{ all } x,$$

then, given the time-preference rates of the two players are r and (1-r) respectively, the observed behaviour represents an equilibrium play of a game, where the players have utility functions characterised by (4.1), and,

$$k_1 = 1 - r + s, \quad k_2 = 1 - s + r.$$

The above exercise has shown:

(a) *If* players do not use history-dependent state variables or history-dependent strategies (more on this later), then the share-preserving exploitation of common-property resources has rather strong implications about the utility functions of the players. In fact, the elasticity forms of the utility functions are determined, up to the relative impatience parameter, r.

(b) We have demonstrated how the method of Lie-transforms can be applied to differential games.

(c) Most importantly, the results of this section are indispensable in addressing the robustness question in the next section.

5. On Robustness

We now come to the third and last step in our quest for robustness. Previously, in the economic literature we are aware of, almost all differential games are solved by appealing to either (a) specific functional forms, or (b) specific behavioural assumptions. By the latter we mean that, having assumed that the players are identical, it is further assumed that like players adopt like strategies in an equilibrium. Neither approach allows us to make statements beyond a negligible subset within the model space:

$$(r,E_1(.),E_2(.)), \tag{5.1}$$

metricised in some routine manner (compare Fudenberg and Tirole (forthcoming)). Furthermore, for approach (b), one cannot conclude that there are any asymmetric equilibria. An exception is that of Judd (1985), who expands the Bellman equations around the point where interaction between players is zero.

One of the reservations often held about the differential game model concerns the fact that very little is known about 'how frequently' such models have any equilibrium at all. Beside some confidence one might draw from the local results of Judd, there is nothing to guarantee that there is any equilibrium in any differential game which would not disappear under some slightest perturbations in the model specification. In other words, there is no proof that any equilibrium is perturbation-proof, or, 'locally robust'. Since functional forms in economics are usually chosen for convenience only, if the non-existence of solutions is the rule and not the exception over the model space, the value of all economic applications of differential games will be dubious.

The crux of the problem is the difficulty in verifying any candidate solution as an equilibrium. As we have seen, the feedback Nash strategy of any differential game is the optimal policy of an N-coupled control problem. For simple (uncoupled) control problems, the Leitmann and Stalford (1972) test is available if the horizon is finite. For the infinite horizon case, works by Mangasarian (1966), Arrow and Kurz (1970), Kamien and Schwartz (1971) as well as Seierstad and Sydsaeter (1977) have all made their contributions. In many applications, the properties of the maximised Hamiltonian are often involved, and most verification criteria are hard to use (Kamien and Schwartz 1981). The only exception is that, with the Ramsey-like models, where the payoff integrand,

$$\exp(-rt)u(c)$$

is a concave function of the control, c, and the dynamic equation:

$$x' + c \leq f(x) \tag{5.2}$$

involves a concave function f of the state variable x. This will be referred to below as the concavity-concavity condition.

Of all the differential game models, the two-person cake-eating problem is the simplest. As we have seen, it resembles the Ramsey model where for any player i the term f(x) is replaced by the negative of the exploitation strategy of the other player, $-p_j(x)$. Complication arises because $-p_j(x)$, unlike f(x), is part of the unknown; $p_j(x)$ is to be determined simultaneously with the equilibrium strategy of player i, $c_i = p_i(x)$. Whether both of the derived forms of $-p_i(x)$ and $-p_j(x)$ would remain concave under small perturbations of the model structure is much more intricate than varying f(x) (for the Ramsey problem), the latter is part of the model structure itself.

In this paper, we experiment with a different approach. Note that to satisfy the concavity-concavity condition, all we need is that:

$$p_i''(x) \geq 0 \text{ for some relevant range of } x, \quad i = 1,2. \tag{5.3}$$

Suppose that (5.3) is satisfied at some 'initial model' in the model space. If it remains valid over all perturbations within some suitably defined neighbourhood of the 'initial model', then we can conclude that the latter is 'locally robust'.

Now we need some initial model as the point of departure. Yet for this purpose, none of the examples in Section 3 is appropriate, since in each case $p_i(x)$ is linear and (5.3) holds as an identity over the entire non-negative range of x. For such a knife-edge case, concavity for the control problem is not likely to hold for all admissible perturbations.

Here our step 2 (Section 4) becomes useful. By state transformation, we have obtained an 'initial model' with H(x) strictly convex, and hence both -H(x) and $-s_jH(x)$ strictly concave, for all j. The concavity-concavity condition is thus satisfied. Using anyone of the uncountably many 'initial models' with their arbitrary shares, arbitrary parametric value for relative impatience and arbitrary H(.) functions, as long as they are smooth and strictly convex, one deduces the corresponding model in the well-defined 'model space' (as specified in (5.1)). Introducing appropriate metrics (based upon the C"-norm) over that model space, one can define neighbourhoods for each, in which the robust existence of a feedback Nash equilibrium is assured by the Mangasarian test.

At long last, we hope that we have established convincingly that the existence of solutions in differential games is a likely outcome, at least for the cake-eating problems.

6. Remarks on Information Structure

In repeated games, trigger strategies may induce self-enforced solutions which improve efficiency. Broadly speaking, three elements are involved: (a) a supportable 'carrot', (b) a credible 'stick', and (c) a scheme linking the reward to some chosen performance standard. The same idea carries over to dynamic games.

Being subgame perfect, the feedback Nash equilibrium obviously satisfies (b). Conceptually, there may be other non-cooperative equilibria one might consider. In our multi-stage game reformulation, the ordered pair ('deplete', 'deplete') seems to qualify as well. Whether a strictly Pareto-dominated equilibrium can be a credible threat, is a philosophical question one must decide. For (c) to work, one needs a simple frame of reference. But both are conceptually simple.

For repeated games, the 'supportable carrots' in (a) form a large class, by the Folk Theorem. In dynamic games, once when history can be used, again infinitely many solutions emerge (Başar 1977). The relationship between these two awaits future study.

For the cake-eating problem, we suggest the following. The literature of resource economics contains two traditions, the state variable may be the level of either 'resources remaining' or 'resources gone'. Should we include both, plus a time variable, then we have a situation denoted as 'closed loop' by Başar. One can readily deduce the average aggregate rate of exhaustion, which may be used as a base to pose threats: 'I shall conserve only if collectively we have all done well, by then'. Of course, other means of introducing history-dependent state variables can also be considered.

Finally, when trigger strategies are considered, the inverse equilibrium problem is greatly complicated. The mere fact that both players followed a 50:50 share in resource exploitation may reflect the players' preferences, or may also reflect some mutual understandings.

7. Conclusion

Differential games and smooth strategy equilibria have their strengths as well as their limitations. Rather than considering such concepts as alternatives to other game models and equilibrium notions, the more fruitful approach seems to be to utilise all available analytic means, singly or in combination, as the situation justifies it. The multi-stage game formulation in Section 3 is offered as an example of this approach.

It is usually perceived that smooth models and continuous controls are necessary building blocks for differential game models. This is not so. Discontinuous value functions are handled in differential games with the analysis of singular surfaces (see Ho and Olsder 1983). Impulse control has been used to depict management-labour relationships (see Leitmann and Chen 1980).

Note

* We are grateful for the helpful comments offered by T. Başar, D.L. Brito, M.D. Intriligator, T. Mitra, R. Sundaram, R. van der Ploeg, E.E.C. van Damme, A.J. de Zeeuw and two anonymous referees. Special thanks are due to S. Tijs, whose discussion at the Tilburg Conference stimulated the two-stage game reformulation in Section 3. We alone are responsible for any errors and shortcomings.

References

Arrow, K.J. and M. Kurz, Public Investment, the Rate of Return and Public Policy, Johns Hopkins University Press, Baltimore, 1970.

Arrow, K.J. and S. Honkapohja (eds), Frontiers of Economics, Basil Blackwell, New York, 1985.

Başar, T., 'Informationally nonunique equilibrium solutions in differential games', SIAM Journal on Control and Optimization, 15, no. 4, 1977, pp. 636-660.

Başar, T. and G.J. Olsder, Dynamic Non-cooperative Game Theory, Academic Press, New York, 1982.

Başar, T., 'A tutorial on dynamic and differential games', in T. Başar (ed.), Dynamic Games and Applications in Economics, Lecture Notes on

Economics and Mathematical Systems, vol. 265, Springer-Verlag, Berlin, 1986.

Becker, G.S., A Treatise on the Family, Harvard University Press, Cambridge, MA, 1981.

Brito, D.L. and M.D. Intriligator, 'A fixed point approach to multi-agent adaptive control', Annals of Economic and Social Measurement, 6, 1977, pp. 137-145.

Clemhout, S., 'A class of homothetic production functions', Review of Economic Studies, 35, 1968, pp. 91-104.

Clemhout, S. and H. Wan, Jr, 'Interactive economic dynamics and differential games', Journal of Optimization Theory and Applications, 27, 1979, pp. 7-30.

Clemhout, S. and H. Wan, Jr, 'Cartelization conserves endangered species?', in Gustav Feichtinger (ed.), Optimal Control Theory and Economic Analysis II, North-Holland, Amsterdam, 1985a.

Clemhout, S. and H. Wan, Jr, 'Resource exploitation and ecological degradation as differential games', Journal of Optimization Theory and Applications, 46, 1985b, pp. 471-481.

Clemhout, S. and H. Wan, Jr, 'Differential games', in J. Eatwell, M. Milgate and P. Newman (eds), The New Palgrave, A Dictionary of Economics, MacMillan, London, 1987.

Damme, E.E.C. van, Refinements of the Nash Equilibrium Concepts, Lecture Notes in Economics and Mathematical Systems, vol. 219, Springer-Verlag, Berlin, 1983.

Dixit, A., 'The role of investment in entry-deterrence', Economic Journal, 90, 1980, pp. 95-106.

Dockner, E., G. Feichtinger and S. Jørgenson, 'Tractable classes of non-zero-sum, open-loop Nash differential games: theory and examples', Journal of Optimization Theory and Applications, 45, 1985, pp. 181-197.

Fleming, W.H. and R.W. Rishel, Deterministic and Stochastic Optimal Control, Springer-Verlag, Berlin, 1975.

Friedman, J.W., 'A non-cooperative equilibrium of supergames', Review of Economic Studies, 38, 1971, pp. 1-12.

Fudenberg, D. and J. Tirole, Dynamic Games of Oligopolies, Harwood, New York, 1985.

Fudenberg, D. and J. Tirole, 'Non-cooperative game theory for industrial organization: an introduction and overview', in R. Schmallensee and R. Willig (eds), The Handbook of Industrial Organization, (forthcoming).

Gale, D., 'On optimal development in a multi-sector model', Review of Economic Studies, 34, 1967, pp. 1-18.

Ho, Y.C. and G.J. Olsder, 'Differential games: concepts and applications', in M. Shubik (ed.), Mathematics of Conflicts, North-Holland, Amsterdam, 1983.

Judd, K., 'Closed-loop equilibrium in a multi-stage innovation race', Discussion paper 647, Kellogg School of Management, Northwestern University, Evanston, 1985.

Kamien, M.I. and N.L. Schwartz, 'Sufficient conditions in optimal control theory', Journal of Economic Theory, 3, 1971, pp. 207-214.

Kamien, M.I. and N.L. Schwartz, Dynamic Optimization, North-Holland, Amsterdam, 1981.

Kemp, M.C. and N.V. Long (eds), Exhaustible Resources, Optimality and Trade, North-Holland, Amsterdam, 1980.

Leitmann, G. and H. Stalford, 'Sufficiency for optimal strategies in Nash equilibrium games', in A.V. Balakrishnan (ed.), Techniques in Optimization, Academic Press, New York, 1972.

Leitmann, G. and S.F.H. Chen, 'Labor-management bargaining models as a dynamic gain', in Optimal Control, Applications and Methods, 1980.

Levhari, D. and L.J. Mirman, 'The great fish war: an example using a dynamic Cournot-Nash solution', The Bell Journal of Economics, 11, 1980, pp. 322-334.

Mangasarian, O.L., 'Sufficient conditions for the optimal control of nonlinear systems', SIAM Journal on Control and Optimization, 4, 1966, pp. 139-152.

Milgrom, P. and J. Roberts, 'Limit pricing and entry under incomplete information', Econometrica, 50, 1982, pp. 443-460.

Nash, J., 'Two-person cooperative games', Econometrica, 21, 1953, pp. 128-140.

Owen, Guillermo, Game Theory, 2nd edition, Academic Press, New York, 1982.

Radner, Roy, 'Collusive behavior in noncooperative epsilon-equilibrium of oligopolies with long but finite lives', Journal of Economic Theory, 22, 1980, pp. 136-154.

Reinganum, J., 'A class of differential games for which open-loop and closed-loop equilibria coincide', Journal of Optimization Theory and Applications, 36, 1982, pp. 253-262.

Rubinstein, A. and M. Yaari, 'Repeated insurance contracts and moral hazard', Journal of Economic Theory, 30, 1983, pp. 74-97.

Rubinstein, A., 'Automata play the repeated prisoners' dilemma', Journal of Economic Theory, 39, 1986, pp. 83-96.

Sato, R., Theory of Technical Change and Economic Invariance Application of Lie Groups, Academic Press, New York, 1981.

Schelling, T.C., The Strategy of Conflict, Harvard University Press, Cambridge, MA, 1960.

Seierstad, A. and K. Sydsaeter, 'Sufficient conditions in optimal control theory', International Economic Review, 18, 1977, pp. 361-397.

Selten, R., 'Spieltheoretische Behandlung eines Oligopolmodells mit Nachfragetragheit', Zeitschrift für die gesamte Staatswissenschaft, 12, 1965, pp. 301-324.

Selten, R., 'Re-examination of the perfectness concept for equilibrium points in extensive games', International Journal of Game Theory, 4, 1975, pp. 25-55.

Shubik, M., Game Theory in the Social Sciences, Concepts and Solutions, The MIT Press, Cambridge, MA, 1982.

Stokey, N., 'The dynamics of industrial-wide learning', in W.P. Heller, R.M. Starr and D.A. Starrett (eds), Essays in Honor of Kenneth J. Arrow, Cambridge University Press, Cambridge, 1985.

Sundaram, R.K., Dynamic Economics and Games: A Strategic Approach to Intertemporal Resource Allocation, Doctoral Dissertation, Economics Department, Cornell University, Ithaca, NY, (forthcoming 1989).

Dynamic Policy Games in Economics
F. van der Ploeg and A.J. de Zeeuw, (Editors)

GAINS AND LOSSES FROM CARTELISATION IN MARKETS FOR EXHAUSTIBLE RESOURCES IN THE ABSENCE OF BINDING FUTURE CONTRACTS*

Alistair Ulph

Department of Economics
University of Southampton
Southampton, SO9 5NH, UK

David Ulph

Department of Economics
University of Bristol
Bristol, BS8 1HY, UK

Introduction

It is now well understood that in modelling imperfect competition (whether by buyers or sellers) in markets for exhaustible resources, where dynamic analysis is essential, the appropriate equilibrium concept depends crucially on whether it is assumed that agents can make binding commitments about their future behaviour (Ulph and Folie 1981; Kemp and Long 1980; Lewis and Ulph 1988; Maskin and Newbery 1978; Newbery 1981; Ulph 1982; Clifford and Crawford 1987). In the specific context of a market where there is a dominant firm sharing the market with a fringe of competitive producers, modelling the equilibrium as an open-loop Stackelberg equilibrium yields policies which in general are time inconsistent and so only appropriate if the dominant firm can precommit itself to a path of future outputs or prices. In the absence of such commitments the appropriate solution is a feedback Stackelberg equilibrium, in which time consistency is imposed, and it is well known that not only can the dominant firm be worse off in such a feedback equilibrium than it is in the open-loop equilibrium, but it can also be worse off than in a competitive equilibrium (Maskin and Newbery 1978; Ulph and Folie 1981).

The models presented in the above literature were developed to throw light on the functioning of markets for resources such as oil, where the dominant firm is usually thought of not as a single producer but as a group of producers. For these models to be applicable to such markets, it is necessary to assume that this group of producers is able to make another set of commitments, namely to act cooperatively to maximise the joint profits of the cartel (or some more general function of individual members' profits). The familiar one-shot model of oligopoly theory shows that producers are generally worse off in a non-cooperative equilibrium than they would be if they could commit themselves to the cooperative solution (see Shapiro (1987) and Ulph (1987) for recent surveys of the extent to which the repeated game version of the oligopoly problem can provide an alternative means of achieving cooperative outcome).

This suggests that to capture the important features of some markets for exhaustible resources, we need to address two rather different sorts of commitments which the producers may or may not be able to enter into, and in this paper we wish to explore the interactions between these two forms of commitments. The analysis is applied to a market for an exhaustible resource where there are a few (in fact, two) large producers, and a large number of small producers who act competitively. We shall consider the outcomes in four scenarios arising from different assumptions about the possibilities of making the two sets of commitments:

Case 1: The large producers act cooperatively to maximise joint profits and can sign long-term contracts with their customers for future supplies.

Case 2: The large producers act cooperatively, but cannot sign long-term contracts with their customers.

Case 3: The large producers act non-cooperatively, but with long-term contracts with customers.

Case 4: The large producers act non-cooperatively, and cannot enter into long-term contracts with customers.

We shall show that the profits of the large producers are greater in Case 1 than in any of the other cases; this shows that if *one* set of commitments can be made, it will always pay to enter into the other set of commitments. But we shall also show that there are parameter values for which profits in Case 4 are greater than in either Case 2 or Case 3, so that, if it is impossible to make one set of commitments, then it may be undesirable to enter into the other set of commitments. The implication is therefore that, other things being equal, we are less likely to observe cartels forming in markets for exhaustible resources where long-term constraints with consumers cannot be signed than in other markets; and equally we are less likely to see long-term contracts between producers and consumers emerging in markets where there are a small number of large, but non-cooperating producers than in other markets.

Similar results have been shown in other areas. For example in the context of international macroeconomic policy coordination, Rogoff (1985), Kehoe (1986), Miller and Salmon (1985) have shown that policy-makers may be better off not cooperating when precommitments with some third party (usually the private sector) are not possible; Oudiz and Sachs (1985), Alesina and Tabellini (1986), Currie, Levine and Vidalis (1987), Canzoneri and Henderson (forthcoming) all show that making precommitments with the private sector may be counter-productive for policy-makers if they cannot cooperate amongst themselves. The same kind of paradoxical results were shown by Ulph (1985) in the context of wage bargaining between unions and a single producer. To the best of our knowledge this paper is the first application of these ideas to markets for exhaustible resources. There is an important question about the significance of these results, namely whether it is really sensible to think of there being *independent* sets of commitments, or whether there are ever only two situations to consider, one where all commitments can be made (Case 1), and the other where no commitments can be made (Case 4). Canzoneri and Henderson (1987) discuss this in the context of international macro-policy coordination, and we shall discuss this in more detail in the concluding section (Section 6) after the structure of the model has been made clear.

The structure of the rest of the paper is as follows: in the next section we set out the structure of the model and calculate the equilibrium and cartel profits for Case 1, where both sets of commitments can be made. The next three sections carry out the same analysis for the other three institutional settings, Cases 2, 3 and 4 respectively. Section

5 compares the payoffs under the four regimes, and demonstrates the possibility of these paradoxical results occurring.

1. The Model and Equilibrium for Case 1 - Cartel Firms Cooperate and Binding Sales Contracts

There is a single homogeneous exhaustible resource, and two periods of time $t = 1,2$. There are two groups of producers, a 'fringe group' and a 'cartel group'; the fringe group consists of a large number of identical firms, whose aggregate output is x_t, $t = 1,2$, and whose aggregate initial reserves are X. The cartel group consists of just two identical producers, whose outputs in period t will be denoted by y_t and z_t respectively. The inverse demand function for the resource in each period is given by

$$P_t = a - x_t - y_t - z_t, \quad t = 1,2. \tag{1.1}$$

The cartel and fringe firms could be distinguished by costs of production, reserves, or discount rates, and we employ only the last two of these. Specifically, we assume that all firms have the same constant per unit cost of producing the resource, which we may as well take to be zero. Denote by δ and ρ the discount factors faced by the fringe and cartel firms respectively, and in general we suppose that $\delta \neq \rho$, reflecting the presence of capital market imperfections[1]. With a finite time horizon there are problems ensuring that resources are fully exhausted, and to simplify the difficulties we assume that the fringe's resources are 'small', and will always be exhausted, whilst the cartel's reserves are large and will never be exhausted: to be precise we shall assume that $(1-\delta)a \leq X \leq a$, while each cartel firm's reserves are greater than 2a, so that even if prices were zero in both periods the cartel firms could never exhaust their reserves, while the fringe's reserves would be insufficient to meet demand in one period. The reason for the lower bound on the fringe's reserves, as we shall see, is to give it sufficient reserves to wish to produce in both periods, and hence be able to arbitrage.

Within this framework let us now turn to the equilibrium in Case 1, where the cartel firms cooperate with each other, (by which we shall simply mean that they act as if they were a single firm whose objective it is to maximise the joint wealth of the two firms), and firms can sign binding contracts for current and future sales. We shall first derive the fringe's supply behaviour and then analyse the cartel's optimal response, so we are computing the open-loop Stackelberg equilibrium.

Suppose that the cartel sets prices P_1, P_2 in periods 1, 2 to which it is committed. The fringe firms will have the following supply correspondence

$$\left.\begin{array}{ll} x_1(P_1,P_2) = X, & P_1 > \delta P_2 \\ x_1(P_1,P_2) = 0, & P_1 < \delta P_2 \\ 0 \le x_1(P_1,P_2) \le X, & P_1 = \delta P_2 \end{array}\right\} , \quad x_2(P_1,P_2) = X - x_1(P_1,P_2). \tag{1.2}$$

The cartel then chooses P_1, P_2 to maximise

$$\pi_1(P_1,P_2) = P_1(a-P_1-x_1(P_1,P_2)) + \rho P_2(a-P_2-x_2(P_1,P_2)). \tag{1.3}$$

Since the supply correspondence $x_1(P_1,P_2)$ is not differentiable we cannot apply standard techniques to solve the cartel's problem, but we can argue as follows. Suppose the optimum of (1.3) occurred at (P_1^*,P_2^*) with $P_1^* > \delta P_2^*$; then a neighbourhood of (P_1^*,P_2^*), N, exists such that for $(P_1,P_2) \in N$, $P_1 > \delta P_2$, and

$$P_1^*(a-P_1^*-X) + \rho P_2^*(a-P_2^*) \ge P_1(a-P_1-X) + \rho P_2(a-P_2). \tag{1.4}$$

This requires that $P_1^* = \frac{a - X}{2}$, $P_2^* = \frac{a}{2}$. However, this is inconsistent with the condition $P_1^* > \delta P_2^*$ as long as $X \ge a(1-\delta)$. Similarly, it cannot be the case that $P_1^* < \delta P_2^*$, so the optimum must have $P_1^* = \delta P_2^*$. But in this case, the fringe is indifferent about its allocation of resources over time, so we can effectively allow the cartel to determine x_1, and x_2 (subject to $x_1 + x_2 = X$).

The problem for the cartel can thus be reformulated as the choice of P_2, x_2 to maximise

$$\pi_1(P_2,x_2) = \delta P_2(a-\delta P_2-X+x_2) + \rho P_2(a-P_2-x_2) \tag{1.5}$$

subject to $a - \delta P_2 - X + x_2 \geq 0$, $a - P_2 - x_2 \geq 0$. The choice of x_2 is immediate. If $\delta > \rho$ the cartel will want x_2 to be as large as possible, so it will set $x_2 = X$ if $P_2 \leq \bar{\bar{P}}_2 \equiv a - X$, and $x_2 = a - P_2$ if $P_2 > \bar{\bar{P}}_2$; similarly, if $\delta < \rho$, the cartel will set $x_2 = 0$ if $P_2 \leq \bar{P}_2 \equiv \frac{a - X}{\delta}$, and $x_2 = X + \delta P_2 - a$ otherwise; if $\delta = \rho$ the choice of x_2 is immaterial (provided it ensures non-negativity of the cartel's output in each period).

We can now substitute the cartel's choice of x_2 into (1.5) and maximise with respect to P_2. Define $P_2^* \equiv \frac{(\delta+\rho)a - \min(\rho,\delta)X}{2(\delta^2+\rho)}$; this is the unconstrained maximum of (1.5) assuming that the non-negativity constraints do not bite; and $\hat{P}_2 \equiv \frac{2a - X}{2(1+\delta)}$, which is the unconstrained optimum when the non-negativity constraints bite, so that the cartel produces nothing in one period. It is readily checked that $\hat{P}_2 < P_2^*$. We can characterise the solution for Case 1 as follows:

PROPOSITION 1. The equilibrium for Case 1 is as follows:

(a) <u>$\delta > \rho$</u>

(i) $\hat{P}_2 < P_2^* \leq \bar{\bar{P}}_2$, $P_2 = P_2^*$, $x_2 = X$, $P_1 = \delta P_2^*$;

(ii) $\hat{P}_2 < \bar{\bar{P}}_2 < P_2^*$, $P_2 = \bar{\bar{P}}_2$, $x_2 = X$, $P_1 = \delta\bar{\bar{P}}_2$;

(iii) $\bar{\bar{P}}_2 \leq \hat{P}_2 < P_2^*$, $P_2 = \hat{P}_2$, $x_2 = a - \hat{P}_2$, $P_1 = \delta\hat{P}_2$.

(b) <u>$\rho > \delta$</u>

(i) $\hat{P}_2 < P_2^* \leq \bar{P}_2$, $P_2 = P_2^*$, $x_2 = 0$, $P_1 = \delta P_2^*$;

(ii) $\hat{P}_2 < \bar{P}_2 < P_2^*$, $P_2 = \bar{P}_2$, $x_2 = 0$, $P_1 = \delta\bar{P}_2$;

(iii) $\bar{P}_2 \leq \hat{P}_2 < P_2^*$, $P_2 = \hat{P}_2$, $x_2 = a - X - \delta\hat{P}_2$, $P_1 = \delta\hat{P}_2$.

(c) <u>$\rho = \delta$</u>

$P_2 = P_2^*$, $X - a - \delta P_2^* \leq x_2 < a - P_2^*$.

In general, for an 'interior' solution, i.e. one where the cartel produces positive outputs in each period, $P_2 = P_2^*$.

Substituting these values for optimal prices in the profit function and rearranging yields that for an interior solution the profits for the cartel in this case are as follows:

$$\pi_1 = \frac{[(\delta+\rho)a - \delta X]^2}{4(\delta^2+\rho)}, \qquad \rho > \delta; \tag{1.6a}$$

$$\pi_1 = \frac{[(\delta+\rho)a - \rho X]^2}{4(\delta^2+\rho)}, \qquad \rho < \delta; \tag{1.6b}$$

$$\pi_1 = \frac{\delta[2a - X]^2}{4(1+\delta)}, \qquad \rho = \delta. \tag{1.6c}$$

As a prelude to the next section it is worth noting that the solution just computed is in general time inconsistent, i.e., if the cartel was not committed to the solution, it would wish to deviate from the solution for the second period. (We consider the case of interior solutions; the argument applies to all cases). Suppose that $\rho > \delta$. Then we have seen that the optimal solution calls for

$$P_2^* = \frac{(\delta+\rho)a - \delta X}{2(\delta^2+\rho)}, \qquad x_1 = X, \qquad x_2 = 0.$$

But in the second period, the fringe has already exhausted its resources, so the cartel would wish to set the static monopoly price $\frac{a}{2}$, which can readily be seen to be above P_2^*; so the cartel, in this case, would want to deviate from the open-loop solution by *raising* the price in the second period. On the other hand, if $\rho < \delta$, the open-loop Stackelberg solution calls for $P_2^* = \frac{(\delta+\rho)a - \rho X}{2(\delta^2+\rho)}$, $x_1 = 0$, $x_2 = X$. But then in period 2 the cartel knows that at any positive price, $x_2 = X$, so the cartel's optimal second period price is just $\frac{a - X}{2} < P_2^*$; so the cartel, having lured the fringe into holding its reserves till the second period, would want to *lower* the price in the second period. Only if $\rho = \delta$ would there be a dynamically consistent solution.

2. The Equilibrium for Case 2 - Cartel Firms Cooperate and No Binding Sales Contracts

We suppose that the two cartel firms continue to act cooperatively, and treat them as if they were a single firm, but assume now that they cannot commit themselves to future sales or prices. As we saw in the last section, the open-loop Stackelberg solution will no longer be appropriate, since, without any precommitment, the cartel will in general wish to deviate from the open-loop solution in the second period. The appropriate solution concept is the feedback Stackelberg solution in which at each point of time, and for each possible state of the game at that time, it is assumed that the agents play their optimal strategies from that point onwards. This involves calculating the Stackelberg equilibrium in period 2 for any outcome in period 1, and then using this to solve for the Stackelberg equilibrium in period 1.

Suppose that in period 1 the fringe had produced x_1, so its remaining reserves in period 2 are $X - x_1$. What will be the Stackelberg equilibrium for the second period given these reserves of the fringe? The cartel knows that at any positive price the fringe will dump all of its reserves on the market, and at a zero price it may do this as well. So the cartel will choose a non-negative price to maximise $P_2(a-X+x_1-P_2)$, for which the solution is clearly

$$P_2(X-x_1) = \frac{a - X + x_1}{2} \geq 0, \tag{2.1}$$

the one-period monopoly price. All firms know that this is the price policy that the cartel will pursue in the second period, given that it has no precommitment.

We now turn to period 1, and consider first the fringe's behaviour. Suppose the cartel has set a price P_1 in period 1. Then, consistent with the view of the fringe as a passive arbitrager of prices in the two periods, the fringe's supply policy will be as follows[2]:

$$x_1(P_1) = X, \quad \text{iff} \quad P_1 > \frac{\delta a}{2}; \tag{2.2a}$$

$$x_1(P_1) = 0, \quad \text{iff} \quad P_1 \leq \frac{\delta(a-X)}{2}; \tag{2.2b}$$

$$x_1(P_1) = \frac{2P_1}{\delta} + X - a, \qquad \text{iff} \qquad \frac{\delta(a-X)}{2} < P_1 < \frac{\delta a}{2}. \tag{2.2c}$$

(2.2c) is derived by setting $P_1 = \delta\left[\frac{a - X + x_1}{2}\right]$ and (2.2a), (2.2b) follow similarly. This supply curve is depicted in Figure 1; unlike Case 1, the supply curve is no longer infinitely elastic (below X).

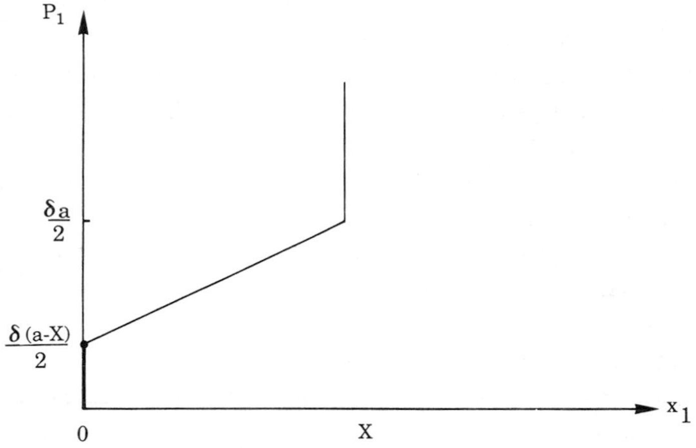

Figure 1: Supply curve of fringe

The first-period problem for the cartel then is to choose P_1 to maximise $\pi_2(P_1)$ subject to $x_1(P_1) \le a - P_1$, where

$$\pi_2(P_1) = P_1[a - P_1 - x_1(P_1)] + \rho\left[\frac{a - X + x_1(P_1)}{2}\right]^2, \tag{2.3}$$

where the second term is the present value of second-period cartel profits, given that it pursues the optimal second-period pricing rule (2.1). Again, the profit function is non-differentiable, but we can proceed as follows. It is readily checked that the optimum price cannot be outside the interval $[\frac{\delta(a-X)}{2}, \frac{\delta a}{2}]$; for example, for prices in the range $0 \le P_1 < \frac{\delta(a-X)}{2}$

$$\pi_2(P_1) = P_1(a-P_1) + \rho\left[\frac{a - X}{2}\right]^2,$$

which takes a maximum at $\frac{a}{2} \geq \frac{\delta(a-x)}{2}$; so it would never pay to set a price below $\frac{\delta(a-x)}{2}$. Similarly for the upper limit.

In general the upper limit on P_1 could be below $\frac{\delta a}{2}$ because of the need to satisfy the constraint $x_1(P_1) \leq a-P_1$, so let

$$\bar{P}_1 = \min[\frac{\delta a}{2}, \frac{\delta}{2+\delta}(2a-X)], \qquad \underline{P}_1 = \frac{\delta(a-X)}{2},$$

then the optimal price must be in the range $[\underline{P}_1, \bar{P}_1]$. Substitute (2.2c) into (2.3) and rearrange to obtain

$$\pi_2(P_1) = [P_1\delta^2(2a-X) - P_1^2(\delta^2+2\delta-\rho)]/\delta^2. \tag{2.4}$$

Note that if $\delta^2 + 2\delta - \rho \leq 0$, then $\pi_2(P_1)$ is strictly increasing in P_1, so the optimal price would be $\bar{P}_1$. If $\delta^2 + 2\delta - \rho > 0$, let

$$\hat{P}_1 = \frac{\delta^2(2a-X)}{2(\delta^2+2\delta-\rho)}, \tag{2.5}$$

where $\hat{P}_1$ is the unconstrained maximum of (2.4). We can put all this together as follows:

PROPOSITION 2. For Case 2, the optimal first-period pricing rule is as follows:

$$\left.\begin{array}{llll} \text{(i)} & \text{if } \delta^2 + 2\delta - \rho \leq 0, & \text{set } P_1 = \bar{P}_1; & \\ \text{(ii)} & \text{if } \delta^2 + 2\delta - \rho > 0, & \text{and } \hat{P}_1 \geq \bar{P}_1, & \text{set } P_1 = \bar{P}_1; \\ \text{(iii)} & \text{if } \delta^2 + 2\delta - \rho > 0, & \text{and } \hat{P}_1 \leq \underline{P}_1, & \text{set } P_1 = \underline{P}_1; \\ \text{(iv)} & \text{if } \delta^2 + 2\delta - \rho > 0, & \text{and } \underline{P}_1 < \hat{P}_1 < \bar{P}_1, & \text{set } P_1 = \hat{P}_1. \end{array}\right\} \tag{2.6}$$

The fringe's first-period supply is:

$$x_1(P_1) = \frac{2P_1}{\delta} + X - a$$

and the second-period price is $P_2 = \dfrac{a - X + x_1(P_1)}{2}$.

The characterisation of equilibrium in this case has been rather more complicated than for Case 1. To provide some more feel for when the various outcomes are likely to occur, it is readily checked that a sufficient though by no means necessary condition for an interior solution $\underline{P}_1 < \hat{P}_1 < \bar{P}_1$ is $\delta > \rho > \delta^2$; i.e. the cartel's discount factor is greater than the fringe's, but not too much greater.

To complete this section, we compare the outcome in the feedback equilibrium with that in the open-loop equilibrium, and to do this we assume that for both equilibria we have the interior solution.
Let P_1^0 denote the first-period price in the open-loop equilibrium, P_1^F the first-period price in the feedback equilibrium and recall that in both equilibria we have $P_1^0 = \delta P_2^0$, $P_1^F = \delta P_2^F$. Then we have the following:

PROPOSITION 3. $P_1^F \gtreqless P_1^0 \Leftrightarrow \rho \gtreqless \delta$

PROOF: see Appendix.

The theorem accords with intuition. We saw at the end of Section 1 that if $\rho < \delta$ the cartel would wish to renege on the open-loop strategy by lowering the second-period price, and in the feedback equilibrium the fringe protects itself against this by putting more output on the market in the first period, lowering prices in both periods relative to their open-loop values, and thereby removing the cartel's incentive to cheat; similarly when $\rho > \delta$, the cartel would wish the renege in the open-loop equilibrium by raising the price in the second period, and again, the fringe, anticipating such a possibility, withholds supply in the first period, raising prices for both periods and again eliminating any further incentive for the cartel to cheat. Finally, if $\rho = \delta$ there is no incentive for the cartel to cheat in the open-loop equilibrium and not surprisingly the open-loop and feedback solutions coincide.

It is clear that where $\rho \neq \delta$ the cartel will be worse off in the feedback equilibrium than in the open-loop equilibrium, i.e. $\pi_2 < \pi_1$. For in both equilibria the cartel is maximising profits over the set of prices $\{(P_1, P_2) : P_1 = \delta P_2\}$; but in the open-loop equilibrium the cartel is also arranging the fringe's output so as to maximise the cartel's profits, while in the feedback equilibrium the fringe chooses its output to prevent the cartel from cheating.

3. The Solution for Case 3 - Cartel Firms Non-cooperative and Binding Sales Contracts

The assumptions underlying Case 3 are that the two firms in the cartel group no longer act cooperatively, but nevertheless they are able to make binding commitments on future prices or sales. By acting non-cooperatively with each other we shall mean that each cartel producer takes as given the outputs (in both periods) of its rival and the supply behaviour of the fringe. So the cartel producers will be acting in a Nash fashion with respect to each other, and as Stackelberg leaders with respect to the fringe.

Note first that, with binding commitment on sales, the fringe firms' supply behaviour will be exactly the same as in Case 1, and so is given by the supply functions $[x_1(P_1,P_2),\ x_2(P_1,P_2)]$ derived in (1.2). We now need to determine which prices will emerge as a Nash equilibrium between the two cartel producers. Suppose then that producer 2 has set output levels (z_1,z_2). Producer 1 will choose outputs (y_1,y_2), or, equivalently, prices (P_1,P_2) to maximise

$$\pi_3(P_1,P_2) = p_1[a - P_1 - x_1(P_1,P_2) - z_1] + \rho P_2[a - P_2 - x_2(P_1,P_2) - z_2]$$

subject to $a - P_1 - x_1(P_1,P_2) - z_1 \geq 0$, $a - P_2 - x_2(P_1,P_2) - z_2 \geq 0$.

The non-differentiability of the fringe's supply correspondence requires us to proceed as in Section 1 by first establishing that an equilibrium must have $P_1 = \delta P_2$, from which it will follow that the cartel producers can effectively choose the fringe's policy to suit themselves. Suppose then that equilibrium occurred with $P_1 > \delta P_2$, so that $x_1 = X$, $x_2 = 0$. Then for all prices within a neighbourhood of the equilibrium the cartel producers can treat the fringe outputs as fixed; hence producer 1 chooses (P_1,P_2) to maximise

$$P[a_1 - z_1 - X - P_1] + \rho P_2[a - z_2 - P_2]$$

(for the moment we ignore the non-negativity output constraints). The optimum then is

$$P_1 = \frac{a - X - z_1}{2}, \qquad P_2 = \frac{a - z_2}{2}.$$

Now $P_1 = a - X - y_1 - z_1$, $P_2 = a - y_2 - z_2$, so in a symmetric Nash equilibrium we would have $P_1 = \frac{a - X}{3}$, $P_2 = \frac{a}{3}$, $y_1 = z_1 = \frac{a - X}{3}$, $y_2 = z_2 = \frac{a}{3}$; note that at this equilibrium outputs are non-negative. However, to be consistent with the requirement that $P_1 > \delta P_2$ requires that $\frac{a - X}{3} > \frac{\delta a}{3}$, or $X < a(1-\delta)$, which we have ruled out by assumption. A similar argument rules out a possible equilibrium with $P_1 < \delta P_2$, so equilibrium requires $P = \delta P$, with the fringe indifferent to its pattern of production over time. As in Section 1, we can imagine that the cartel producers effectively choose the fringe's output to suit themselves, provided they ensure that $P_1 = \delta P_2$.

We can reformulate the problem of the first cartel producer as being to choose P_2, x_1, to maximise

$$\pi_3(P_2,x_1) \equiv \delta P_2[a - \delta P_2 - x_1 - z_1] + \rho P_2[a - P_2 - z_2 - X + x_1] \tag{3.1}$$

subject to $a - \delta P_2 - x_1 - z_1 \geq 0$, $a - P_2 - z_2 - X + x_1 \geq 0$.
The analysis now proceeds along lines very similar to those in Case 1, and we shall sketch it only for the case $\rho > \delta$. For any P_2 the first producer will want to make x_1 as large as possible, and so will set $x_1 = \min(X, a-\delta P_2-z_1)$. There are going to be two possibilities for a Nash equilibrium - an interior one, in which $x_1 = X$, $y_1 = z_1 > 0$, and a corner solution in which $x_1 \leq X$, $y_1 = z_1 = 0$. For the interior case, setting $x_1 = X$ in (3.1) yields an expression for profits

$$\pi_3(P_2) = P_2[\delta(a-z_1-X) + \rho(a-z_2)] - P_2^2(\delta^2+\rho), \tag{3.2}$$

which yields an optimal price

$$P_2 = \frac{(\delta+\rho)a - \delta X - \delta z_1 - \rho z_2}{2(\delta^2+\rho)}. \tag{3.3}$$

To clear the market in both periods requires

$$a - y_2 - z_2 = P_2 = \left[\frac{(\delta+\rho)a - \delta X - \delta z_1 - \rho z_2}{2(\delta^2+\rho)}\right], \tag{3.4}$$

$$a - y_1 - z_1 - X = \delta P_2 = \delta\left[\frac{(\delta+\rho)a - \delta X - \delta z_1 - \rho z_2}{2(\delta^2+\rho)}\right]. \tag{3.5}$$

For a symmetric Nash equilibrium we set $y_2 = z_2$, $y_1 = z_1$, so that (3.4) and (3.5) give us two equations in z_1 and z_2, which we solve to yield

$$\left.\begin{aligned} y_1 = z_1 &= \frac{a[2\delta^2 + 3\rho - \rho\delta] - X[2\delta^2 + 3\rho]}{6(\delta^2+\rho)}, \\ y_2 = z_2 &= \frac{a[3\delta^2 - \delta + 2\rho] + \delta X}{6(\delta^2+\rho)}. \end{aligned}\right\} \tag{3.6}$$

Putting (3.6) into (3.3) we get as the interior solution for price

$$P_2 = \frac{a(\delta+\rho) - \delta X}{3(\delta^2+\rho)} = \frac{2}{3} P_2^*,$$

where P_2^* was defined in Case 1.

Now consider the corner solution case. Suppose that $z_1 = 0$ and set $x_1 = a - \delta P_2$ in (3.1) to get

$$\pi_3(P_2) = \rho P_2[2a - X - z_2 - (1+\delta)P_2]. \tag{3.7}$$

Maximising (3.7) with respect to P_2 yields

$$P_2 = \frac{(2a-X) - z_2}{2(1+\delta)} \tag{3.8}$$

and by market clearing

$$P_2 = a - x_2 - z_2 - y_2. \tag{3.9}$$

Setting $x_2 = X - x_1$, $y_2 = z_2$ in (3.9) and combining with (3.8)

$$P_2(1+\delta) = \frac{(2a-X) - z_2}{2} = 2a - X - 2z_2,$$

from which we deduce

$$y_2 = z_2 = \frac{2a - X}{3},$$

$$P_2 = \frac{(2a-X)}{3(1+\delta)} = \frac{2}{3}\hat{P}_2, \qquad (3.10)$$

where $\hat{P}_2$ was defined in Case 1.

This sketch suffices to show that the equilibrium for Case 3 can be characterised along lines very similar to those in Case 1 as follows:

PROPOSITION 4. The equilibrium for Case 3 is as follows:

(a) $\underline{\delta > \rho}$

(i) $\frac{2}{3}\hat{P}_2 < \frac{2}{3}P_2^* \leq \bar{\bar{P}}_2$, $\quad P_2 = \frac{2}{3}P_2^*$, $\quad x_2 = X$, $\quad P_1 = \delta P_2$;

(ii) $\frac{2}{3}\hat{P}_2 < \bar{\bar{P}}_2 < \frac{2}{3}P_2^*$, $\quad P_2 = \bar{\bar{P}}_2$, $\quad x_2 = X$, $\quad P_1 = \delta P_2$;

(iii) $\bar{\bar{P}}_2 \leq \frac{2}{3}\hat{P}_2 < \frac{2}{3}P_2^*$, $\quad P_2 = \frac{2}{3}\hat{P}_2$, $\quad x_2 = a - P_2$, $\quad P_1 = \delta P_2$.

(b) $\underline{\rho > \delta}$

(i) $\frac{2}{3}\hat{P}_2 < \frac{2}{3}P_2^* \leq \bar{P}_2$, $\quad P_2 = \frac{2}{3}P_2^*$, $\quad x_2 = 0$, $\quad P_1 = \delta P_2$;

(ii) $\frac{2}{3}\hat{P}_2 < \bar{P}_2 < \frac{2}{3}P_2^*$, $\quad P_2 = \bar{P}_2$, $\quad x_2 = 0$, $\quad P_1 = \delta P_2$;

(iii) $\bar{P}_2 \leq \frac{2}{3}\hat{P}_2 < \frac{2}{3}P_2^*$, $\quad P_2 = \frac{2}{3}\hat{P}_2$, $\quad x_2 = a - X - \delta P_2$, $\quad P_1 = \delta P_2$.

(c) $\underline{\rho = \delta}$

$$P_2 = \frac{2}{3}P_2^*, \qquad X - a + \delta P_2 \leq x_2 \leq a - P_2.$$

With the exception of cases (a)(ii) and (b)(ii) (where the outcome and hence the profits would be the same as in corresponding equilibria in Case 1), prices are two-thirds of the prices that would exist in the corresponding equilibrium in Case 1, and cartel outputs are four-thirds of those in Case 1, so that profits will be eight-ninths of the corresponding expression for profits in Case 1. In particular in the 'interior' solutions [(a)(i), (b)(i), (c)] profits from the cartel are

$$\pi = \frac{2[a(\delta+\rho) - \min(\delta,\rho)X]^2}{9(\delta^2+\rho)}, \tag{3.11}$$

which should be compared with (1.6). This is very similar to the kind of relationship between outputs, prices and profits in simple textbook comparisons of Cournot and monopoly outcomes.

4. The Solution for Case 4 - Cartel Firms Non-cooperative and No Binding Sales Contracts

We assume that the cartel producers are unable to commit themselves either to future prices or sales, or to cooperating with each other. The solution for this case will therefore combine features from the previous two models.

We shall begin by computing the equilibrium in period 2 for any level of stocks remaining for the fringe; this will require computing a symmetric Nash equilibrium between the two cartel producers. By determining the equilibrium second-period price for any remaining stock of the fringe, we can derive the first-period supply behaviour of the fringe that will result from its arbitrage activities, and we shall see that for any first-period price the fringe will be willing to supply at least as much first-period output as in the supply function we computed for Case 2. As in Case 3, we can use this supply function to determine the first-period equilibrium in which each cartel producer acts in Nash fashion with respect to each other, but as a Stackelberg leader with respect to the fringe. For reasons we shall see this last stage of the analysis turns out not to be completely straightforward.

We begin with second-period equilibrium. Suppose that the fringe had produced x_1 in period 1, leaving $x_2 = X - x_1$ resources for period 2. Again, it is understood by all agents that the fringe will supply all of this to the market at any positive price, and it may also supply it at a zero price. Producer 1 therefore can take as given x_2 and z_2. Clearly, if $x_2 - z_2 \geq a$ the first producer will produce nothing; if $x_2 + z_2 < a$, then the profits to the first producer are $P_2(a-P_2-x_2-z_2)$ and clearly the optimal policy for producer 1 is to set

$$P_2 = \frac{1}{2}(a-z_2-x_2),$$

which requires producing $y_2 = \frac{1}{2}(a-z_2-x_2)$.
So producer 1's reaction function is

$$\left.\begin{aligned} y_2 &= 0, && \text{if} \quad z_2 \geq a - x_2; \\ y_2 &= \frac{1}{2}(a-x_2) - \frac{1}{2}z_2, && \text{if} \quad z_2 < a - x_2 \end{aligned}\right\} \tag{4.1}$$

and a symmetric equilibrium would yield

$$P_2 = \frac{a - x_2}{3}, \qquad y_2 = z_2 = \frac{a - x_2}{3},$$

with profits for each producer of $\frac{(a-x_2)^2}{9}$.

Now turn to period 1 and the determination of the fringe's supply function. If the fringe produces x_1 in this period the price in the next period will be

$$P_2 = \frac{a - X + x_1}{3} \tag{4.2}$$

and, as in Section 2, viewing the fringe as a purely arbitraging agent, we get the following supply behaviour by the fringe in period 1.

$$\left.\begin{aligned} x_1(P_1) &= X, && \text{if} \quad P_1 \geq \frac{\delta a}{3}; \\ x_1(P_1) &= 0, && \text{if} \quad P_1 \leq \frac{\delta(a-X)}{3}; \\ x_1(P_1) &= \frac{3P_1}{\delta} + X - a, && \text{if} \quad \frac{\delta(a-X)}{3} \leq P_1 \leq \frac{\delta a}{3}. \end{aligned}\right\} \tag{4.3}$$

From (2.2) and (4.3) first-period supply curves for the fringe for Cases 2 and 4 are shown in Figure 2.

At any given price, the fringe is willing to supply at least as much current output when the cartel firms act non-cooperatively as when they act cooperatively. We now turn to the last stage - determining equilibrium in period 1. To economise on notation, we shall drop time subscripts, since all the relevant variables refer to period 1. Consider the problem facing the first producer; he takes as given z, the current output of the

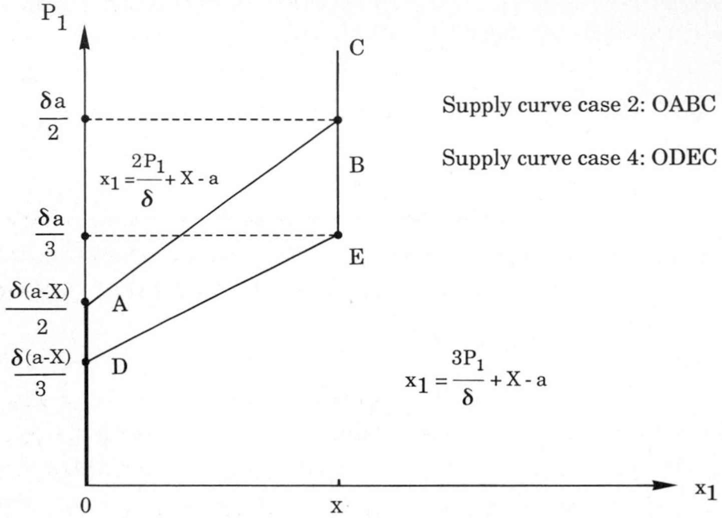

Figure 2: Comparison of fringe supply curves Cases 2 and 4

second producer, and the supply behaviour of the fringe x(P) as represented in (4.3). Thus the problem for the first producer is to choose an output level y, or, equivalently, a price P to maximise

$$\pi_4(P|z) \equiv P(a-P-z-x(P)) + \rho\,\frac{[a - X + x(p)]^2}{9}, \tag{4.4}$$

subject to the constraint that $a - P - z - x(P) \geq 0$. To take account of the constraint, define $\bar{P}(z)$ as the maximum price that producer 1 can set in the first period, given production z by producer 2; then $\bar{P}(z)$ is given by $\bar{P}(z) + x(\bar{P}(z)) = a - z$; $\bar{P}(z)$ is shown in Figure 3a and it is obvious that, as z increases, $\bar{P}(z)$ falls.

Carrying out the maximisation in (4.4) for each value of z will define producer 1's reaction function, from which we can proceed to calculate a (symmetric) Nash equilibrium. However, there are complications, because the profit function in (4.4) is not quasi-concave, and so the reaction function may be discontinuous, which could threaten the existence of a Nash equilibrium. The reason for the non-concavity of $\pi_4(P|z)$ is partly the inclusion of the second-period profits, and partly the nature of the first-period residual demand curve facing producer 1 (Figure 3b). A more detailed discussion of this can be found in the Appendix.

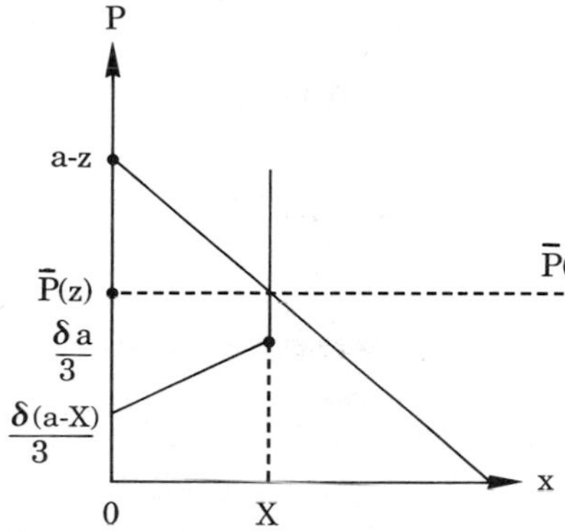

Figure 3a: Determination of $\bar{P}(z)$

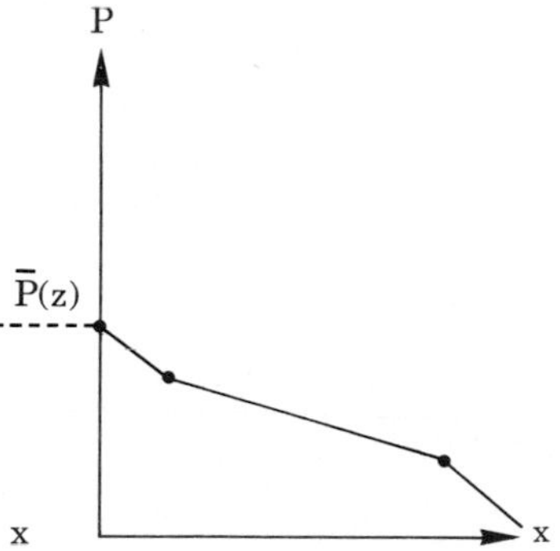

Figure 3b: Residual demand curve

Figure 4 shows a typical reaction function, consisting of linear segments which are downward sloping (or horizontal) with upward discontinuities. It is clear that a symmetric Nash equilibrium will always exist; the problem is rather the possibility of multiple equilibria. The next proposition excludes this possibility.

PROPOSITION 5. There is a unique symmetric Nash equilibrium with a first-period price which lies in the range $[\frac{\delta(a-X)}{3}, \frac{\delta a}{3}]$.

PROOF: See Appendix.

We can now characterise the symmetric Nash equilibrium. This will be rather similar to the characterisation for Case 2.

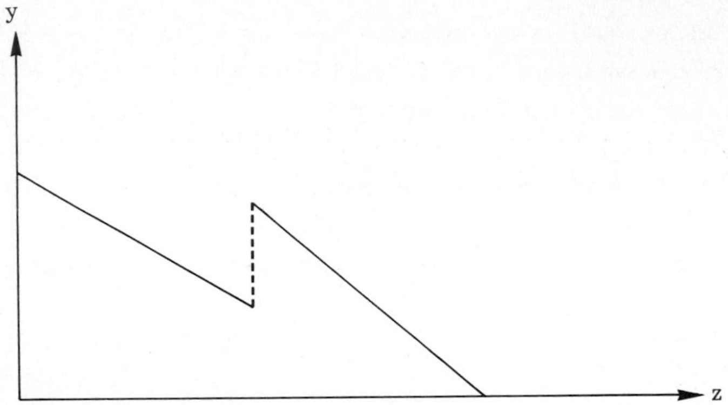

Figure 4: Typical reaction function

Define

$$\bar{\bar{P}} \equiv \min\left[\frac{\delta(2a-X)}{3-\delta}, \frac{\delta a}{3}\right], \qquad \underline{\underline{P}} \equiv \frac{\delta(a-X)}{3}$$

and

$$\hat{P} \equiv \frac{\delta^2(2a-X)}{(3\delta^2+9\delta-4\rho)}.$$

Then we have

PROPOSITION 6. The equilibrium for Case 4 can be characterised as follows:

(i) if $\delta_2 + 3\delta - 2\rho \leq 0$, $P_1 = \bar{\bar{P}}$;

(ii) if $\delta^2 + 3\delta - 2\rho > 0$ and $\hat{P} \geq \bar{\bar{P}}$, then $P_1 = \bar{\bar{P}}$;

(iii) if $\delta^2 + 3\delta - 2\rho > 0$ and $\hat{P} \leq \underline{\underline{P}}$, then $P_1 = \underline{\underline{P}}$;

(iv) if $\delta^2 + 3\delta - 2\rho > 0$ and $\underline{\underline{P}} < \hat{P} < \bar{\bar{P}}$, then $P_1 = \hat{P}$.

First-period output for the fringe is $x_1(P_1)$ and second-period price is

$$\frac{a - X + x_1(P_1)}{3}$$

PROOF: See Appendix.

The profits associated with this equilibrium for each cartel member are $\pi_4(P|z)$, where $z = \frac{1}{2}\,[a = P_1 - x_1(P_1)]$.

For the interior solution, $P_1 = \hat{P}$, the profits of each cartel member are

$$\frac{\delta^2(2a-X)^2(\delta^2+3\delta-\rho)}{(3\delta^2+9\delta-4\rho)^2}$$

5. Comparison of the Solutions in the Four Cases

We begin by collecting the results of Sections 1-4 on the profits of each firm in the cartel for the four cases for interior solutions.

Case 1: Firms cooperate, binding contracts on future sales.

$$\pi_1 = \frac{[(\delta+\rho)a - \min(\delta,\rho)X]^2}{8(\delta^2+\rho)};$$

Case 2: Firms cooperate, no binding contracts on future sales.

$$\pi_2 = \frac{\delta^2(2a-X)^2}{8(\delta^2+2\delta-\rho)};$$

Case 3: Firms do not cooperate, binding contracts on future sales.

$$\pi_3 = 8/9\ \pi_1;$$

Case 4: Firms do not cooperate, no binding contracts on future sales.

$$\pi_4 = \frac{\delta^2(2a-X)^2(\delta^2+3\delta-\rho)}{(3\delta^2+9\delta-4\rho)^2}.$$

It is clear that $\pi_3 < \pi_1$, and we showed in Section 2 that $\pi_2 \leq \pi_1$. The same argument can be used to show that $\pi_4 \leq \pi_1$; for we saw in Section 4 that a symmetric Nash equilibrium must have first-period prices in the range $[\frac{\delta(a-X)}{3}, \frac{\delta a}{3}]$, for which the second-period price must be such that $P_1 = \delta P_2$. But in Case 1 the cartel firms chose price *and* fringe outputs from the set of prices $\{(P_1,P_2);\ P_1 = \delta P_2\}$ to maximise total cartel profits, while in Case 4 the fringe chooses its own output policy, and the cartel firms are not maximising joint cartel profits; both of these features must lead to $\pi_4 \leq \pi_1$.

What is of interest, then, is the relative rankings of π_2, π_3 and π_4. Such comparisons are complicated by the fact that we are interested not only in interior solutions (i.e. when both fringe and cartel firms produce in both periods), but also in corner solutions. However, since we are interested more in demonstrating the rankings that can occur, rather than characterising precisely when each would occur (a relatively unrewarding exercise given the simplicity of the example we are considering) we have chosen simply to compute the profits in the four cases for a wide range of parameter values. The relevant parameters are the two discount rates, δ and ρ, and the ratio of fringe reserves to demand, $s = X/a$, where s must be in the range $(1-\delta) \leq s \leq 1$.

Before considering the numerical calculations, it should be fairly clear what configurations of parameters are likely to be needed to ensure that $\pi_4 > \pi_2$ or $\pi_4 > \pi_3$. We have seen that, relative to the outcome with full commitment, absence of cooperation by the two cartel producers leads to the cartel producing too much, thereby lowering prices. The inability to sign long-term contracts with customers would lead a fully-cooperative cartel to drive down prices when $\rho < \delta$, but to drive up prices when $\rho > \delta$. This suggests that when $\rho < \delta$ the absence of the two forms of precommitment are going to reinforce each other, leaving the cartel very much worse off in Case 4 than in any of the other cases. On the other hand, when $\rho > \delta$, the absence of the two forms of precommitment pull in opposite directions, so that when neither form of precommitment is made one may end up with prices that may not be too different from those prevailing when both forms of commitment are present. So to obtain the results we are looking for, we should focus on parameter values where $\rho > \delta$. The failure of the large producers to cooperate has a fairly marked effect on cartel profits (reducing them to 8/9 of their Case 1 value), so we are likely to need values of ρ and δ which produce comparable effects on cartel profits and it turns out that this requires ρ to be significantly greater than δ^3.

Table 1: Values of π_2, π_3 and π_4 for four combinations of parameter values δ, ρ and s

Parameter set number	Parameters			Relative profits		
	δ	ρ	s	π_2	π_3	π_4
(i)	.54	.96	.90	.955	.889	.983
(ii)	.56	.90	.90	.952	.889	.839
(iii)	.56	.96	.90	.952	.889	.919
(iv)	.90	.60	.90	.851	.889	.603

Table 1 shows the values of π_2, π_3 and π_4 (relative to π_1) for four combinations of parameter values; the parameter sets chosen illustrate all the possible rankings of π_2, π_3 and π_4 that occurred in the numerical calculations. Parameter set (i) confirms that there are parameter values for which π_4 exceeds both π_2 and π_3, so that if it is impossible to undertake either set of commitments then it is undesirable for the cartel producers to undertake the other set of commitments. As indicated above, we need ρ significantly above δ to ensure this result.

Parameter set (ii) confirms that the margin between ρ and δ needs to be quite large, for even with quite a significant margin of ρ above δ, π_4 is less than both π_2 and π_3. Comparing parameter set (iii) and parameter set (i) we see that even a slight narrowing of the gap between ρ and δ leads to π_4 less than π_2, though still above π_3. We were unable to find parameter values for which $\pi_3 > \pi_4 > \pi_2$. In this sense, then, it is more likely to pay the producers to commit themselves to cooperating with each other than to commit themselves to long-term contracts with customers in the absence of the other set of commitments.

Finally parameter set (iv) confirms that when $\delta > \rho$, the two precommitments reinforce each other, so that the inability to make both sets of commitments leaves the cartel very much worse off than the inability to make either set of commitments by itself.

6. Conclusions

We have argued that in modelling imperfect competition in markets for exhaustible resources it is necessary to take account of two sets of commitments that non-competitive producers may wish to undertake - commitments to long-term contracts for prices or supplies to customers and commitments to other large producers to act cooperatively. While profits will be greatest if both commitments can be made, if for some reason one set of commitments cannot be made, it may no longer be profitable to undertake the other set of commitments. One then concludes that in markets for exhaustible resources one will be less likely to observe cartels if it is impossible to make long-term contracts with consumers, and it will be less likely that long-term contracts will be found if producers cannot cooperate with each other.

However, before drawing such conclusions we need to explore more carefully what is meant by making each set of commitments, and in particular whether it is reasonable to assume that the ability to make one set of commitments can be treated independently of the other. The usual notion of making a commitment is entering into a legally binding contract, but then it has to be asked why, if it is possible to make a legally binding contract for one set of commitments, it is not possible for another. In the context of our model, if we supposed in Case 3 that the two cartel producers could sign contracts with consumers to supply the quantities (y_1,y_2), (z_1,z_2) why could they not sign contracts to produce the outputs implicit in Case 1, and hence achieve the maximum profits? Conversely, if the producers can sign legally binding contracts with each other about their production plans in each period (Case 2), why can they not sign such contracts with consumers, albeit for a longer time period? In short, it might be argued that, since what is involved in either set of commitments is an ability to make a legally binding contract about the amount of output to be produced, if it is possible to enter such a contract with one other party it ought to be possible to achieve the Case 1 outcome.

We would argue that this need not be the case. Suppose for example that contracts between a producer and his customers took place within the jurisdiction of a single country but because producers were located in different countries to make legally binding contracts between producers would require some international mechanism for enforcing contracts. In such a case, the ability to sign contracts with customers need not imply that it is also possible to sign contracts with other producers. Nor is it the case that being able to sign contracts with customers alone is sufficient to achieve the fully cooperative solution. For while it is true that both producers *could* sign contracts with their customers to produce the outputs implied by the Case 1 solution, it clearly cannot be supposed that they will do so in the absence of any means of enforcing an agreement between the producers. For if one producer does sign a contract with his customers to produce the outputs appropriate to Case 1, it will pay the other producer to renege on any verbal agreement and sign an agreement with his customers to supply the outputs implied by the two-period 'reaction function' discussed in Section 3. Both producers know this, and so the contracts entered into with customers will be those implied by the Case 3 solution.

Equally, even if in any one period producers could sign legally enforceable contracts among themselves about what outputs they will produce, it does not follow that they could sign such contracts over long periods of time and hence provide the commitments of concern to the fringe. One reason why this might be the case is that the producers are in fact governments that can only enter into agreements for the duration of their office.

In discussing similar issues in connection with international macro-policy coordination, Canzoneri and Henderson (1987) argue that to make the "paradoxical results", that partial precommitment may be undesirable, interesting it is necessary to answer "the question why the policy-makers precommit to the partial precommitment but not to the full precommitment policy... To explain why, if indeed explanation is possible, the institutional structures ... will have to be described in some detail." We believe that the above provides examples of institutional structures where partial precommitment but not full precommitment would be possible.

Of course legally binding contracts are not the only form of precommitment, and there is now a considerable literature on how repeated games, reputation effects and trigger mechanisms may be used to achieve the same outcome as achieved by precommitment through legally binding contracts. Canzoneri and Henderson (1987) show how a trigger mechanism can be used to enforce a full precommitment outcome and note that this could not be used to enforce the partial precommitment outcomes if these yielded payoffs lower than the no-precommitment outcome. The implication is that the inability to enforce partial precommitment is irrelevant because the trigger mechanism will achieve the full precommitment outcome.

However, it is less clear how far this would translate to the context of this paper, for trigger mechanisms require the ability to enforce punishment strategies for long periods of time, and with an exhaustible resource the ability of producers to punish each other by expanding production becomes increasingly limited as reserves become exhausted.

To conclude we would argue that our results can be defended because it is possible to think of institutional settings in which some forms of precommitment could be made but not others, in which case demonstrating that it may not be in the interests of producers to undertake such partial precommitment is a result of some interest. To assess whether other mechanisms for achieving precommitment outcomes could be exploited would require careful analysis because the exhaustibility of resources imposes natural limitations on the nature of punishment strategies, and this is a line of research that would be well worth exploring.

Notes

* We are grateful to Alan Ingham and participants in the Conference, especially Matt Canzoneri, John Driffill and the discussant Cees Withagen, for comments on an earlier version of this paper. Remaining errors are our own.

1. The assumption of imperfect capital markets may be implausible in a real world application. But as already noted we could have assumed perfect capital markets (equal discount rates) and instead have assumed differences in extraction costs. It turns out to be slightly

easier to work with differences in discount rates, for when costs vary the critical sizes of the fringe's reserves also vary.

2. It might seem that we are assuming rather great coordination powers for a passive price-taking fringe. For faced with a price P_1 by the cartel, any individual firm in the fringe needs to form some view of what other firms in the fringe will produce in period 1 in order to work out what price the cartel will set next period and hence work out its profit-maximising supply decision. One approach is simply to note that the supply function in (2.2) is the only one that is consistent with fringe producers forming rational expectations about future prices set by the cartel, without saying how such expectations are formed. Another is to think of the fringe consisting of n identical producers each taking as given the price function of the cartel (2.1) and the final period supplies of all other fringe producers and consider the resulting symmetric Nash equilibrium amongst fringe producers. Letting n tend to infinity yields the supply behaviour in (2.2). We are grateful to Cees Withagen for this point.

3. It turns out that the margin between δ and ρ required to ensure that π_4 is greater than π_2 or π_3 also generates corner solutions in which the cartel produces only in the second period.

References

Alesina, A. and G. Tabellini, 'Rules and discretion with non-coordinated monetary and fiscal policies', (mimeo), 1986.

Canzoneri, M. and D. Henderson, 'Is sovereign policy-making bad?', (mimeo), Georgetown University (to appear in Carnegie-Rochester Conference Series), 1987.

Canzoneri, M. and D. Henderson, Noncooperative Monetary Policies in Interdependent Economies, (forthcoming).

Clifford, N. and V. Crawford, 'Short-term contracts and strategic oil reserves', Review of Economic Studies, 54, 1987, pp. 311-324.

Currie, D., P. Levine and N. Vidalis, 'Cooperative and non-cooperative rules for monetary and fiscal policy in an empirical two-bloc model', in R. Bryant and R. Portes (eds), Global Macroeconomics, MacMillan, London, 1987.

Kehoe, P., 'International policy cooperation may be undesirable', Staff Report 103, Federal Reserve Bank of Minneapolis, 1986.

Kemp, M. and N. Long (eds), Exhaustible Resources, Optimality and Trade, North-Holland, Amsterdam, 1980, Chapters 16, 17, 18.

Lewis, T. and A. Ulph, 'A survey of game-theoretical models of trade and exhaustible resources', in J. Lesourne and H. Sonnenschein (eds), Fundamentals of Pure and Applied Economics, Harwood, (forthcoming 1988).

Maskin, E. and D. Newbery, 'Rational expectations with market power: the paradox of the disadvantageous tariff on oil', Working Paper 227, MIT, 1978.

Miller, M. and M. Salmon, 'Policy coordination and dynamic games', in W. Buiter and R. Marston (eds), International Economic Policy Coordination, Cambridge University Press, Cambridge, 1985.

Oudiz, G. and J. Sachs, 'International policy coordination in dynamic macroeconomic models', in W. Buiter and R. Marston (eds), International Economic Policy Coordination, Cambridge University Press, Cambridge, 1985.

Newbery, D., 'Oil prices, cartels and the problem of dynamic inconsistency', Economic Journal, 91, 1981, pp. 617-646.

Rogoff, K., 'Can international monetary policy cooperation be counterproductive?', Journal of International Economics, 18, 1985, pp. 199-217.

Shapiro, C., 'Theories of oligopoly behaviour', Discussion Paper 126, Woodrow Wilson School, Princeton, 1987.

Ulph, A., 'Modelling partially cartelised markets for exhaustible resources', in W. Eichorn et al. (eds), Economic Theory of Exhaustible Resources, Physica-Verlag, 1982, pp. 269-295.

Ulph, A., 'The incentives to make commitments in wage bargains', Discussion Paper 8509, University of Southampton, Southampton, 1985.

Ulph, A., 'Recent developments in oligopoly theory from a game-theory perspective', Journal of Economic Surveys, 1, 1987, pp. 149-172.

Ulph, A. and M. Folie, 'Dominant firm models of resource depletion', in D. Currie, D. Peel and W. Peters (eds), Microeconomic Analysis, Croom-Helm, London, 1981, pp. 77-106.

Appendix: Proofs of Some Propositions

PROOF OF PROPOSITION 3.

(i) $\underline{\delta > \rho}$

$$P_1^F = \frac{\delta^2(2a-X)}{2(\delta^2+2\delta-\rho)}, \qquad P_1^0 = \frac{\delta[(\delta+\rho)a - \rho X]}{2(\delta^2+\rho)},$$

$$P_1^F < P_1^0 \Leftrightarrow (\delta^3+\rho\delta)(2a-X) < (\delta^2+2\delta-\rho)[(\delta+\rho)a - \rho X].$$

Rearranging and collecting terms yields

$$P_1^F < P_1^0 \Leftrightarrow (\delta-\rho)[(1-\delta)\delta a + (\delta^2-\rho)X] > 0.$$

The first factor is positive, while the second factor is greater than $(1-\delta)\delta a + (\delta\rho-\rho)X = (1-\delta)(\delta a-\rho X) > 0$.

(ii) $\underline{\delta = \rho}$

$$P_1^F = \frac{\delta(2a-X)}{2(1+\delta)} = P_1^0.$$

(iii) $\underline{\delta < \rho}$

$$P_1^F = \frac{\delta^2(2a-X)}{2(\delta^2+2\delta-\rho)}, \qquad P_1^0 = \frac{\delta[(\delta+\rho)a - \delta X]}{2(\delta^2+\rho)}$$

Similar calculations as employed in (i) yield

$$P_1^F > P_1^0 \Leftrightarrow \delta a(1-\delta) + \delta(a-X) + (a\rho-\delta X) > 0$$ which must hold. Q.E.D.

PROPOSITION A1. The profit function

$$\pi_4(P|z) \equiv P(a-P-z-x(P)) + \delta\,\frac{[a - X + x(P)]^2}{9}$$

is not quasi-concave, so the associated reaction function may be discontinuous. However, discontinuities involve upward jumps in the reaction function.

PROOF: Because the supply function x(P) defined in (4.3) consists of three segments, we can write the profit function as follows:

$$0 \le P \le \frac{\delta(a-X)}{3} : \pi_4(P|z) = \pi_4^1(P|z) \equiv P(a-z) - P^2 + \rho\,\frac{(a-X)^2}{9}, \qquad \text{(A.1a)}$$

$$\frac{\delta(a-X)}{3} \le P \le \frac{\delta a}{3} : \pi_4(P|z) = \pi_4^2(P|z) \equiv P(2a-X-z) - \frac{P^2}{2\delta}(\delta^2+3\delta-\rho), \qquad \text{(A.1b)}$$

$$\frac{\delta a}{3} \le P \le a \quad \pi_4(P|z) = \pi_4^3(P|z) \equiv P(a-X-z) - P^2 + \rho\,\frac{a^2}{9}. \qquad \text{(A.1c)}$$

The continuity of the supply function guarantees that the profit function is continuous; that it violates quasi-concavity may be seen by considering the following case. Suppose that $X < a$, and $\bar{P}(0) \le \frac{\delta a}{3}$, so producers can never consider charging a price above $\frac{\delta a}{3}$, and so $\pi_4^3(P|z)$ is irrelevant. Further suppose that $\rho = \delta^2 + 3\delta < 1$, so that $\pi_4^2(P|z)$ is a strictly increasing linear function. It is readily seen that $\bar{P}(z) = \frac{\delta}{3+\delta}(2a-X-z)$. Finally, the unconstrained maximum of π_4^1 occurs at $P^* = \frac{a-z}{2}$, and we shall assume that

$$z > a(1-2/3\delta) + 2/3\delta X, \qquad \text{(A.2)}$$

so that $P^* < \frac{\delta(a-X)}{3}$. Putting this all together, for z satisfying (A.2) the payoff function will be as shown in Figure A1.

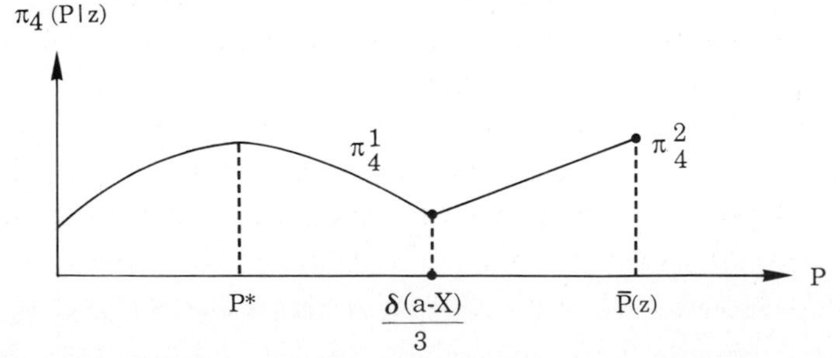

Figure A1: Payoff function $\pi_4(P|z)$

In fact we have drawn Figure A1 for the special case of $z = \hat{z}$ where $\hat{z}$ is such that $\pi^1(P^*|\hat{z}) = \pi^2(\bar{P}(\hat{z})|\hat{z})$, and it is clear that for $z > \hat{z}$, $\pi_2^1(P^*|z) > \pi_4^2(\bar{P}(z)|z)$ while for $z < \hat{z}$, $\pi_4^1(P^*|z) < \pi_4^2(\bar{P}(z)|z)$.

So for $z > \hat{z}$, the optimum is $P^* = \frac{a - z}{2}$, which yields the reaction function $y = \frac{a - z}{2}$; while for $z < \hat{z}$ the optimum is $\bar{P}(z)$ and the reaction function is $y = 0$. Thus the reaction function for this case is shown in Figure A2 as the broken curve ABCD.

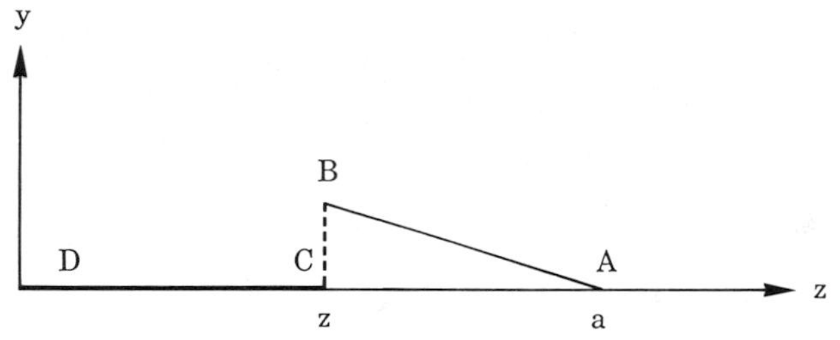

Figure A2: Reaction function

We have demonstrated the lack of quasi-concavity and the resulting discontinuous reaction function for a special case. It is clear that (A.1) consists of three quadratic functions defined over their relevant ranges of P, each with its own local maximum, which may be a boundary point. If, for each value of z, the global maximum lay within the same segment, we would have a continuous (piecewise) linear reaction function. Problems will arise only if we jump from the local maximum in one range to the local maximum in another as z varies. We see from (A.1a) - (A.1c) that z enters the three quadratics in the same way, as a term $-Pz$. So an increase in z will have more effect on profits in the higher range of P than in the lower range, so as z increases we can only jump from a local maximum in a higher range of P to a local maximum in a lower range of P. This means we must be jumping to higher values of y, so if there are discontinuities in reaction function they must involve upward jumps, as exemplified by Figure A2.

Q.E.D.

PROOF OF PROPOSITION 5.

$(\tilde{P},\tilde{z})$ is a symmetric Nash equilibrium (S.N.E.) if

$$\pi_4(\tilde{P}|\tilde{z}) \geq \pi_4(P|\tilde{z}), \qquad 0 \leq P \leq \bar{P}(\tilde{z}),$$

and

$$\tilde{z} = \frac{1}{2}\,(a-x(\tilde{P})-\tilde{P}),$$

i.e. $\tilde{P}$ is a best response to $\tilde{z}$ and when both firms produce $\tilde{z}$ the market clears at price $\tilde{P}$ in period 1. Suppose $\tilde{P}$ does not lie in the range $[\frac{\delta(a-X)}{3}, \frac{\delta a}{3}]$; for example suppose $\tilde{P} > \frac{\delta a}{3}$, $\tilde{z} = \frac{1}{2}\,(a-\tilde{P}-X)$. For this to be a S.N.E., then $\tilde{P}$ must be an unconstrained maximum of $\pi_4^3(P|\tilde{z})$ in (A.1c). This implies that $\tilde{P} = \frac{1}{2}(a-X-\tilde{z}) = a - X - 2\tilde{z}$, so that $\tilde{z} = 1/3(a-X) = \tilde{P}$. But to have $P > \frac{\delta a}{3}$ would require $X < a(1-\delta)$, which we have ruled out. A similar argument rules out the possibility that $\tilde{P} < \frac{\delta(a-X)}{3}$. Q.E.D.

PROOF OF PROPOSITION 6.

Proposition 5 shows that the S.N.E. $(\tilde{P},\tilde{z})$ must lie in the range $[\frac{\delta(a-X)}{3}, \frac{\delta a}{3}]$. It must also satisfy the condition $\tilde{P} \leq \bar{P}(\tilde{z})$. But if $\tilde{P} = \bar{P}(\tilde{z})$, then $\tilde{y} = 0$, so in a *symmetric* Nash equilibrium, the relevant constraint must be $\tilde{P} \leq \bar{P}(0)$. So the relevant upper boundary is $\bar{\bar{P}}$, and the relevant lower boundary $\underline{\underline{P}}$. If we consider the unconstrained maximum of $\pi_4^2(P|\tilde{z})$ we get

$$\tilde{P} = \frac{\delta^2(2a-X-\tilde{z})}{2(\delta^2+3\delta-\rho)};$$

solving with

$$\tilde{z} = \frac{1}{2}\,[a - x(\tilde{P}) - \tilde{P}],$$

we have as the interior equilibrium

$$\hat{P} = \frac{\delta^2(2a-X)}{[3\delta^2+9\delta-4\rho]}, \qquad \hat{z} = \frac{[2a-X](\delta^2+3\rho-2\rho)}{[3\delta^2+9\delta-4\rho]}.$$

Clearly for this to be an interior equilibrium requires $\delta^2 + 3\delta - 2\rho > 0$.

Q.E.D.

Dynamic Policy Games in Economics
F. van der Ploeg and A.J. de Zeeuw, (Editors)

STRATEGIC WAGES POLICY AND THE GAINS FROM COOPERATION*

Stephen J. Turnovsky

Department of Economics
University of Washington
Seattle, WA 98195, USA

Marcelo Bianconi

Department of Economics
University of Illinois
Urbana, IL 61801, USA

Introduction

The policies of different countries in the world economy with regard to wage indexation have been varied. High inflation countries such as Brazil and Israel have long histories of adopting wage indexation as part of their macroeconomic stabilisation policies; over 20 years in the former and 30 years in the latter[1]. Wage indexation has also been widely adopted in the more moderate inflation countries of Western Europe, although recently there has been some movement in favour of less complete wage indexation towards more financial indexation[2]. By contrast, the United States has never followed official indexation rules, although private wage contracts can, and do, incorporate wage indexation and cost of living adjustments.

The analysis of wage indexation has been extensively studied both in the context of closed economies and for small open economies; see e.g., Gray (1976), Fischer (1977), Flood and Marion (1982), Marston (1984). A standard result of this literature is that the optimal degree of wage indexation is to index fully for demand shocks but to index only partially in the face of supply shocks. In the open economy, an important conclusion is that the optimal degree of wage indexation depends critically upon the form of exchange rate regime. In this regard, Flood and Marion (1982) compared the optimal degrees of wage indexation under alternative forms of fixed and flexible exchange rates. This approach has been extended more recently by Turnovsky (1983, 1987) and Aizenman and Frenkel (1985, 1986) to analyse the interdependence between wage indexation on the one hand, and more general forms of monetary policy rules, or forms of exchange market intervention rules, on the other.

In a world economy it is clear that the economic performance of one country will depend not only upon the form of wages policy adopted in that country, but also upon the form of wages policy pursued abroad. The determination of the optimal degree of wage indexation in the multi-country context necessarily involves strategic behaviour.

This paper addresses this issue in a two-country stochastic model of a world economy in which both economies are subjected to stochastic disturbances in demand and supply and expectations are rational. Both non-cooperative Nash and Pareto-optimal cooperative equilibria are considered. The optimal degrees of indexation in the two equilibria are compared and the gains from cooperation are assessed. In view of the dependence of the degree of indexation on the exchange rate regime, we determine the optimal degrees of wage indexation under both flexible and fixed exchange rate regimes. In the former case we show how, in general, non-cooperative Nash behaviour leads to overindexation of wages relative to the Pareto-optimal cooperative equilibrium. The gains from cooperation do exist, but for plausible parameter values they appear to be numerically small. In the fixed exchange rate regime, we show how the non-cooperative and the cooperative equilibrium coincide. Each country pursuing its own independent welfare will in fact lead to a Pareto-optimal outcome.

1. The World Economy

The analysis is based on the following two-country stochastic macroeconomic model in which, for simplicity, the two countries are assumed to be structurally identical[3]. There is a single traded good and, with no impediments to trade, purchasing power parity (PPP) holds. The financial assets consist of two national monies held by the respective domestic residents, and a traded bond. Assuming no impediments to financial trade and risk neutrality, uncovered interest parity (UIP) also holds. Expressed in deviation form, the model can be summarised by the following set of equations:

$$(1-d_1)(Y_t+Y_t^*) = -d_2[R_t - [\mathscr{E}_t(P_{t+1}) - P_t] + R_t^* - [\mathscr{E}_t(P_{t+1}^*) - P_t^*]] + u_t, \tag{1.1}$$

$$P_t = P_t^* + E_t, \tag{1.2}$$

$$M_t - P_t = \alpha_1 Y_t - \alpha_2 R_t, \tag{1.3a}$$

$$M_t^* - P_t^* = \alpha_1 Y_t^* - \alpha_2 R_t^*, \tag{1.3b}$$

$$R_t = R_t^* + \mathscr{E}_t(E_{t+1}) - E_t, \tag{1.4}$$

$$Y_t = az[P_t - \mathscr{E}_{t-1}(P_t)] + v_t, \tag{1.5a}$$

$$Y_t^* = az^*[P_t^* - \mathscr{E}_{t-1}(P_t^*)] + v_t^*, \tag{1.5b}$$

where

$$z \equiv 1 - \tau, \qquad z^* \equiv 1 - \tau^*$$

and

Y_t = real output, expressed in logarithms, measured in deviation form about its natural rate level,

P_t = price of output, expressed in logarithms,

E_t = exchange rate (measured in terms of units of domestic currency per unit of foreign currency), measured in logarithms,

R_t = nominal interest rate, expressed in natural units,

M_t = nominal money supply, expressed in logarithms,

$\mathscr{E}_t$ = expectation, conditioned on information at time t,

u_t = stochastic disturbance in world demand,

v_t = stochastic disturbance in supply.

Domestic variables are unstarred; foreign variables are denoted by asterisks. We shall also refer to these as Country 1 and Country 2, respectively.

Equation (1.1) describes equilibrium in the world commodity market. Aggregate output depends upon the real interest rate in the two economies, which under the assumptions of UIP and PPP are equal, and the stochastic disturbance in world demand. The absence of impediments to world trade is contained in the PPP condition (1.2). The money market equilibrium conditions in the two economies are described by (1.3a), (1.3b), where the money stocks are measured as logarithmic deviations about some constant equilibrium levels. These equations are standard and require no further comment. The perfect substitutability between domestic and foreign bonds is specified by the UIP condition (1.3).

Finally, output in each economy is described by a Lucas supply function. Namely, the deviation in output from its natural rate level is postulated to be a positive function of the unanticipated change in the price level, as well as the stochastic supply (or productivity) shock. The degrees of wage indexation, τ, τ^* which are the policy decisions we are considering, are incorporated in the parameters z, z*, thereby influencing the slopes of the respective aggregate supply curves. Full wage indexation, $\tau = \tau^* = 1$, corresponds to $z = z^* = 0$, while zero indexation implies $z = z^* = 1$. We shall assume $z \geq 0$, $z^* \geq 0$[4].

While several alternative motivations can be given for the supply functions (1.5a), (1.5b), the simplest is in terms of the one-period wage contract model of Gray (1976), with an underlying Cobb-Douglas production function. Specifying the latter in its logarithmic form

$$Y_t = (1-\vartheta)N_t + \varepsilon_t,$$

where N denotes employment measured in logarithms, leads to supply functions of the form (1.5a), (1.5b), with[5]

$$a \equiv \frac{1-\vartheta}{\vartheta}, \qquad v_t \equiv \frac{\varepsilon_t}{\vartheta}.$$

The stochastic variables u_t, v_t and v_t^* are assumed to be independently distributed over time, with zero means and finite variances[6]. Moreover, while supply and demand shocks are assumed to be uncorrelated, the two supply disturbances may, or may not, be correlated. The stochastic properties are summarised by

$$\mathcal{E}(u_t) = \mathcal{E}(v_t) = \mathcal{E}(v_t^*) = 0, \qquad (1.6)$$

$$\mathcal{E}(u_t^2) = \sigma_u^2, \quad \mathcal{E}(v_t^2) = \sigma_v^2, \quad \mathcal{E}(v_t^{*2}) = \sigma_v^2, \quad \mathcal{E}(v_t v_t^*) = \sigma_{vv*} = \sigma_v \sigma_{v*} \rho.$$

The case where $\rho = 0$ characterises country-specific supply disturbances, while $\rho = 1$ denotes a worldwide supply shock.

Under these stochastic conditions, the rational expectations solution to (1.1) - (1.5) implies that all expectations are simply zero, so that

$$\mathcal{E}_t(P_{t+1}) = \mathcal{E}_t(P^*_{t+1}) = \mathcal{E}_t(E_{t+1}) = 0. \tag{1.7}$$

Equations (1.1) - (1.7) describe the stochastic structure of the world economy. Wage contracts introduce rigidities into the economy, thereby leading to welfare losses relative to a frictionless economy in which wages are fully flexible and labour markets clear. The objective of the indexation scheme is in effect to undo these rigidities due to the contracts and to attempt to replicate as closely as possible the behaviour of the frictionless economy[7]. An important consequence of the stochastic specification and the implied stationarity of expectations is that the dynamics will be of a repeated nature. In other words, the problem can be solved statically in each period, which of course rules out any potential problems of time inconsistency.

It is well known that for the Cobb-Douglas production function specified above, and with labour immobile internationally, the frictionless levels of output in the respective economies are

$$\tilde{Y}_t = \left(\frac{1+n}{1+n\vartheta}\right)\varepsilon_t = \left(\frac{1+n}{1+n+a}\right)v_t, \tag{1.8a}$$

$$\tilde{Y}^*_t = \left(\frac{1+n}{1+n\vartheta}\right)\varepsilon^*_t = \left(\frac{1+n}{1+n+a}\right)v^*_t, \tag{1.8b}$$

where n is the elasticity of supply of labour with respect to the real wage. The formal objectives are then to choose the indexation parameters τ, τ^* (or z, z^*) to minimise the variances of output about their respective frictionless levels, namely[8]

$$\mathcal{E}_t[Y_t - \tilde{Y}_t]^2 \equiv \Omega(z,z^*), \qquad \mathcal{E}_t[Y^*_t - \tilde{Y}^*_t]^2 \equiv \Omega^*(z,z^*).$$

2. Strategic Wage Indexation under Flexible Exchange Rates

Under a perfectly flexible exchange rate regime, $M_t = M_t^* = 0$, in which case (1.1) - (1.5), (1.7) may be solved for outputs Y_t, Y_t^* as follows

$$Y_t = a^F(z,z^*)v_t + b^F(z,z^*)v_t^* + c^F(z,z^*)u_t, \tag{2.1a}$$

$$Y_t^* = b^F(z^*,z)v_t + a^F(z^*,z)v_t^* + c^F(z^*,z)u_t, \tag{2.1b}$$

where

$$a^F(x,y) = \frac{X_2y + X_3}{X_1xy + X_2(x+y) + X_3} > 0 \qquad x = z,z^*, \qquad y = z,z^*, \qquad x \neq y,$$

$$b^F(x,y) = \frac{axX_4}{X_1xy + X_2(x+y) + X_3} < 0,$$

$$c^F(x,y) = \frac{ax(X_5y+X_6)}{X_1xy + X_2(x+y) + X_3} > 0,$$

and

$$X_1 \equiv 2a^2(\frac{\alpha_1}{\alpha_2})[(1-d_1)] + d_2\frac{\alpha_1}{\alpha_2}] > 0, \qquad X_4 \equiv -(1-d_1)\frac{(1+\alpha_2)}{\alpha_2} < 0,$$

$$X_2 \equiv a_1[\frac{(1+\alpha_2)}{\alpha_2}][(1-d_1) + 2d_2\frac{\alpha_1}{\alpha_2}] > 0, \qquad X_5 \equiv \frac{a\alpha_1}{\alpha_2} > 0,$$

$$X_3 \equiv 2d_2\frac{(1+\alpha_2)}{\alpha_2} > 0, \qquad X_6 \equiv \frac{(1+\alpha_2)}{\alpha_2} > 0.$$

The symmetry of these solutions reflects the symmetry of the underlying structure. In both economies, the impacts of the disturbances u_t, v_t and v_t^* depend upon the degrees of wage indexation both at home and abroad. Differentiating the coefficients a^F, b^F, c^F yields

$$\frac{\partial a^F(x,y)}{\partial x} = -\frac{(X_2y+X_3)(X_1y+X_2)}{\Delta_F^2} < 0, \qquad \frac{\partial a^F(x,y)}{\partial y} = \frac{a^2X_4^2z}{\Delta_F^2} > 0,$$

$$\frac{\partial b^F(x,y)}{\partial x} = \frac{aX_4(X_2y+X_3)}{\Delta_F^2} < 0, \qquad \frac{\partial b^F(x,y)}{\partial y} = -\frac{aX_4z(X_1z+X_2)}{\Delta_F^2} > 0,$$

$$\frac{\partial c^F(x,y)}{\partial x} = \frac{a(X_5z^*+X_6)(X_2z^*+X_3)}{\Delta_F^2} > 0, \qquad \frac{\partial c^F(x,y)}{\partial y} = \frac{a^2zX_4(X_5z+X_6)}{\Delta_F^2} < 0,$$

and

$$\Delta_F \equiv X_1xy + X_2(x+y) + X_3 > 0.$$

From these equations we see that a positive worldwide demand disturbance raises output in both economies. If, for a given world demand disturbance, Country 1 increases its degree of wage indexation (i.e., lowers z), this will tend to lower the impact of this demand shock on the domestic economy, while increasing its effect on output abroad. This is because more indexation in the domestic economy will reduce the flexibility of the domestic real wage, thereby shifting more of the adjustment within the domestic economy away from output to the price level. Given PPP, the higher domestic price level will tend to raise the price level abroad, thereby stimulating foreign output. By symmetry, an increase in indexation abroad (lower z*) will shift the demand shock from the foreign economy to the domestic economy.

A positive domestic supply shock raises domestic output, while lowering the domestic price level. Given PPP, this reduces the price level abroad, thereby causing a decline in the level of foreign output. An increase in the degree of domestic wage indexation exacerbates both the increase in domestic output and the decline abroad. This is because, as the degree of wage indexation increases, the reduced flexibility of the domestic real wage means that more of the domestic supply disturbance is borne by domestic output. The larger increase in output stimulates the demand for money which, with the domestic stock of money fixed, requires a larger drop in the domestic price level for the domestic money market to obtain equilibrium. The larger fall in the domestic price level leads, via PPP to a larger fall in the foreign price level, and hence to a larger decline in the level of foreign output. An increase in the level of indexation abroad will mitigate the effect of the domestic supply shock on both domestic and foreign output. This is because more indexation in the foreign economy reduces the flexibility of the foreign real wage, thereby shifting the adjustment away from output to the foreign price level. Given PPP, this means a larger price adjustment and a smaller quantity adjustment in the domestic economy as well. The effects of a foreign supply shock and their response to indexation are analogous.

Letting

$$\varphi \equiv \frac{1 + n}{1 + n + a},$$

so that the frictionless levels of output in the two economies may be written as

$$\tilde{Y}_t = \varphi v_t, \qquad \tilde{Y}^*_t = \varphi v^*_t,$$

the objective functions of the policy-makers in the domestic and foreign economies are respectively

$$\Omega(z,z^*) \equiv [a^F(z,z^*) - \varphi]^2\sigma_v^2 + b^F(z,z^*)^2\sigma_{v^*}^2 + 2[a^F(z,z^*) - \varphi]b^F(z,z^*)\sigma_{vv^*} + c^F(z,z^*)^2\sigma_u^2, \tag{2.2a}$$

$$\Omega^*(z,z^*) \equiv b^F(z^*,z)^2\sigma_v^2 + [a^F(z^*,z) - \varphi]^2\sigma_{v^*}^2 + 2[a^F(z^*,z) - \varphi]b^F(z^*,z)\sigma_{vv^*} + c^F(z^*,z)^2\sigma_u^2. \tag{2.2b}$$

The optimal policy confronting each of the policy-makers is to choose their respective degree of wage indexation to minimise their cost functions, (2.2a), (2.2b). We now proceed to analyse these policies under both non-cooperative Nash and Pareto-optimal cooperative behaviour.

2.1 Non-cooperative Behaviour

Under non-cooperative behaviour, each policy-maker chooses his respective degree of indexation, taking the behaviour of his opponent as remaining fixed. This leads to the optimality conditions

$$\frac{\partial\Omega}{\partial z} = 0, \tag{2.3a}$$

$$\frac{\partial\Omega^*}{\partial z^*} = 0. \tag{2.3b}$$

Performing these calculations we obtain

$$\begin{aligned}\frac{\partial\Omega}{\partial z} &= [a^F(z,z^*) - \varphi]a_1^F(z,z^*)\sigma_v^2 + b^F(z,z^*)b_1^F(z,z^*)\sigma_{v^*}^2 \\ &+ [b^F(z,z^*)a_1^F(z,z^*) + [a^F(z,z^*) - \varphi]b_1^F(z,z^*)]\sigma_{vv^*} \\ &+ c^F(z,z^*)c_1^F(z,z^*)\sigma_u^2 = 0,\end{aligned} \tag{2.4a}$$

$$\begin{aligned}\frac{\partial\Omega}{\partial z^*} &= b^F(z^*,z)b_1^F(z^*,z)\sigma_v^2 + [a^F(z^*,z) - \varphi]a_1^F(z^*,z)\sigma_{v^*}^2 \\ &+ [b^F(z^*,z)a_1^F(z^*,z) + [a^F(z^*,z) - \varphi]b_1^F(z^*,z)]\sigma_{vv^*} \\ &+ c^F(z^*,z)c_1^F(z^*,z) = 0,\end{aligned} \tag{2.4b}$$

where $a_1^F(z,z^*) \equiv \partial a^F(z,z^*)/\partial z$, etc. Substituting for the functions $a^F(.)$, etc., and the partial derivatives yields the reaction functions

$$z = \frac{(1-\varphi)(X_2z^*+X_3)[(X_1z^*+X_2)\sigma_v^2 - aX_4\sigma_{vv^*}]}{\varphi(X_1z^*+X_2)^2\sigma_v^2 + a^2X_4^2\sigma_{v^*}^2 - aX_4(X_1z^*+X_2)(1+\varphi)\sigma_{vv^*} + a^2(X_5z^*+X_6)^2\sigma_u^2} \tag{2.5a}$$

$$z^* = \frac{(1-\varphi)(X_2z+X_3)[(X_1z+X_2)\sigma_{v^*}^2 - aX_4\sigma_{vv^*}]}{\varphi(X_1z+X_2)^2\sigma_{v^*}^2 + a^2X_4^2\sigma_v^2 - aX_4(X_1z^*+X_2)(1+\varphi)\sigma_{vv^*} + a^2(X_5z+X_6)^2\sigma_u^2} \tag{2.5b}$$

From these two equations one can establish that[9]

$$\left[\frac{dz}{dz^*}\right]_1 > 0 \qquad \left[\frac{dz^*}{dz}\right]_2 > 0, \tag{2.6}$$

so that the reaction functions in the two economies are both upward sloping. That is, a policy-maker in one country will respond to increased indexation abroad by increasing his own rate of wage indexation. The intuitive reasoning for this follows from the fact that increased indexation abroad increases the vulnerability of output in the domestic economy to all stochastic disturbances, which, however, can be alleviated by increased indexation in the domestic economy.

It would appear from the non-linearity of the reaction functions (2.5a), (2.5b) that the possibility of non-unique Nash equilibria exists. And indeed, an example of where this may occur is presented below. While further analysis of the general case (2.5a), (2.5b) is intractable, a number of special cases are worth noting.

(i) If the only stochastic disturbances are in worldwide demand shocks ($\sigma_u^2 > 0$, $\sigma_v^2 = \sigma_v^{*2} = 0$), it is clear that the optimal solutions to (2.5a), (2.5b) are

$$z = z^* = 0, \qquad \text{i.e., } \tau = \tau^* = 1. \tag{2.7}$$

That is, both economies should index wages fully. This, of course, is a direct extension of the familiar closed economy-small open economy result and follows directly from the form of the supply function and the fact that demand shocks have an impact on it through fluctuations in the price level.

(ii) If there are worldwide demand shocks accompanied by supply disturbances specific to Country 1 ($\sigma_u^2 > 0$, $\sigma_v^2 > 0$, $\sigma_{v*}^2 = 0$), then the optimum is

$$z^* = 0, \tag{2.8a}$$

$$z = \frac{(1-\varphi)X_2X_3\sigma_v^2}{\varphi X_2^2\sigma_v^2 + a^2X_6^2\sigma_u^2}. \tag{2.8b}$$

In this case, the foreign economy should index its wage fully, $\tau^* = 1$, while the domestic economy should invoke only partial indexation. As far as the foreign economy is concerned, the domestic supply shock manifests itself as a price disturbance and hence requires complete indexation, along with the demand shock. The partial indexation in the domestic economy is analogous to the result for the closed economy, with the partial degree of indexation trading off the variances of the demand and supply disturbances. Note that it is possible for $\tau < 0$, and examples of this occur in some of the numerical results presented in Section 4 below.

(iii) With supply shocks present in both economies ($\sigma_v^2 > 0$, $\sigma_{v*}^2 > 0$), the solutions to (2.5a), (2.5b) involve partial indexation in the two countries. For example, in the case of a worldwide supply shock and no demand shock ($\sigma_v^2 = \sigma_{v*}^2 = \sigma_{vv*} > 0$, $\sigma_u^2 = 0$), the solutions reduce to $z = z^*$ where z is the unique positive solution to the quadratic equation

$$\varphi X_1 z^2 + [(2\varphi-1)X_2 - aX_4]z - (1-\varphi)X_3 = 0.$$

On the other hand, for country-specific supply shocks of equal variance and no demand shocks ($\sigma_v^2 = \sigma_{v*}^2 > 0$, $\sigma_{vv*} = \sigma_u^2 = 0$), the optimal indexation is $z = z^*$ where z is the solution to the cubic equation

$$\varphi X_1^2 z^3 + X_1 X_2(3\varphi-1)z^2 + [(2\varphi-1)X_2^2 - (1-\varphi)X_1 X_3 + a^2 X_4^2]z - (1-\varphi)X_2 X_3 = 0.$$

In this case, while there is definitely one positive solution, the possibility of three positive solutions for z and z* cannot be ruled out[10].

The criterion underlying these results ignores any welfare costs associated with unstable prices. This is the standard assumption throughout the indexation literature. In principle, such costs could be incorporated by modifying Ω to say

$$\Omega \equiv \lambda \mathscr{E}_t (Y_t - \tilde{Y}_t)^2 + (1-\lambda)\sigma_p^2, \qquad 0 < \lambda < 1,$$

where σ_p^2 is the variance of the price level, and similarly for Ω*. This will obviously influence the optimal degree of indexation. For example, in the case of worldwide demand disturbances, when full indexation in both economies was shown to be optimal and to lead to the perfect stabilisation of output, the fluctuations stemming from the underlying random shocks are fully borne by prices, leading to a large variance in the price level. If the policy-maker attaches some positive weight to this in his objective function, he will be willing to trade some reduction in price variance against additional variance in output. This will involve some reduction in the degree of wage indexation, to below unity.

2.2 Cooperative Equilibrium

We now assume that the policy-makers in the two economies collude and jointly set their degrees of wage indexation z, z* to minimise their aggregate welfare loss function $W = \Omega + \Omega^*$. Differentiating W with respect to z, z* yields the optimality conditions

$$\frac{\partial W}{\partial z} = \frac{\partial \Omega}{\partial z} + \frac{\partial \Omega^*}{\partial z} = 0, \tag{2.9a}$$

$$\frac{\partial W}{\partial z^*} = \frac{\partial \Omega}{\partial z^*} + \frac{\partial \Omega^*}{\partial z^*} = 0, \tag{2.9b}$$

which upon evaluation become

$$\begin{aligned}\frac{\partial W}{\partial z} \equiv\ & [(a^F(z,z^*)-\varphi)a_1^F(z,z^*) + b^F(z^*,z)b_2^F(z^*,z)]\sigma_v^2 \\ & + [(a^F(z^*,z)-\varphi)a_2^F(z^*,z) + b^F(z,z^*)b_1^F(z,z^*)]\sigma_{v^*}^2 \\ & + [b^F(z,z^*)a_1^F(z,z^*) + b^F(z^*,z)a_2^F(z^*,z) + [a^F(z,z^*) - \varphi]b_1^F(z,z^*) \\ & + [a^F(z^*,z) - \varphi]b_2^F(z^*,z)]\sigma_{vv^*} \\ & + [c^F(z,z^*)c_1^F(z,z^*) + c^F(z^*,z)c_2^F(z^*,z)]\sigma_u^2 = 0,\end{aligned} \tag{2.10a}$$

$$\begin{aligned}\frac{\partial W}{\partial z^*} \equiv\ & [(a^F(z,z^*)-\varphi)a_2^F(z,z^*) + b^F(z^*,z)b_1^F(z^*,z)]\sigma_v^2 \\ & + [(a^F(z^*,z) - \varphi)a_1^F(z^*,z) + b^F(z,z^*)b_2^F(z,z^*)]\sigma_{v^*}^2 \\ & + [b^F(z,z^*)a_2^F(z,z^*) + b^F(z^*,z)a_1^F(z^*,z) + [a^F(z,z^*) - \varphi]b_2^F(z,z^*) \\ & + [a^F(z^*,z) - \varphi]b_1^F(z^*,z)]\sigma_{vv^*} \\ & + [c^F(z,z^*)c_2^F(z,z^*) + c^F(z^*,z)c_1^F(z^*,z)]\sigma_u^2 = 0.\end{aligned} \tag{2.10b}$$

Solving this pair of equations for z, z* yields the optimal degrees of indexation in the Pareto-optimal cooperative equilibrium. Again, these equations are highly non-linear so that multiple solutions may exist. When this occurs, the one yielding the highest value for W is obviously chosen.

2.3 Comparison between the Cooperative and Non-cooperative Equilibria

Further investigation of the cooperative equilibrium can best be achieved by comparison with the non-cooperative Nash equilibrium. To do this, we evaluate $\frac{\partial W}{\partial z}, \frac{\partial W}{\partial z^*}$, at the Nash equilibrium. Specifically,

$$\left.\frac{\partial W}{\partial z}\right|_N = \left.\frac{\partial \Omega}{\partial z}\right|_N + \left.\frac{\partial \Omega^*}{\partial z}\right|_N,$$

$$\left.\frac{\partial W}{\partial z^*}\right|_N = \left.\frac{\partial \Omega}{\partial z^*}\right|_N + \left.\frac{\partial \Omega^*}{\partial z^*}\right|_N,$$

and since at the Nash equilibrium

$$\left.\frac{\partial \Omega}{\partial z}\right|_N = \left.\frac{\partial \Omega^*}{\partial z^*}\right|_N = 0,$$

we have

$$\left.\frac{\partial W}{\partial z}\right|_N = \left.\frac{\partial \Omega^*}{\partial z}\right|_N, \qquad (2.11a)$$

$$\left.\frac{\partial W}{\partial z^*}\right|_N = \left.\frac{\partial \Omega}{\partial z^*}\right|_N. \qquad (2.11b)$$

Comparing (2.11) with (2.9) it is evident that, when a country indexes non-cooperatively, it fails to take account of the fact that its wages policy generates an externality which affects the welfare of the other country. In particular, the non-cooperative level of wage indexation, $\tau^N = 1 - z^N$ say, is too large or too small relative to the cooperative level, $\tau^C = 1 - z^C$ say, according to whether $\left.\frac{\partial \Omega^*}{\partial z}\right|_N < 0$ or > 0, respectively. Aggregate welfare costs can be reduced if τ is decreased in the former case and increased in the latter. An analogous statement applies with respect to the degree of foreign indexation, τ^*.

To consider the comparison further, we can show that

$$\left.\frac{\partial W}{\partial z}\right|_N = \left.\frac{\partial \Omega^*}{\partial z}\right|_N = a_2^F(z^*,z)\{(\frac{aX_4}{X_1z+X_2} - \frac{(X_1z^*+X_2)}{aX_4})[b^F(z^*,z)\sigma_v^2$$

$$+ (a^F(z^*,z)-\varphi)\sigma_{vv^*}] + c^F(z^*,z)[\frac{a(X_5z+X_6)}{X_1z+X_2} + \frac{X_5z^*+X_6}{X_4}]\sigma_u^2\}, \tag{2.12a}$$

$$\left.\frac{\partial W}{\partial z^*}\right|_N = \left.\frac{\partial \Omega}{\partial z^*}\right|_N = a_2^F(z,z^*)\{[\frac{aX_4}{X_1z^*+X_2} - \frac{(X_1z+X_2)}{aX_4}][b^F(z,z^*)\sigma_{v^*}^2$$

$$+ [a^F(z,z^*)-\varphi]\sigma_{vv^*}] + c^F(z,z^*)[\frac{a(X_5z^*+X_6)}{X_1z^*+X_2} + \frac{X_5z+X_6}{X_4}]\sigma_u^2\}, \tag{2.12b}$$

from which the following conclusions can be drawn[11].

(i) In the case of a worldwide demand disturbance and no supply shocks ($\sigma_u^2 > 0$, $\sigma_v^2 = \sigma_{v^*}^2 = 0$), at the non-cooperative Nash equilibrium $c^F(z,z^*) = c^F(z^*,z) = 0$, and hence

$$z = z^* = 0, \quad \text{i.e., } \tau = \tau^* = 1.$$

In this case, (2.12a) and (2.12b) reduce to

$$\left.\frac{\partial \Omega^*}{\partial z}\right|_N = \left.\frac{\partial \Omega}{\partial z^*}\right|_N = 0,$$

implying

$$z^N = z^C, \quad z^{*N} = z^{*C}.$$

Accordingly, the cooperative equilibrium leads to the same degree of indexation as the non-cooperative, namely full indexation $\tau = \tau^* = 1$.

(ii) If the only disturbances are supply shocks in Country 1 ($\sigma_v^2 > 0$, $\sigma_{v^*}^2 = \sigma_u^2 = 0$), the Nash equilibrium (2.4a), (2.4b) implies

$$a^F(z,z^*) = \varphi, \quad b^F(z^*,z) = 0,$$

in which case

$$\left.\frac{\partial \Omega^*}{\partial z}\right|_N = \left.\frac{\partial \Omega}{\partial z^*}\right|_N = 0,$$

and again the cooperative and Nash equilibria coincide.

(iii) Combining (i) and (ii) so that the worldwide demand shocks are accompanied by supply disturbances in Country 1, the Nash equilibrium implies

$$b^F(z^*,z) = c^F(z^*,z) = 0, \qquad \text{i.e., } z^* = 0.$$

Substituting this value into (2.12a), (2.12b), we obtain

$$\left.\frac{\partial\Omega^*}{\partial z}\right|_N = 0, \qquad \left.\frac{\partial\Omega}{\partial z^*}\right|_N < 0.$$

The non-cooperative and cooperative values of z coincide; however, the non-cooperative value of τ^* is greater than the Pareto-optimal value.

In other words, the partial wage indexation characteristic of the Nash equilibrium in the economy experiencing the supply disturbances remains appropriate from the Pareto-optimal viewpoint. The complete indexation $\tau^* = 1$ of the other country is now too great. Overall welfare W will be increased if this latter country reduces its degree of indexation. While this will increase welfare losses in that economy, thereby making it worse off, the improved welfare in the economy experiencing the supply shocks will more than compensate, bringing about the potential for an overall improvement in global welfare.

(iv) If the three disturbances u, v, and v^* are uncorrelated, so that both countries experience country-specific supply shocks, then we can show

$$\left.\frac{\partial\Omega^*}{\partial z}\right|_N < 0, \qquad \left.\frac{\partial\Omega}{\partial z^*}\right|_N < 0,$$

so that the non-cooperative Nash equilibrium implies overindexing relative to the cooperative equilibrium, in both economies.

Figure 1 illustrates the relationship between the non-cooperative equilibrium for this case. Under non-cooperative behaviour, the equilibrium is at A, the point of intersection of the two reaction functions. The cooperative equilibrium is at B, the point of tangency of the two objective functions. The figure illustrates clearly how moving from A to B involves increasing both z and z^*, i.e. reducing the degree of indexation.

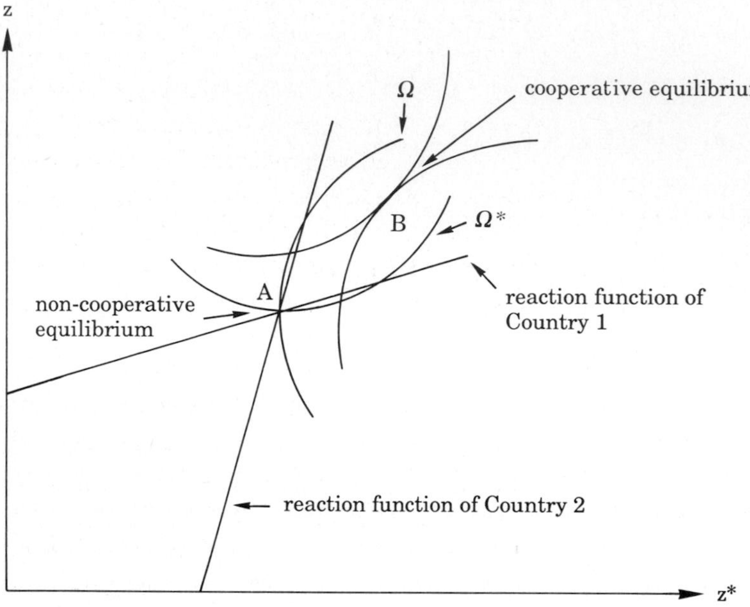

Figure 1: Non-cooperative and cooperative equilibria: perfectly flexible exchange rate

(v) In the case of worldwide supply shocks accompanied by worldwide demand shocks, we can show

$$\left.\frac{\partial\Omega^*}{\partial z}\right|_N = [a^F(z^*,z) - \varphi + b^F(z^*,z)][a_2^F(z^*,z) + b_2^F(z^*,z)]\sigma_v^2$$

$$+ c^F(z^*,z)c_2^F(z^*,z)\sigma_u^2,$$

$$\left.\frac{\partial\Omega}{\partial z^*}\right|_N = [a^F(z,z^*) - \varphi + b^F(z,z^*)][a_2^F(z,z^*) + b_2^F(z,z^*)]\sigma_v^2$$

$$+ c^F(z,z^*)c_2^F(z,z^*)\sigma_u^2.$$

Evaluating these expressions at the Nash equilibrium, they can be shown to equal zero, implying that non-cooperative behaviour will lead to the Pareto-optimal cooperative outcome.

3. Optimal Strategic Wage Indexation under Fixed Exchange Rates

In principle, the exchange rate can be fixed in an infinite number of ways, depending upon how the monetary authorities agree to adjust their respective money stocks to accommodate to the various stochastic shocks. In discussing the fixed exchange rate, we shall follow Turnovsky and d'Orey (1986) in assuming that the policy-makers agree to peg the exchange rate by adjusting their respective money stocks equally in response to the disturbances. This was shown to be superior to a natural alternative where each monetary authority accommodates to the disturbances originating in that country[12].

Fixing the exchange rate in this way, the solutions for output in the two economies are given by

$$Y_t = a^P(z,z^*)v_t + b^P(z,z^*)v_t^* + c^P(z,z^*)u_t, \tag{3.1a}$$

$$Y_t^* = b^P(z^*,z)v_t + a^P(z^*,z)v_t^* + c^P(z^*,z)u_t, \tag{3.1b}$$

where

$$a^P(x,y) = \frac{\delta_1 + \delta_2 y}{\delta_1 + \delta_2(x+y)} > 0 \qquad x = z,z^*, \qquad y = z,z^*, \qquad x \neq y,$$

$$b^P(x,y) = \frac{-\delta_2 x}{\delta_1 + \delta_2(x+y)} < 0,$$

$$c^P(x,y) = \frac{a\alpha_2 x}{\delta_1 + \delta_2(x+y)} > 0,$$

and

$$\delta_1 = 2d_2\frac{(1+\alpha_2)}{\alpha_2} > 0,$$

$$\delta_2 = a[(1-d_1) + \frac{d_2\alpha_1}{\alpha_2}] > 0.$$

These solutions are analogous to (2.1) under flexible exchange rates, and imply the same qualitative responses to the various disturbances. In addition, the impacts of these disturbances are affected by indexation in the same way as under flexible rates.

The objective functions to be minimised now become

$$\Omega(z,z^*) \equiv [a^P(z,z^*) - \varphi]^2\sigma_v^2 + b^P(z,z^*)^2\sigma_{v^*}^2$$

$$+ 2[a^P(z,z^*) - \varphi]b^P(z,z^*)\sigma_{vv^*} + c^P(z,z^*)^2\sigma_u^2, \tag{3.2a}$$

$$\Omega^*(z,z^*) \equiv b^P(z^*,z)^2\sigma_{v^*}^2 + [a^P(z^*,z) - \varphi]^2\sigma_v^2$$

$$+ 2[a^P(z^*,z) - \varphi]b^P(z^*,z)\sigma_{vv^*} + c^P(z^*,z)^2\sigma_u^2 \tag{3.2b}$$

and both non-cooperative and cooperative behaviour shall be considered.

3.1 Non-cooperative Behaviour

The non-cooperative equilibrium, obtained by setting

$$\frac{\partial\Omega}{\partial z} = \frac{\partial\Omega^*}{\partial z^*} = 0,$$

leads to the optimality conditions

$$\frac{\partial\Omega}{\partial z} \equiv [a^P(z,z^*) - \varphi]a_1^P(z,z^*)\sigma_v^2 + b^P(z,z^*)b_1^P(z,z^*)\sigma_{v^*}^2$$

$$+ [b^P(z,z^*)a_1^P(z,z^*) + [a^P(z,z^*) - \varphi]b_1^P(z,z^*)]\sigma_{vv^*}$$

$$+ c^P(z,z^*)c_1^P(z,z^*)\sigma_u^2 = 0, \tag{3.3a}$$

$$\frac{\partial\Omega^*}{\partial z^*} \equiv b^P(z^*,z)b_1^P(z^*,z)\sigma_v^2 + [a^P(z^*,z) - \varphi]a_1^P(z^*,z)\sigma_{v^*}^2$$

$$+ [b^P(z^*,z)a_1^P(z^*,z) + [a^P(z^*,z) - \varphi]b_1^P(z^*,z)]\sigma_{vv^*}$$

$$+ c^P(z^*,z)c_1^P(z^*,z)\sigma_u^2 = 0. \tag{3.3b}$$

Evaluating these expressions, we obtain the following linear reaction functions

$$z = \frac{(1-\varphi)\delta_2(\delta_1+\delta_2 z^*)(\sigma_v^2+\sigma_{vv^*})}{\varphi\delta_2^2\sigma_v^2 + \delta_2^2\sigma_{v^*}^2 + \delta_2^2(1+\varphi)\sigma_{vv^*} + a^2\alpha_2^2\sigma_u^2}, \tag{3.4a}$$

$$z^* = \frac{(1-\varphi)\delta_2(\delta_1+\delta_2 z)(\sigma_{v^*}^2+\sigma_{vv^*})}{\varphi\delta_2^2\sigma_v^2 + \delta_2^2\sigma_{v^*}^2 + \delta_2^2(1+\varphi)\sigma_{vv^*} + a^2\alpha_2^2\sigma_u^2}. \tag{3.4b}$$

Since $1 - \varphi > 0$, we have

$$\text{sgn}\left[\frac{dz}{dz^*}\right]_1 = \text{sgn}(\sigma_v^2+\sigma_{vv^*}), \qquad \text{sgn}\left[\frac{dz^*}{dz}\right]_2 = \text{sgn}(\sigma_{v^*}^2+\sigma_{vv^*}).$$

It is clear that these reaction functions will be upward sloping, certainly as long as the supply shocks are non-negatively correlated. However, in the case where the supply shocks are strongly negatively correlated, it is possible for one, but not both, reaction functions to be downward sloping. The intuition remains as under flexible exchange rates.

Solving this pair of equations yields a unique non-cooperative pair of indexation parameters z, z^*. Qualitatively the results remain essentially as under flexible exchange rates. If the only disturbance is a worldwide demand shock, this calls for full indexation in both economies. If the supply disturbances are specific to Country 1, then Country 2 should index fully, setting $z^* = 0$, while Country 1 should index partially in accordance with

$$z = \frac{(1-\varphi)\delta_1\delta_2\sigma_v^2}{\varphi\delta_2^2\sigma_{v^*}^2 + a^2\alpha_2^2\sigma_u^2}. \tag{3.5}$$

Comparing (3.5) with (2.8b) we find that indexation in Country 1 under flexible exchange rates may be greater than or less than indexation under fixed exchange rates, depending upon the relative variances σ_v^2 and σ_u^2.

With supply shocks in both economies, then partial indexation in both economies is appropriate.

3.2 Cooperative Equilibrium

As before, the cooperative equilibrium, where joint welfare costs are being minimised, is described by

$$\frac{\partial W}{\partial z} \equiv \frac{\partial \Omega}{\partial z} + \frac{\partial \Omega^*}{\partial z} = 0, \tag{3.6a}$$

$$\frac{\partial W}{\partial z^*} \equiv \frac{\partial \Omega}{\partial z^*} + \frac{\partial \Omega^*}{\partial z^*} = 0, \tag{3.6b}$$

leading to a pair of equations in z, z^* directly analogous to (2.10a) and (2.10b), with $a^P(.)$ replacing $a^F(.)$, etc. Evaluating the resulting expressions, the following relationships can be established:

$$\frac{\partial \Omega}{\partial z} = -2(\delta_1+\delta_2 z^*)\frac{\Phi}{\Delta_p^3}, \qquad \frac{\partial \Omega}{\partial z^*} = 2\delta_2 z\frac{\Phi}{\Delta_p^3}, \tag{3.7a}$$

$$\frac{\partial \Omega^*}{\partial z^*} = -2(\delta_1+\delta_2 z)\frac{\Phi^*}{\Delta_p^3}, \qquad \frac{\partial \Omega^*}{\partial z} = 2\delta_2 z^*\frac{\Phi^*}{\Delta_p^3}, \tag{3.7b}$$

where

$$\Delta_p \equiv \delta_1 + \delta_2(z+z^*) > 0,$$

$$\Phi \equiv \delta_2[(\delta_1+\delta_2 z^*)(1-\varphi) - \varphi\delta_2 z]\sigma_v^2 - z\delta_2^2\sigma_{v^*}^2$$
$$+ \delta_2[(\delta_1+\delta_2 z^*)(1-\varphi) - \delta_2(1+\varphi)z]\sigma_{vv^*} - a^2\alpha_2^2 z\sigma_u^2,$$

$$\Phi^* \equiv -z^*\delta_2^2\sigma_v^2 + \delta_2[(\delta_1+\delta_2 z)(1-\varphi) - \varphi\delta_2 z^*]\sigma_{v^*}^2$$
$$+ \delta_2[(\delta_1+\delta_2 z)(1-\varphi) - \delta_2 z^*(1+\varphi)]\sigma_{vv^*} - a^2\alpha_2^2 z^*\sigma_u^2.$$

With this notation, the non-cooperative equilibrium can be written as

$$\Phi = 0, \tag{3.8a}$$

$$\Phi^* = 0, \tag{3.8b}$$

while the cooperative equilibrium becomes

$$-(\delta_1+\delta_2 z^*)\Phi + \delta_2 z^*\Phi^* = 0, \tag{3.9a}$$

$$\delta_2 z\Phi - (\delta_1+\delta_2 z)\Phi^* = 0. \tag{3.9b}$$

Subtracting these last two equations leads to

$$(\Phi^* - \Phi)\Delta_p = 0$$

and, since $\Delta_p \neq 0$, this last equation implies

$$\Phi = \Phi^*.$$

Setting $\Phi = \Phi^*$ in the cooperative equilibrium, (3.9a) and (3.9b) reduce to

$$\Phi = 0 = \Phi^*,$$

which is precisely the non-cooperative equilibrium.

Hence we obtain the proposition that under a fixed exchange rate regime, the unique cooperative and non-cooperative equilibria coincide, both being given by the solutions to the linear equations (3.4a), (3.4b). Under such an exchange rate system, when the policy-maker acts as a non-cooperative Nash agent and optimises independently with respect to his own rate of wage indexation, setting $\partial\Omega/\partial z = 0$, at the same time he succeeds in eliminating the impact of the foreign wage indexation on his welfare, i.e. $\partial\Omega/\partial z^* = 0$, as well. With the externality caused by foreign wages policy thereby eliminated, there are no further gains from cooperation on wage indexation. In other words, cooperating by fixing the exchange rate, eliminates any further gains from cooperating on wages policy.

The equilibrium is illustrated in Figure 2, where the point of intersection A of the reaction functions is the non-cooperative outcome. The slopes of the indifference curves for Country 1, say, are given by

$$\frac{dz}{dz^*} = \frac{\delta_2 z}{\delta_1 + \delta_2 z^*}$$

and consist of a family of straight lines. The cooperative equilibrium occurs where these pass through the point A.

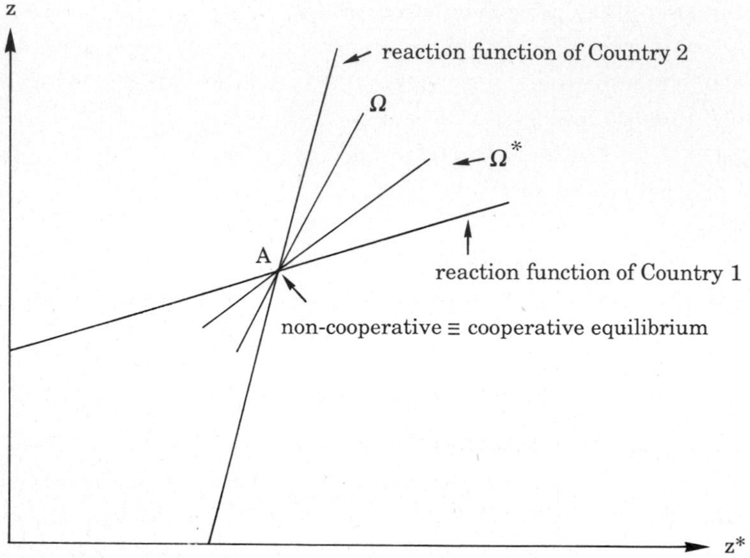

Figure 2: Non-cooperative and cooperative equilibria: fixed exchange rate

4. Numerical Analysis

While we have been able to characterise the optimal solutions for indexation in some detail, they remain complex functions of the underlying parameters of the model. To gain further insights into the general welfare implication of the different strategic equilibria under the different exchange rate regimes, we resort to numerical analysis.

Table 1 lists the set of parameter values underlying our numerical work. These have been chosen on the basis of reasonable empirical evidence. Specifically, the elasticity of demand for world output with respect to actual world output $d_1 = 0.65$; the semi-elasticity of the demand for real output with respect to the real interest rate, $2d_2 = 0.5$; the income elasticity of the demand for money $\alpha_1 = 1$; the semi-elasticity of the demand for money with respect to the nominal interest rate $\alpha_2 = 0.5$; the capital share in total output produced by the underlying production function $\vartheta = 0.4$ implying $a = 1.5$; and the elasticity of the supply of labour with respect to the expected real wage is $n = 0.15$.

Although these base parameters seem plausible and are similar to values chosen for other simulation studies of this kind, they are nevertheless arbitrary[13]. In view of this we have varied the parameter values quite widely, although these other cases are not reported.

Table 1: Base parameter set

d_1	= 0.65
d_2	= 0.25
α_1	= 1.00
α_2	= 0.5
ϑ	= 0.4 (i.e. a = 1.5)
n	= 0.15

Table 2 considers the non-cooperative and cooperative equilibria for both: (i) a perfectly flexible exchange rate and (ii) a fixed exchange rate, under alternative assumptions regarding the variances of the demand and supply disturbances. As a base case we normalise these variances to be 25. However, other larger values are also considered. Some of the results reported in Table 2 are simply numerical verifications of the formal propositions obtained in previous sections. Other cases offer further insights, not apparent from the formal analysis. And in all cases, some notions of the relative magnitudes involved are obtained.

In case (i) where the domestic supply shock is the only disturbance, perfect stabilisation about the frictionless level of output is possible, with the implied minimum welfare costs being zero. This is because each economy is experiencing only a single disturbance and given that the stabilisation authority setting the degree of wage indexation observes the current price level, he can from this information infer this disturbance exactly, and therefore achieve perfect stability. Since the domestic supply shock manifests itself in the foreign economy as a demand shock, this calls for full indexation abroad, but only partial, and for this parameter set, a very low degree of wage indexation domestically.

Table 2: Non-cooperative and cooperative equilibria for perfectly flexible and fixed exchange rates

	σ_v^2	σ_{v*}^2	ρ	σ_u^2		Perfectly Flexible Exchange Rate					Fixed Exchange Rate			
						τ	τ^*	Ω	Ω^*		τ	τ^*	Ω	Ω^*
(i)	25	0	0	0	N≡C	.0338	1	0	0	N≡C	-.5345	1	0	0
(ii)	25	25	0	0	N:	.0258	.0258	.1071	.1071	N≡C	.2327	.2327	4.0049	4.0049
					C:	-.0150	-.0150	.1047	.1047					
(iii)	25	25	1	0	N≡C	.2327	.2327	0	0	N≡C	.2327	.2327	0	0
(iv)	25	0	0	25	N:	.5733	1	2.8378	0	N≡C	.6337	1	4.6501	0
					C:	.5733	.9779	2.8175	.0100					
(v)	25	25	0	25	N:	.5368	.5368	2.6536	2.6536	N≡C	.7042	.7042	5.6430	5.6430
					C:	.5027	.5027	2.6449	2.6449					
(vi)	25	25	1	25	N≡C	.5731	.5731	2.0591	2.0591	N≡C	.5731	.5731	2.0591	2.0591
(vii)	25	0	0	50	N:	.7261	1	4.1909	0	N≡C	.7920	1	5.8842	0
					C:	.7261	.9883	4.1790	.0059					
(viii)	50	0	0	25	N:	.4080	1	3.4488	0	N≡C	.4085	1	6.5521	0
					C:	.4080	.9667	3.4043	.0218					
(ix)	25	25	0	50	N:	.7047	.7047	4.0329	4.0329	N≡C	.8168	.8168	6.3300	6.3300
					C:	.6867	.6867	4.0268	4.0268					
(x)	50	25	0	25	N:	.3683	.5344	3.1784	2.6516	N≡C	.5041	.7520	8.7117	6.1829
					C:	.3341	.4875	3.1529	2.6520					
(xi)	25	25	1	50	N≡C	.7042	.7042	3.2760	3.2760	N≡C	.7042	.7042	3.2760	3.2760
(xii)	50	25	1	25	N≡C	.4383	.5794	2.5429	1.9006	N≡C	.4190	.5891	3.0742	1.5371

Furthermore, with the number of policy instruments equal to the number of disturbances, the strategic problem degenerates and all equilibria coincide.

Cases (ii) and (iii) introduce simultaneous supply shocks in the two economies. In (ii) they are uncorrelated and are therefore country-specific. For this parameter set extremely low indexation is required and in the case of flexible exchange rates, the non-cooperative equilibrium leads to overindexation relative to the cooperative equilibrium. In the latter, negative indexation is optimal. This is a consequence largely of the low value of n = 0.15, assumed, and which is not inconsistent with available empirical evidence[14]. In this case, the frictionless economy responds relatively little to productivity shocks. Real wages must move more strongly countercyclically to the shocks to prevent output in the contract economy from rising too much and this requires overindexation of wages. Under fixed exchange rates, the non-cooperative and cooperative equilibria coincide, as we have shown they must. Case (iii), in which the supply disturbances impinge equally on the two economies and are perfectly correlated, describes a worldwide supply shock. In this case, each country is in effect facing a single shock, which can be fully inferred from observed price movements, so that the optimal indexation leads to perfect stability.

Cases (iv) - (vi) introduce demand disturbances having equal variance to supply disturbances. In all instances this increases the optimal degree of wage indexation. In cases (iv) and (v) there are now two independent disturbances facing each economy, so that perfect stabilisation is not possible with a single policy instrument. The comparison of the non-cooperative and cooperative equilibria in (iv) illustrates one of our previous results: namely, the domestic economy should maintain its non-cooperative equilibrium level of indexation, while the foreign economy should no longer index fully. While this adjustment leads to a small increase in welfare costs for the foreign economy, it leads to greater welfare improvements for the domestic economy, with potential overall welfare gains. Case (v) illustrates the example of overindexation under flexible rates in both economies, with modest gains to both countries to be obtained from cooperation.

The remaining six cases vary the relative magnitudes of the demand and supply disturbances and need no explicit comment.

Viewing the table as a whole, we can make the following general observations.

(i) In the case of flexible exchange rates, the welfare gains in going from the non-cooperative to the cooperative equilibrium are extremely small. We have evaluated these gains over a wide range of parameter sets and find this to be invariably the case. This finding is generally consistent with the small gains from cooperation typically found with respect to monetary policy in models of this type[15]. The reason for this stems from the fact that the effects of the various shocks on output in each economy are dominated by that country's indexation, rather than the indexation being pursued abroad. In other words, the degree of interaction between the policy instruments is small, so that there are relatively small gains from international cooperation[16].

(ii) The comparison of fixed and flexible exchange rates indicates that in general, with optimal indexation, the flexible rate regime is superior to the fixed. This is analogous to the findings of Flood and Marion (1982) for the small open economy. The optimal degree of indexation under flexible exchange rates can be either greater or less than under fixed exchange rate, depending upon the relative magnitudes of the disturbances. In case (xii) where the perfectly correlated supply shock has a larger variance domestically, the domestic economy should index more under flexible exchange rates, while the foreign economy should index more under fixed exchange rates.

(iii) In the case where the supply shocks are of equal variances and perfectly correlated (a worldwide supply shock), cases (iii), (vi), (xi), the optimal degrees of wage indexation under non-cooperative and cooperative behaviour and fixed and flexible exchange rates all coincide. To see this, we may note that, in general, the solution for the exchange rate under flexible exchange rates is given by the expression

$$E_t = \frac{\frac{1}{a} X_1[zv_t^*-z^*v_t] + 2\alpha_1 \frac{d_2}{\alpha_2} X_6(v_t^*-v_t) + X_5(z^*-z)u_t}{X_1 zz^* + X_2(z+z^*) + X_3},$$

which depends in part upon differentials in the supply disturbances and in part upon differentials in indexation policy. In the case of a worldwide supply shock $v = v^*$ (accompanied by a possible worldwide demand shock), symmetry makes it clear that the optimal indexation will be identical for the two economies ($z = z^*$). In this case, even in a potentially flexible exchange rate regime, the optimal indexation will ensure that the exchange rate will in fact be fixed. The two exchange rate regimes will therefore coincide. The further result that there are no gains from cooperation under flexible exchange rates follows from the fact that this is so under fixed exchange rates.

5. Monetary Policy as an Alternative

The model we have been considering has analysed wage indexation in the absence of monetary disturbances. Under these conditions, we can show that, provided the monetary authorities in each economy can observe, say, their respective domestic price levels and interest rates, then monetary policy is not only superior to wage indexation, but can stabilise output perfectly. Specifically, suppose that the money stocks in the two economies are adjusted in accordance with the rules

$$M = \left(1 - \frac{\alpha_1 az\varphi}{1-\varphi}\right)P - \alpha_2 R, \qquad (5.1a)$$

$$M^* = \left(1 - \frac{\alpha_1 az\varphi}{1-\varphi}\right)P^* - \alpha_2 R^*. \qquad (5.1b)$$

According to these rules, the monetary authority in each economy should contract the money supply in response to an increase in the domestic interest rate, by an amount equal to the elasticity of demand $\alpha_2 R$, while it should accommodate to an increase in the domestic price level, though less than proportionately[17]. Such a rule will generate an excess supply of money

$$-\alpha_1\left[\frac{az\varphi}{1-\varphi} P + Y\right]$$

and for the money market equilibrium to be maintained, the domestic price level and output must move to satisfy

$$\frac{az\varphi}{1 - \varphi} P + Y = 0. \qquad (5.2)$$

Now, with stationary expectations, and with $\tilde{Y} = \varphi v_t$, the aggregate supply function (1.5a) may be written as

$$Y = azP + v = azP + \frac{\tilde{Y}}{\varphi}. \tag{5.3}$$

Combining equations (5.2) and (5.3), we see that

$$Y = \tilde{Y} \tag{5.4}$$

and the same applies abroad.

In other words, the simple monetary rules, (5.1a), (5.1b), generate price movements such that output in each economy will exactly track that of the corresponding frictionless economy. No cooperation is required and the degree of indexation can be arbitrary. Observe that the higher the degree of indexation (the smaller z), the more sensitive money policy must be, in response to price movements. This is because with higher indexation, real wages are less flexible in bringing about changes in output, thereby increasing the scope for monetary intervention.

Are we to conclude that wage indexation is an inappropriate instrument for stabilisation policy? Not at all. The superiority of monetary policy in the present example depends critically upon the absence of all stochastic disturbances from the monetary sector. This assumption was made purely for convenience and for the following reason. Since all forms of demand disturbances, irrespective of origin, call for full indexation, and since the interesting comparison insofar as indexation is concerned is between demand and supply disturbances, the demand disturbances were made as simple as possible in order to focus on this dichotomy. It is clear that a model having disturbances in: (i) output demand, (ii) money demand, and (iii) supply, will assign a non-redundant role to wage indexation.

6. Conclusion

This paper has analysed wage indexation policies in a strategic context. The results are extremely simple to summarise.

Under flexible exchange rates, increased wage indexation typically generates a negative externality abroad, with the result that the Nash non-cooperative equilibrium typically leads to overindexation relative to the Pareto-optimal cooperative equilibrium. Under fixed exchange rates, the retaliatory action of the foreign economy is able to eliminate these externalities, in which case the non-cooperative and cooperative equilibria coincide.

Based on our numerical calculations it appears that the gains from cooperation under flexible exchange rates are extremely small (while of course they have shown to be zero under fixed rates). In terms of the comparison of fixed versus flexible exchange rates, our results suggest that for the demand and supply shocks we consider, flexible exchange rates are superior in the sense of yielding lower welfare costs, by a substantial margin. This finding is consistent with previous results obtained for the small open economy. Overall, our results, together with the previous results obtained using this type of model to analyse monetary cooperation, suggest that there is little to be gained from cooperating either on monetary or wages policies. A system of flexible exchange rates, with each country pursuing its own independent wages policy will lead to a reasonable outcome.

Of course the simplicity of the present model should not be overlooked and several directions for extension suggest themselves. Firstly, the assumption of a single traded commodity is obviously restrictive. Relaxing this assumption may assign a more critical role to demand shocks. Secondly, the symmetry of the economies, both in structure and in objectives, may tend to bias the results in favour of non-cooperative behaviour. Thirdly, a consideration of more general types of disturbances, such as permanent shocks, may be of interest. Finally, the interaction of wage indexation with monetary policy, and the optimal coordination of these policies, is an important topic for further analysis.

Notes

* The authors are grateful to the discussant Theo van de Klundert and a reviewer for their helpful comments.

1. See Simonsen (1983) and Fischer (1984).

2. See Emerson (1983).

3. The assumption of symmetric economies, although obviously restrictive, is typical of the two-country policy coordination literature; see, e.g., the papers in Buiter and Marston (1985).

4. In principle, the case of overindexation $\tau > 1$, $\tau^* > 1$, ($z < 0$, $z^* < 0$) cannot be ruled out. However, since it never arises in any of our numerical simulations, we do not consider it.

5. For a derivation of the aggregate supply function along these lines, see, e.g., Turnovsky (1987).

6. The exclusion of monetary shocks involves no essential loss of generality, insofar as indexation policy is concerned. This is because they influence output through price fluctuations in the supply function in precisely the same way as does the world aggregate demand shock u. No new margin of impact is added.

7. The welfare justification for this in terms of appropriate surplus triangles is given by Aizenman and Frenkel (1985).

8. We should draw attention to the parallel between what is being done in this paper, namely choosing indexation strategies z, z*, in response to observed price movements, and Buiter and Eaton (1985), who consider optimal exchange rate management rules in a two-country setting, conditional on observed movements in the current exchange rate.

9. The reaction functions will be positively sloped as long as the supply shocks are non-negatively correlated.

10. The fact that the product of the three roots to this cubic equation is positive implies that there is either one or three positive roots. A sufficient condition for a unique positive solution for z is that $\varphi > \frac{1}{3}$, since in that case the sum of the roots will be negative. For $\varphi < \frac{1}{3}$, the possibility of three positive roots arises. For the base parameter set used in the numerical work, $\varphi = 0.43 > \frac{1}{3}$, so the solution is unique.

11. By direct evaluation we can show

$$\frac{aX_4}{X_1z + X_2} - \frac{(X_1z^*+X_2)}{aX_4} > 0 \qquad \frac{a(X_5z+X_6)}{X_1z + X_2} + \frac{X_5z^* + X_6}{X_4} < 0.$$

12. For further discussion of this point see Turnovsky and d'Orey (1986).

13. See, e.g., the numerical studies in Buiter and Marston (1985).

14. Our choice of n = 0.15 is based in part on empirical estimates obtained by MaCurdy (1981).

15. See, e.g., Oudiz and Sachs (1985) and Turnovsky and d'Orey (1986).

16. More formally one can consider this by evaluating the relative effects of indexation.

17. Since M is in logarithms and R is in natural units, the coefficient α_2 is a semi-elasticity. The corresponding interest elasticity is $\alpha_2 R$.

References

Aizenman, J. and J.A. Frenkel, 'Optimal wage indexation, exchange market intervention and monetary policy', American Economic Review, 75, 1985, pp. 402-423.

Aizenman, J. and J.A. Frenkel, 'Supply shocks, wage indexation and monetary accommodation', Journal of Money, Credit and Banking, 19, 1986, pp. 304-322.

Buiter, W.H. and J. Eaton, 'Policy decentralization and exchange rate management', in J.S. Bhandari (ed.), Exchange Rate Management under Uncertainty, MIT Press, Cambridge, MA, 1985.

Buiter, W.H. and R. Marston (eds), International Economic Policy Coordination, Cambridge University Press, Cambridge, U.K., 1985.

Emerson, M., 'A view of current European indexation experiences', in R. Dornbusch and M. Simonsen (eds), Inflation, Debt and Indexation, MIT Press, Cambridge, MA, 1983.

Fischer, S., 'Wage indexation and macroeconomic stability', in K. Brunner and A. Meltzer (eds), Stabilization of the Domestic and International Economy, Carnegie-Rochester Conference Series, 5, North-Holland, Amsterdam, 1977.

Fischer, S., 'The economy of Israel', in K. Brunner and A. Meltzer (eds), Monetary and Fiscal Policies and Their Applications, Carnegie-Rochester Conference Series, 20, North-Holland, Amsterdam, 1984.

Flood, R. and N. Marion, 'The transmission of disturbances under alternative exchange rate regimes with optimal indexing', Quarterly Journal of Economics, 97, 1982, pp. 43-66.

Gray, J.A., 'Wage indexation: a macroeconomic approach', Journal of Monetary Economics, 2, 1976, pp. 225-235.

MaCurdy, T.E., 'An empirical model of labor supply in a life-cycle setting', Journal of Political Economy, 89, 1981, pp. 1059-1085.

Marston, R.C., 'Real wages and the terms of trade: alternative indexing rules for an open economy', Journal of Money, Credit and Banking, 16, 1984, pp. 285-301.

Oudiz, G. and J. Sachs, 'International policy coordination in dynamic macroeconomic models', in W. Buiter and R. Marston (eds), International Economic Policy Coordination, Cambridge University Press, Cambridge, U.K., 1985.

Simonsen, M.H., 'Indexation: current theory and the Brazilian experience', in R. Dornbusch and M. Simonsen (eds), Inflation, Debt and Indexation, MIT Press, Cambridge, MA, 1983.

Turnovsky, S.J., 'Wage indexation and exchange market intervention in a small open economy', Canadian Journal of Economics, 16, 1983, pp. 574-592.

Turnovsky, S.J., 'Optimal monetary policy and wage indexation under alternative disturbances and information structures', Journal of Money, Credit and Banking, 19, 1987, pp. 157-180.

Turnovsky, S.J. and V. d'Orey, 'Monetary policies in interdependent economies with stochastic disturbances: a strategic approach', Economic Journal, 96, 1986, pp. 696-721.

Dynamic Policy Games in Economics
F. van der Ploeg and A.J. de Zeeuw, (Editors)

OPTIMAL CHOICE OF MONETARY POLICY INSTRUMENTS IN A SIMPLE TWO-COUNTRY GAME*

Matthew B. Canzoneri

Department of Economics
Georgetown University
Washington DC 20057, USA

Dale W. Henderson

Department of Economics
Georgetown University
Washington DC 20057, USA,
Board of Governors of the
Federal Reserve System and the
National Bureau of Economic Research

Introduction

In a justly celebrated article, Poole (1970) asked whether a rational policy-maker would choose the interest rate or the money supply as his instrument of monetary policy. Poole's answer is well known: if the policy-maker is sure of private sector behaviour, he will be indifferent about the choice of an instrument; the policy-maker faces the same tradeoff between target variables no matter which instrument he selects. If, however, the policy-maker is uncertain about supplies of or demands for goods and money, and views them as random variables at the time he must act, then he will not be indifferent about the choice of an instrument; the probability distribution of target variables depends upon the instrument he selects.

Poole's analysis was conducted in a closed economy with a fixed fiscal policy. There was only one policy-maker, the monetary authority, and Poole's problem was that of a single controller. If we extend his analysis by adding a fiscal policy-maker or foreign policy-makers with conflicting objectives, then we have a macroeconomic game. Policy-makers are not indifferent about their choice of instrument in a game situation, even if there is no uncertainty about private sector behaviour[1].

In this paper we ask which instrument a rational policy-maker would choose in a simple two-country game. The game is essentially a two-country version of the Barro and Gordon (1983) game; in each country, the policy-maker's inability to precommit with respect to the private sector results in an inflation bias. There is no uncertainty about private sector behaviour, but instrument selection matters because it is an important strategic consideration. Each policy-maker cares about inflation and employment, and while a policy-maker's choice of instrument does not affect his own inflation-employment tradeoff, it does affect his opponent's. Letting policy-makers choose both instruments and instrument values, we find that there are many Nash solutions to this game. If there are N instruments to choose from, there are N^2 Nash solutions.

The macroeconomic literature suggests that there may be a large number of instruments to choose from. Poole (1970) lets his policy-maker choose between the money supply, the interest rate, and a 'combination' policy (essentially a money supply curve). Barro and Gordon (1983) have their policy-maker set the inflation rate. Considering just these possibilities, we have four instruments and sixteen distinct Nash solutions.

This multiplicity of solutions is problematic; so we also want to ask whether there are ways in which some of the solutions can be eliminated. We consider three approaches. Firstly, one might argue on economic grounds that a variable such as the inflation rate cannot serve as an instrument. One might also argue that supply curves are not legitimate instruments. However, even if these arguments are accepted (and the latter is quite controversial), we are still left with interest rates and money supplies, and four Nash solutions. Secondly, we note that the policy-makers themselves prefer some of the outcomes to others; we suggest that certain institutions may help policy-makers coordinate upon the preferred solutions.

Finally, the work of Klemperer and Meyer (1986) has shown that even a little uncertainty of the Poole type may eliminate most of the solutions[2]. In most macroeconomic applications, policy-makers will face some uncertainty; leaving it out, perhaps for the sake of simplicity, may be a serious modelling error. This observation suggests that it would be very interesting to combine the original Poole view of instrument selection with the strategic view. With uncertainty about private sector behaviour, instrument selection would play both a strategic role and a stabilisation role, and we may be left with only one Nash solution.

The rest of the paper is divided into three sections. In Section 1 we outline a two-country version of the Barro and Gordon game, and we illustrate the four Nash solutions that result when policy-makers get to choose values for their interest rates or their money supplies. We also identify a certain fragility in the multiplicity of solutions. In Section 2 we illustrate the proliferation of solutions as we add inflation and Poole's combination policy to the list of instruments. We also discuss some of the consequences. In Section 3 we discuss three macroeconomic approaches to the multiplicity problem. One works on the fragility identified in Section 1.

1. The Money Supply versus the Interest Rate

We begin with a game in which the policy-maker in each country can choose a value for his money supply or his interest rate. We will see that there are four Nash solutions to this game[3]. But first, we must describe the model.

1.1 A Simple Two-country Model

The model is a simple extension of the one used in Canzoneri and Henderson (1988); therefore, our description can be brief. Each country produces one good and two assets, money and bonds. The goods are imperfect substitutes; the bonds are perfect substitutes; and the moneys are not traded internationally.

Production functions are given by

$$y = \bar{y} + (1-\alpha)n \quad \text{and} \quad y^* = \bar{y} + (1-\alpha)n^*, \tag{1.1}$$

where $\bar{y} \equiv \log[1/(1-\alpha)]$ and α is less than one[4]. All variables (except interest rates) are in logs. y and n are home output and employment. *'s denote foreign country variables. Units are defined so that the natural rate of employment is equal to zero (in logs) in each country; so, $\bar{y}$ is the natural rate of output in each country.

Profit maximising firms hire until the marginal product of labour equals the real product wage,

$$w - p = -\alpha n \quad \text{and} \quad w^* - p^* = -\alpha n^*. \tag{1.2}$$

w is the home nominal wage. p is the home currency price of the home good. We will explain how wages are set when we describe the game between policy-makers; for now, they are just fixed parameters.

Money markets are described by the Cambridge equations

$$m - p = y - \bar{y} \quad \text{and} \quad m^* - p^* = y^* - \bar{y}. \tag{1.3}$$

The log of velocity has been set equal to $\bar{y}$ in each country; this achieves some algebraic simplicity. m and m^* are the money supplies that may be chosen as instruments; if interest rates are chosen instead, then m and m^* become endogenous variables.

The consumer price indices, q and q^*, and the inflation rates, π and π^*, are given by

$$\begin{aligned} q &= .5p + .5(p^*+e) = p + .5z = \pi, \\ q^* &= .5p^* + .5(p-e) = p^* - .5z = \pi^*. \end{aligned} \tag{1.4}$$

e is the home currency price of foreign exchange, and $z \equiv p^* + e - p$ is the terms of trade. For algebraic simplicity, we have assumed that home and foreign goods have equal weight in consumers' market baskets. We have normalised on last period's price levels ($q_{-1} = q^*_{-1} = 0$); so, price levels and inflation rates are the same thing in the current period.

Demands for the two goods are given by

$$\begin{aligned} y &= \bar{y} + \delta z + .5\varepsilon[(y-\bar{y}) + (y^*-\bar{y})] - .5\nu(r+r^*), \\ y^* &= \bar{y} - \delta z + .5\varepsilon[(y-\bar{y}) + (y^*-\bar{y})] - .5\nu(r+r^*). \end{aligned} \tag{1.5}$$

These demands have been log-linearised around the natural rates of output. r and r^* are real rates of interest. The nominal interest rates, i and i^*, may be chosen as instruments; they are given by

$$i = r + (q_{+1}-q) = r + \pi_{+1} \quad \text{and} \quad i^* = r^* + (q^*_{+1}-q^*) = r^* + \pi^*_{+1}. \qquad (1.6)$$

Since home and foreign bonds are perfect substitutes,

$$i = i^* + (e_{+1}-e), \qquad (1.7)$$

and (1.6) and (1.7) imply that real interest rates equalise across countries.

The policy-makers care about inflation and employment, so we must solve the model for π, π^*, n and n^* (in terms of the instruments the policy-makers have selected) and calculate the inflation-employment tradeoffs, τ and τ^*. There are four possibilities. In an (m,m^*) equilibrium, both policy-makers choose money supplies as their instruments; so i and i^* are determined by the model. In an (i,i^*) equilibrium, i and i^* are the instruments; m and m^* are endogenous. The policy-makers need not make the same choice. In an (m,i^*) equilibrium, m and i^* are the instruments; and in an (i,m^*) equilibrium, i and m^* are the instruments. We describe these equilibria separately. In each case, we have set $(1-\varepsilon)/2\nu = 1$ and $(1-\alpha)/4\delta = 1$, for algebraic simplicity.

In an *(m,m^*) equilibrium*, the policy tradeoffs are given by

$$\pi = (1+\alpha)m - m^* - \alpha w + w^*, \qquad \pi^* = (1+\alpha)m^* - m - \alpha w^* + w,$$

$$n = m - w, \qquad n^* = m^* - w^*, \qquad (1.8)$$

$$\tau_{m^*} = (d\pi/dm)/(dn/dm) = 1 + \alpha, \qquad \tau^*_m = (d\pi^*/dm^*)/(dn^*/dm^*) = 1 + \alpha.$$

Home employment depends entirely upon home money (and the home wage); foreign monetary policy does not affect home employment. This is because we left the nominal interest rates out of home money demand and set the real income elasticity equal to one. Foreign monetary policy does affect home inflation. An increase in m^* increases foreign employment and output; this causes an excess supply of foreign goods, which is accommodated by a decrease in the relative price of foreign goods. At home, the price of imported goods falls, decreasing inflation. τ_{m^*} is the inflation-employment tradeoff faced by the home policy-maker when his opponent is fixing m^*.

The foreign reduced forms are symmetric to the home reduced forms. τ_m^* is the inflation-employment tradeoff faced by the foreign policy-maker when the home policy-maker is fixing m.

In an *(i,i*) equilibrium*, the policy tradeoffs are given by

$$\pi = -\Delta(2+\alpha)(i-q_{+1}) + \eta(i^*-q_{+1}^*) + \eta(w+w^*),$$

$$\pi^* = -\Delta(2+\alpha)(i^*-q_{+1}^*) + \eta(i-q_{+1}) + \eta(w^*+w),$$

$$n = -2\Delta(i-q_{+1}) - \alpha\Delta(i^*-q_{+1}^*) - 2w - \alpha\Delta w^*, \qquad (1.9)$$

$$n^* = -2\Delta(i^*-q_{+1}^*) - \alpha\Delta(i-q_{+1}) - 2w^* - \alpha\Delta w,$$

$$\tau_{i*} = (d\pi/di)/(dn/di) = 1 + .5\alpha,$$

$$\tau_i^* = (d\pi^*/di^*)/(dn^*/di^*) = 1 + .5\alpha,$$

where $\Delta \equiv 1/(4-\alpha^2)$ (> 0) and $\eta \equiv \Delta[2-(1+\alpha)\alpha]$ (> 0). Here, foreign monetary policy does spill over to home employment. To decrease i*, the foreign policy-maker must allow his money supply to grow. This causes an excess supply of foreign goods. Both the relative price of foreign goods and the real interest rate fall. The fall in foreign prices lowers home inflation, and in equation (1.6) this effect dominates; there is upward pressure on the home interest rate. Thus when the foreign policy-maker decreases i*, the home policy-maker must let m grow to keep i fixed, and this is expansionary at home.

The most important thing to note here is that the home policy-maker's inflation-employment tradeoff is flatter when the foreign policy-maker is fixing i*; that is, $\tau_{i*} < \tau_{m*}$. When the home policy-maker decreases i to increase employment, the foreign policy-maker must let m* grow to keep i* from rising. This increases the supply of foreign output, puts downward pressure on the relative price of foreign goods, and mitigates the home inflation.

Once again, the foreign reduced forms are symmetric to the home reduced forms. τ_i^* is the inflation-employment tradeoff faced by the foreign policy-maker when the home policy-maker is fixing i.

In an *(m,i*) equilibrium*, the policy tradeoffs are given by

$$\pi = (1+.5\alpha)m + .5(i^*-q^*_{+1}) - .5\alpha w + .5w^*,$$

$$\pi^* = -.5(1+\alpha)(i^*-q^*_{+1}) - 5(\eta/\Delta)m + .5(\eta/\Delta)w + .5(1-\alpha)w^*,$$

$$n = m - w, \tag{1.10}$$

$$n^* = -.5(i^*-q^*_{+1}) + .5\alpha m - .5(w+\alpha w^*),$$

$$\tau_{i*} = (d\pi/dm)/(dn/dm) = 1 + .5\alpha,$$

$$\tau^*_m = (d\pi^*/di^*)/(dn^*/di^*) = 1 + \alpha.$$

Here, the reduced forms are, of course, asymmetric. An (m,i^*) solution mixes elements of the (m,m^*) and (i,i^*) equilibria. Foreign monetary policy does not affect home employment, but home expansion increases foreign employment, because the foreign policy-maker has to let m^* grow to keep i^* fixed.

An *(i,m^*) equilibrium* is completely symmetric to an (m,i^*) equilibrium. One simply interchanges the home and foreign variables.

The important thing to note here is that a policy-maker's choice of instrument does not affect his own inflation-employment tradeoff, but it does affect his opponent's. No matter which instrument he chooses, the home policy-maker faces the steep tradeoff, $\tau_{m*} = 1 + \alpha$, when the foreign policy-maker fixes m^*. And no matter which instrument he chooses, the home policy-maker faces the flat tradeoff, $\tau_{i*} = 1 + .5\alpha$, when the foreign policy-maker fixes i^*.

Now we can see why Poole's observations about a single controller do not apply to a Nash game player. Suppose the foreign policy-maker's actions were somehow set beforehand. The home policy-maker's inflation-employment tradeoff would be fixed; absent uncertainty, he would be indifferent about instrument selection. This is Poole's result. However, in a Nash game situation the foreign policy-maker's play is not fixed beforehand; the home policy-maker may be able to elicit a favourable tradeoff via strategic instrument selection and its effect on his opponent's tradeoff.

1.2 The Two-country Game

The game we use to illustrate the instrument selection problem focuses upon the observations just made, and the focus may be too sharp. Each player's payoff will depend entirely upon the slope of his inflation-employment tradeoff, and thus the instrument chosen by his opponent; in this respect, the game we have chosen is quite special.

The game is based on a two-country version of Barro and Gordon's (1983) inflation bias model. The policy-makers' utility functions are

$$U = -\sigma(n-\bar{n})^2 - \pi^2 \quad \text{and} \quad U^* = -\sigma(n^*-\bar{n}^*)^2 - \pi^{*2}. \tag{1.11}$$

They would like zero inflation and positive employment rates, $\bar{n}$ and $\bar{n}^*$. Agents in the private sector want zero employment rates (in logs), and they set the nominal wages, w and w*, to achieve their goals. Why do policy-makers want higher employment rates than the wage setters? In Barro and Gordon (1983) and the literature that followed, several answers have been given: income taxes may distort the labour-leisure decision, making the 'natural rate' of employment too low, or monopolistic forces in the labour market may seek real wages that are too high for employment of the entire labour force. In either case, $\bar{n}$ and $\bar{n}^*$ represent fixed distortions. The policy-makers can do nothing to affect them.

Wage setters get their way in this game. They know the policy-makers' utility functions; so they can set wage inflation just high enough that the policy-makers will give them the employment rates they want. More precisely, letting x and x* be the instruments the policy-makers have chosen, the wage setters can calculate the policy-makers' first order conditions,

$$\begin{aligned} U_x &= -2\sigma(n-\bar{n})\frac{dn}{dx} - 2(\pi)\frac{d\pi}{dx} = 0, \\ U^*_{x^*} &= -2\sigma(n^*-\bar{n}^*)\frac{dn^*}{dx^*} - 2(\pi^*)\frac{d\pi^*}{dx^*} = 0, \end{aligned} \tag{1.12}$$

and they can set π and π^* (via their choices of w and w*) high enough that the policy-makers will want to set n and n* equal to zero.

Setting n and n* equal to zero in (1.12), we can calculate the inflation rates imposed by the wage setters in each country,

$$\pi = \sigma\bar{n}/\tau_{x*} \quad \text{and} \quad \pi^* = \sigma\bar{n}^*/\tau^*_x, \tag{1.13}$$

where $\tau_{x*} \equiv (d\pi/dx)/(dn/dx)$ and $\tau^*_x \equiv (d\pi^*/dx^*)/(dn^*/dx^*)$. If the inflation-employment tradeoff is flat, wage setters have to impose a high inflation rate to get their way; if the tradeoff is steep, a low inflation rate will do.

The resulting utilities (or payoffs) for the policy-makers are

$$U = -\sigma\bar{n}^2 - (\sigma\bar{n}/\tau_{x*})^2 \quad \text{and} \quad U^* = -\sigma\bar{n}^{*2} - (\sigma\bar{n}^*/\tau^*_x)^2. \tag{1.14}$$

As stated above, each policy-maker's payoff depends entirely upon his inflation-employment tradeoff, a tradeoff imposed on him by his opponent's choice of instrument. The payoff does not even depend upon the value of his opponent's instrument, just on the instrument itself[5].

We can thus measure the policy-makers' payoffs by τ_{x*} and τ^*_x. A steeper tradeoff leads to a lower inflation rate and to higher utility. The payoffs for the four equilibria described in Subsection 1.1 are given in the matrix below. It will be recalled that $\tau_{m*} = \tau^*_m > \tau_{i*} = \tau^*_i$.

foreign country

home country	m^*	i^*
m	τ_{m*}, τ^*_m	τ_{i*}, τ^*_m
i	τ_{m*}, τ^*_i	τ_{i*}, τ^*_i

All four equilibria $-(m,m^*)$, (m,i^*), (i,m^*) and $(i,i^*)-$ are Nash solutions to the game in which policy-makers choose values for either their money supply or their interest rate. Consider, for example, the solution (m,i^*), represented by the box in the north-east corner. If the foreign policy-maker chooses i^* as his instrument, the home policy-maker is indifferent between choosing m and i: he gets τ_{i*} either way. Since he can do no better by choosing i, (m,i^*) is a Nash solution. In a similar manner, the other three boxes can also be shown to be Nash solutions[6].

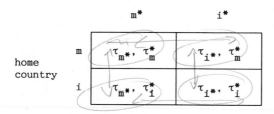

It is interesting to note that there is a certain fragility to this multiplicity of solutions; this observation will be relevant to our discussion in Section 3. Consider once again the solution (m,i*). The home policy-maker is indifferent between choosing m and i as his instrument, but he must actually choose m if (m,i*) is to be a solution. If the game structure were somehow altered so that the home policy-maker had even a slight preference for i, then (m,i*) would no longer be a Nash solution.

2. The Great Multiplicity of Potential Nash Solutions and Its Consequences

Are the money supply and the interest rate the only instruments the policy-makers have to choose from? The macroeconomic literature suggests that there may be many more choices. Barro and Gordon (1983) let their policy-maker set the inflation rate directly. Poole (1970) suggests that policy-makers can choose supply curves: his 'combination' policy is a money supply curve on the interest rate.

We can calculate the inflation-employment tradeoffs imposed by these instrument selections, and we can compare them to the tradeoffs discussed in the last section:

$$\begin{aligned} \tau_{\pi*} &= \tau^*_{\pi} = 1 + \left[2 - \frac{2}{\alpha(1+\alpha)}\right](1/2)\alpha \\ &< \tau_{i*} = \tau^*_{i} = 1 + (1/2)\alpha \\ &< \tau_{\varphi*} = \tau^*_{\varphi} = 1 + (2/3)\alpha \\ &< \tau_{m*} = \tau^*_{m} = 1 + \alpha, \end{aligned} \tag{2.1}$$

where φ is the choice parameter in Poole's combination policy[7].

We can construct a four by four payoff matrix and show that there are now sixteen Nash solutions to our game. The money supply produces the smallest inflation biases; Barro and Gordon's inflation rate produces the biggest inflation biases.

Is there any reason to stop here? We might consider Taylor's (1985) 'accommodative' policy, which is a money supply curve on the price level instead of the interest rate. We might also combine the Poole and Taylor policies and consider a money supply curve on both the interest rate and the price level. We might further consider any endogenous variable or any money supply curve on any combination of the endogenous variables as a potential instrument. Are there any restrictions that we ought to place on the set of instruments? If not, we will indeed obtain a very large set of Nash solutions. We will return to this question in Section 3.

Before going on, however, we would like to make some observations. There is a growing macroeconomic literature that uses the game-theoretic approach. Almost universally, the game analyst chooses the instruments; game players choose values for their pre-assigned instruments. Instruments are often chosen on the basis of analytical convenience, and there is a wide diversity of instruments used in the literature[8].

Our first observation is that there is no reason for the results of various studies to be consistent, or even comparable, if the analysts have chosen different instruments. As we have seen, the same game has many solutions if the instruments are chosen arbitrarily.

Our second (and related) observation is about attempts to assess the empirical relevance of this growing literature. Are the inefficiencies of Nash solutions big enough for us to force policy-makers to give up their sovereignty and to 'cooperate' with one another? Can the Barro-Gordon model of inflation bias explain the periods of high inflation various countries have experienced? The literature's answers to such questions may be biased by the analyst's choice of instruments. For example, we have shown that the size of the Barro-Gordon inflation bias may depend crucially upon the instruments being used at the time[9].

3. Reducing the Multiplicity of Solutions

Multiple solutions are the bane of modern game theory. Indeed, much of the current research in game theory is motivated by this problem. We will not attempt to extend this theoretical literature; rather, we will proceed in a direction in which we may have some comparative advantage. We will ask whether macroeconomic applications themselves suggest any resolution of the problem.

We take three different approaches to this question. Firstly, we ask whether in the real world players have already found a way to coordinate upon the better equilibria. Secondly, we ask whether there are restrictions that ought to be placed on the set of admissable instruments. Since the number of solutions goes up with the square of the number of instruments, this seems a profitable approach to pursue. And finally, we ask whether the multiplicity of solutions will survive in more realistic game structures; for example, Klemperer and Meyer (1986) have shown that adding uncertainty will reduce the number of solutions significantly in duopoly games.

3.1 Coordinating on Efficient Nash Solutions

In the game in Section 1, the (m,m*) solution is (weakly) preferred to the other three by both policy-makers. Have policy-makers found some way to coordinate themselves on the better Nash solutions? In Canzoneri and Henderson (1988), we suggest that supranational institutions like the IMF and the OECD provide a forum in which sovereign policy-makers may be able to do just that. Indeed, since the demise of the Bretton Woods system, this may be the major reason for these institutions' existence. In international macroeconomic applications, the multiplicity problem may already have found an institutional resolution[10].

3.2 Restricting the Set of Instruments

It was suggested in Section 2 that a policy-maker might use virtually any variable in the model as an instrument, or any money supply curve. We think that it is possible to rule out some variables on economic grounds, and the use of supply curves raises serious methodological issues. One could argue that interest rates and money supplies are the only true instruments in the game described above.

Policy-makers can be identified with the markets in which they intervene. If a policy-maker is 'big' in his own market, he can set either the price or the quantity transacted. If our monetary policy-maker intervenes in the market for short-term government bonds, then it seems clear that the interest rate on short-term government bonds is a valid instrument; the policy-maker can peg this rate by announcing that he will buy or sell government bonds at an appropriate price. To conclude that 'the' interest rate in a simple macroeconomic model is a valid instrument is another matter; however, one may be able to appeal to a term structure argument. It may be reasonable to include the interest rate and a monetary aggregate in the set of instruments for most macroeconomic games.

Can variables in other markets (markets in which the policy-maker does not intervene) serve as instruments? In a world of perfect certainty, it may be reasonable to assume that a 'big' player can set the value of any variable in any market by imposing the appropriate price (or quantity) in his own market. However, a macroeconomic policy-maker does not live in a world of perfect certainty, whether or not the uncertainty is modelled explicitly; he cannot calculate the appropriate price to be set in his own market.

It is sometimes argued that a policy-maker can observe 'indicators' of variables in other markets while those markets are actually clearing. Using these indicators, a monetary policy-maker might be able to find the money supply that pegs the rate of inflation, or output. Similarly, the policy-maker might be able to use the indicators to play a supply curve. The monetary policy-maker may be able to peg a money-interest rate pair along some fixed schedule, or a money-inflation pair.

There are two potential problems with the indicator approach. The first is that the indicators may not actually be available to allow it to be practiced. One might question whether information about real variables or the aggregate price level comes in quickly enough for these variables to be used as instruments or in supply curves; money-interest rate supply curves might avoid this problem.

The second problem is a methodological one. Some game theorists object to the indicator approach on the same grounds that they object to conjectural variations. If one player is reacting to information about an endogenous variable or another player's instrument setting, then they argue that the game should be modelled as a sequence of moves. The result of the correctly specified extensive form game may not be the supply curve Nash solution; indeed, there may be no extensive form game that results in the supply curve Nash solution.

We see merit in this argument, but we also note that supply curve solutions and conjectural variation solutions remain popular in the industrial organisation literature[11]. This does appear to be a methodological issue, albeit an important one. We thought it should be mentioned here, but we do not think that macroeconomic applications will shed any new light on it.

3.3 Adding Uncertainty

Poole's (1970) original concern was with policy-making under uncertainty; he showed that instrument selection matters when the policy-maker has to act before private supplies and demands are fully known. This kind of uncertainty is surely part of most macroeconomic games in the real world; its absence in abstract studies is presumably due to the analyst's desire for simplicity.

The work of Klemperer and Meyer (1986) suggests that these analysts may be throwing the baby out with the bath water. They showed that even some uncertainty of the Poole type can dramatically reduce the number of Nash solutions in a duopoly game. Their approach exploits the fragility of the solutions that was noted in Section 1. Recall once again the proof that (m,i*), the north-east corner of the payoff matrix, is a Nash solution. If the foreign policy-maker chooses i* as his instrument, the home policy-maker is indifferent between m and i; however, he must actually choose m if (m,i*) is to be a Nash solution. Adding even a bit of uncertainty may give the policy-maker a marginal preference for i and eliminate (m,i*) as a solution.

Thus, we seem to have come full circle. Poole's original approach to the instrument selection problem may be crucial; uncertainty may be necessary for a sensible game specification, even if it is not the main focus of attention. This possibility is a good reason for trying to synthesise the Poole literature and the literature on international policy coordination.

Notes

* We would like to thank Edward Green, John Roberts, Carl Ross, Stephen Turnovsky, Ning Zhu, conference participants and two anonymous referees for helpful comments on the material presented here. The usual disclaimer applies.

1. Some may find this result rather surprising, given the popularity of Poole's result for a single controller. However, we know from the work of Cournot (1838) and Bertrand (1883) that it matters whether duopolists set prices or quantities; instrument selection has been a

subject of controversy in the industrial organisation literature for years.
Recently, it has also become a concern in the macroeconomic literature. Giavazzi and Giovannini (1985) and Turnovsky and d'Orey (1986) discuss instrument selection in monetary policy games between countries. Tabellini (1987) discusses a game between monetary and fiscal policy-makers in a closed economy. They all find a multiplicity of solutions, corresponding to various assignments of instruments to the policy-makers.

2. Klemperer and Meyer analysed a game between duopolists who produce differentiated products. Absent uncertainty, there are four Nash solutions. If, however, the duopolists are uncertain about demand, the Cournot solution is the unique solution when marginal cost curves slope upward, and the Bertrand solution is the unique solution when marginal cost curves slope downward.

3. This game is analogous to a game in which duopolists can set either a price or a quantity. Our four Nash solutions are analogous to the solutions Singh and Vives (1984) and Klemperer and Meyer (1986) find, absent uncertainty.

4. In levels (rather than logs), the production functions are

$$Y = \left[\frac{1}{1-\alpha}\right] K^{\alpha} N^{(1-\alpha)} \quad \text{and} \quad Y^* = \left[\frac{1}{1-\alpha}\right] K^{*\alpha} N^{*(1-\alpha)},$$

where K and K* are capital stocks. The capital stocks are set equal to one.

5. Suppose for example that $\bar{n}^*$ is increased. π^* will be higher, and x^* will take a different value, but the home policy-maker will be unaffected, as long as the foreign policy-maker continues to use the same instrument. Inflation rate differentials are absorbed by exchange rate changes since the model is super-neutral.

6. The proof is somewhat simplified by the fact that payoffs do not depend on the actual values policy-makers choose for their

instruments. As noted above, this is a special feature of our game. More generally, the payoffs will depend upon both instrument choice and instrument settings; see, for example, Turnovsky and d'Orey's (1986) game.

In the more general case, we can take our four boxes to represent the Nash solutions to the games in which instruments are allocated beforehand and policy-makers just choose instrument settings. Klemperer and Meyer (1986) call them 'candidate solutions' to the game in which players choose both instruments and instrument settings. Consider once again the proof that the north-east box is a Nash solution to the game in which players choose both instruments and instrument settings. When we ask whether the home policy-maker can do better with the interest rate than the money supply, we can no longer simply refer to the south-east box. In that box, the foreign policy-maker (generally) sets i^* at a different value than he does in the north-east box. However, when the correct comparison is made, we reach the same conclusion. The home policy-maker is indifferent between setting the money supply and the interest rate, because his policy tradeoffs are fixed when the foreign policy-maker's instrument is set.

7. In levels, the Poole policy is $M = \Phi\exp(i)$. In logs, we have $m = \varphi + i$. So, our choice parameter is an intercept term rather than a slope. The tradeoff is obtained by solving for the reduced forms for inflation and employment in terms of φ and φ^*.

8. Giavazzi and Giovannini (1985) add the exchange rate to the list considered above.

9. For what it is worth, if $\alpha = 1/4$, then (2.1) implies that $1/\tau_{\vartheta*}$ is equal to .19 while $1/\tau_{m*}$ is equal to 1.25. So, the home inflation bias is about 6.5 times higher if the foreign policy-maker chooses Barro and Gordon's inflation rate rather than the money supply. The home inflation bias is about 1.1 times higher if the foreign policy-maker chooses the interest rate rather than the money supply.

10. Of course, if the game is repeated, the players themselves may be able to achieve the better outcomes through the use of trigger mechanisms or reputational strategies. (In fact, Friedman (1985) shows that a

multiplicity of solutions to the one-shot game may actually be helpful in that it allows trigger mechanisms to work in finitely repeated games.) The literature following Barro and Gordon (1983) suggests that there may be a Nash solution to the repeated game that eliminates the inflation biases entirely.

In the duopoly literature, Singh and Vives (1984) suggest a two-stage game in which the policy-makers commit to instruments in the first stage and select instrument values in the second. However, this resolution is not very appealing in macroeconomic applications. We do not observe anything like the first stage; we do not see policy-makers credibly committing themselves to instruments before they set instrument values.

All of these approaches differ from the one in the main text; they suggest new Nash solutions rather than eliminating old ones. The coordination problem remains.

11. See Klemperer and Meyer (1987) and the papers they refer to. See Chapter 5 of Friedman (1983) for a critique of conjectural variation solutions.

References

Barro, Robert and David Gordon, 'Rules, discretion and reputation in a model of monetary policy', Journal of Monetary Economics, 12, 1983, pp. 101-121.

Bertrand, J., 'Revue de la théorie mathématique de la richesse sociale et des recherches sur les principes mathématiques de la théorie des richesses', Journal des Savants, 1883, pp. 499-508.

Canzoneri, Matthew and Dale Henderson, 'Is sovereign policy-making bad?', Carnegie-Rochester Series on Public Policy, vol. 28, 1988.

Cournot, A., Recherches sur les principes mathématiques de la théorie des richesses, Paris, 1838.

Friedman, James, Oligopoly Theory, Cambridge University Press, Cambridge, 1983.

Friedman, James, 'Cooperative equilibria in finite horizon non-cooperative supergames', Journal of Economic Theory, vol. 2, 1985, pp. 390-398.

Giavazzi, F. and A. Giovannini, 'Monetary policy interactions under managed exchange rates', CEPR Discussion paper no. 123, 1985.

Klemperer, Paul and Margaret Meyer, 'Price competition vs. quantity competition: the role of uncertainty', Rand Journal of Economics, vol. 17, no. 4, Winter 1986, pp. 618-638.

Klemperer, Paul and Margaret Meyer, 'Supply function equilibria under uncertainty', (unpublished manuscript), Stanford Graduate School of Business, 1985.

Poole, William, 'Optimal choice of monetary policy instruments in a simple stochastic macro-model', Quarterly Journal of Economics, vol. 84, 1970, pp. 197-216.

Singh, Nirvikar and Xavier Vives, 'Price and quantity competition in a differentiated duopoly', Rand Journal of Economics, vol. 15, no. 4, Winter 1984, pp. 546-554.

Tabellini, Guido, 'Optimal monetary instruments and policy games', (unpublished manuscript), U.C.L.A., August 1987.

Taylor, John, 'International coordination in the design of macroeconomic policy rules', European Economic Review, vol. 28, 1985, pp. 53-81.

Turnovsky, Stephen and Vasco d'Orey, 'A strategic analysis of the choice of monetary instruments in two interdependent economies', (unpublished manuscript), University of Illinois, 1986.

Dynamic Policy Games in Economics
F. van der Ploeg and A.J. de Zeeuw, (Editors)

SERVICING THE PUBLIC DEBT: THE ROLE OF EXPECTATIONS*

Guillermo A. Calvo

Department of Economics
University of Pennsylvania
Philadelphia, PA 19104-6297, USA

Introduction

As one looks around the world one is impressed by the wide variety of languages, cultures and even perceptions of the same phenomena. However, the topic of the government budget is one of the few where the range of issues and the degree of emotions appear to find a common denominator. The government budget lies at the basis of political campaigns and plays a significant role in the evaluation of government policy.

Recently economic theory has begun to catch up with political reality by not only studying the optimality of fiscal and monetary policy in a context in which explicit account is taken of the government's budget constraint -the cradle of political disputes- but it has gone a step further by examining the time consistency of optimal policy, i.e. the issue of whether it is optimal to keep promises that were optimal to make in the past (e.g. during the electoral campaign). The latter lies at the heart of the 'credibility' dilemma faced by any serious politician.

Time inconsistency of optimal policy has received a great deal of attention in the literature (see, for example, Kydland and Prescott 1977; Calvo 1978a and b; Barro and Gordon 1983a and b; Lucas, Jr and Stokey 1983, Persson, Persson and Svensson 1987, among others). Most of the attention, however, was directed at (a) the identification of the factors responsible for time inconsistency, (b) mechanisms to ensure time consistency, and (c) the characterisation of optimal policy when present planners take into account their inability to make future commitments - which leads to the equilibrium concept first examined in macroeconomics by

Phelps and Pollak (1968). The latter has become the dominant equilibrium concept in this literature (see Rogoff 1987).

Phelps-Pollak equilibria were studied and developed much further in several influential articles (e.g. Kydland and Prescott 1977; Barro and Gordon 1983a and b); most of the examples, however, exhibit unique equilibrium solutions. Non-uniqueness was mentioned in Phelps (1975) and Calvo (1978b), and is one of the central subjects of recent game-theoretic models with an infinite horizon (see Rogoff 1987) but, in all fairness, it must be said that non-uniqueness tends to be deemed more a theoretical possibility -reflecting, perhaps, the fact that the models are not entirely correct- rather than a characteristic of empirically relevant models.

The central topic of these notes is the discussion of a set of empirically motivated examples where non-uniqueness of Phelps-Pollak equilibria is clearly exhibited. The possible empirical relevance of the non-uniqueness issue becomes apparent when examining the role of interest-bearing government debt. The events of the 1970s and 1980s suggest very strongly that when governments become strapped for funds, they tend to rely more heavily on bonds' issuance. In fact, Barro (1979) suggests that this may even be optimal if governments are faced with a temporary income fall, or a temporary increase in government expenditures. However, the consequent taxation postponement is not free from 'credibility' problems: will the additional debt be paid off in full, will the government find it optimal to resort to higher inflation or currency devaluation to diminish the burden of the debt, etc.? When these questions are posed in terms of more precise language they translate into the following: is debt repudiation -directly, say through interest rate taxes, or indirectly through inflation- a characteristic of Phelps-Pollak equilibria? Some answers can be found in Fischer (1983), Bohn (1987), Grossman and Van Huyck (1987), and the literature on sovereign countries' debt (see the recent survey by Eaton, Gersovitz and Stiglitz 1986). In this paper we pursue the discussion enquiring, specifically, whether the mere existence of government obligations may not be responsible for the existence of multiple Phelps-Pollak equilibria. This appears to be likely because expected (partial) debt repudiation would tend to be reflected in the interest rate on government bonds (increasing it), while the higher the burden of the debt, the higher would be the temptation to repudiate it. Thus, it should be possible to generate an equilibrium with low interest and low repudiation, coexisting with a high-interest, high-repudiation equilibrium.

Our examples give strong support to the above conjecture: multiple solutions are possible even if our examples assume a finite horizon, and the existence of government bonds may be the triggering factor for non-uniqueness.

The implications for policy could be staggering; for, our results suggest that postponing taxes (i.e. falling into debt) may generate the seeds of indeterminacy; it may, in other words, generate a situation in which the effects of policy are at the mercy of people's expectations - gone would be the hopes of leading the economy along an 'optimal' path.

For the sake of the exposition, we will first discuss these issues in terms of non-monetary models with one representative individual. In Section 1 we will examine a two-period model, where the debt is contracted in the first period and repaid in the second; taxes are distorting and, hence, the government has an incentive to renege on the debt. In order to get an equilibrium with a positive public debt, we assume that debt repudiation is costly, and that the cost is proportional to the amount being repudiated. In addition, we assume that individuals know the relevant model; hence, since there is no uncertainty, the equilibrium net rate of interest on public bonds (adjusted for debt repudiation) equals the rate of return on capital (the opportunity cost of private funds). The main result of the section is that if an equilibrium with a positive public debt exists, there are in general two equilibrium points: a 'good', Pareto-efficient, equilibrium in which there is no debt repudiation, and a 'bad', Pareto-inefficient, equilibrium where debt is partially repudiated.

In Section 2 we focus on a monetary economy with non-indexed bonds. Obviously, in this context inflation is equivalent to some form of repudiation, but *negative* repudiation has to be allowed for since price deflation cannot be ruled out. In order to cast the example in terms of a standard monetary model, we follow Barro and Gordon (1983a and b) and modify the previous model by assuming that price changes are costly. This is enough to give results that are qualitatively similar to the ones in the non-monetary model. Typical of a monetary economy, however, the two equilibria are Pareto-inefficient. At the (relatively) good equilibrium, inflation and the nominal interest rate on government bonds are lower than at the bad equilibrium. In addition, we show that, if instead the nominal return on government bonds were fully indexed to the price level, then the first-best solution with precommitment can be attained, which suggests that, if inflation is the only means of debt repudiation, indexation of the public debt could lead the economy to a Pareto-superior outcome.

In Section 3 the analysis is extended to an open economy where foreigners hold a positive share of total public debt. The main purpose of this short section is to establish a link with the relatively well-developed theory of sovereign borrowing. We show that multiple equilibria still can occur in this new context, and that the effect on the bond interest rate of increasing foreigners' participation in that market depends on whether the economy settles down to the good or to the bad equilibrium.

Finally, Section 4 summarises some of the central findings, and discusses some extensions and suggestions for further research.

1. Debt Repudiation

There are two periods: period 0 and period 1, and two types of agents: identical competitive consumers (or individuals) and the government. In period 0 the government borrows b per capita units of output with a (gross) interest factor[1] R_b, i.e. in period 1 consumers will receive R_b units of output per unit of bond they hold *and which has not been repudiated*. Therefore, if consumers expect that a proportion ϑ of total bonds will be repudiated, $0 \leq \vartheta \leq 1$, the *net* interest factor would be[2]:

$$(1-\vartheta)R_b.$$

We assume that consumers can accumulate physical capital with a constant net interest factor equal to $R > 1$; hence, in a perfect foresight equilibrium with positive stocks of capital and government bonds, consumers should be indifferent between these two types of assets, and, consequently

$$(1-\vartheta)R_b = R. \tag{1.1}$$

The budget constraint of the government in period 1 is

$$x = (1-\vartheta)bR_b + g + \alpha\vartheta bR_b, \tag{1.2}$$

where b, x and g are the per capita stock of bonds, taxes and government expenditure, respectively, and α stands for the per capita cost per unit of repudiated debt[3] ($0 \leq \alpha < 1$). Thus, in other words, taxes are required to finance debt repayment, $(1-\vartheta)bR_b$, government expenditure, g, and the costs of debt repudiation, $\alpha\vartheta bR_b$.
Furthermore, we assume that g is exogenous[4].

By (1.2),

$$\vartheta bR_b = \frac{bR_b + g - x}{1 - \alpha}. \tag{1.3}$$

In period 1 individuals consume all their wealth; thus, assuming that government expenditure does not directly affect private consumption in period 1, c,

$$c = y - z(x) + kR + (1-\vartheta)bR_b - x, \tag{1.4}$$

where y is endowment income, z(x) is a function representing the 'deadweight' cost of taxation[5], and k is per capita physical capital[6]. We assume

$$z(0) = z'(0) = 0, \tag{1.5a}$$

$$z''(x) > 0 \text{ for all } x, \tag{1.5b}$$

$$\lim_{x\to\infty} z'(x) = \infty = -\lim_{x\to-\infty} z'(x). \tag{1.5c}$$

The last Inada-type condition will simplify the presentation of our results.

Employing (1.3) in (1.4), we get

$$c = y - z(x) + kR + bR_b - (bR_b+g-x)/(1-\alpha) - x. \tag{1.6}$$

Consequently, a 'benevolent' government that tries to maximise c in period 1 subject to its budget constraint, (1.2), and taking R_b as given (recall that, by assumption, R_b is negotiated at time 0), will choose x so as to minimise

$$z(x) - \frac{\alpha}{1 - \alpha} x \tag{1.7}$$

subject to (1.2), and $0 \leq \vartheta \leq 1$. In other words, the problem is to minimise (1.7) by choosing x such that the associated ϑ in budget constraint (1.2) is in the interval [0,1]. This condition is equivalent to restricting x in the following manner:

$$g + \alpha bR_b \leq x \leq g + bR_b. \tag{1.8}$$

Note that the left-most expression in (1.8) corresponds to total debt repudiation, $\vartheta = 1$, in which case taxes are equal to government consumption, g, plus the cost of total repudiation, αbR_b. On the other hand, the right-most expression corresponds to no repudiation, $\vartheta = 0$; thus taxes have to be equal to g plus debt repayment.

For the sake of definiteness, we will assume $g > 0$ and $b > 0$, unless otherwise stated; thus, by (1.5), if $R_b > 0$ (the only relevant case for the model of this section), the minimisation of (1.7) subject to (1.8) is attained at some unique $x > 0$. Note that, due to (1.8), the solution will depend on g, and, most importantly for our discussion here, it will also depend on R_b, the interest factor on bonds (which, as argued above, is a predetermined variable in period 1).

The maximum problem for the government in period 1 is depicted in Figure 1[7]. In the figure we portray the two functions associated with constraint (1.8). Given R_b, the government is thus constrained to choose x between the two straight lines stemming from g on the vertical axis. If x^* is located as in Figure 1, the government will be able to attain the unconstrained maximum, x^*, if R_b lies between $\underline{R}$ and $\bar{R}$. On the other hand, if $R_b < \underline{R}$, the maximum will be attained on the upper bound (where there is no repudiation, $\vartheta = 0$), while if $R_b > \bar{R}$, the maximum lies on the lower bound (where repudiation is total, $\vartheta = 1$). Consequently, the set of best responses or 'reaction function' for the government in period 1, given R_b, is depicted by the heavy line of broken segments in Figure 1. Note that when $R_b \leq \underline{R}$ the government will be induced to repudiate none of its debt (i.e. set $\vartheta = 0$), whereas if $R \geq \bar{R}$ repudiation will be total (i.e., $\vartheta = 1$). In between $\underline{R}$ and $\bar{R}$, repudiation will be partial, and -by (1.2), and recalling that in this region $x = x^*$- the repudiation share, ϑ, will increase with R_b; thus, in other words, *the optimal repudiation share in* *period 1 is an increasing function of the interest rate contracted in period 0.*

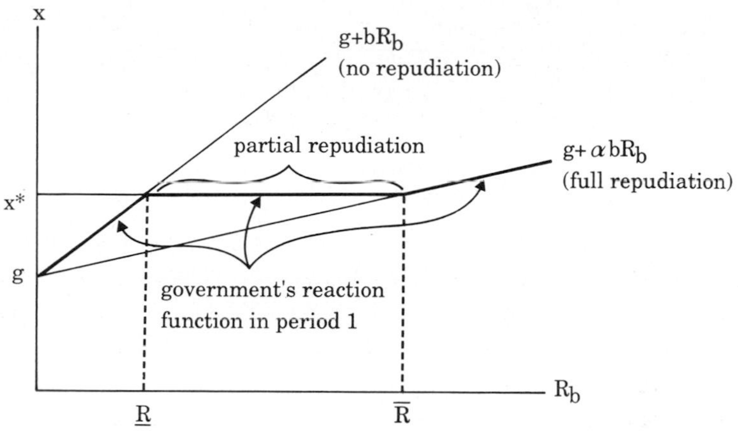

Figure 1: Determination of government's reaction function in period 1

We will be interested in an equilibrium concept in which individuals at time 0 are able to predict the optimal government policy in period 1 (i.e. the optimal government decision about x and ϑ at time 1 as discussed above) with perfect certainty. Under these circumstances (1.1) holds and, hence, by (1.2),

$$x = g + (1-\alpha)bR + \alpha bR_b. \tag{1.9}$$

The latter is a 'consistency condition' that must be satisfied by the government's budget constraint at equilibrium, where, by definition, the public can predict exactly the repudiation share, ϑ, and it is indifferent between holding bonds or capital (i.e. equation (1.1) is satisfied). Note, incidentally, that since ϑ is non-negative, (1.1) implies that equation (1.9) is only relevant over the range where $R_b \geq R$, i.e. where the interest rate on public bonds exceeds or equals that of physical capital.

The consistency condition and the government's reaction function are depicted in Figure 2 for the case in which $x^* > g + bR$. Equilibria are found at points of intersection; in the present case these are E^0 and E^1.

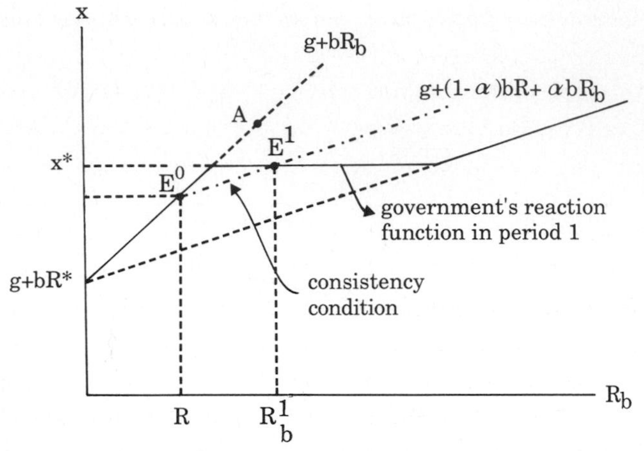

Figure 2: Determination of equilibrium

At E^0 the interest factor on bonds, R_b, is equal to that on capital, R, meaning that the public expects no repudiation; on the other hand, the government's optimal response in period 1 is to set $x = g + bR$, which, as indicated in Figures 1 and 2, lies on the no-repudiation section of its reaction function. Expectations are, thus, fulfilled. Note that at this equilibrium solution the government would wish to increase x above $g + bR$ and towards x^*, but that is impossible because it would call for setting $\vartheta < 0$ (negative repudiation), which has been ruled out by assumption[8].

In the other equilibrium, E^1, repudiation is partial and, thus, the associated interest factor, denoted R_b^1 in Figure 2, is larger than that on capital, R. At this equilibrium, the government is able to attain the unconstrained optimum value of x, x^*.

Our previous discussion covered the case in which $x^* > g + bR$. If, contrariwise, $x^* < g + bR$, the curve depicting the consistency condition would stem from a point like A in Figure 2; it is easy to see that the latter and the government's reaction function will never cross, because the slope of the consistency-condition curve is equal to that of the right-most section of the reaction function. Consequently, there is no equilibrium with a positive stock of bonds.

Finally, in the borderline case where $x^* = g + bR$, equilibrium is unique and $R_b^1 = R = \underline{R}$. The following proposition summarises our findings:

PROPOSITION 1. If $x^* > g + bR$, then two equilibrium solutions exist; one of the solutions exhibits no repudiation, while in the other the public debt is partially repudiated. On the other hand, if $x^* < g + bR$, there is no equilibrium, and in the borderline case that $x^* = g + bR$, equilibrium is unique and there is no repudiation.

Our model has several interesting implications. In the first place, note that, by (1.7), x^* is an increasing function of the cost of repudiation, α; hence, given the initial stock of debt, there is some critical value for the cost of repudiation below which no equilibrium with a positive amount of bonds would exist. The possibility of non-existence of equilibrium is intuitively clear for the case $\alpha = 0$; for, a benevolent government would repudiate 100 per cent of the debt given that there are no direct repudiation costs, and that setting $\theta = 1$ eliminates the deadweight cost of taxes required to service the debt. But, of course, this cannot be an equilibrium with a positive stock of bonds. In addition to confirming this basic intuition, our example shows that the non-existence problem could arise with a positive α, and that the critical value for the latter depends positively on the value of the outstanding debt.

The most important implication of the analysis, however, is that problems do not necessarily go away when repudiation costs are set above the critical level; for, in such a case the economy will normally exhibit two equilibria: a non-repudiation equilibrium in which taxes equal $g + bR$ (recall Figure 2), and another equilibrium in which the debt is partially repudiated and taxes are set at $x^* > g + bR$. Note that, by (1.1) and (1.4), in equilibrium we have:

$$c = y - z(x) + (k+b)R - x. \tag{1.10}$$

Therefore, these two solutions can be Pareto-ranked, and the non-repudiation solution is the dominant one. Unfortunately, however, without further restrictions, the economy could end up at any one of these equilibria. The interest factor in the 'good' equilibrium is always R; however, the value of R_b and θ at the 'bad' equilibrium (E^1 in Figure 2) are sensitive to changes in b. Somewhat paradoxically, as it can easily be established employing Figure 2, at the bad equilibrium *the bond interest factor is smaller the larger is the total outstanding government debt*. It should be noted, however, that the consumption cost of being at the bad equilibrium is independent of total debt[9] (because $x = x^*$, and the latter does not depend on b). But, on the other hand, x^* depends positively on α; therefore, our analysis reveals that while repudiation costs are important for ensuring the existence of equilibria with a positive stock of bonds, by (1.5), (1.7) and (1.10), the larger are the repudiation costs, the larger will also be the consumption costs associated with the bad equilibrium. Thus, *although increasing the costs of repudiation enhances the 'credibility' of the government in the capital markets, the latter may be bought at the cost of lower consumption if the economy ends up at the bad equilibrium.*

The way the above 'game' has been structured is consistent with situations in which the government at time 0 auctions off b, and lets the market free to determine the associated interest factor, R_b. An alternative[10] would be for the government at time 0 to refuse to sell bonds at interest factors which are equal to or exceed R_b^1 (recall Figure 2). Thus, under our assumptions it follows that the only possible equilibrium would be $R_b = R$, the first best. This is an important observation which suggests that free auctioning of the public debt may be dominated by a system in which the government stops selling bonds after the implied interest rates go beyond certain bounds. This observation will take up further relevance when we discuss it in the context of the next section.

2. Money and Non-indexed Debt

The concept of partial repudiation takes a more familiar form in the context of a monetary model, because when variables are expressed in real terms, changes in the rate of inflation imply changes in the real value of assets which are not indexed to the price level. Two important assets of this kind are (high-powered) money and nominal government debt. The literature has paid a great deal of attention to the former (e.g. Barro and Gordon 1983a and b; Lucas and Stokey 1983, Calvo 1978a and b), but there is growing awareness about the importance of understanding the role of nominal debt (e.g. Bohn 1987; Grossman and Van Huyck 1987; Persson, Persson and Svensson 1987). As far as I know, however, none of the available papers addresses the issue of non-uniqueness of equilibria, which is the main focus of the following discussion.

To minimise the use of new notation, we redefine R_b as the nominal interest factor on nominal non-indexed bonds (i.e. $R_b = 1 + i$, where i is the nominal interest rate from periods 0 to 1). Thus, if we let P_t stand for the price level in period t = 0, 1, then the *real* interest factor on period-0 bonds would be:

$$R_b P_0/P_1. \tag{2.1}$$

We can, therefore, think of the ratio P_0/P_1 as the share of the debt which is not repudiated in period 1; hence, using the notation of the previous section, we will write

$$P_0/P_1 = (1-\vartheta). \tag{2.2}$$

We define the rate of inflation between periods 0 and 1, π, as follows:

$$\pi = \frac{P_1 - P_0}{P_0}. \tag{2.3}$$

Thus, by (2.2) and (2.3),

$$\vartheta = \frac{\pi}{1 + \pi}. \tag{2.4}$$

Consequently, each rate of inflation, π, $-1 < \pi$, is associated with a unique rate of repudiation, ϑ. We are thus entitled to carry out our discussion in terms of ϑ instead of π. Note, however, that, contrary to the previous section, ϑ could be negative because it is only constrained to satisfy:

$$-\infty < \vartheta \leq 1. \tag{2.5}$$

In line with our previous results, it is easy to convince oneself that if the costs of inflation/repudiation are nil, then a social welfare maximiser will repudiate 100 per cent of the debt, i.e. he will set $\vartheta = 1$ or, equivalently, $\pi = \infty$. Therefore, the existence of a well-defined interior equilibrium solution requires, once again, the introduction of (social) repudiation costs. As a matter of fact, one could translate the model of Section 2 in monetary terms using (2.4), and interpret those costs as being related to, for example, the Olivera-Tanzi effect. However, I believe it will be more useful to develop the analysis in terms of a more conventional monetary model in which inflation costs directly affect the consumers' utility functions (see Barro and Gordon 1983a and b), and in which explicit account is taken of the inflation tax on high-powered money.

Let the supply of high-powered money in period t, t = 0, 1, be denoted by M_t. For the sake of simplicity, we assume that the monetary authorities can directly determine the price level, P, by, for example, setting the exchange rate. Furthermore, we assume that the demand for money satisfies[11]:

$$M/P = \kappa, \ \kappa > 0. \tag{2.6}$$

The revenue from inflation is conventionally defined as the amount of real resources that the government can obtain by the associated sale of high-powered money; thus, in period 1 it would be given by

$$\frac{M_1 - M_0}{P_1} = (M_1/P_1) - (M_0/P_0)(P_0/P_1) = \kappa\vartheta, \tag{2.7}$$

where the last equality follows from (2.2) and (2.6).

The government budget constraint in period 1 is given by

$$x = (1-\vartheta)bR_b + g - \kappa\vartheta. \tag{2.8}$$

This is similar to (1.2) above, except that inflation is assumed not to be costly for the government, and the inflation tax is subtracted from total government expenditure (inclusive of debt service) in order to calculate the amount of required conventional taxes.

Effective consumption, c, is defined as follows:

$$c = y - z(x) + kR + (1-\vartheta)bR_b - x - \kappa\vartheta - \aleph(\vartheta), \tag{2.9}$$

where $\aleph(.)$ is the inflation-cost function. Again, this is very similar to (1.4) above, except that we have quite naturally subtracted the inflation tax, and, as discussed at the outset, we assume that inflation is reflected in a direct welfare cost for consumers.

We assume

$$\aleph(0) = \aleph'(0) = 0 \tag{2.10a}$$

$$\aleph''(\vartheta) > 0 \text{ for all } \vartheta. \tag{2.10b}$$

We will first study the optimal problem with precommitment, i.e. the problem of maximising c with respect to ϑ *in period 0*. Since we maintain the assumption of perfect foresight, equation (1.1) -the Fisher equation- holds. Therefore, the above-mentioned problem can be formally stated as follows:

$$\max_{\vartheta \le 1} c$$

subject to (1.1), (2.8) and (2.9)[12]. The latter is equivalent to

$$\min_{\vartheta \le 1}[z(g+bR-\kappa\vartheta) + \aleph(\vartheta)], \tag{2.11}$$

which, by (1.5) and (2.10) has a unique solution, denoted ϑ^{FB} (for 'first best'). Since the function in (2.11) is strictly convex, one can readily prove the following useful proposition:

PROPOSITION 2. Assume that (1.1) holds, and let c^i be the effective consumption associated with ϑ^i, i = 1, 2; then, if $\vartheta^{FB} \le \vartheta^1 < \vartheta^2$, we have that $c^2 < c^1$.

In other words, the above proposition states that, if inflation is higher than its first-best level, then social welfare -as measured by effective consumption- is a decreasing function of inflation.

We now turn to the second-best situation which is the focus of our analysis. The government is not able to precommit the inflation level, and, therefore, the government maximises social welfare in period 1, taking the interest rate factor R_b and period-0 inflationary expectations as given. Recalling (2.9), this problem is equivalent to

$$\underset{\vartheta\leq 1}{\text{Min}}\ F(\vartheta;R_b) \equiv \underset{\vartheta\leq 1}{\text{Min}}[z(g+b(1-\vartheta)R_b-\kappa\vartheta) + \aleph(\vartheta)]. \tag{2.12}$$

Note that in the first-best problem (2.11) the government takes (1.1) into account because the government is maximising from the perspective of period 0 and consumers would not be in an (interior) equilibrium if the Fisher equation does not hold. In (2.12), however, the government controls ϑ taking R_b as given, because it maximises effective consumption in period 1 in an environment in which R_b has been negotiated in the previous period (i.e. period 0), and, by assumption, R_b is not contingent on future policy or events.

By (2.12), at an interior[13] (second-best) optimum we have:

$$F_\vartheta \equiv -z'(x)(bR_b+\kappa) + \aleph'(\vartheta) = 0, \tag{2.13}$$

implying, by (1.5) and (2.10), that optimal $\vartheta > 0$. The second-order condition is always satisfied, because F is strictly convex with respect to ϑ. Also, note that, by (1.5) and (2.10), the minimisation problem (2.12) always has a solution, and, by strict convexity, the solution is unique; we denote it ϑ^{SB} (for 'second best'). By (2.13), there is some function $\varphi(.,.)$, such that

$$\vartheta^{SB} = \varphi(\overset{+}{bR_b},\overset{+}{g}), \tag{2.14}$$

where signs over the variables indicate those of the corresponding partial derivatives at an interior solution. Consequently, the (second-best) rate of inflation is an increasing function of nominal debt service, bR_b, and government expenditure, g.

An important implication of the above is that, if there is a positive stock of government bonds, b, then ϑ^{SB} is an increasing function of the nominal interest rate factor, R_b; but, by Fisher equation (1.1), equilibrium ϑ is also an increasing function of R_b and thus -like in Figure 1- the two schedules (i.e. the government's reaction function φ and the Fisher equilibrium relationship) are upward sloping, which, once again, opens the door for multiple equilibria.

It is important to note that, in the absence of government debt (i.e. $b = 0$), equilibrium will be unique because ϑ^{SB} would be independent of R_b. Thus, in the present simple context, the familiar inflation tax on high-powered money plays no significant role in causing non-uniqueness[14].

In order to complete the non-uniqueness argument, the next step will be to show a simple example of non-uniqueness when $b > 0$. Consider the case in which

$$\aleph(\vartheta) = \frac{\beta}{2}\vartheta^2. \tag{2.15}$$

Therefore, by (1.1) and (2.13), we have

$$z'(x) = \beta \frac{\vartheta}{bR/(1-\vartheta) + \kappa} \tag{2.16}$$

and, by (1.1) and (2.8), we get

$$x = bR + g - \kappa\vartheta. \tag{2.17}$$

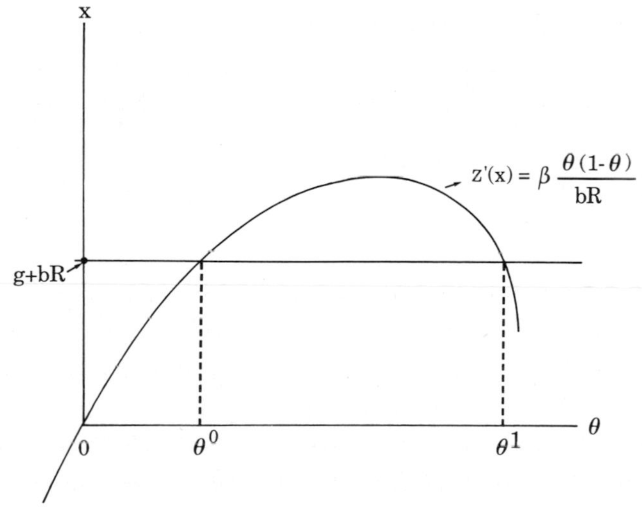

Figure 3: Monetary example

Equilibrium relationships (2.16) and (2.17) are depicted in Figure 3 for the limit case in which the demand for money is zero, i.e. $\kappa = 0$. By continuity, it is quite clear that multiplicity of solutions would continue to hold for κ in some neighbourhood of 0. It is, however, very interesting to note that in the present example uniqueness would prevail if κ is sufficiently large[15]. This is perfectly consistent with our previous observation that the existence of high-powered money is conducive to uniqueness. The result is also highly suggestive; since the value of κ may have much to do with the inflationary history of a country, the above result indicates that *multiple solutions may be a bigger problem for countries which have recently suffered from high inflation*[16].

By (2.11), the first-order condition for a first-best optimum is

$$-z'(g+bR-\kappa\vartheta)\kappa + \aleph'(\vartheta) = 0. \tag{2.18}$$

Thus, recalling that in Section 2 we assumed $g > 0$ and $b > 0$, we have $\vartheta^{FB} > 0$. On the other hand, recalling (2.8), the first-order condition for a second-best optimum is at equilibrium, -i.e., when (1.1) holds-,

$$-z'(g+bR-\kappa\vartheta)(bR+\kappa) + \aleph'(\vartheta) = 0. \tag{2.19}$$

Note that, by (1.5), (2.10), (2.18) and (2.19), the first- and second-best optima satisfy $\kappa\vartheta < g + bR$, implying that in neither one of these optima will the inflation tax be enough to finance total government expenditures. Consequently, by (1.5), (2.10), (2.18) and (2.19), we have, at equilibrium,

$$\vartheta^{SB} > \vartheta^{FB}. \tag{2.20}$$

In other words, we have shown that optimal inflation with precommitment is lower than in any of the equilibrium solutions obtained under no precommitment. Consequently, recalling Proposition 2, we deduce that equilibria without precommitment can be ranked according to their associated inflation rates: given any two of these equilibria, the one exhibiting the largest rate of inflation yields the smallest social welfare (as measured by effective consumption, see (2.9)). In terms of the example associated with Figure 3, therefore, we are entitled to call ϑ^0 the 'good', and ϑ^1 the 'bad' equilibrium[17].

Price indexation of government debt has important effects on this economy since it removes the inflation incentives associated with the debt burden. With full price indexation and an interest-insensitive demand for money (i.e. constant κ, as in the present model), it is easy to see that the no-precommitment equilibrium coincides with the first-best[18].

An alternative to indexation -which was discussed at the end of the previous section- is to put bounds on interest rates; this could ensure that the solution settles at ϑ^0 in Figure 3 rather than at ϑ^1. However, one can easily show that such a solution is inferior to bond indexation, because the latter results in lower inflation[19], recall Proposition 2 and (2.20)[20].

As the example depicted in Figure 3 shows, an increase in the cost of inflation (i.e. an increase in β, recall (2.15)), has ambiguous results on welfare. A rise in β causes the curve in Figure 3 to shift upwards, raising inflation in the bad equilibrium, and lowering it in the good one. Clearly, net consumption, c, will decrease in the bad equilibrium (because β and inflation go up). In the good equilibrium (i.e. ϑ^0), on the other hand, the picture is less clear, because inflation goes down, which tends to be welfare improving. However, if $\kappa = 0$, a simple manipulation using (2.16) and (2.17) shows that welfare increases with β. Thus, as in the previous section, the effects of increasing the costs of inflation/repudiation are ambiguous: they could be welfare improving in the good equilibrium, but they definitely lower welfare in the bad equilibrium.

Our example sheds some light on the issue studied by McCallum (1984) of whether monetary policy could be separated from fiscal considerations. His discussion has to do with the long-run (literally when $t \to \infty$) feasibility of policies that keep money supply at a constant level while running a fiscal deficit. In our model the relationship between the rate of inflation and fiscal policy is very direct for the case of non-indexed bonds (still the dominant kind of government bonds in the U.S. and several other countries), and confirms and complements McCallum's insight that there are no grounds for expecting fiscal policy to have no monetary implications even though, for instance, the monetary authority promises to keep a constant price level (or a constant money supply in a set-up where the latter is explicitly modelled). In our model this happens because the government may not commit itself *credibly* to zero inflation in the presence of non-indexed debt, since the level of the latter determines the set of equilibrium inflation rates that could be sustained *ex post*[21]. This relationship between the stock of government bonds and inflation, incidentally, will hold true even if the equilibrium is unique (see Bohn 1987).

Our results add a pessimistic note to the view that price controls might help leading the economy to the 'good' solution[22], which appears to have played some role in the design of the recent 'heterodox' stabilisation plans in Argentina, Brazil and Israel. This is so, because in our example the government has direct control on the price level, but, once again, non-uniqueness arises due to the fact that its *ex-post* behaviour is not immune to *ex-ante* expectations. As a matter of fact, our previous discussion suggests that interest-rate pegging of some sort may be as much a crucial ingredient of a credible stabilisation effort as price controls are, and that interest-rate pegging could in some occasions be all that is needed for credibility.

3. International Debt: a Short Detour

Borrowing and lending among sovereign states has recently received considerable attention (see, for instance, the recent survey by Eaton, Gersovitz and Stiglitz 1986), so a few words establishing the connection between the present paper and that type of literature may be in order.

A common characteristic of our examples is that the 'size of the penalty' (i.e. the cost of repudiation) is a function of the degree of repudiation; in the example of Section 2 the cost was proportional to the value of the debt, whereas in that of Section 3 the cost was simply a function of the fraction that was repudiated. In the international debt literature, on the other hand, it is typically assumed that the cost of repudiation bears no relationship to the size of the debt. This explains why it was relatively easy for us to generate multiple equilibria while in that literature the equilibrium is typically unique[23].

The presence of foreign debt adds an interesting twist to our previous models. Thus, for example, we could assume that only a proportion γ, $0 \leq \gamma \leq 1$, of the total public debt is owned by domestic residents, while $(1-\gamma)$ is owned by foreigners whose welfare is of no concern to the local authorities. Thus equation (1.4) now becomes

$$c = y - z(x) + kR + \gamma(1-\vartheta)bR_b - x \quad (1.4')$$

and (2.9) is similarly modified. One can now examine the relationship between γ and the equilibrium outcomes. This is a straightforward exercise which, however, shows that the results depend very strongly on the model. In the model of Section 1, an increase in foreign ownership of the public debt (i.e. a fall in γ) induces a fall in the bond interest rate at the bad equilibrium, but no change at the good one. On the other hand, in the monetary model of Section 2 (with $\kappa = 0$), interest rates in both equilibria are affected, rising in the bad equilibrium and falling in the good one. There does not seem, therefore, to be a clear-cut relationship between the participation of foreigners in the official bonds market, and the degree of repudiation or inflation.

4. Concluding Remarks

The central message that is conveyed by this paper is that expectations may play a crucial role in the determination of equilibrium when the government debt is auctioned off to the public, and there is no attempt to manage expectations, or to peg interest rates on the government debt. In our examples we saw that the nominal interest rate is not simply a passive reflection of people's inflationary expectations, but rather that the nominal interest rate is actually one of the main determinants of inflation. Consequently, a credible anti-inflationary policy would have to implement rules to prevent nominal interest rates to become unduly high. The two simple mechanisms that were suggested in our discussion were: (i) price indexation of the public debt, and (ii) refraining from issuing new government bonds when their interest rate exceeds some well-defined bounds. In more general terms, however, our discussion pointed to the advisability of governments taking a more active stand on nominal interest rates. In my opinion, this implication of the formal analysis is likely to be particularly relevant in situations where the stabilisation programme is launched in the midst of very high inflation.

The analysis has been conducted in terms of models with one representative consumer because so much of the related literature has been couched in this form (prominently Barro 1979 and Lucas and Stokey 1983). However, I suspect that one of the important reasons for debt repudiation to be costly (other than due to 'reputation' costs) is the fact that not all individuals are alike and, therefore, the incidence of repudiation is not uniform[24]. Consider, for example, a model of the type discussed by Sargent and Wallace (1982) where only a subset of total population holds non-interest bearing public debt (say, cash), while the rest of society holds high-denomination non-indexed bonds. For the sake of the argument, suppose, in addition, that everybody pays the same amount of taxes. Clearly, if the planner adheres to utilitarian principles, for example, debt repudiation could be costly (or beneficial), because the latter would be an instrument of wealth redistribution. In that context, the planner may end up repudiating less than 100 per cent of the debt (say, held by the 'rich') because of the loss it would cause cash-holders (the 'poor'). I think the analysis of these types of models should provide us with a deeper understanding of these issues. It is my feeling, however, that the central insights of this note will carry over to those models.

Another interesting extension would be to introduce uncertainty. Note, first, that the above two-period examples would not exhibit random equilibria, because once the interest rate is determined in period 0, there is only one optimum response for the government in period 1. An easy extension, however, would be to make the repudiation cost, α, random. Thus, if individuals are risk neutral, for example, R_b *times* the expected repudiation share would in equilibrium equal the interest factor on capital, R; the repudiation shares for each state of nature, on the other hand, would depend on R_b (as in our previous analysis). Therefore, the equilibrium values of R_b will be deeply intertwined with the probability distribution of α. Clearly, since R_b is just one number, we will observe situations where *ex post* the *actual* net return on bonds exceeds (or falls short of) that of physical capital. Consequently, these models could help explain phenomena like the high *ex-post* real interest rates observed at the beginning of anti-inflationary programmes (see, for instance, Dornbusch 1985; Sachs 1986).

Finally, an important extension of the analysis would be to allow for more than two periods[25], and the simultaneous existence of explicit repudiation (e.g. interest rate taxes) and inflation.

Notes

* I have greatly benefited from comments received at Johns Hopkins University, Georgetown University, the Macro Lunch Group of the University of Pennsylvania, MIT, and the Research Department of the International Monetary Fund. I am particularly indebted to Matt Canzoneri, Sara Guerschanik-Calvo, Joseph Harrington, Jr, Elhanan Helpman, Nissan Leviatan, Maury Obstfeld, Assaf Razin, Sweder van Wijnbergen and two anonymous referees. The research on this paper was partly done while I was a visiting scholar at the Research Department of the International Monetary Fund, and it was partially funded by the National Science Foundation. However, any opinions expressed are entirely my own and not those of any of the above institutions. This paper has already been published in the *The American Economic Review*, 78, 4, September 1988, pp. 647-661.

1. Let r be an interest rate; we define the corresponding interest factor as (1+r).

2. Repudiation is a catchall word in this paper that includes anything from open repudiation to a tax on interest.

3. α could be thought of as transaction costs associated with debt repudiation (legal fees, etc., when repudiation is open). In Section 4 other types of costs are discussed. It should be stressed, however, that in this paper we are interested in examining the 'mechanics' associated with these types of costs as a prelude to a more substantive analysis where those costs will be subject to closer scrutiny.

4. In a more realistic model, the expected net return on capital will also be a function of expected government policy (through expected capital levies, for example). The relationship between the latter and 'capital flight' has recently been explored by Eaton (1987).

5. Alternatively, one could follow Barro (1979) and assume that z(x) measures tax collection costs; under this interpretation, z(x) should be included in the r.h.s. of (1.2).

6. There is no real need to keep track of the non-negativity of c, because in this model one can always ensure that by setting endowment income, y, sufficiently large.

7. I am very grateful to Elhanan Helpman for suggesting Figures 1 and 2, which greatly improved the intuitive appeal of the presentation.

8. This type of constraint will be relaxed in Section 2. However, one simple way to extend the present example to allow for $\vartheta < 0$ would be to assume that negative repudiation is also costly. It is easy to see that this would remove any incentive from the government at time 1 to set $\vartheta < 0$, because the latter would involve bigger tax distortions and repudiation costs than if $\vartheta = 0$.

9. This invariance does not hold in the model discussed in Section 4.

10. This fine point was suggested to me by Assaf Razin.

11. The following simple form is sufficient for conveying the central insights of this section. Extensions are possible; however, see note 14.

12. This is like the optimisation problem examined in Phelps (1973). Its solution differs from Milton Friedman's Optimum Quantity of Money ($\vartheta = 0$ in the present context) because, contrary to Friedman, we assume that taxes are distorting.

13. In what follows we will concentrate on interior solutions (i.e. $\vartheta < 1$), corresponding to cases in which the inflation rate is less than infinity (recall (2.4)).

14. This result could be extended to the case in which the demand for money is sensitive to the rate of interest if the elasticity of $z'(x)$ with respect to x is less than unity, and the inflation tax does not exceed regular taxes, the normal case. Our proof, however, relies on the existence of more than two periods, and will, therefore, not be presented here. For an infinite-horizon model of non-uniqueness along the present lines, but without government bonds, see Obstfeld (1988).

15. The exact condition is $\kappa > bR + g$, i.e. real monetary balances must exceed total government expenditure, including the inflation-adjusted service on the public debt.

16. This point emerged during a useful conversation with Sweder van Wijnbergen.

17. Multiple equilibria are by no means a necessary feature of these models. Uniqueness would, in fact, prevail if, for example, $\aleph(\vartheta) = \pi^2$; the latter is related to the work of Barro and Gordon (1983a, b) and Bohn (1987). For a somewhat detailed discussion of these issues, see Calvo (1987).

18. Indexation would not suffice for attaining the first-best solution if the demand for money is sensitive to the rate of interest. I conjecture, however, that there are relevant examples where one could still show that debt indexation increases social welfare.

19. This is not intended to be a thorough analysis of the welfare economics of bond indexation since there are some important aspects of the issue which have not been taken into account. For example, as pointed out to me by Nissan Liviatan, it has been argued that indexation may reduce the base of the inflation tax because in such a case bonds become better substitutes for domestic money. This aspect is not covered by our discussion because κ was assumed to be independent of the degree of indexation.

20. Bounds on interest rates may be particularly difficult to implement when there is an active private capital market. See Calvo (1987) for some discussion on this issue.

21. Note that our arguments establish a link between the stock of non-indexed debt and inflation, in contrast with McCallum (1984) who emphasised the relation between fiscal deficits and inflation.

22. For recent models that could be employed to support that point of view, see Bruno and Fischer (1985) and Kiguel (1986).

23. An exception is the recent work of Eaton (1987) where, however, the issue of debt repudiation is not central to the analysis.

24. See Rogers (1986) and Calvo and Obstfeld (1987) for models which highlight the link between time inconsistency and wealth distribution.

25. For some progress on this front, see Calvo (1987).

References

Barro, Robert J., 'On the determination of the public debt', Journal of Political Economy, 87, 5, October 1979, pp. 940-971.

Barro, Robert J. and David B. Gordon, 'A positive theory of monetary policy in a natural-rate model', Journal of Political Economy, 91, 4, August 1983a, pp. 589-610.

Barro, Robert J. and David B. Gordon, 'Rules, discretion and reputation in a model of monetary policy', Journal of Monetary Economics, 12, 1, July 1983b, pp. 101-122.

Bohn, Henning, 'Why do we have nominal government debt?', Department of Finance, The Wharton School, University of Pennsylvania, Revised Version, April 1987, Journal of Monetary Economics, forthcoming January 1989, pp. 127-140.

Bruno, Michael and Stanley Fischer, 'Expectations and the high inflation trap', (unpublished manuscript), September 1985.

Calvo, Guillermo A., 'Optimal seigniorage from money creation: an analysis in terms of the optimum balance of payments problem', Journal of Monetary Economics, 4, August 1978a, pp. 503-517.

Calvo, Guillermo A., 'On the time consistency of optimal policy in a monetary economy', Econometrica, 46, November 1978b, pp. 1411-1428.

Calvo, Guillermo A., 'Staggered prices in a utility maximizing framework', Journal of Monetary Economics, 12, 3, September 1983, pp. 383-398.

Calvo, Guillermo A., 'Controlling inflation: the problem of non-indexed debt', in S. Edwards and F. Larraín (eds), Debt Adjustment and Recovery: Latin America's Prospect for Growth and Development, Basil Blackwell, New York, forthcoming.

Calvo, Guillermo A. and Maurice Obstfeld, 'Optimal time consistent fiscal policy with finite lifetimes: analysis and extensions', CARESS Working Paper No. 87-09, University of Pennsylvania, March 1987. A shorter version with the same main title was published in Econometrica, vol. 56, March 1988, pp. 411-432.

Dornbusch, Rudiger, 'Stopping hyperinflation: lessons from the German experience in the 1920's', NBER Working Paper No. 1675, May 1985.

Eaton, Jonathan, 'Public debt guarantees and private capital flight', The World Bank Economic Review, 1, May 1987, pp. 377-396.

Eaton, Jonathan, Mark Gersovitz and Joseph E. Stiglitz, 'The pure theory of country risk', European Economic Review, 30, 1986, pp. 481-513.

Fischer, Stanley, 'Welfare aspects of government issue of indexed bonds', in R. Dornbusch and M.H. Simonsen (eds), Inflation, Debt and Indexation, The MIT Press, Cambridge, MA, 1983, pp. 223-246.

Friedman, Milton, The Optimum Quantity of Money and Other Essays, Aldine Publishing Company, Chicago, 1969.

Grossman, Herschel I. and John B. Van Huyck, 'Nominally denominated sovereign debt, risk shifting and reputation', NBER Working Paper No. 2259, May 1987.

Kiguel, Miguel, 'Stability, budget deficits and the monetary dynamics of hyperinflation', (unpublished manuscript), June 1986.

Kydland, Finn and Edward C. Prescott, 'Rules rather than discretion: the inconsistency of optimal plans', Journal of Political Economy, 85, June 1977, pp. 473-493.

Lucas, Robert E., Jr and Nancy L. Stokey, 'Optimal fiscal and monetary policy in an economy without capital', Journal of Monetary Economics, 12, 1, July 1983, pp. 55-94.

McCallum, Bennett T., 'Are bond-financed deficits inflationary? a Ricardian analysis', Journal of Political Economy, 92, February 1984, pp. 123-135.

Obstfeld, Maurice, 'A theory of capital flight and currency depreciation', (unpublished manuscript), January 1988.

Persson, Mats, Torsten Persson and Lars E.O. Svensson, 'Time consistency of fiscal and monetary policy', Econometrica, 55, November 1987, pp. 1419-1432.

Phelps, Edmund S., 'Inflation in the theory of public finance', Swedish Journal of Economics, 75, 1973, pp. 67-82.

Phelps, Edmund S., 'The indeterminacy of game-theoretic equilibrium in the absence of an ethic', in E.S. Phelps (ed.), Altruism, Morality and Economic Theory, Russell Sage Foundation, New York, 1975, pp. 87-106.

Phelps, Edmund S. and Robert A. Pollak, 'On second-best national saving and game-equilibrium growth', Review of Economic Studies, 35, 1968, pp. 185-199.

Rogers, Carol Ann, 'The effect of distributive goals on the time inconsistency of optimal taxes', Journal of Monetary Economics, 17, 1986, pp. 251-269.

Rogoff, Kenneth, 'Reputation, coordination and monetary policy', The Hoover Institution, Working Paper in Economics E-87-14, March 1987.

Sachs, Jeffrey, 'The Bolivian hyperinflation and stabilisation', NBER Working Paper No. 2073, November 1986.

Sargent, Thomas J. and Neil Wallace, 'The real-bills doctrine versus the quantity theory: a reconsideration', Journal of Political Economy, 90, December 1982, pp. 1212-1236.

Dynamic Policy Games in Economics
F. van der Ploeg and A.J. de Zeeuw, (Editors)

MONETARY POLICY IN MODELS WITH CAPITAL*

Finn E. Kydland

Graduate School of Industrial Administration
Carnegie-Mellon University
Pittsburgh, PA 15213, USA

Introduction

Over the past ten or twenty years there has been a clear trend in the direction of modelling aggregate phenomena, whether in a growth or a business-cycle context, as environments in which households and firms make optimal decisions. Such abstractions, especially when assuming competitive equilibria, imply considerable discipline in the sense that it is possible to construct models of quite complex dynamic phenomena with very few free parameters. If a model can be quantitatively restricted by empirical relations that are determined separately from the phenomena being modelled, it generally stands a better chance of giving a useful answer to the question being addressed.

In terms of thinking about policy, the introduction of optimising government initially seemed to offer the possibility of similar scientific benefits. So far, however, our models have raised more questions than they have answered. From a normative point of view, with a government objective, one can certainly determine the optimal policy within a given model. The problem lies in the implementation. As shown by Kydland and Prescott (1977), this government plan, in a dynamic economic environment without commitment, is intertemporally inconsistent. If the plan is implemented today, the government will generally have an incentive to change it in the future. Alternatively, if the time-consistent plan is used, then the results may be very inferior relative to the optimal plan with commitment.

From a positive standpoint, unless one can demonstrate that a commitment mechanism exists, the no-commitment time-consistent equilibrium would appear to be the candidate for a framework for understanding intertemporal policy-making. But this outcome, in some models, can be almost unbelievably bad for society, and it is hard to imagine that there would not be attempts to set up institutional arrangements, or pass laws that are difficult to change, in order that superior policies may be implemented.

To study the nature of monetary policy with or without commitment, including the possibility of commitment arising endogenously, basically two types of models have been used in the literature. One emphasises the role of money for the purpose of stabilisation policy due to a tradeoff between inflation and unemployment[1]. The other takes a public-finance approach[2]. In Section 1, I discuss why the former model is not in the spirit described above. The public-finance view, on the other hand, is a serious framework to build upon and is firmly grounded in the economic tradition described at the beginning of this introduction.

In order to evaluate policies, including both the optimal and the time-consistent ones, it is necessary to be able to determine the competitive equilibrium, given a policy rule that, generally, is a function of the aggregate state of the economy. In Section 2, a direct method which emphasises computability is illustrated for a particularly simple dynamic tax example, but in the context of a competitive industry. In Section 3, the aggregate general equilibrium case is outlined, and the example of a monetary policy rule is described. Section 4 discusses equilibrium definitions and other issues for the case in which the policy rule is chosen by an optimising government.

A major theme of this paper is that capital-theoretic issues are central to time inconsistency. This emphasis is maintained throughout the paper. At the end of each of Sections 3 and 4, I discuss models of money as a medium of exchange in which the demand for money is clearly dependent on the state of the aggregate economy. In Section 4, in particular, I informally outline a theory which would represent an attempt to account for high-frequency movements of the rental price of liquidity, but which also offers a temptation for policy-makers to excessively tax a form of accumulated capital, in this case in the household.

1. Time Inconsistency and Monetary Policy

In this section, I discuss two approaches that have been used for analysing time-consistency issues in the context of monetary policy. One, which is based on an expectational Phillips curve, suffers from at least two drawbacks. The first is that the level of the parameters is such that there is no economic reason why they would be even approximately policy invariant, especially under repeated play. Another related problem is that the model is not formulated in terms of parameters that economists are confident about measuring and restricting so as to get an idea of the quantitative importance of time inconsistency. The public-finance approach, on the other hand, is explicit, the models have parameters that can be measured, and monetary policy changes can imply real changes through any one of several channels. I predict that this, so far largely ignored, area will be an important topic for future research.

1.1 The Inflation-Unemployment Example

An example used in Kydland and Prescott (1977) is the following. The monetary authority maximises

$$-\pi_t^2 - \omega(u_t - u^* + u^o)^2, \qquad \omega, u^o > 0,$$

where u^* is the natural unemployment rate, π_t is the inflation rate, ω expresses the relative weights on the two terms, and the presence of the parameter u^o suggests that, for any given π_t, the preferred value of u is less than u^* (see our Figure 1 on p. 479). The Phillips curve is assumed to be linear:

$$u_t = -\lambda(\pi_t - \pi_t^e) + u^*,$$

where π_t^e is the expected inflation rate as of the beginning of period t. Substituting for u_t, the monetary objective can be written as

$$-\pi_t^2 + \omega[\lambda(\pi_t - \pi_t^e) - u^o]^2.$$

Some variations on this formulation have been used, for example making the natural unemployment rate stochastic as in Barro and Gordon (1983b), or making the second term linear, or letting both terms take a more general functional form; letting the optimal inflation rate be zero is without loss of generality.

This example demonstrates that, if people make their decisions first on the basis of expectations π_t^e, then the government will have an incentive to fool them by choosing $\pi_t > \pi_t^e$, thereby temporarily lowering the unemployment rate. In the long run, however, such a policy would lead to above-optimal inflation.

Barro and Gordon (1983a) made the important observation that the government can, in some cases, support lower inflation through reputation. Others have assumed that policy-maker type, whether high or low-inflation, is uncertain to the public, and various other forms of uncertainty have been introduced.

While this example serves to demonstrate the possible severity of time inconsistency within a framework that most economists are familiar with, it also has obvious weaknesses. For example, results have been derived for repeated play that depend on the parameters of this model. There is, however, no basis for arguing that the parameters are invariant to government policy, such as high versus low-inflation policy. The slope of the Phillips curve surely will depend crucially on the policy that individuals expect the government to follow. An example of a story behind it is an island model. This is not a likely basis for an invariant expectational Phillips curve. Justifications for why a positive value of u^o could be in the interest of the public have also been proposed. For example, it has been suggested that other tax distortions may become less severe as a result of unanticipated inflation. This is not unreasonable, but there is no economic foundation for arguing that the nature of these distortions is the same for high as for low-inflation policy.

Another strike against the model and its more elaborate variants is that, at least for the US over the last thirty years, it is not empirically plausible. If one detrends real GNP and the aggregate price level, whether measured by the GNP deflator or the Consumer Price Index, the price level clearly has been countercyclical[3]. This fact is illustrated in Figure 1. Using price changes (not in logs) rather than the price level, the measured cyclical inflation rate is slightly positively correlated with cyclical real GNP, but with a lag of three or four quarters. These empirical features suggest that monetary authorities have not played a significant role in generating output or employment movements in a way suggested by the model under consideration.

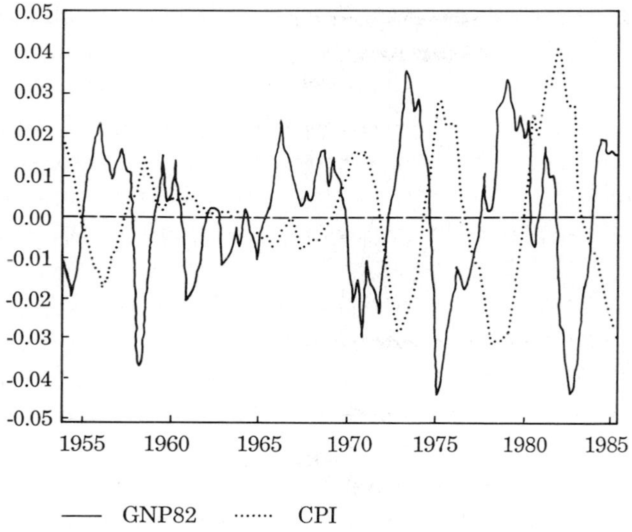

Figure 1: Per cent deviation, real GNP & CPI

There is also a recent literature which considers cooperative arrangements among countries. Some of these models ignore the optimising behaviour by private individuals and focus instead on the game among countries. This approach makes questions of commitment to cooperative arrangements (for example, through trigger-like strategies) quite similar to some of the literature in industrial organisation. Ignoring whether or not one can commit versus the atomistic inhabitants of the countries could make cooperation seem advantageous when it really is not. In contrast, Kehoe (1987) shows in a public-finance model with utility-maximising consumers and benevolent governments that, without commitment versus private agents, the cooperative solution may be inferior for reasons similar to those explaining why the time-consistent solution can be very suboptimal within a given country[4].

1.2 A Public-Finance Perspective

In contrast with this type of model of monetary policy-making, models of fiscal policy have been much more explicit in their specification of what decisions people make and what problems they solve. Our own main example (1977), involving specifically the investment tax credit, was of that type, as was our 1980 public-finance model (and Fischer's illuminating two-period version of it) in which the government can use different tax rates on labour and capital income in order to finance varying government expenditures. The result is that the government, without any commitment mechanism, would tax capital too heavily, as it is inelastically supplied in the short run, and thus would make future saving too low. More recently, the possibility that sustainable equilibria could arise that are not the limit of finite-horizon equilibria has been studied[5].

The omission of productive capital from many models removes a feature that was instrumental in producing large differences between time-consistent and optimal policy rules in our 1977 paper. Intuitively, the durability of capital must be an important reason. Investors would like to know tax rates on capital income many years into the future. An unexpected increase in the tax rate has little effect on the quantity of capital services supplied in the short run, but would affect savings and therefore growth in the longer run and have profound effects on the welfare of the society.

Does money play a significant role in promoting or discouraging growth? The usual examples of such a role are the inflation tax, which most people probably regard as quantitatively small under usual circumstances[6], and the tax on bondholders resulting from an unexpected increase in inflation.

Slightly more subtle, perhaps, but potentially quite important, is the possible increase in tax burden on capital due to interaction with the fiscal tax system. Examples are the value of depreciation write-offs for tax purposes or changes in the progressiveness of labour-income tax, assuming they are non-indexed. An increase in the progressiveness can be regarded as an increase in the tax on human capital[7]. Obviously, the net effect depends on what other simultaneous fiscal changes are made. An interesting and important empirical question is whether higher inflation tends to be associated with a significantly higher relative tax burden on physical or human capital and therefore tends to reduce growth.

2. Industry Equilibrium with Tax Policy

A prerequisite for any evaluation of policies is a method for determining competitive equilibrium, given a policy rule. Especially at the aggregate level, the assumption that households and firms are atomistic and do not behave strategically is essential. Any other assumption is probably unrealistic and leaves room for too many possibilities that are hard to evaluate and that leave too many degrees of freedom.

A method for computing competitive equilibrium enables one to compare alternative policy rules, such as the optimal policy rule (if it could credibly be committed to) as opposed to the time-consistent one. One could perhaps also evaluate simple rules which may be easier to implement while being not much inferior to the usually more complex optimal commitment policy.

In this section, I illustrate the determination of competitive equilibrium with tax policy in a particularly simple dynamic environment that we can think of as a competitive industry. This is a slightly simplified version of the main example used in Kydland and Prescott (1977). I compare the direct solution procedure with solving a social planner's problem, and point out that this latter method cannot be used when there are government policy rules that depend upon the state of the economy. In the next section, then, the more interesting case of an aggregate general equilibrium is considered.

In this model, investment planned in period t, x_t, and carried out in that period and the next, does not become productive until period t + 2. Thus, the law of motion for the firm-specific productive capital is

$$k_{t+1} = (1-\delta)k_t + x_{t-1}, \tag{2.1}$$

and in the aggregate

$$K_{t+1} = (1-\delta)K_t + X_{t-1}, \tag{2.2}$$

where δ is the physical rate of depreciation. The investment rate in period t is then

$$i_t = \psi x_t + (1-\psi)x_{t-1}, \tag{2.3}$$

where ψ is the fraction of the investment effort induced by plan x_t in the same period. Investment expenditures in period t are $qi_t + \gamma(i_t-\delta k_t)^2$, with a tax offset of $Z_t i_t$, where Z is the investment tax credit. Thus, the model combines cost of adjustment with the feature that it takes multiple periods before planned additions to the capital stock become productive[8]. These dynamic elements, and especially the time-to-build feature, turned out to have significant implications for the nature of time inconsistency in the model.

The cash-flow function of the typical firm is

$$P_t k_t - (q-Z_t)i_t - \gamma(i_t-\delta k_t)^2,$$

where units are chosen such that one unit of capital produces one unit of output[9]. The inverse aggregate demand function is assumed to be linear:

$$P_t = A_t - bK_t, \tag{2.4}$$

where b is positive, and A_t is a stochastic shift parameter that is subject to the first-order autoregressive process

$$A_{t+1} = \rho A_t + \varepsilon_t, \qquad -1 < \rho < 1, \tag{2.5}$$

where ε is a positive independent random variable with mean μ and constant variance. Finally, we assume that the investment tax credit is chosen according to the rule

$$Z_t = z_0 + z_1 K_t + z_2 X_{t-1} + z_3 A_t. \tag{2.6}$$

Defining $R(k_t,x_{t-1},x_t,K_t,A_t,z_t)$ to be the objective function after we have substituted for i_t and P_t from (2.3) and (2.4), the typical firm's objective is to maximise

$$E \sum_{t=0}^{T} \beta^t R(k_t,x_{t-1},x_t,K_t,A_t,Z_t), \qquad 0 < \beta < 1,$$

where T could be infinity. Let $v_t(k_t,x_{t-1},K_t,X_{t-1},A_t)$ be the value to the firm of pursuing optimal decision rules for the remainder of the horizon, given the state of the economy at the beginning of period t. These functions satisfy the recursive relationship

$$v_t(k_t, x_{t-1}, K_t, X_{t-1}, A_t)$$

$$= \max_{x_t} E[R(k_t, x_{t-1}, x_t, K_t, A_t, Z_t) \tag{2.7}$$

$$+ \beta v_{t+1}(k_{t+1}, x_t, K_{t+1}, X_t, A_{t+1})],$$

for all t, given relations (2.1), (2.2), (2.5) and (2.6), along with expectation of future prices. These expectations can be expressed in terms of the expected laws of motion of industry-wide investment:

$$X_t = D_t^e(K_t, X_{t-1}, A_t, \pi_t),$$

which map uniquely into expectations of the process determining future prices through equations (2.2), (2.4) and (2.5).

Assuming now that the quadratic v_{t+1} has already been determined, one obtains a first-order condition at time t which implies a decision rule of the form

$$x_t = d_{0t} + d_{1t}k_t + d_{2t}x_{t-1} + d_{3t}K_t + d_{4t}X_{t-1} + d_{5t}A_t + d_{6t}X_t + d_{7t}Z_t, \tag{2.8}$$

where d_{it}, $i = 0,\dots,7$, are the coefficients that are obtained for time period t. Note that this individual decision rule is made a function of the aggregate decision, X_t, in the industry. In order to get the aggregate or per-firm behavioural rule, which will also be the basis for the firms' expectations, we impose the conditions that $x_t = X_t$, $k_t = K_t$, and $x_{t-1} = X_{t-1}$, yielding

$$X_t = \frac{d_0}{1 - d_{6t}} + \frac{d_{1t} + d_{3t}}{1 - d_{6t}} K_t + \frac{d_{2t} + d_{4t}}{1 - d_{6t}} X_{t-1} + \frac{d_{5t}}{1 - d_{6t}} A_t + \frac{d_{7t}}{1 - d_{6t}} Z_t$$

$$\equiv D_t(K_t, X_{t-1}, A_t, Z_t). \tag{2.9}$$

The linearity of the decision rules allows us to aggregate in this way, so that the aggregate or per-firm values of the state variables contain the necessary information.

If $D_t \neq D_t^e$, aggregate behaviour will give rise to price distributions that are different from the expected distributions on the basis of which the individual decisions were made. In equilibrium, expectations are rational, and we therefore close the model by requiring that $D_t = D_t^e$ for all t. From a computational point of view, this can be handled by requiring that this condition hold at each iteration of the recursive procedure outlined above. To complete the computations for period t, then, we substitute for the linear relations (2.1), (2.2), (2.5) and (2.6), and the linear individual and aggregate behavioural rules, (2.8) and (2.9), in the right-hand side of the functional equation (2.7). The resulting function is quadratic and depends only on the individual and aggregate state of the economy at time t and represents the value function to be used in determining the (equilibrium) behaviour in period t - 1. Thus, this procedure incorporates the assumption that agents' expectations of future price distributions are rational.

For the infinite-horizon case, we can think of the above description as outlining one step in the successive approximations, the limit of which is generally a stationary decision rule. For this framework outlined, the aggregate behaviour of economic agents is then given by the relation

$$X_t = D(K_t, X_{t-1}, A_t, Z_t),$$

the coefficients of which are the same in every period.

In view of the results of Lucas and Prescott (1971), this procedure may appear unnecessarily complicated. Assuming for the moment that $Z_t = z^* =$ constant in every period, they showed that a competitive industry such as the one above behaves in equilibrium as if maximising a certain consumer surplus. Thus, we might consider solving this stand-in problem, which is to maximise

$$E \sum_{t=0}^{T} \beta^t S_t,$$

where

$$S_t = \int_0^{K_t} (A_t - bu)du - (q-z^*)I_t - \gamma(I_t - \delta K_t)^2,$$

subject to

$$K_{t+1} = (1-\delta)K_t + X_{t-1},$$

$$A_{t+1} = \rho A_t + \varepsilon_t,$$

and where

$$I_t \equiv \psi X_t + (1-\psi)X_{t-1}.$$

This is a problem of smaller dimension the solution of which can be obtained by standard recursive methods. When the policy variable depends on aggregate industry behaviour, however, this simpler method is not immediately applicable. Since all firms are small, each firm assumes that it has no effect on future policies. Of course, if all firms invest less now, future capital stock will be lower, thus most likely future tax credits will increase. In the stand-in problem, this effect of current decisions on future taxes is recognised, and the competitive equilibrium therefore does not correspond to the solution of that maximisation problem, given the policy rule.

From an empirical standpoint, as pointed out by Lucas (1976), attempts at estimating equations like (2.9) and using them for policy evaluation will fail because the coefficients will not be invariant to changes in the policy rule (2.6). Furthermore, it is unlikely that this is a quantitatively unimportant phenomenon, especially in environments with structural dynamics such as the one considered here.

3. Dynamic Competitive Equilibrium with Government Policy

In this section, we outline a more general framework. It is capable of dealing with a variety of general equilibrium models with optimising households and firms facing government policy which depends on their aggregate behaviour. We concentrate on consumers' maximisation, although implicit is also firms' maximisation. The consumers are thought of as renting the input factors, including capital, to the firms.

In the spirit of thinking about computable models the quantitative, and not just qualitative, properties of which can be studied, we assume that the structure of the model is such that maximisation and equilibrium result in linear decision rules. This will typically require that a quadratic approximation be made for the utility function around its steady state which can usually be determined analytically. The utility function may be indirect in the sense that a budget or resource constraint has been substituted. In examples without policy in which this approach has been compared with exact methods, the properties have been very similar. A factor is that most aggregate fluctuations around their growth paths are small in terms of percentage. This formulation permits a great deal of quantitative discipline in that prior knowledge from outside the model can be used to restrict the parameters. Examples are capital depreciation rates, long-run ratios of key variables, including factor shares, elasticity of long-run labour supply, and so on.

Let x_t be the vector of decision variables for the representative consumer at time t, and y_t be the individual-specific vector of endogenous state variables summarising all the information needed for making decisions at time t. Typical examples are capital stocks or money holdings at the beginning of the period, although in some cases variables dated before t may have to be included. Also, let X_t and Y_t be the corresponding aggregate variables. For example, if y_t includes the agent's capital stock, then the aggregate capital stock is an element of Y_t. The laws of motion for the state variables are given by the linear equations

$$y_{t+1} = f(y_t, x_t) \tag{3.1}$$

$$Y_{t+1} = F(Y_t, X_t). \tag{3.2}$$

Generally, the function f will be the same as F. In addition, there may be state variables the paths of which are determined by autonomous processes. These variables are assumed to follow an autoregressive process

$$W_{t+1} = \Omega W_t + \eta_t, \tag{3.3}$$

where Ω is a matrix of fixed coefficients, and η is a random vector with fixed variance. Examples are technology shocks with serial correlations. Finally, Z_t is a vector of policy variables assumed to be determined by a linear policy rule

$$Z_t = G(Y_t, W_t), \tag{3.4}$$

which incorporates the government budget constraint and is correctly anticipated. Examples of variables in Z are tax rates, government purchases, or the change in the nominal money stock.

The consumer is assumed to maximise the indirect utility function

$$E \sum_{t=0}^{T} \beta^t u(x_t, y_t, P_t, Z_t),$$

which is obtained after having substituted for the private budget constraint. The price vector, P_t, is included because of this substitution. Relations determining the dynamic motion of prices will be endogenously determined.

The value function, $v_t(y_t, Y_t, W_t)$, denotes the (equilibrium) expected discounted value or utility at time t for a consumer in initial state y_t when pursuing optimal decision rules, and the initial aggregate state is (Y_t, W_t). Implicit in this value function is the assumption of rational expectations about future prices in the sense that their expected distributions are those generated by the equilibrium laws of motion of the economy. The decision rules and corresponding value functions can be determined recursively from the relation

$$v_t(y_t, Y_t, W_t) = \max_{x_t} E[u(x_t, y_t, P_t, Z_t) + \beta v_{t+1}(y_{t+1}, Y_{t+1}, W_{t+1})],$$

$$t = 0, 1, \ldots, T, \tag{3.5}$$

subject to constraints (3.1) - (3.4).

Assuming now that v_{t+1} has already been determined, and taking account of equations (3.1) - (3.4), the first-order conditions for a maximum at time t determine linear decision rules of the form

$$x_t = d_t(y_t,Y_t,W_t,X_t,P_t,Z_t). \tag{3.6}$$

As in Section 2, we note that the aggregate X_t is included in the right-hand side. These individual decision rules can be aggregated. It is convenient to think of X_t and Y_t in per-consumer terms. Thus, in the aggregate, we have $x_t = X_t$ and $y_t = Y_t$. Therefore

$$X_t = d_t(Y_t,Y_t,W_t,X_t,P_t,Z_t),$$

which can be written as

$$X_t = D_t(Y_t,W_t,P_t,Z_t). \tag{3.7}$$

The prices must be such that markets are cleared. These prices will depend on the aggregate state, i.e.,

$$P_t = P_t(Y_t,W_t,Z_t). \tag{3.8}$$

For example, if borrowing and lending are possible, then the price of these loans (which implicitly defines the interest rate) must be such that aggregate net loans are zero in every period. Or, as a second example, if consumers hold money from one period to the next, then the equilibrium price of money in terms of goods must be such that the aggregate amount of money that individuals wish to hold is equal to the amount supplied. The supply of money can in general depend on the state of the economy.

From a computational point of view, as in the preceding section, the equilibrium condition is required to hold at each iteration of the recursive procedure outlined above. To complete the computations for period t, therefore, we substitute for the linear laws of motion, (3.1) - (3.4), and the linear individual and aggregate behavioural rules, (3.6) and (3.7), in the right-hand side of the functional equation (3.5). The resulting function is quadratic and depends only on the individual and aggregate states (y_t,Y_t,W_t), and represents the value function to be used in determining the (equilibrium) behaviour in period $t - 1$. Thus, this procedure incorporates the assumption that agents' expectations of future price distributions are rational.

If v_{t+1} is quadratic, a quadratic function is maximised at time t subject to linear constraints. The optimal decision rules are then linear, and the new value function, v_t, is quadratic. By definition, v_{T+1} is zero and therefore trivially quadratic, and so all v_t are quadratic by backward induction.

We summarise this discussion in the following

DEFINITION. An equilibrium is a sequence of decision rules (3.6) and a sequence of price functions, $\{P_t(Y_t,W_t,Z_t)\}_{t=0}^T$, such that, for each individual, the decision rules solve recursively the functional equations (3.5) subject to laws of motion (3.1) - (3.4), the expected behaviour of the aggregate variables in each period, $D_t(Y_t,W_t,P_t,Z_t)$, which must be consistent with aggregation (or average) of the individual decision rules, and such that prices determined by the functions $P_t(Y_t,W_t,Z_t)$ clear markets for all t.

In this paper, we assume stationary models in the sense that utility functions and laws of motion are the same in every period. For infinite-horizon models, such structures generally yield stationary decision rules which we obtain by determining the limit as the horizon becomes large. For the framework outlined above, the aggregate behaviour of economic agents is then given by the relation

$$X_t = D(Y_t,W_t,P_t,Z_t),$$

the coefficients of which are the same in every period, and similarly for the price relations.

An example is the business-cycle model with money used in Kydland (1987). If n_t is hours of work in period t and T is the total time allocation per period, then net leisure in period t is $T - n_t + \ell(P_t m_t)$, where $\ell' > 0$ and $\ell'' < 0$, and m_t is the nominal quantity of money held by the typical household at the beginning of period t. The price level, P_t, is the inverse of the conventional price level. Thus, there is a tradeoff in the household between real money and leisure.

With this money-holding motive embedded in a real business cycle model, the resulting demand for money can be written as

$$m_t^d = m^d(y_t,Y_t,M_t,P_t),$$

which in the aggregate becomes

$$M_t^d = M^d(Y_t, P_t).$$

For this market to clear, the price level must satisfy

$$M^d(Y_t, P_t) = M^s(Y_t),$$

where M^s is an unchanging monetary policy rule. The resulting price function, $P(Y_t)$, is used by rational consumers in forming expectations about future price distributions. If M^d and M^s are both linear, then $P(Y_t)$ is also linear.

By keeping the model computable, it is possible to compare its covariance properties to those of the data. The aggregate behavioural relations, the laws of motion for the state variables, the equilibrium price relations, and the policy rules together form a system of difference equations. From this set of stochastic equations, repeated draws can be made of the same length as the data series available, and similar statistics can be computed for the artificial economy and the data. This, indeed, was the purpose for which the above-mentioned model of money as a medium of exchange was used. In particular, it is consistent with the observed countercyclical price level (conventionally defined) illustrated in Figure 1.

4. Optimising Government

So far, we have described the determination of equilibrium, given an exogenous policy function, without describing where the policy came from. This is a prerequisite for dealing with the case in which policy is determined from optimisation by the government. That is, the government wishes to maximise a social objective function

$$E \sum_{t=0}^{T} \beta_z^t S(X_t, Y_t, Z_t), \qquad 0 < \beta_z < 1,$$

subject to its budget constraint. For simplicity of notation, we have included the exogenous shocks in Y_t. If distributional considerations are not an issue, then a common abstraction is one in which all consumers are alike. In that case, a natural candidate for S is the equal-weighted or average utility function with $\beta_z = \beta$. It is well known that, in a dynamic environment such as one with productive capital, the optimal plan without commitment is still time inconsistent[10]. This is the case so long as, for example, tax rates are chosen by the policy-maker and allocations are selected by consumers.

The extension of our definition of equilibrium to include a time-consistent government continues to be recursive. Let $R_t(Y_t) = \Sigma_{\tau=t}^{T}\beta_z^{\tau-t}S(X_\tau,Y_\tau,Z_\tau)$ given that policy is selected consistently from time t on and the economy is competitive. Also, for any given Z_t, let $X_t = D_t(Y_t,P_t,Z_t)$ and $P_t = P_t(Y_t,Z_t)$ represent the competitive equilibrium resulting from solving the functional equation (3.5) subject to constraints (3.1) - (3.3) and after aggregation as described in going from equation (3.6) to (3.7). Then

$$R_t(Y_t) = \max_{Z_t} E[S(X_t,Y_t,Z_t) + \beta_z R_{t+1}(Y_{t+1})],$$

subject to $X_t = D_t(Y_t,P_t,Z_t)$ and the government budget constraint. The resulting solution is of the form $Z_t = G_t(Y_t)$.

The infinite-horizon case is now trickier. If there is a time-consistent equilibrium, one can be found by taking the limit of the above procedure. There may, however, be other equilibria that depend on how the policy-maker has behaved up until that time. A definition of a time-consistent stationary policy rule for the infinite horizon is given in Kydland and Prescott (1977, p. 481).

Note the contrast with the standard inflation-unemployment model. In that model without structural dynamics in the form of, for example, capital accumulation, time inconsistency arises because private agents make their decisions before the government does. It is more reasonable to consider environments in which, on day one of each time period, the government chooses tax rates and other policy variables, and, given these choices by the government, households and firms subsequently make their decisions for that time period. With capital accumulation of some form or another being a part of the model, time consistency is still an important consideration. This is because some private decisions in period t affect the state of the economy in the future and in the aggregate determine these tax rates through the tax policies. At the same time, period-t decisions are affected in an important way by these (expected) future tax rates.

A typical example is where government expenditures can be financed by taxing labour and capital income. The standard result is that, unless one can commit to the optimal plan (sometimes called the Ramsey plan), capital will be taxed too heavily. It is important to realise, however, that it is not necessary that capital be taxed directly for time consistency to be an issue. It will play a role so long as the quantity of what is being taxed is chosen as a function of some form of capital. For example, labour supply may depend on already accumulated capital. If so, that dependence gives rise to a time-inconsistency problem even if only the labour income is taxed. Another example is the case of intertemporally non-separable utility in leisure, which can be interpreted as a stand-in for households' allocation of part of their non-market time to, perhaps unobserved, capital in the households, such as quality of children, health, and so on.

The model of money as a medium of exchange outlined in the preceding section has the property that the demand for money is highly dependent on aggregate state variables, including physical capital and perhaps also unobserved capital in the household. It is possible to construct reasonable models of money that have a direct capital-theoretic element. Assume that there are at least two distinct ways of carrying out transactions. In the language of household production theory, one can think of the inputs as being real money, the allocation of time in that period, and the input of a form of household capital that results from previous uses of time. Whenever a significant change is made in the method households use for payment, such as one which significantly economises on the use of cash, there is probably some degree of learning taking place over a period of time as people gain experience with the new method.

Given that it takes time to accumulate this experience, one would expect considerably more movement in the rental price of liquidity services than otherwise. This would be consistent with the empirical puzzle of excess volatility of short-term interest rates relative to the standard demand for money function as demonstrated clearly in Lucas (1987), especially in his Figure 5.

Whenever a capital stock is being accumulated, an insight of the time-inconsistency literature is that it will be tempting for the government to tax it excessively, in this case indirectly. Whether this phenomenon can be of quantitatively significant magnitude in such a context is an interesting question for future research.

5. Conclusion

This paper has been concerned with monetary policy in environments in which dynamics are important due to capital-theoretic elements. These are also environments in which there is considerable scope for the phenomenon commonly referred to as the time inconsistency of optimal policy. In this context, three themes were elaborated on. The first is the importance of computable models that can be quantitatively restricted and in which the quantitative importance of the phenomena under study can be addressed. Such models could then be used, for example, as a basis for an assessment of the value of having a commitment mechanism.

The second theme is that two-player games, or games in which the decision problems of individuals in the economy are not explicitly formulated, are likely to be of little value in understanding aggregate government policy. An appropriate framework is one in which atomistic people's optimisation problems are explicitly formulated. In such models, unlike representative agent models the equilibrium of which can be determined by solving a stand-in planner's problem, the distinction between individual decision and state variables on the one hand and their aggregate counterparts on the other becomes important. Equilibria with optimising governments can then be used to obtain insights into many issues related to the operation of government policy.

The third theme is that incentives for capital accumulation are at the heart of time inconsistency. In particular, while most people may accept that view in the context of fiscal policy, it is less common in discussions of monetary policy. I argue that, in this sense, there is not really an important distinction between monetary and fiscal policy. Inflation is likely to affect capital-accumulation decisions, both physical and human. I also gave other examples of model features in the context of money which have capital-theoretic elements. The empirical relevance of such features is an important topic for future research.

Notes

* I have benefited from comments by Patrick Kehoe and Torsten Persson. The paper was written while the author was visiting the Federal Reserve Bank of Minneapolis. The views expressed herein are those of the author and not necessarily those of the Federal Reserve Bank of Minneapolis or the Federal Reserve System.

1. For some surveys, see Barro (1985), Blackburn and Christensen (1987), Chari, Kehoe and Prescott (1988), and Rogoff (1987).

2. See Calvo (1978), Lucas and Stokey (1983), and Persson, Persson, and Svensson (1987).

3. These results are from Kydland (1987).

4. See also van der Ploeg (1987).

5. See Chari and Kehoe (1988a,b).

6. This argument is made in Kydland (1983).

7. See, however, Cooley and Hansen (1987).

8. The cost-of-adjustment assumption is often used in industry or firm models so as to make investment expenditures smooth over time. This is probably inappropriate at the aggregate level, and certainly not necessary for the purpose mentioned above. In aggregate equilibrium, the real interest rate will adjust and affect the willingness to substitute between present and future consumption.

9. In the original model, labour was an input as well. This input had no intertemporal features, however, and therefore did not play a role for the issue of time inconsistency.

10. See Kydland and Prescott (1980).

References

Barro, R.J., 'Recent developments in the theory of rules versus discretion', Working Paper 12, University of Rochester, 1985.

Barro, R.J. and D.B. Gordon, 'Rules, discretion and reputation in a model of monetary policy', Journal of Monetary Economics, 12, 1983a, pp. 101-121.

Barro, R.J. and D.B. Gordon, 'A positive theory of monetary policy in a natural rate model', Journal of Political Economy, 91, 1983b, pp. 589-610.

Blackburn, K. and M. Christensen, 'Monetary policy and policy credibility: theories and evidence', Working Paper, 1987.

Calvo, G.A., 'On time consistency of optimal policy in a monetary economy', Econometrica, 46, 1978, pp. 1411-1428.

Chari, V.V. and P.J. Kehoe, 'Sustainable plans', Research Department Working Paper 377, Federal Reserve Bank of Minneapolis, 1988a.

Chari, V.V. and P.J. Kehoe, 'Sustainable plans and debt', Research Department Working Paper 399, Federal Reserve Bank of Minneapolis, 1988b.

Chari, V.V., P.J. Kehoe and E.C. Prescott, 'Time consistency and policy', Research Department Staff Report, Federal Reserve Bank of Minneapolis, 1988.

Cooley, T.F. and G.D. Hansen, 'The inflation tax and the business cycle', Working Paper, 1987.

Fischer, S., 'Dynamic inconsistency, cooperation and the benevolent dissembling government', Journal of Economic Dynamics and Control, 2, 1980, pp. 93-107.

Kehoe, P.J., 'International policy cooperation may be undesirable', Research Department Staff Report 103, Federal Reserve Bank of Minneapolis, 1986.

Kydland, F.E., 'Implications of dynamic optimal taxation for the evolution of tax structures: a comment', Public Choice, 41, 1983, pp. 229-235.

Kydland, F.E., 'The role of money in a business cycle model', Working Paper, Carnegie-Mellon University, 1987.

Kydland, F.E. and E.C. Prescott, 'Rules rather than discretion: the inconsistency of optimal plans', Journal of Political Economy, 85, 1977, pp. 473-491.

Kydland, F.E. and E.C. Prescott, 'Dynamic optimal taxation, rational expectations and optimal control', Journal of Economic Dynamics and Control, 2, 1980, pp. 79-91.

Lucas, R.E., Jr, 'Econometric policy evaluation: a critique', in K. Brunner and A.H. Meltzer (eds), The Phillips Curve and Labor Markets, North-Holland, Amsterdam, 1976.

Lucas, R.E., Jr and E.C. Prescott, 'Investment under uncertainty', Econometrica, 39, 1971, pp. 659-681.

Lucas, R.E., Jr and N.L. Stokey, 'Optimal fiscal and monetary policy in an economy without capital', Journal of Monetary Economics, 12, 1983, pp. 55-93.

Lucas, R.E., Jr, 'Money demand in the United States: a quantitative review', Working Paper, Carnegie-Rochester Conference on Public Policy, 1987.

Persson, M., T. Persson and L.E.O. Svensson, 'Time consistency of fiscal and monetary policy', Econometrica, 55, 1987, pp. 1419-1431.

Ploeg, F. van der, 'International policy coordination in interdependent monetary economies', Discussion Paper 169, Centre for Economic Policy Research, London, 1987.

Rogoff, K., 'Reputation, coordination and monetary policy', Working Paper E-87-14, Hoover Institution, 1987.

Dynamic Policy Games in Economics
F. van der Ploeg and A.J. de Zeeuw, (Editors)

MACROECONOMIC POLICY GAMES WITH INCOMPLETE INFORMATION: SOME EXTENSIONS*

John Driffill

Department of Economics
University of Southampton
Southampton SO9 5NH, UK
and
CentER for Economic Research
Tilburg University
5000 LE Tilburg, The Netherlands

Introduction

In recent work on the inflationary bias in macroeconomic policy (Backus and Driffill 1985), the choice of policy has been modelled as a game between the private sector of the economy and the government, in which the private sector has incomplete information about the government's preferences. The private sector does not know whether the government is committed to a non-inflationary policy or whether it is maximising an objective function which puts negative weight on inflation and positive weight on expanding output above the natural level. The macroeconomic model which is used is a static and deterministic one which embodies the 'price-surprise' model of output in its simplest form: in each period the excess of output above the natural rate is proportional to the inflation surprise. The only source of uncertainty in the model arises from the randomising strategies which the government may choose. The government is assumed to choose the actual rate of inflation in each period, and the private sector 'chooses' the expected rate of inflation.

The analysis of this as a finitely repeated game, drawing heavily on the work of Kreps and Wilson (1982), produces a sequential equilibrium in which the non-committed government imitates the committed government until the end of the game draws close. In each period of the game, the government has a 'reputation': the probability with which the private sector agents believe that the government is committed to zero inflation; and this belief is updated each period by Bayes' rule according to the event observed (inflation/no inflation) and the strategies which each possible type of government would adopt at that stage of the game. Since a committed government is known never to inflate, and since the private sector perfectly monitors the government's actions, the observation of inflation immediately reduces the government's reputation to zero. The cost associated with losing one's reputation in this way is sufficiently great to deter the non-committed government from causing inflation, until the end of the game approaches. As the game draws near its end, the government may become indifferent between inflating and not inflating, in which case it may pursue a randomising strategy, mixing the strategies (inflate/do not inflate). Conditional on the realisation of no inflation when randomising, its reputation in the next period will be higher. In the papers by Backus and Driffill (1985a) and Barro (1986) the increase in reputation which occurs is just sufficient to offset the effects of the increased tendency of the non-committed government to inflate as time goes by, so that overall the expected inflation rate (or its mean value) remains constant during the period of time when the government is randomising.

The main result from this analysis is that the uncertainty in the minds of the private sector is sufficient to induce the uncommitted government to adhere to the policy of the committed government for most of the game. No formal constitutional amendment or restriction on government freedom of action is needed in order to achieve the socially efficient outcome, except near the end of the game.

The results of those papers may be sensitive to some of the restrictive assumptions made about the beliefs and information of private sector agents and the strategies which are open to the government. For example, Vickers (1986) modifies the structure of the game slightly by introducing two different types of government that each give some weight to employment in their objective function, but differ in the amount. This contrasts with the assumption of an uncommitted and a committed government used by Barro (1986) and by Backus and Driffill (1985a). Comparison of this analysis with Backus and Driffill shows that the assumed 'committed' player simplifies the problem and makes it easier to get a pooling equilibrium rather than a separating equilibrium. The player who is committed to zero inflation always wants to play zero under any circumstances whatever, and consequently any other action immediately identifies its perpetrator as being uncommitted. The uncommitted player then has effectively two choices of action in each period of time: (i) zero inflation and (ii) his best response to the public's expectation. The scope for pooling exists, because the committed player has no interest in the action an uncommitted player would take and does not attempt to take an action which would distinguish him from an uncommitted player. By contrast, in Vickers' formulation, the player who cares less about unemployment has an incentive to take actions which separate him from the other type of player. Vickers shows that pooling equilibria can in a wide class of situations be ruled out. In a two-period game, the two types of players take different actions in the first period so that the type is completely revealed in the second period. In the first period, the less concerned (about unemployment) player chooses an inflation rate which is so low that a more concerned player would not wish to imitate his behaviour. This result contrasts sharply with the pooling equilibrium of the Backus and Driffill formulation. It suggests that one should investigate the way alternative assumptions about private agents' priors affect the solutions of the games.

In Section 1 below the analysis of Vickers is extended to include cases where pooling equilibria are possible. In addition, in Section 2, a situation in which private agents believe that governments may come in more than two types is considered. In this case, separating and pooling equilibria are possible, depending on how similar the possible government types are.

One stark result of the game in which private agents can monitor perfectly the actions of the government, and where there is no uncertainty in the execution of policy actions is that, if the inflation rate ever deviates from zero, the government's reputation immediately and irrevocably falls to zero. This result is too strong for the real world, where governments have only indirect control over the rate of inflation, many random events intervene its determination, and the private sector may not be able to monitor the government's actions independently of the final outcome. Thus it would be interesting to examine a model which embodies these factors.

In Section 3 of the paper this is attempted. It is assumed that the government is either committed to zero inflation or uncommitted, as before. A government is assumed to take one of two actions with respect to inflation -intend zero inflation, or intend inflation- and the actual outcome is not certain to be the one intended. There is a chance that the opposite of the intended outcome may occur. The private sector can observe only the final outcome, the actual inflation rate, and cannot tell whether or not it was intended.

In this situation, application of Bayes' rule to the evolution of reputation shows that the observation of inflation does not immediately reduce reputation to zero, since it can always occur even if the government is committed. In a two-period game it now results that the uncommitted government will always play either a pure strategy (intend inflation) or a mixed strategy in the first period, such that it is indifferent between inflating and not inflating. Its reputation improves if no inflation occurs and deteriorates if some inflation occurs.

It appears that a government with a moderately good reputation is likely to put more probability on intending zero inflation than is a government with either a very good or a very poor reputation, since near the extremes it is not possible for the government to influence its reputation much and so the cost of inflating is lower than for middling reputations. It further appears that even if the probability of error is small, so that actual inflation is very likely to equal intended inflation, then the committed government will not pursue the pure strategy of intending zero inflation, but will always mix to some extent. This shows that the ability to get close to the efficient outcome depends on the information and belief structure to a considerable degree.

The analysis of this model is carried out for a two-period game. Even for the very simple structure proposed here, the analysis becomes so complicated as to prevent general results for a T-period game (T greater than 2) from being derived.

The model discussed in Section 3 is related to work by Canzoneri (1985) and by Söderström (1985) in that it includes, as they have done, imperfect monitoring of government actions. Söderström analyses a game between a government and a centralised labour union in which the government monitors the union's action with error, but is fully informed about the union's objectives. As here, only two outcomes are possible for each player. The union sets wages, and can either be aggressive or passive. The government sets monetary policy, which can be either accommodatory or non-accommodatory. Söderström examines an infinitely repeated game and uses a solution proposed by Rubinstein (1979), which induces the union to play a passive wage strategy in each period of time. The government 'punishes' the union by not accommodating wage increases if they have occurred frequently enough in the past. The critical frequency of occurrence is a diminishing function of the duration of the game, and approaches the frequency of naturally occurring (exogenous) wage shocks as the game proceeds. This result suggests imperfect monitoring alone is not enough to cause inefficient government behaviour.

Canzoneri (1985) analyses a somewhat different model where the government has private and incommunicable information about money demand. In his model the money stock (government's control variable) can vary continuously rather than taking on just two discrete values. The private sector responds by anticipating inflation for a 'reversionary period' if it exceeds some critical value in a period. This happens randomly, and thus induces occasional apparent breakdowns of cooperation between the private sector and the government. Meanwhile, the government is discouraged from causing inflation in each period, a result which parallels that of Söderström.

Section 4 of the paper contains some conclusions.

1. Differing Tastes: Two Types, Many Strategies

In this part of the paper the structure used by Vickers (1986) is adopted. Consider a two-period game played between the private sector and the government. In each period the government chooses an inflation rate x_{T-1}, x_T; and the private sector forms expectations of that period's inflation rate x^e_{T-1}, x^e_T. There are two potential governments which differ in the weight they put on output in their objective functions. The per period payoff for government of type i is

$$u_i = -x_t^2/2 + c_i(x_t - x_t^e), \tag{1.1}$$

where $t = T-1$, T and $0 < c_1 < c_2$. Thus the game runs for periods T-1 and T. Both types of government care somewhat about output, but type 2 cares more than type 1. This is basically the same set-up as Backus and Driffill (1985a) and Barro (1986), except the taste difference replaces the committed/uncommitted distinction, and we allow any action on the real line, rather than a choice from just two. As in those models, the private sector is assumed to attach an initial probability to the event that the government is of type 1, p_{T-1}, at the start of period T-1, which it updates as the game proceeds. The government knows its own type. We look for a sequential equilibrium of the game.

In the final period, T, the government takes x_T^e as being fixed and clearly sets $x_T = c_i$.

Thus the payoff in the final period for a government of type i is

$$u_i(T,x_T^e) = c_i^2/2 - c_i x_T^e.$$

Thus the total payoff for government of type i over both periods of the game, given that in T-1 the private sector expects inflation x_{T-1}^e is

$$U_i = -x_{T-1}^2/2 + c_i(x_{T-1}-x_{T-1}^e) + c_i^2/2 - c_i x_T^e. \tag{1.2}$$

The real action in this game comes in the first period (T-1) when the government chooses an inflation rate x_{T-1} taking x_{T-1}^e as given, but taking into account the way in which the private sector forms its expectations in period T as a function of the inflation rate observed in T-1.

U_i will be used to denote the utility of government of type i which takes action x_{T-1} in period T-1, and c_i in T, when the private sector forms expectations x_T^e of inflation in T (x_{T-1}^e is taken as some fixed number). Effectively we are considering utility effects of action taken after x_{T-1}^e has been chosen. Thus only changes in x_{T-1} and x_T^e affect the value of $U_i(x_{T-1},x_T^e)$. Note that the value of x_{T-1}^e does not affect the ranking over (x_{T-1},x_T^e) combinations for any player.

The private sector will form expectations which are rational, and since there are two discrete government types, they can use a step function, such that $x_T^e = x_1$ if $x_{T-1} \le x^*$ and $x_T^e = x_2$ if $x_{T-1} > x^*$, for some values of x_1, x_2 and x^*.

Two possibilities are (i) a separating equilibrium and (ii) a pooling equilibrium. In the separating equilibrium, following Vickers, we have expectations formed by

$$x_T^e = \begin{bmatrix} c_1 \text{ if } x_{T-1} \le k_B \\ c_2 \text{ if } x_{T-1} > k_B \end{bmatrix} \tag{1.3a}$$

where k_B is defined by

$$U_2(k_B,c_1) = U_2(c_2,c_2) \tag{1.3}$$

and that the type-2 government is indifferent between inflating at rate c_2 and being identified as type 2 on the one hand, and choosing low inflation k_B and being identified as of type 1. We assume that the type-2 government then chooses inflation rate c_2 in this case. At the same time, the type-1 government must find it in its interest to choose the lower rate of inflation k_B in T-1, and thus be identified as of type 1. The condition

$$U_1(k_B,c_1) > U_1(c_1,c_2) \tag{1.4}$$

must therefore be satisfied.

A separating equilibrium is illustrated in Figure 1, which follows Vickers (1986). The indifference curves of a government of type i in (x_{T-1},x_T^e) space are parabolae which peak at $x_{T-1} = c_i$. The slope of the indifference curves of U_i defined by (1.2) above is

$$\left.\frac{dx_T^e}{dx_{T-1}}\right|_{U_i \text{ const}} = 1 - x_{T-1}/c_i, \tag{1.5}$$

so they all have a slope equal to unity at $x_{T-1} = 0$. In the figure, U_2 is the indifference curve of the type-2 player through (c_2,c_2). It cuts the vertical axis at $(0,c_2/2)$. Thus for $c_1 > c_2/2$ we have a separating equilibrium in the positive quadrant. k_B is defined as above by (1.3). For $c_1 > c_2/2$, (1.4) is automatically satisfied.

Now consider a pooling equilibrium. In this case expectations are formed as follows

$$x_T^e = \begin{cases} \bar{c}, & x_{T-1} \le \ell \\ c_2, & x_{T-1} > \ell \end{cases} \tag{1.6}$$

where $\bar{c} \equiv pc_1 + (1-p)c_2$
and both types of government play $x_{T-1} = \bar{c}$. For this to hold in equilibrium, we have

$$U_2(\ell,\bar{c}) \geq U_2(c_2,c_2) \tag{1.7}$$

and

$$U_1(\ell,\bar{c}) \geq U_1(c_1,c_2). \tag{1.8}$$

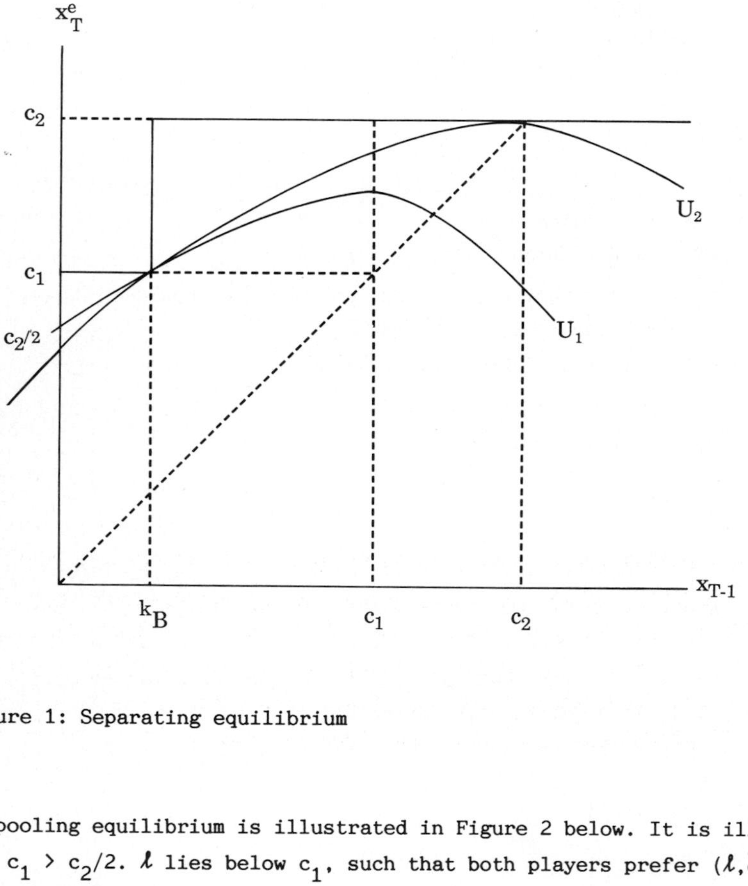

Figure 1: Separating equilibrium

A pooling equilibrium is illustrated in Figure 2 below. It is illustrated for $c_1 > c_2/2$. ℓ lies below c_1, such that both players prefer $(\ell,\bar{c})$ to any other outcome.

A pooling equilibrium does not always exist since there does not always exist an ℓ which satisfies (1.7) and (1.8) above, for $\ell \leq c_1$. As is clear from Figure 2, if $\bar{c}$ is sufficiently close to c_2 because p is sufficiently small, then no $\ell \leq c_1$ may exist such that the type-2 government prefers $(\ell,\bar{c})$ to (c_2,c_2).

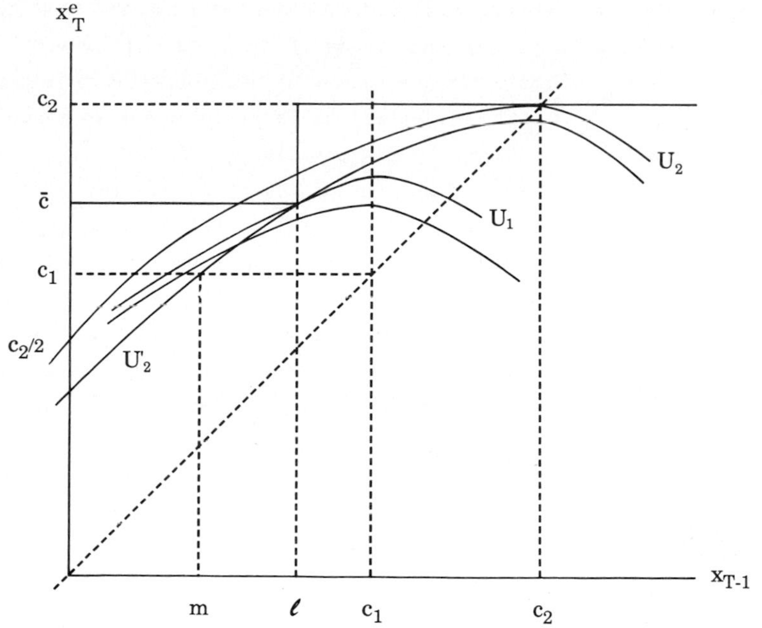

Figure 2: Pooling equilibrium

Vickers rejects pooling equilibria because it is always possible for the type-1 government to defect by choosing a low rate of inflation m such that, if the government could play m and thereby convince the public that it was of type 1, and have the public expect $x^e_T = c_1$, only a type-1 player would find it advantageous to do so. Thus m lies just to the left of the type-2 indifference curve through $(\ell,\bar{c})$. Thus we have

$$U_2(\ell,\bar{c}) > U_2(m,c_1), \tag{1.9}$$

but

$$U_1(\ell,\bar{c}) < U_1(m,c_1). \tag{1.10}$$

Since in the positive orthant the indifference curves of the type-1 government have smaller slopes than those of the type-2 government, such an m always exists, and the pooling equilibrium can always be rejected.

Thus for $c_2 \geq c_1 \geq c_2/2$ a separating equilibrium exists as defined above in (1.3) and (1.4), and no pooling equilibria exist.

For $c_1 < c_2/2$, however, things look different because we can in fact find pooling equilibria which do not fall victim to Vickers' defection argument (above) for rejection, and in some circumstances these appear to dominate the separating equilibrium.

Consider the following equilibria. For $c_1 < c_2/2$ and $\bar{c} > c_2/2$ a pooling equilibrium with mixing exists. The type-2 government plays $x_{T-1} = 0$ with probability q and $x_{T-1} = c_2$ with probability (1-q). The type-1 government plays $x_{T-1} = 0$ certainly. Contingent on $x_{T-1} = 0$ having been observed the probability of the government being of type 1 is

$$\hat{p} = \frac{p}{p + (1-p)q} \tag{1.11}$$

and the expected inflation rate in T is therefore $\hat{p}c_1 + (1-\hat{p})c_2$, q is chosen so that this expected inflation rate is $c_2/2$, i.e. so that

$$\hat{p}c_1 + (1-\hat{p})c_2 = c_2/2.$$

The private sector forms expectations

$$x_T^e = \begin{cases} c_2/2 & \text{if } x_{T-1} \leq 0 \\ c_2 & \text{if } x_{T-1} > 0. \end{cases}$$

Given these expectations, the type-1 government prefers the outcome $(0, c_2/2)$ and the type-2 government is indifferent between $(0, c_2/2)$ and (c_2, c_2) and chooses a random strategy as described above.

This pooling equilibrium is proof against the defection argument since the indifference curve of the type-1 player through $(0, c_2/2)$ is below that of the type-2 player which passes through the same point, except at $x_{T-1} = 0$ where they coincide, as Figure 3 illustrates.

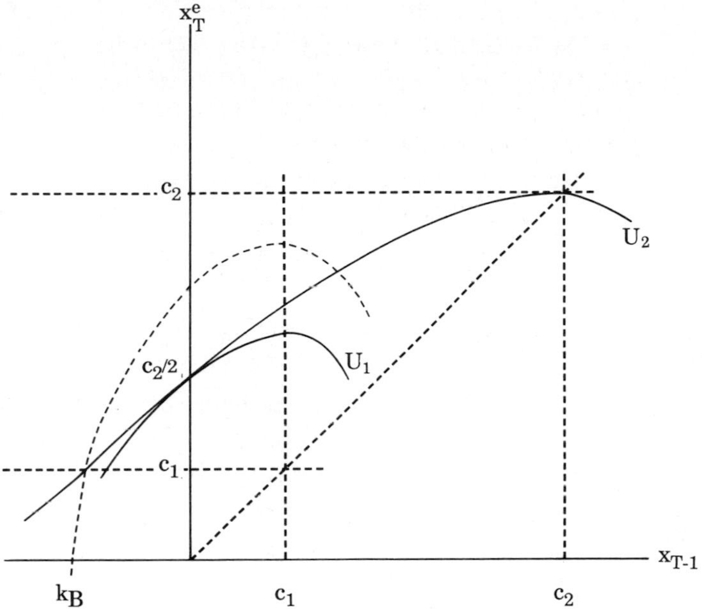

Figure 3: Pooling equilibrium with mixing when $c_1 < c_2/2$ and $\bar{c} > c_2/2$

For the case where $c_1 \leq \bar{c} < c_2/2$ an equilibrium exists similar to the last one but in pure strategies. Expectations are formed by

$$x_T^e = \begin{cases} \bar{c} & \text{if } x_{T-1} \leq \ell \\ c_2 & \text{if } x_{T-1} > \ell. \end{cases} \tag{1.12}$$

For the type-1 governments

$$U_1(\ell,\bar{c}) \geq U_1(c_1,c_2) \tag{1.13}$$

and, for the type-2 governments,

$$U_2(\ell,\bar{c}) \geq U_2(c_2,c_2), \tag{1.14}$$

where $0 \le \ell \le c_1$. In order to prevent defection by type-1 governments, a third condition must be satisfied. There must be no value of x_{T-1} which for $x_T^e = c_1$ is preferred to the pooling outcome $(\ell, \bar{c})$ by type 1 but not by type 2. Thus if j is defined by

$$U_2(j_2, c_1) = U_2(\ell, \bar{c}), \tag{1.15}$$

we have

$$U_1(j, c_1) \le U_1(\ell, \bar{c}) \tag{1.16}$$

These two equations place an upper limit on the value of ℓ. Note that j is necessarily negative, as Figure 4 illustrates, because the indifference curves of type 1 are flatter than those of type 2 to the right of the vertical axis, and steeper to the left of the vertical axis.

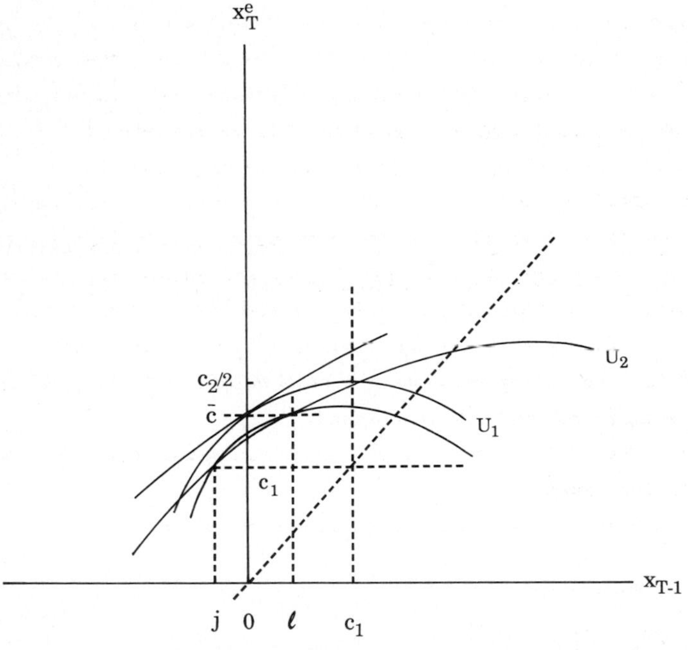

Figure 4: Pooling equilibrium in pure strategies with $c_1 < c_2/2$ and $\bar{c} < c_2/2$

From (1.15) and (1.16) it can be deduced that

$$\ell \le (\bar{c}-c_1)/2$$

or

$$\ell \le (1-p)(c_2-c_1)/2. \tag{1.17}$$

In addition, we have the condition that $\ell \le c_1$.

The higher is the value of ℓ, within the constraints of (1.17) and $\ell \le c_1$, the greater the payoff to each type of government, taking the value of x^e_{T-1} as given. But if initial expectations are taken into account, and noting that $x_{T-1} = x^e_{T-1} = \ell$ for both types of government in this equilibrium, it is clear that both types of players are best off when $\ell = 0$. On grounds of equilibrium dominance, this would therefore be the chosen equilibrium from among these pooling equilibria.

In the Appendix it is shown that in the case where $c_1 \le c_2/2$ and $\bar{c} \le c_2/2$, the pooling equilibrium above dominates the separating equilibrium, where the separating equilibrium exists. All players in the game -governments of both types, and agents in the private sector- prefer the outcome under the pooling equilibrium. In the case where $c_1 > c_2/2$ but $\bar{c} \ge c_2/2$, the pooling equilibrium does not dominate the separating equilibrium, nor is it dominated by the separating equilibrium. Both types of government prefer the pooling equilibrium, but the private sector may for some parameter combinations prefer the separating outcome. Note that the separating equilibrium only exists for $c_1 \ge c_2/9$ in any event.

Consequently, separating equilibria can be ruled out for the first case ($c_1 \le \bar{c} \le c_2/2$) but not for the second.

In summary, the equilibria for a game with two government types can be reduced to the following:

(i) For $c_1 \ge c_2/2$ only a separating equilibrium exists with

$$x^e_T = \begin{cases} c_1 \text{ if } x_{T-1} \le k_B \\ c_2 \text{ if } x_{T-1} > k_B \end{cases}$$

and type-1 governments play $x_{T-1} = k_B$

type-2 governments play $x_{T-1} = c_2$.

(ii) For $c_1 < c_2/2$ but $\bar{c} \geq c_2/2$, a partial pooling equilibrium exists with

$$x_T^e = \begin{cases} c_2/2 & \text{if } x_{T-1} \leq 0 \\ c_2 & \text{if } x_{T-1} > 0 \end{cases}$$

type-1 plays $x_{T-1} = 0$
type-2 plays $x_{T-1} = 0$ with probability q and
$x_{T-1} = c_2$ with probability (1-q)
such that $c_2/2 = c_1\hat{p} + (1-\hat{p})c_2$
where $\hat{p} \equiv p/(p+(1-p)q)$.

For some combinations of parameters (c_1, c_2 and p) a separating equilibrium may also exist.

(iii) For $c_1 < \bar{c} < c_2/2$, a pooling equilibrium exists with expectations

$$x_T^e = \begin{cases} \bar{c} & \text{if } x_{T-1} \leq 0 \\ c_2 & \text{if } x_{T-1} > 0. \end{cases}$$

Both type 1 and type 2 play $x_{T-1} = 0$.

The pooling equilibrium proposed for $c_1 < c_2/2$ holds good as $c_1 \to 0$. By contrast the separating equilibrium is only available for $c_1 \geq c_2/9$, since at that point the constraint (1.4) begins to bind, as Vickers points out. Note that as $c_1 \to 0$, the pooling equilibrium proposed is continuous with the equilibrium in Backus and Driffill (1985a) and Barro (1986). In the limit as $c_1 \to 0$ in the above pooling equilibrium, type 2 plays $x_{T-1} = 0$ if $p \geq \frac{1}{2}$ so that $\bar{c} \leq c_2/2$. If $p < \frac{1}{2}$ then type 2 plays $x_{T-1} = 0$ with probability q such that the *ex-post* probability of type 1, contingent on $x_{T-1} = 0$, is $\hat{p} = \frac{1}{2}$.

2. Many Types

This part of the paper considers how the game is affected when private agents believe at the start of the game that the government's preference for employment (reflected in the parameter c_i) is drawn from a distribution which has some bounded support. As before, a two-period game is considered.

Suppose at T-1 the policy-maker could be of any type c_i in some range, $[\underline{c},\bar{c}]$. Can a separating equilibrium be found? As before, it is assumed that the private sector agents form expectations x_T^e based on their observations of actual inflation at time T-1, x_{T-1}. Let the expectation be represented by the function

$$x_T^e = f(x_{T-1}). \tag{2.1}$$

If the equilibrium is separating, then for each type c_i there is an optimal choice of x_{T-1} given f(.) which is different for each c_i. Thus in equilibrium it must be true that

$$f(x_{T-1}(c)) = c \tag{2.2}$$

for all $c \in [\underline{c},\bar{c}]$, since $x_{T-1}(c)$ reveals the agent's true type c.

If the function $f(x_{T-1})$ is such that x_{T-1} minimises cost, then it satisfies an additional condition. Cost for player of type i is, as in (1.2) above

$$U_i = -x_{T-1}^2/2 + c(x_{T-1}-x_{T-1}^e) + c^2/2 - cf(x_{T-1}). \tag{2.3}$$

Providing f(.) is differentiable and continuous, at an optimum the first order condition is satisfied:

$$\partial U_i/\partial x_{T-1} = -x_{T-1} + c - cf'(x_{T-1}) = 0 \tag{2.4}$$

and

$$\partial^2 U_i/\partial x_{T-1}^2 = -1 - cf''(x_{T-1}) < 0. \tag{2.5}$$

So $f(x_{T-1})$ is a function which for all $c \in [\underline{c},\bar{c}]$ satisfies (2.2) and (2.4) and (2.5). Combining (2.2) and (2.4) gives a differential equation in f:

$$\frac{df(x)}{dx} = 1 - \frac{x}{f(x)}. \tag{2.6}$$

Thus f(x) is a function which has a slope of +1 when x = 0 (f(0) > 0), diminishing to 0 at x = f(x). To tie down the constant of integration, we can set $f(x) = \bar{c}$ when x = f(x). This means that the agent with the highest value of $c(\bar{c})$ playes $x_{T-1} = \bar{c}$: it is not in his interests to reduce x_{T-1} to attempt to signal a lower c.

Having used the upper bound on $\bar{c}$ to position f(.), the lower bound on c is determined by the intersection of f(x) with the x-axis. At this point the player $\underline{\underline{c}}$ sets $x_{T-1}(\underline{\underline{c}}) = 0$. This is illustrated in Figure 5.

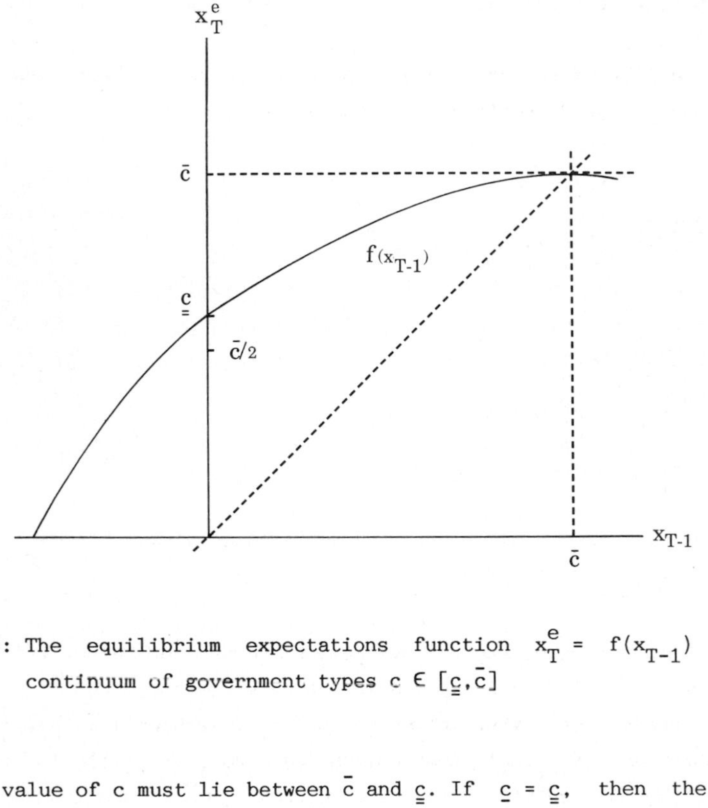

Figure 5: The equilibrium expectations function $x^e_T = f(x_{T-1})$ with a continuum of government types $c \in [\underline{\underline{c}},\bar{c}]$

The value of c must lie between $\bar{c}$ and $\underline{\underline{c}}$. If $c = \underline{\underline{c}}$, then the player with the lowest value of c sets $x_{T-1} = 0$. This restricts the possible values of c to a narrow range, since $\underline{\underline{c}} > \bar{c}/2$. (This is because the $\bar{c}$ player has an indifference curve passing through $(\bar{c},\bar{c})$ on the diagram which also passes through $(0,\bar{c}/2)$, and $f(x_{T-1})$ lies above this indifference curve except at $(\bar{c},\bar{c})$ where they coincide.)

It is not possible to use the part of the function f(.) lying in the NW quadrant where $x \leq 0$ and $f(x) \geq 0$ to induce players with a $c < \underline{\underline{c}}$ to choose a point on that part of the curve, because the second order condition (2.5) is not satisfied on f(x) for $x < 0$. Points of tangency here are maxima of the cost function, not minima. The second order condition (2.5) is satisfied for $c \in [\underline{\underline{c}},\bar{c}]$ where $x_{T-1}(c) \in [0,\bar{c}]$.

The above procedure defines a value $\underline{\underline{c}}$ as a function of $\bar{c}$. If there were players of type $c < \underline{\underline{c}}$ then the above separating equilibrium would not survive. Governments of type $c < \underline{\underline{c}}$ would choose $x_{T-1} = 0$ and the private sector belief $\underline{\underline{c}} = f(0)$ as defined above would not be rational. In this case it may be possible to find a part pooling/part separating equilibrium.

An equilibrium for this case is postulated as follows. Expectations are formed by the discontinuous function

$$x_T^e = \begin{cases} \hat{c} \text{ if } x_{T-1} = 0 \\ f(x_{T-1}) \text{ if } x_{T-1} \in (\tilde{x}_{T-1},\bar{c}] \end{cases} \tag{2.7}$$

where

$$\hat{c} = \int_{\bar{c}}^{\tilde{c}} cp(c)dc/\int_{\bar{c}}^{\tilde{c}} p(c)dc \tag{2.8}$$

and

$$\tilde{c} = f(\tilde{x}_{T-1}). \tag{2.9}$$

In this equilibrium, the private sector expects inflation at a rate $\hat{c}$ if it observes $x_{T-1} = 0$, and expects inflation given by the $f(.)$ function derived above for higher inflation in T-1. Governments with $c > \tilde{c}$ prefer to choose an (x_{T-1},x_T^e) combination on $(x_{T-1},f(x_{t-1}))$ in the range $x_{T-1} \in (\tilde{x}_{T-1},\bar{c}]$ rather than to choose $(0,\hat{c})$, and conversely for governments with $c \leq \tilde{c}$.

At the boundary between the two regions is the government of type $\tilde{c}$ that is indifferent between $(0,\hat{c})$ and $(\tilde{x}_{T-1},f(\tilde{x}_{T-1}))$. Thus, $\tilde{c}$, $\tilde{x}_{T-1}$ and $\hat{c}$ satisfy the condition that

$$U_{\tilde{c}}(0,\hat{c}) = U_{\tilde{c}}(\tilde{x}_{T-1},f(\tilde{x}_{T-1})) \tag{2.10}$$

where $U_{\tilde{c}}(.)$ is the utility of agent of type $\tilde{c}$ as defined by equation (1.2).

In Figure 6, $\hat{c}$ is plotted on the vertical axis, and against it on the horizontal axis is plotted (i) $\tilde{c}$, the highest value of c such that a government of type c prefers or is indifferent to the combination $(0,\hat{c})$ to any point on the expectations curve $(x_{T-1}, f(x_{T-1}))$, and (ii) the mean value of c from those values less than or equal to $\tilde{c}$.

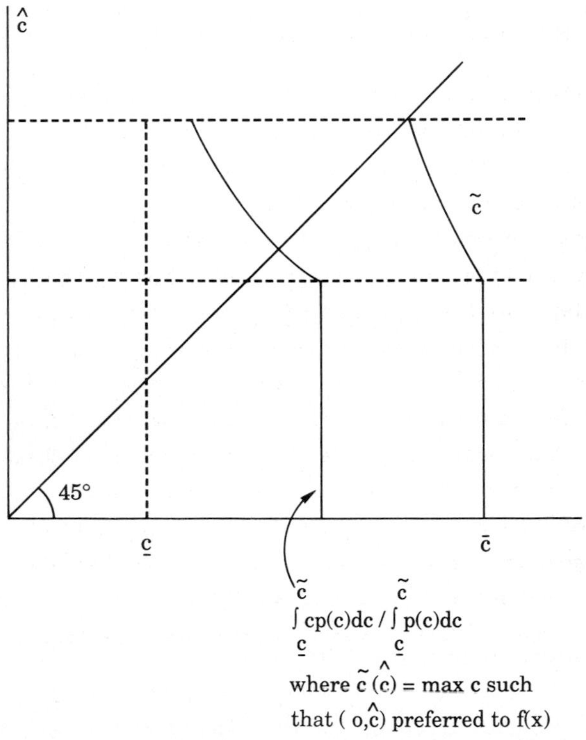

Figure 6: Hybrid pooling/separating equilibrium with a continuum of government types

At $\hat{c} = \underline{\underline{c}}$, all government types with $c \le \underline{\underline{c}}$ prefer the combination $(0,\hat{c})$ to a point on the curve, and the mean value of c for these types will be less than $\hat{c}$. As $\hat{c}$ is reduced, the value of $\tilde{c}$ rises, until $\hat{c} = \bar{c}/2$ when all types prefer $(0,\hat{c})$.

Thus there will always be a unique value of $\hat{c}$ which satisfies (2.8).

At the equilibrium, all players $c \le \tilde{c}$ prefer $x_{T-1} = 0$, $x_T^e = \hat{c}$. The average value of c for these players is $\hat{c}$, and consequently private sector expectations are rational. For players $c > \tilde{c}$, a pair $(x_{T-1}, x_T^e = f(x_{T-1}))$ is preferred and they choose a value of x_{T-1} which identifies their true type.

If $\int_{\underline{c}}^{\bar{c}} cp(c)dc \leq \bar{c}/2$, then the average type over all players is less than $\bar{c}/2$, and all players choose to play $x_{T-1} = 0$, $x_T^e = \hat{c}$ where $\hat{c} = \int_{\underline{c}}^{\bar{c}} cp(c)dc$. In this case there is complete pooling.

In Vickers (1986), pooling equilibria are dominated, because some players would have an incentive to defect, play some other x_{T-1}, to persuade the public that they are of a particular type. However, this does not appear to be the case in this instance.

The difference between the result here and Vickers' result is that here the pooling equilibrium occurs with $x_{T-1} = 0$, and in order to achieve separation, a player with a low value of c would have to play a negative inflation rate in T-1, which would give a worse outcome than the pooling equilibrium. However, in Vickers the pooling occurs with a positive inflation rate in T-1, and the low-c player can achieve separation by playing a lower but still positive inflation rate. In that case, the separating deviation pays off better than the pooling equilibrium.

The analysis of this section suggests that the reputational discipline on non-committed governments works when private sector beliefs are more general than in Backus and Driffill (1985). The crucial element is a sufficiently wide disparity in the range of government preferences.

3. Exogenous Uncertainty

This part of the paper examines what happens when the simple model of Backus and Driffill (1985a) is perturbed by the addition of an exogenous random element. The following structure is assumed.

Governments are of two types. Type 1 ('dry') are committed to zero inflation and their preferences in each period could be represented by the function

$$u_{1t} = -x_t^2,$$

where x_t is the rate of inflation in period t. Type 2 ('wet') care about inflation and unemployment and have the following preferences in each period:

$$u_{2t} = -x_t^2/2 + c(x_t - x_t^e),$$

where x_t^e is the private sector's expectation of inflation in period t.

It is assumed as before that only two outcomes for the actual inflation rate are ever observed, either $x_t = 0$ or $x_t = c$. However, it is here assumed that governments do not have perfect control over the actual inflation rate. With some small probability $(1-\pi)$ the government hits the wrong button, so that, if it intends to create inflation equal to c, then c occurs with probability π and zero occurs with probability $(1-\pi)$, and conversely if zero inflation is intended. $\pi > \frac{1}{2}$, so that what is intended is more likely to occur than not. The structure adopted here follows closely that of Söderström (1985) in having two potential outcomes for government behaviour in each period. However, in Söderström, the government's objectives are known for sure. (In his set-up the player who is equivalent to the government here is his trade union.) Another difference between the present set-up and Söderström is that the private sector is assumed to be able to 'choose' any point on the real line when they form expectations, which they do rationally. As before, the game runs until a last period when t = T. The government attempts to maximise the expected value of the sum of the payoffs received up to the end of the game. Thus at time s the government maximises

$$\sum_{t=s}^{T} u_{it}.$$

The private sector enters period t with the belief that with probability p_t the government is of type 1 and with probability $(1-p_t)$ of type 2. Its beliefs are updated using Bayes' rule. Thus if the type-2 player is known to play the strategy of intending zero inflation with probability q_t and intending inflation equal to c with probability $(1-q_t)$, then the private sector updates its beliefs such that

$$p_{t+1}(x_t=0) = \frac{\pi p_t}{\pi p_t + (1-p_t)\tilde{q}_t}, \tag{3.1a}$$

where $\tilde{q} \equiv \pi q_t + (1-q_t)(1-\pi)$, if $x_t = 0$ is observed and

$$p_{t+1}(x_t=c) = \frac{(1-\pi)p_t}{(1-\pi)p_t + (1-p_t)(1-\tilde{q}_t)}, \tag{3.1b}$$

if $x_t = c$ is observed.

The probability of observing inflation equal to c at time t is $(1-\pi)p_t + (1-p_t)(1-\tilde{q}_t)$ and consequently the expected inflation is

$$x_t^e = c[p_t(1-\pi) + (1-p_t)(1-\tilde{q}_t)]. \tag{3.2}$$

Thus the set-up here is exactly the same as in Backus and Driffill (1985a), except that actions are not always carried out as intended due to this element of exogenous uncertainty. This change in the model has significant effects. Providing π is strictly less than one, there is always a positive chance of observing the high inflation outcome, even if the government is actually of type 1 (dry). Consequently, this observation no longer identifies the government as being unmistakably wet and reduces its reputation to zero. Reputation is reduced by a high inflation outcome, but not destroyed. From equation (3.1b) above, it is seen that if $q_t < 1$ so that $\tilde{q}_t < \pi$, and if $\pi < 1$, then conditional on $x_t = c$, $p_{t+1} < p_t$. But if $p_t > 0$, then $p_{t+1} > 0$.

If the realisation is $x_t = 0$, which is always possible regardless of the type of government or strategy played, reputation is not worsened, and improves if the type-2 player is known to play the zero intended inflation strategy with probability less than one ($q_t < 1$).

The greater the amount of noise in the system (i.e. the lower the value of π) the less does the revised reputation differ from the old one, given any initial reputation and strategy choice q_t. In the limit as $\pi_t \to \frac{1}{2}$, the players have no control over the outcome and no observation can change reputation. Of course, there is then no effective difference between the two types of government. Neither has any control at all.

The solution of the game is now considered. In the final period, T, the type-2 player always intends inflation c, and the type-1 player intends zero inflation. The private sector's expectation is

$$x_T^e = c(p_T(1-\pi)+(1-p_T)\pi).$$

The payoff to the wet (type-2) player is

$$-cx_T^e$$

with probability $1-\pi$, and

$$-c^2 + c(c-x_T^e)$$

with probability (π). Hence his expected final period payoff is

$$V_T(p_T) = -c^2(p_T(1-\pi)+(1-p_T)\pi) + \pi c^2/2$$

$$= c^2 p_T(2\pi-1) - \pi c^2/2.$$

Now consider period T-1.

If the wet plays 'intend inflation' equal to zero with probability q_{T-1}, his payoff in T-1 is

$$W_{T-1} = \tilde{q}_{T-1}\{u_2(0,x_{T-1}^e) + V(p_T|x_{T-1} = 0)\}$$

$$+ (1-\tilde{q}_{T-1})\{u_2(c,x_{T-1}^e) + V(p_T|x_{T-1} = c)\}, \tag{3.3}$$

where $u_2(0,x_{T-1}^e) = -cx_{T-1}^e$ and $u_2(c,x_{T-1}^e) = c^2/2 - cx_{T-1}^e$. p_T is determined by equations (3.1a) and (3.1b) above. The government chooses $\tilde{q}_{t-1}$ in the range $\pi \geq \tilde{q}_{t-1} \geq 1-\pi$ to maximise W_{T-1}, taking the private sector's expectations of future inflation as being fixed, since in a sequential equilibrium the strategies (q_{T-1},x_T^e) form a Nash equilibrium pair. Thus the equilibrium values of $\tilde{q}_{T-1}$ satisfy

(i) $\tilde{q}_{T-1} = \pi$ if $u_2(0,x_{T-1}^e) + V(p_T|x_{T-1} = 0)$

$> u_2(c,x_{T-1}^e) + V(p_T|x_{T-1} = c)$,

(ii) $\pi \geq \tilde{q}_{T-1} \geq 1 - \pi$ if

$$u_2(0,x_{T-1}^e) + V(p_T|x_{T-1} = 0) = u_2(c,x_{T-1}^e) + V(p_T|x_{T-1} = c)$$

for some $\tilde{q}_{T-1} \in [\pi,1-\pi]$,

(iii) $\tilde{q}_{T-1} = 1 - \pi$ if $u_2(0,x^e_{T-1}) + V(p_T|x_{T-1} = 0)$

$$< u_2(c,x^e_{T-1}) + V(p_T|x_{T-1} = c). \qquad (3.4)$$

The equilibrium value of $\tilde{q}_{T-1}$ depends on both π and p_{T-1}. It is clear that there is never an equilibrium with $\tilde{q}_{T-1} = \pi$, i.e. with the 'wet' government playing exactly the same strategy as the 'dry' government and intending zero inflation with probability one. In this case p_T would be equal to p_{T-1} regardless of the realisation of x_{T-1}, and the expected payoff from intending zero inflation would be clearly less than from intending inflation equal to c. This result is clearly at variance with the results of Backus and Driffill (1985a) where with a sufficiently good reputation in T-1, the wet player would mimic the dry. The reason for the difference is that the occurrence of high inflation does not now totally ruin the government's reputation. It is no longer the case that $p_T = 0$ if $x_{T-1} = c$.

We now turn to the solution to the wet government's problem at date T-1. From (3.1a) and (3.1b), $p_T(x_{T-1} = 0)$ is a decreasing function of $\tilde{q}_{T-1}$ and $p_T(x_{T-1} = c)$ is an increasing function. $V(T,p_T)$ is a linear increasing function of p_T. If a value $\tilde{q}_{T-1} \in [\pi,1-\pi]$ exists such that equality (3.4) (ii) above is satisfied, then this is the unique solution. If not, then the solution involves $\tilde{q}_{T-1} = (1-\pi)$ and the government prefers the high inflation outcome to the low inflation outcome.

The inequalities (3.4) above reduce to the following

$$(2\pi-1)c^2(p_T(x_{T-1} = 0) - p_T(x_{T-1} = c)) - c^2/2 \begin{cases} > 0; & \tilde{q}_{T-1} = \pi \\ = 0; & \pi \le \tilde{q}_{T-1} \le 1-\pi \\ < 0; & \tilde{q} = (1-\pi). \end{cases} \qquad (3.5)$$

It is clear from (3.5) that for the equality to be satisfied we must have $\pi \ge 3/4$. This is a necessary, not sufficient, condition. No wet would ever depart from intending inflation in T-1 if this condition were not satisfied.

It is shown below that for a given value of p_{T-1}, the equilibrium value of q_{T-1} is decreasing in π for $q_{T-1} > 0$, and that for given π, q_{T-1} at first rises with p_{T-1} and then falls. Thus the relationship is as illustrated in Figure 7. In Figure 7b the curve shifts upwards as $\bar{u}$ is increased from 3/4 towards 1. Below some critical value $\underline{p}_{T-1}$, and above a higher critical value $\bar{p}_{T-1}$, the wet government does not randomise but plays the strategy of intending to cause inflation with probability one. At intermediate values of p_{T-1}, randomisation occurs. The reason for this result is that the difference in reputation $p_T(x_{T-1} = 0)$ and $p_T(x_{T-1} = c)$ is wider at intermediate values of p_{T-1} than at extreme values. As $p_{T-1} \to 1$ from below and as $p_{T-1} \to 0$, the difference $p_T(x_{T-1} = 0) - p_T(x_{T-1} = c)$ approaches zero. Because inflating does not injure one's reputation so much if it is either very bad or very good already, there is less disincentive to doing it.

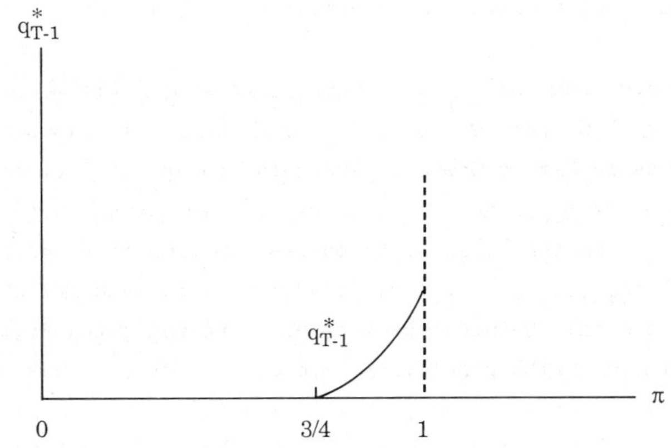

Figure 7a: Relationship between the optimum mixing (q^*_{T-1}) and the probability of error (π)

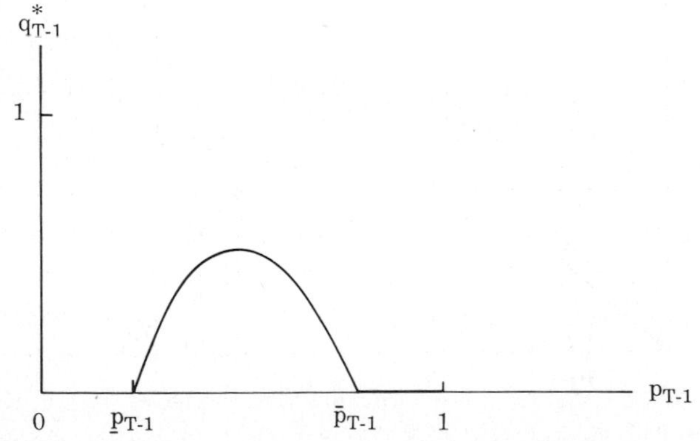

Figure 7b: Relationship between the optimum mixing (q^*_{T-1}) and the initial reputation (p_{T-1})

If the wet government is randomising in T-1, the equality

$$p_T(x_{T-1} = 0) - p_T(x_{T-1} = c) = \frac{1}{2(2\pi-1)} \tag{3.6}$$

must be satisfied, where $p_T(x_{T-1} = 0)$ and $p_T(x_{T-1} = c)$ are determined by equations (3.1a) and (3.1b) above. The left-hand side of (3.6) is a decreasing function of q_{T-1} for $q_{T-1} \in [0,1]$ and $p_{T-1} \in (0,1)$. At $q_{T-1} = 1$, it equals zero, and it reaches a maximum at $q_{T-1} = 0$. Define the LHS of (3.6) as $F(p_{T-1}, q_{T-1}, \pi)$, so we have

$$F(p_{T-1}, q_{T-1}, \pi) \equiv p_T(x_{T-1} = 0) - p_T(x_{T-1} = c). \tag{3.7}$$

F(.) is decreasing in q_{T-1}. $F(0, q_{T-1}, \pi) = 0$, $F(1, q_{T-1}, \pi) = 0$, and $F(p_{T-1}, q_{T-1}, \pi) > 0$ for $0 < p_{T-1} < 1$ and $q_{T-1} < 1$. Thus F(.) can be illustrated as in Figure 8 where each curve in (p_{T-1}, F) space is drawn for a given value of q_{T-1}, and successively higher curves correspond to lower values of q_{T-1}. In the diagram, randomisation occurs for values of p_{T-1} in the interval $(\underline{p}_{T-1}, \bar{p}_{T-1})$. q_{T-1} at first rises and then falls as p_{T-1} rises inside the interval. Outside the interval, the wet government always plays 'intend inflation' with probability one.

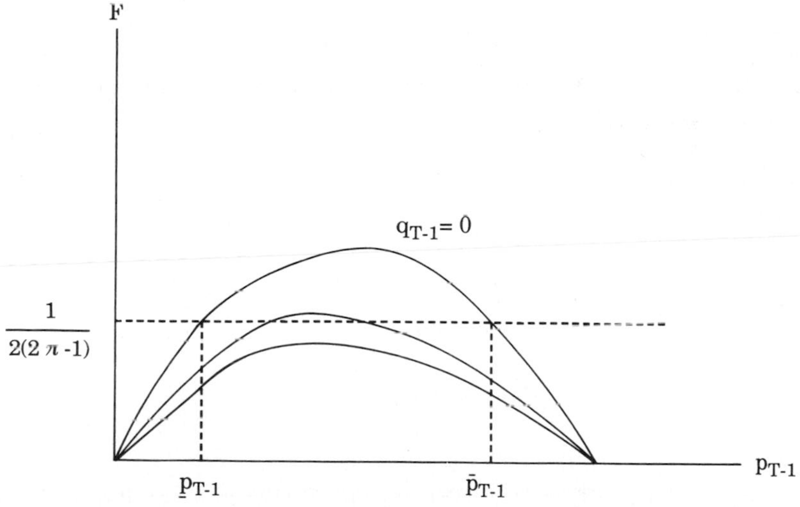

Figure 8: Initial reputation (p_{T-1}) and the difference (F) between posterior reputations in the event of zero inflation and in the event of high inflation

The reputation of the government in period T, $p_T(x_{T-1} = 0)$ or $p_T(x_{T-1} = c)$, is an increasing function of p_{T-1}. This is clearly true for $p_{T-1} \leq \underline{p}_{T-1}$ and $p_{T-1} \geq \bar{p}_{T-1}$, since for these values the optimal $q_{T-1} = 0$ and (3.1a) and (3.1b) immediately indicate that this is so. For $\underline{p}_{T-1} < p_{T-1} < \bar{p}_{T-1}$ this assertion may be proved as follows.

Define

$$F^{o}(p_{T-1}, q_{T-1}, \pi) \equiv p_T(x_{T-1} = 0)$$

and

$$F^{c}(p_{T-1}, q_{T-1}, \pi) \equiv p_T(x_{T-1} = c) \tag{3.8}$$

from (3.1a) and (3.1b). Then

$$\frac{dp_T(x_{T-1} = 0)}{dp_{T-1}} = \frac{\partial F^{o}}{\partial p_{T-1}} + \frac{\partial F^{o}}{\partial p_{T-1}} \frac{dq_{T-1}}{dp_{T-1}} \tag{3.9}$$

and

$$\frac{dp_T(x_{T-1} = 0)}{dp_{T-1}} = \frac{\partial F^{c}}{\partial p_{T-1}} + \frac{\partial F^{c}}{\partial q_{T-1}} \frac{dq_{T-1}}{dp_{T-1}}. \tag{3.10}$$

Since $\dfrac{dp_T(x_{T-1} = 0)}{dp_{T-1}} = \dfrac{dp_T(x_{T-1} = c)}{dp_{T-1}}$ when (3.6) is satisfied, and the government is randomising,

$$\frac{dq_{T-1}}{dp_{T-1}} = -\left[\frac{\partial F^{o}/\partial p_{T-1} - \partial F^{c}/\partial p_{T-1}}{\partial F^{o}/\partial q_{T-1} - \partial F^{c}/\partial q_{T-1}}\right]. \tag{3.11}$$

Substituting (3.11) into (3.9) gives

$$\frac{dp_T(x_{T-1} = 0)}{dp_{T-1}} = \frac{\partial F^{o}}{\partial p_{T-1}} - \frac{\partial F^{0}/\partial p_{T-1} - \partial F^{c}/\partial p_{T-1}}{1 - F_q^{c}/F_q^{o}}. \tag{3.12}$$

Since $F_q^c > 0$ and $F_q^o < 0$, the denominator $(1-F_q^c/F_q^o)$ is greater than one, and clearly the whole RHS in (3.12) is positive. Applying the same treatment to (3.10) confirms that $\frac{dp_T}{dp_{T-1}}(x_{T-1} = c)$ is also positive.

Thus an improvement in reputation at the start of period T-1 results in an improvement in the conditional reputations in period T.

To take the analysis beyond the penultimate period of the game T-1, it is necessary to compute the value function for the government with reputation p_{T-1} entering period T-1, $V(T-1,p_{T-1})$. Whereas for period T, the corresponding function $V(T,p_T)$ is a linear function of p_T, it does not appear to be linear for T-1, and indeed it is not clear that the value function will be monotonically increasing in the reputation p_{T-1}. The reason is as follows:

$$V_1(T-1,p_{T-1}) = \max_{q_{T-1}} W_{T-1},$$

where W_{T-1} is defined in (3.3) above. Expectations of inflation in T-1 are given by (3.2) above for t = T-1.

The optimal choice of q_{T-1} is non-monotonic in p_{T-1}: there may be a range over which q_{T-1} is falling in p_{T-1}. Over this range x_{T-1}^e is rising in p_{T-1}. Consequently, as (3.3) indicates, the effect of the improved reputation in period T may be offset by the effect of higher inflation expectations in T-1. Thus it is not clear that the value function at T-1 is monotonic in reputation T-1, and it does not seem straightforward to extend this analysis beyond two periods.

4. Conclusions

This paper has attempted a number of generalisations of simple models of macroeconomic policy with incomplete information, with the purpose of finding out how sensitive their implications are to changes in assumptions. The basic result of the simple analysis (Backus and Driffill 1985a; Barro 1986) is that the reputation effect can constrain a government to mimic the behaviour of a government which is committed to a zero-inflation strategy, so long as the government has a sufficiently long time-horizon or a sufficiently long period of time remaining in office.

In Section 1 of the paper that simple analysis is extended, following Vickers (1986) to allow for a weaker form of uncertainty about the government's preferences, namely the private sector is unsure about the weight the government places on employment: it may be higher or lower, but it is not zero. It then appears that if the two possible types are relatively similar, they take actions at the start of the game which distinguish the true type of government. The government which is less concerned about employment and output initially signals its type in instituting an inflation rate which is so low (though positive) that the more concerned government would not want to imitate it. If, however, the two possible types of government are relatively dissimilar, a pooling equilibrium is possible in which both types initially institute a zero inflation rate and the true type is only revealed in the last period of the game.

Thus this result supports the Backus/Driffill result. It appears that it is not necessary for the public to believe that the government may be 100 per cent committed to zero inflation for the reputational constraint to induce zero inflation, only that the government may care little enough about output.

The result may appear paradoxical in that separation occurs for relatively similar government types and not for relatively dissimilar types. The reason for this is that the less a government cares about employment, the less 'budgeable' it is. That is to say that it is less willing to deviate from its preferred inflation rate in exchange for a given reduction in the private sector's inflation expectation in the next period. Hence it may be unwilling to set an inflation rate low enough to prevent the more caring government from imitating its action.

Zero inflation emerges in pooling equilibria even when both possible government types have an inflationary bias because, in a pooling equilibrium, the actual and expected inflation rates in the first period are equal, for all types of government, and, when there are no inflationary surprises, all types of government prefer zero inflation to any other. The private sector is modelled formally as being indifferent among alternative fully anticipated inflation rates. Consequently a pooling outcome with zero inflation dominates other pooling equilibria.

Section 2 of the paper extends the same analysis to allow for any possible type of government within some range. In this case, the separating equilibrium applies over a narrower range of types of government, since for each type of government, the adjacent type (with a lower c-value) chooses a low enough inflation rate to separate itself from the next higher type of government. Zero inflation is played by a government with a relatively high preference for employment and inflation. No type of government uses a less-than-zero inflation rate in equilibrium to identify its type. If the range of possible types is wider than the pure separating equilibrium can accommodate, a hybrid pooling/separating equilibrium may emerge with the most inflationary governments separated, but the least inflationary governments pooled. Thus this is an example where, although there is an infinity of possible government types, and an infinity of actions, each type does not take a different action in order to identify itself uniquely. Only the most inflationary governments are exposed.

In Section 3 the simple Backus/Driffill model is extended in a completely different direction. Exogenous noise is introduced into the model, so that the appearance of some inflation is no longer incontrovertible evidence of an uncommitted or inflationary government. It may simply be a random occurrence when the government has, with imperfect controls, attempted to achieve zero inflation. Under these circumstances the incentive for the uncommitted government to imitate the one committed to zero inflation is weakened considerably. In the penultimate stage of the game, an uncommitted government with either a very poor or a very good reputation will intend to cause inflation, and a government with a middling reputation will mix inflating and not inflating, but no uncommitted government will intend zero inflation with certainty.

The simple change to the model made by adding uncertainty about the effects of policy complicates the analysis considerably. Only a two-period game has been analysed in this paper.

It appears from the tentative analysis in this paper that the reputational constraints on macroeconomic policy remain effective when the private sector's beliefs about possible government types are generalised, but imperfect monitoring of government actions weakens those constraints considerably.

Note

* This paper was written while the author was Houblon-Norman Research Fellow at the Bank of England. The work reflects views solely of the author and not necessarily of the Bank. The paper has benefited from comments received in seminars at Aarhus, Bristol, Exeter, Hull and LSE.

References

Backus, D.K. and E.J. Driffill, 'Inflation and reputation', American Economic Review, vol. 75, no. 3, 1985a, pp. 530-538.

Backus, D.K. and E.J. Driffill, 'Rational expectations and policy credibility following a change in regime', Review of Economic Studies, vol. LII, 1985b, pp. 211-221.

Barro, Robert J., 'Reputation in a model of monetary policy with incomplete information', Journal of Monetary Economics, vol. 17, 1986, pp. 3-20.

Canzoneri, M.B., 'Monetary policy games and the role of private information', American Economic Review, vol. 75, no. 5, December 1985, pp. 1056-1070.

Cukierman, A. and A.H. Meltzer, 'A theory of ambiguity, credibility and inflation under discretion and asymmetric information', Econometrica, vol. 54, no. 5, September 1986, pp. 1099-1128.

Kreps, D. and R. Wilson, 'Reputation and incomplete information', Journal of Economic Theory, vol. 27, 1982, pp. 253-279.

Rogoff, K.D., 'Reputational constraints on monetary policy', (mimeo), July 1986.

Rubinstein, A., 'An optimal conviction policy for offences that may have been committed by accident', in S.J. Brams, A. Scholter and G. Schwodiauer (eds), Applied Game Theory, Physica-Verlag, Wurzburg, 1979.

Söderström, H.T., 'Union militancy, external shocks, and the accommodation dilemma', Scandinavian Journal of Economics, vol. 87, no. 2, 1985, pp. 335-351.

Vickers, J., 'Signalling in a model of monetary policy with incomplete information', Oxford Economic Papers, vol. 38, 1986, pp. 443-455.

Appendix

In this Appendix we investigate whether, for the cases in Section 1 of the paper where $c_1 < c_2/2$, the proposed pooling equilibria dominate the separating equilibrium, when both exist.

In the separating equilibrium (1.3a) above, the equilibrium strategies are

$$
\begin{aligned}
&x_{T-1(1)} = k_B \\
&x_{T-1(2)} = c_2 \\
&x^e_{T-1} = pk_B + (1-p)c_2 \\
&x_{T(1)} = c_1 \\
&x_{T(2)} = c_2 \\
&x^e_T = \begin{cases} c_1 \text{ if } x_{T-1} \le k_B \\ c_2 \text{ if } x_{T-1} > k_B. \end{cases}
\end{aligned}
\tag{A.1}
$$

Thus the utilities over the whole game are

$$
\begin{aligned}
U^s_1 &\equiv U_1(x^e_{T-1}, x_{T-1}, x^e_T) = -k_B^2/2 + c_1(1-p)(k_B-c_2) - c_1^2/2 \\
U^s_2 &\equiv U_2(x^e_{T-1}, x_{T-1}, x^e_T) = -c_2^2 + c_2 p(c_2-k_B).
\end{aligned}
\tag{A.2}
$$

In the pure pooling equilibrium which obtains when $c_1 < c_2/2$ and $\bar{c} \le c_2/2$, we have in equilibrium

$$
\begin{aligned}
&x_{T-1(1)} = x_{T-1(2)} = x^e_{T-1} = 0 \\
&x^e_T = \bar{c} = pc_1 + (1-p)c_2 \\
&x_{T(1)} = c_1 \\
&x_{T(2)} = c_2
\end{aligned}
\tag{A.3}
$$

and the utilities are correspondingly

$$U_1^p \equiv U_1(x_{T-1}^e, x_{T-1}, x_T^e) = -c_1^2/2 + c_1(c_1-c_2)(1-p)$$
$$U_2^p \equiv U_2(x_{T-1}^e, x_{T-1}, x_T^e) = -c_2^2/2 + c_2 p(c_2-c_1). \tag{A.4}$$

It is clear that $U_1^p \geq U_1^s$ and $U_2^p \geq U_2^s$ and thus that the pooling equilibrium dominates the separating equilibrium for both government types.

(For the case of the type-2 government, subtraction of (A.2) from (A.4) yields an expression which gives on rearrangement

$$U_2^p - U_2^s = c_2(c_2/2-c_1+k_B) - c_2(1-p)(k_B-c_1).$$

The second term, $c_2(1-p)(k_B-c_1)$ is clearly negative. The first term is positive because $c_2/2 - c_1 \geq -k_B$ when $c_1 \leq c_2/2$, as reference to Figure 3 shows. In Figure 3, U_2 cuts the vertical axis at 45°, but the U_2 curve is strictly concave, thus $c_2/2 - c_1 \geq -k_B$.)

If private sector expectational errors are examined, it is found that the sum of expected squared errors over the two periods are smaller in the pooling equilibrium. Thus all players in the game prefer the pooling equilibrium to the separating equilibrium in this case.

Now turn to the case where $c_1 < c_2/2$ but $\bar{c} > c_2/2$ and there is a mixed pooling solution. The equilibrium strategies are now

$$x_{T-1(1)} = 0$$

$$x_{T-1(2)} = \begin{cases} 0 \text{ with probability } q \\ c_2 \text{ with probability } 1-q \end{cases}$$

$$x_{T-1}^e = c_2(1-p)(1-q)$$

$$x_{T(1)} = c_1$$

$$x_{T(2)} = c_2 \tag{A.5}$$

$$x_T^e = c_2/2 = \hat{p}c_1 + (1-\hat{p})c_2 \text{ if } x_{T-1} = 0$$

and c_2 if $x_{T-1} > 0$,

where $\hat{p} = \dfrac{p}{p + (1-p)q}$.

Now the utilities are

$$U_1^M = -c_1c_2(1-p)(1-q) - c_1^2/2 + c_1(c_1-c_2/2)$$
$$\tag{A.6}$$
$$U_2^M = -c_2^2(1-p)(1-q).$$

It can be shown that $U_2^M - U_2^s \geq 0$ and $U_1^M - U_1^s \geq 0$. Subtracting (A.2) from (A.6) for type 2 gives

$$U_2^M - U_2^s = c_2^2(1-p)q + c_2pk_B. \tag{A.7}$$

By (1.11) we deduce that

$$\frac{p}{p + (1-p)q} = \frac{c_2/2}{c_2 - c_1}$$

and hence

$$p + (1-p)q = 2p\,\frac{c_2 - c_1}{c_2}. \tag{A.8}$$

Substituting for $(1-p)q$ in (A.6) gives

$$U_2^M - U_2^s = c_2^2\left(2p\,\frac{c_2-c_1}{c_2} - p\right) + c_2pk_B$$
$$= c_2p(c_2-2c_1+k_B).$$

As it was shown above that $k_B \geq -c_2/2 + c_1$, it is clear that $U_2^M - U_2^s \geq 0$.

Consider now $U_1^M - U_1^s$. Subtracting (A.2) from (A.6) gives

$$U_1^M - U_1^s = -c_1c_2(1-p)(1-q) + c_1(c_1-c_2/2)$$
$$+ k_B^2/2 - c_1(1-p)(k_B-c_2)$$

and we use (A.8) again to substitute out q yielding

$$U_1^M - U_1^S = -c_1((1-2p)c_2+2pc_1) + c_1(c_1-c_2/2) + k_B^2/2 - c_1(1-p)(k_B-c_1)$$

$$= -c_1(1-2p)(c_2/2-c_1) - c_1k_B(1-p) + k_B^2/2$$

$$\geq -c_1(c_2/2-c_1) - c_1k_B + k_B^2/2. \qquad (A.9)$$

From the definition (1.3) of k_B we derive the condition

$$k_B^2/2 - c_2k_B - c_2^2/2 + c_1c_2 = 0$$

which, when subtracted from (A.9), yields

$$U_1^M - U_1^S \geq (c_1-c_2)(-k_B+c_1-c_2/2) \geq 0,$$

since both bracketed terms, (c_1-c_2) and $(-k_B+c_1-c_2/2)$, are negative.

Hence both types of government prefer the mixed pooling equilibrium to separating when $c_1 \leq c_2/2$ and $\bar{c} \geq c_2/2$. However, it does not appear to be the case that the private sector prefers the mixed pooling equilibrium to the separating equilibrium. In the mixed-pooling outcome, the private sector makes an error of $c_2(1-p)(1-q)$ with probability $p + (1-p)q$, and $c_2(1-(1-p)(1-q))$ with probability $(1-p)(1-q)$ in the first period. And in the second period, it makes no error if $x_{T-1} = c_2$ was observed in the first. But if $x_{T-1} = 0$ was observed in the first period, then it makes an error of $c_2 - c_2/2$ with probability $(1-\hat{p})$ and $(c_1-c_2/2)$ with probability $\hat{p}$ in the second period.

The expected value of squared expectational errors in the mixed-pooling case ($\equiv -U_p^M$) gives

$$-U_p^M = 2p(c_2-c_1)(c_2-2p(c_2-c_1)) + p(c_2-c_1)(c_2/2-c_1)$$

which compares with the value in the separating equilibrium of

$$-U_p^S = p(1-p)(k_B-c_2)^2.$$

Thus this equilibrium may not dominate the separating equilibrium, although it is not dominated by it, and so the separating equilibrium cannot be ruled out on grounds of equilibrium dominance in the case $c_1 \leq c_2/2$, $\bar{c}(\equiv c_1p+(1-p)c_2) > c_2/2$.

INDEX